CERES™
Celestial Legend
Volume 7: Maya
Shôjo Edition

STORY & ART BY YUU WATASE

English Adaptation/Gary Leach

Translation/Lillian Olsen
Touch–Up Art & Lettering/Bill Schuch
Cover & Graphics Design/Hidemi Sahara
Editor/Avery Gotoh

Editor in Chief, Books/Alvin Lu
Editor in Chief, Magazines/Marc Weidenbaum
VP of Publishing Licensing/Rika Inouye
VP of Sales/Gonzalo Ferreyra
Sr. VP of Marketing/Liza Coppola
Publisher/Hyoe Narita

Printed in Canada

Published by VIZ Media, LLC
P.O. Box 77010 • San Francisco CA 94107

Shôjo Edition

10 9 8 7 6 5

First printing, April 2004
Fifth printing, March 2007

www.viz.com
store.viz.com

VIZ GRAPHIC NOVEL

CERES™

Celestial Legend

Vol. 7: Maya

Story and Art by
Yuu Watase

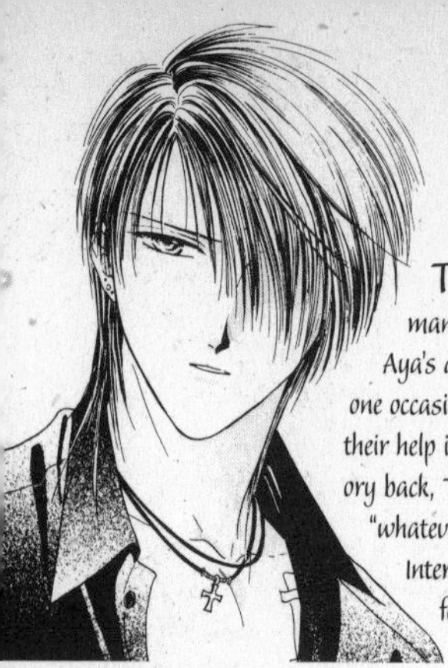

TÔYA: Mysterious man who's come to Aya's aid on more than one occasion. In exchange for their help in getting his memory back, Tôya works doing "whatever" for Mikage International... At least for now.

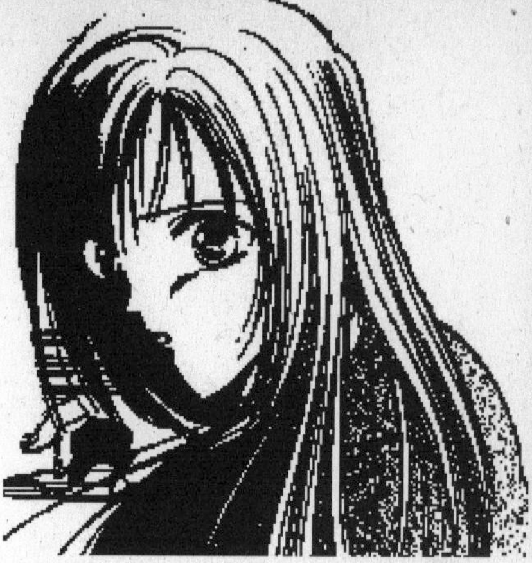

AYA MIKAGE: Ceres is taking over sixteen-year-old Aya Mikage's mind and body. To prevent Ceres from destroying the entire Mikage clan, Aya's own family is trying to kill her. Despite all the turmoil, Aya finds herself falling in love with Tôya—a man hired by Kagami to keep an eye on her.

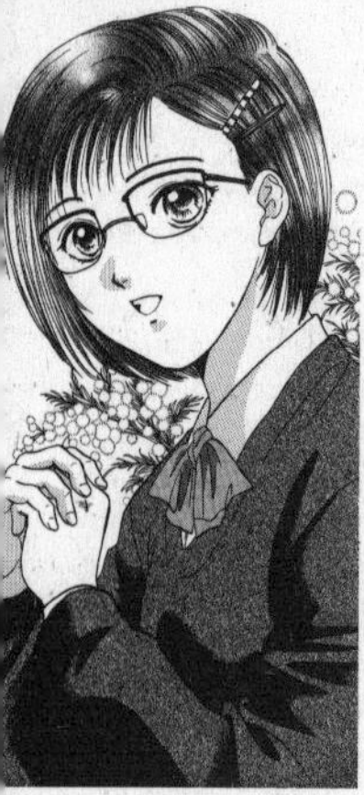

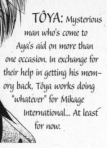

MAYA HIROBE: Pretty and popular student (and an unknowing C-Genome!) at Aya and Yûhi's new high school. Her underlying frustration at a past romance gone wrong summons forth the "ghost dog"—a spooky, angry, white avenger—which she then inadvertently turns upon the targets of her emotion.

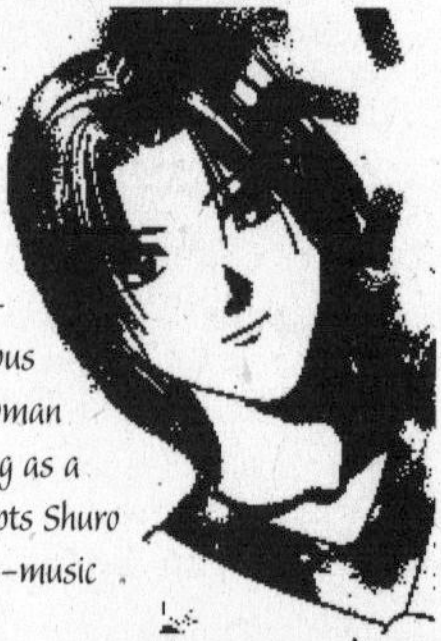

SHURO: Surviving member of the beautiful, androgynous Japan pop duo, GeSANG. A woman (with ten'nyo ancestry) passing as a man, her agent's urging prompts Shuro to consider a return to the pop-music scene, this time as a solo act.

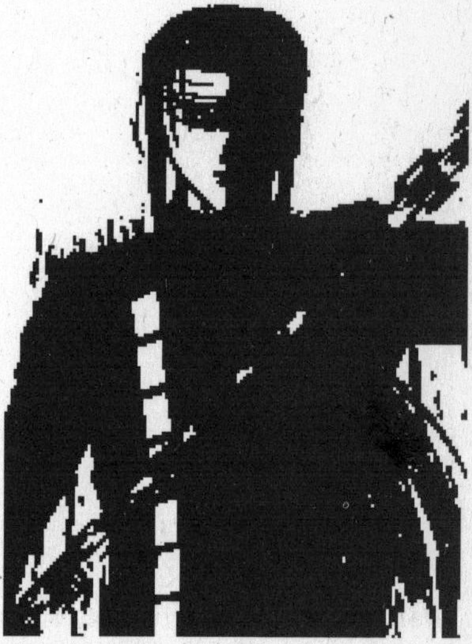

YÛHI: Sixteen-year-old brother-in-law to Suzumi. A skilled martial artist and aspiring chef, Yûhi has been asked (ordered, more like) to serve as Aya's watchful protector and guardian...his own feelings for her notwithstanding.

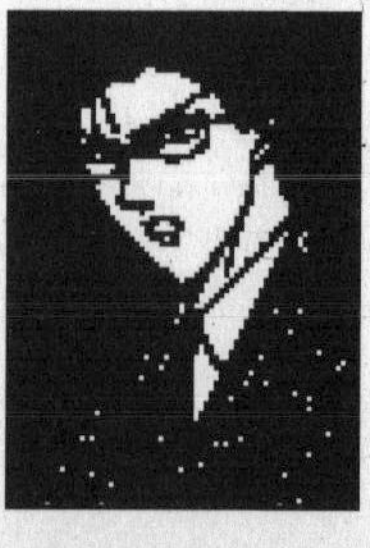

KAGAMI: Although the Mikage family wants to kill off Ceres through Aya, Kagami—head of Mikage International's research and development department—has put into motion his own agenda: C-Project, a plan to gather descendants of ten'nyo and use their power.

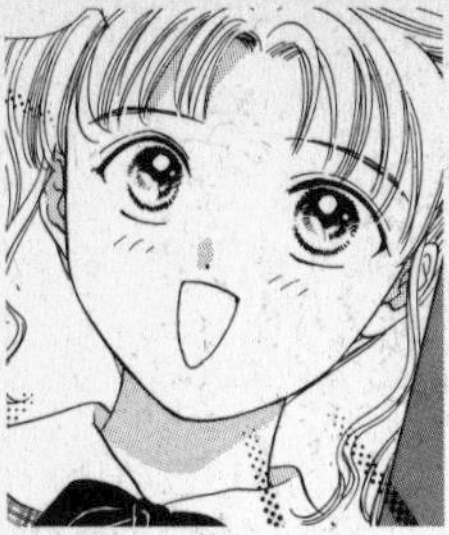

CHIDORI: Awakened to her own, unsuspected celestial powers only after her younger brother was put into mortal danger, Chidori Kuruma was at first another target of Kagami, but was spared by the compassion of Tôya. Deceptively young in appearance (she looks like a grade-schooler but is actually in high school, just like Aya), Chidori has since decided to help Aya and the others in the search for Ceres' missing hagoromo.

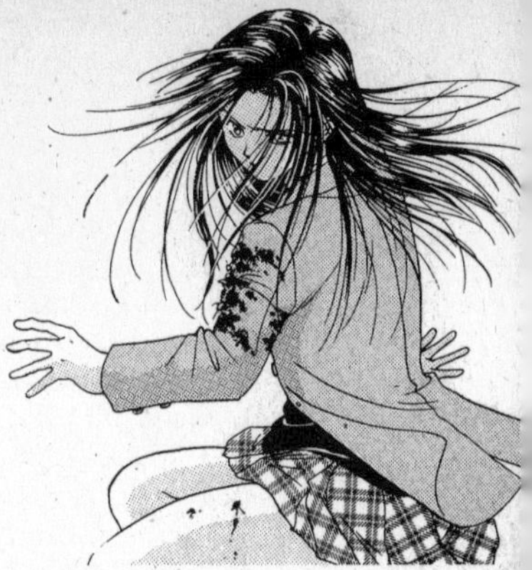

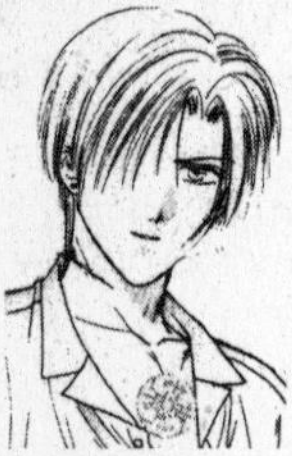

AKI MIKAGE: Aya's twin brother. While the consciousness of Ceres is taking over Aya, Aki is showing signs of bearing the consciousness of the founder (progenitor) of the Mikage family line. Placed under confinement by the Mikage family to keep him separated from Aya, still nothing will keep him from her....

CERES: Once upon a time...long, long ago...a ten'nyo named Ceres descended to Earth. Her hagoromo or "feathered robes" stolen, Ceres—unable to return to the heavens—was forced by the human thief to become his wife and bear his children...thus beginning the Mikage family line. Awakened after aeons of waiting—and anger—Ceres wants her hagoromo back and vows to use all her celestial powers to avenge herself against the descendants of the man who wronged her.

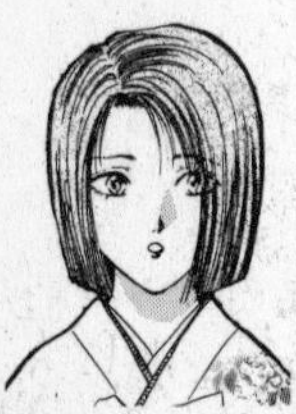

SUZUMI: Instructor of traditional Japanese dance and descendant of ten'nyo or "celestial maidens" herself. A big sister figure, Suzumi has welcomed Aya into her household, and is more than happy to provide her with all the protection, assistance and support that she can.

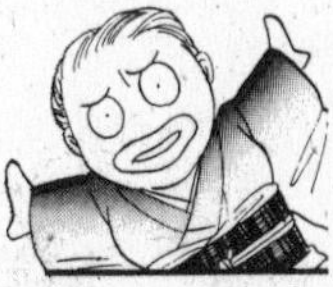

MRS. Q (ODA-KYÛ): Eccentric yet loyal-to-a-fault servant of the Aogiri household.

You may have noticed some unfamiliar people and things mentioned in CERES. VIZ left these Japanese pop-culture references as they originally appeared in the manga series. Here's an explanation for those who may not be so J-Pop savvy:

Page 22: A "translation" into Japanese, Assam's language (speech style) is rendered deliberately stilted

Page 49: "Tokyo Disneyland" is actually located in Chiba

Page 53: Okinawan variants of the by-now familiar-to-Ceres-fans "ten'nyo" legend

Page 85: Said to be a combination of the Spanish words alivio (relaxation) and villa (country house), the Hotel Alivila is a famous Okinawa luxury resort

Page 103: "Tamahome" is the male romantic lead in Watase's "other" popular series, "Fushigi Yûgi (The Mysterious Play)"

Page 120: During the Jomon Period (ca. 10,000 BC to 300 BC) in Japan, the inhabitants were hunter-gatherers and fishermen. The Jomon pottery that comes from this time is typified by rope pattern designs

Page 130: A popular recreational activity dating far, far back into Japanese history, otsukimi or "moon-viewing" is usually enjoyed with various snacks—in this case, some earthy-tasting "dirt dumplings" whipped up by Yûhi

Page 131: "Song to Fly," the 1998 album by anime fan-favorite composer Yoko Kanno (Macross Plus, Please Save My Earth)

Page 174: "Puri-kura"—kind of like the usual photo booths found at airports, arcades, etc., except what "Print Club" machines do is print the photos on handy, postage stamp-sized stickers

CERES • CELESTIAL GAG PAGE (If you don't want your illusions spoiled, skip this!)

•Tōya's Past•

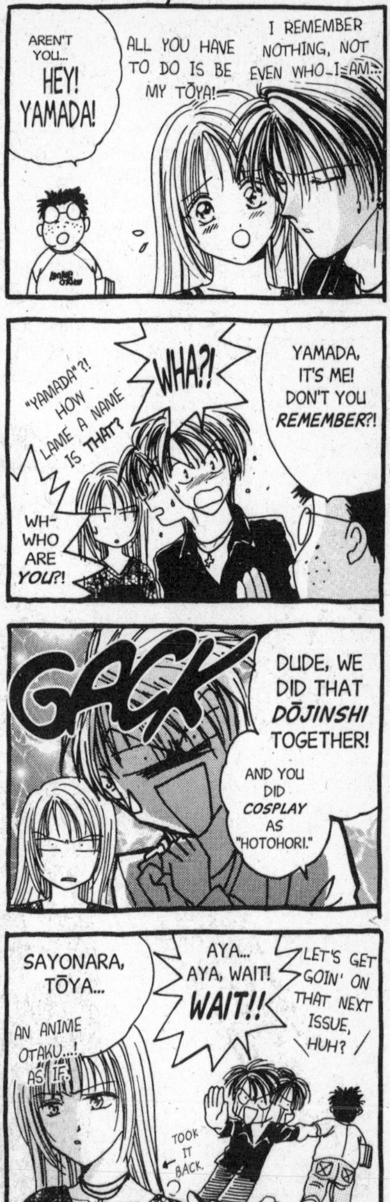
I REMEMBER NOTHING, NOT EVEN WHO I AM...
ALL YOU HAVE TO DO IS BE MY TŌYA!
AREN'T YOU... HEY! YAMADA!
YAMADA, IT'S ME! DON'T YOU *REMEMBER*?!
WHA?!
"YAMADA"?! HOW LAME A NAME IS *THAT*?
WH-WHO ARE *YOU*?!
DUDE, WE DID THAT *DŌJINSHI* TOGETHER!
AND YOU DID *COSPLAY* AS "HOTOHORI."
GACK
LET'S GET GOIN' ON THAT NEXT ISSUE, HUH?
AYA... AYA, WAIT! WAIT!!
SAYONARA, TŌYA...
AN ANIME OTAKU...! AS IF.
TOOK IT BACK.

•Refer to Vol. 5!•

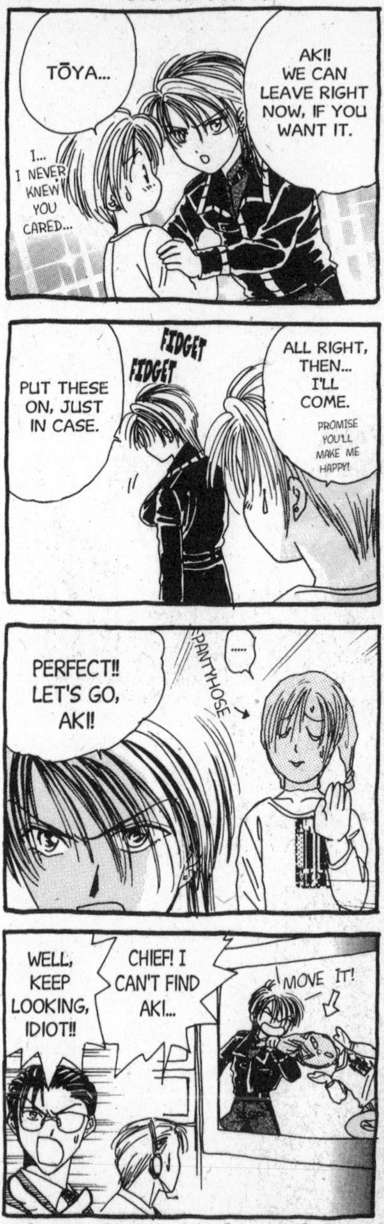
AKI! WE CAN LEAVE RIGHT NOW, IF YOU WANT IT.
TŌYA...
I... I NEVER KNEW YOU CARED...
ALL RIGHT, THEN... I'LL COME.
PROMISE YOU'LL MAKE ME HAPPY!
FIDGET FIDGET
PUT THESE ON, JUST IN CASE.
......
PANTYHOSE
PERFECT!! LET'S GO, AKI!
MOVE IT!
CHIEF! I CAN'T FIND AKI...
WELL, KEEP LOOKING, IDIOT!!

Ideas by Assistant "H." I swear, I almost died laughing when she told me.
To all the Yamadas, anime otaku, and Tōya fans out there–forgive me!!
...Okay, the pantyhose-part was mine.

TO BE **CONTINUED** (?)

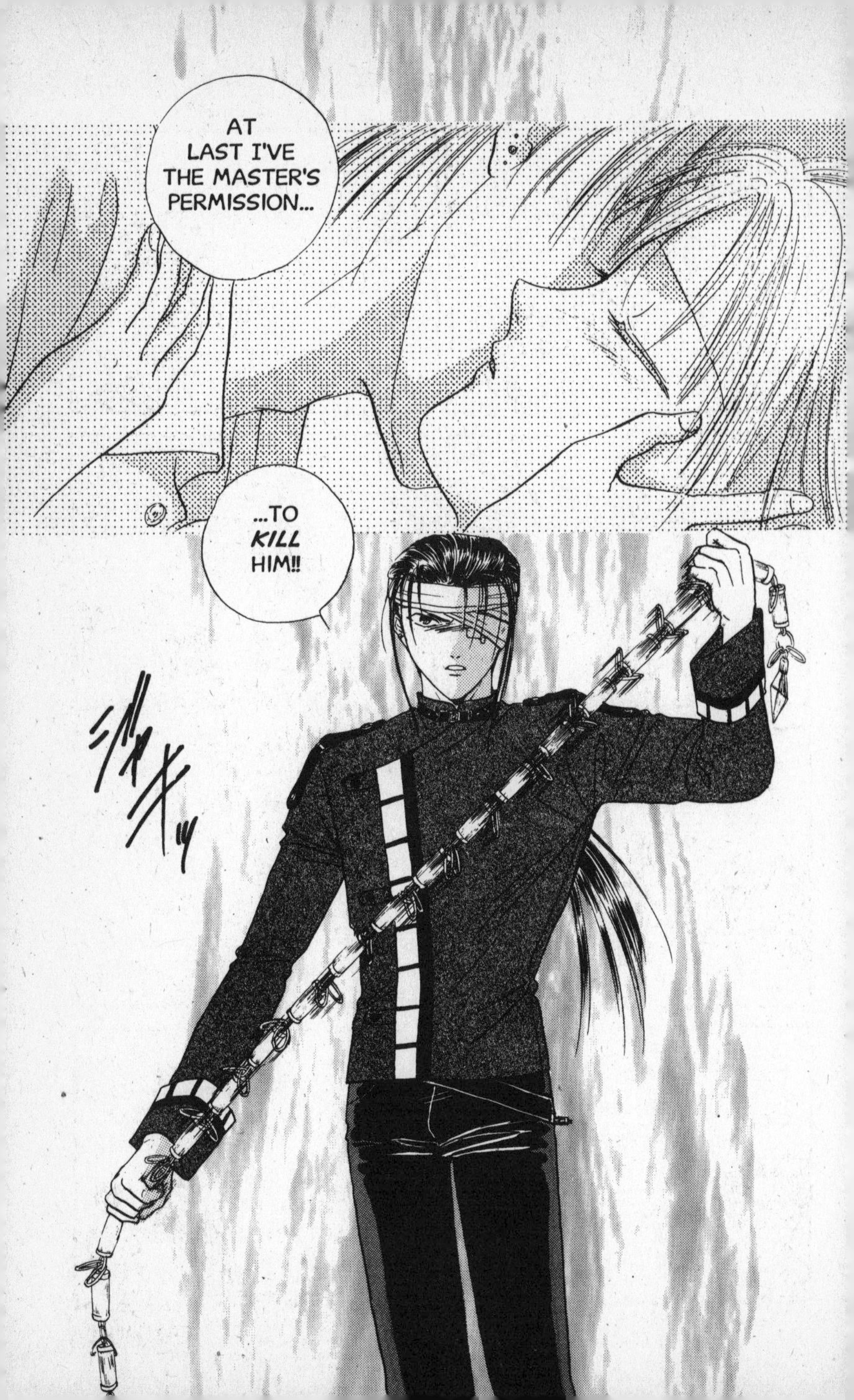
AT LAST I'VE THE MASTER'S PERMISSION...
...TO *KILL* HIM!!

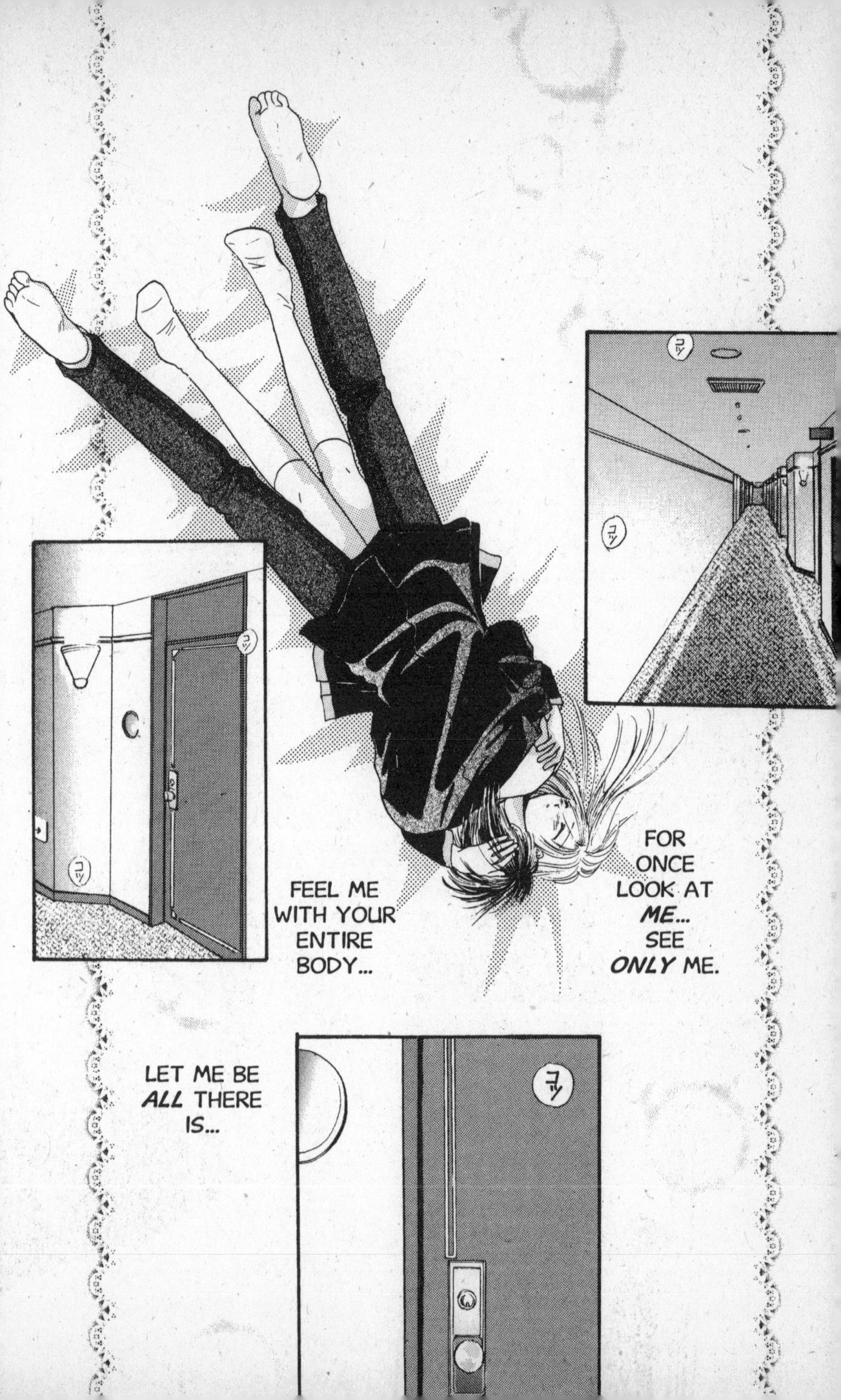

コッ
コッ
FOR ONCE LOOK AT ME... SEE ONLY ME.
コッ
コッ
FEEL ME WITH YOUR ENTIRE BODY...
コッ
LET ME BE ALL THERE IS...

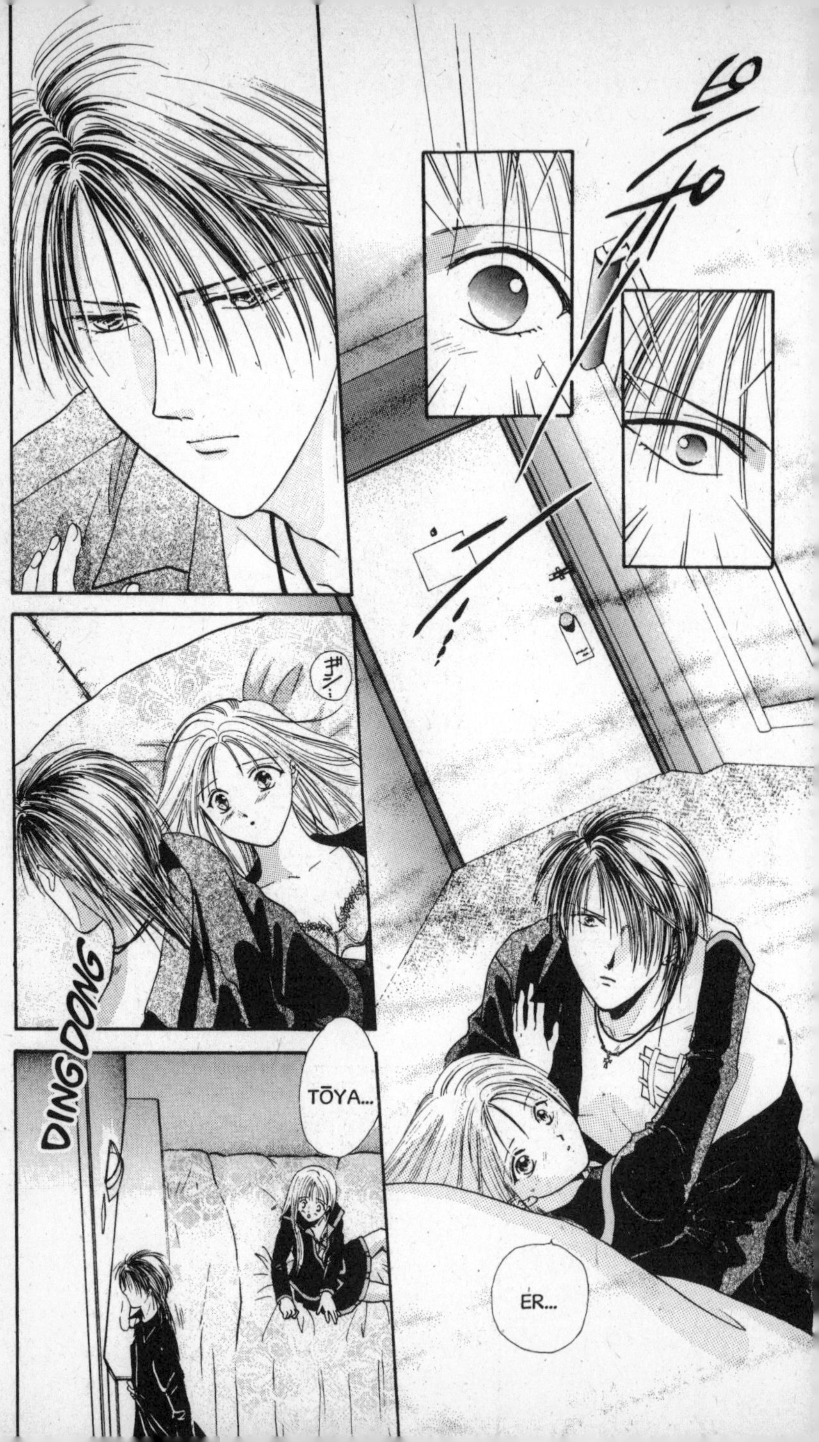
TŌYA...
ER...
DING DONG

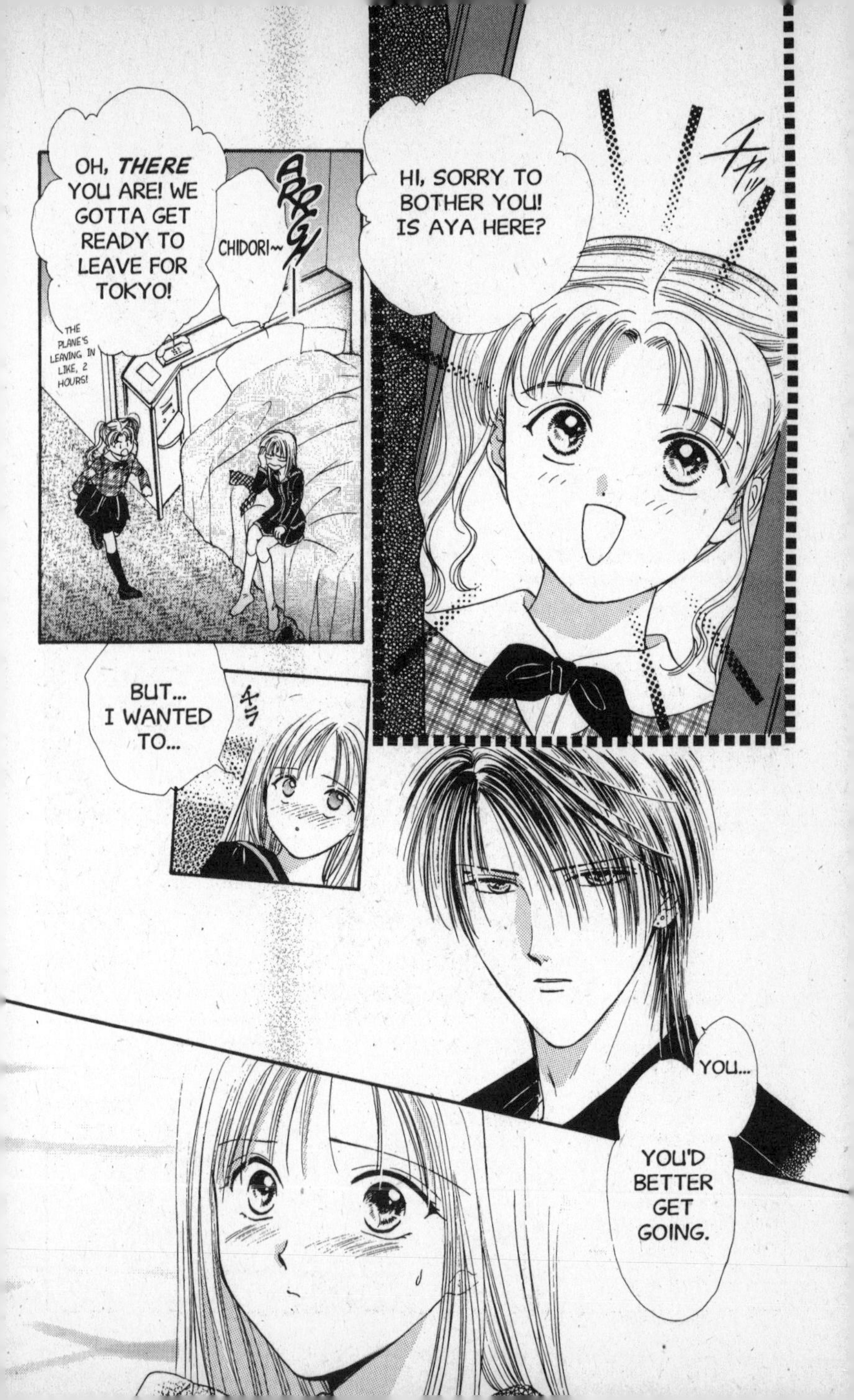
HI, SORRY TO BOTHER YOU! IS AYA HERE?
ARRGH
CHIDORI~
OH, THERE YOU ARE! WE GOTTA GET READY TO LEAVE FOR TOKYO!
THE PLANE'S LEAVING IN LIKE, 2 HOURS!
BUT... I WANTED TO...
YOU...
YOU'D BETTER GET GOING.

Ceres: 7

Hey, everyone! We meet again. The printing of [the Japan-released] Volume 6 made me a little sad, in that some of my writing here was blurred. Maybe people who can't press down hard enough oughtn't use nib pens.... (I write with such little force that I never form calluses, no matter how much I draw.) My grip is about 25kg on my right, 15 on my left. I'm so weak~~
Now, then. Let's start with the Okinawa autograph session. Thanks so much to all who came! It was at a bookstore in a department store called "Palette Kumoji" (I think), and I was happy so many could come.
I took pictures with most who showed, and I don't usually do that. Why did I, this time...? Back when I took my assistants there on the research trip for Volume 6, I thought it was a wonderful place—and I felt it this time, too. I'm seriously jealous of Okinawans who get to live surrounded by such natural beauty all the time. One of my assistants, "M," is totally mad for Okinawa. ☺ She chose to take her own vacation there, and has declared that someday she's going to retire there, too. ☺ I've always been interested in Okinawan folk songs, and so one night we went to a folk bar. Once again, I thought it was wonderful.
This most recent trip was actually my third time. The first time, I learned about Okinawa's painful history—it was a profound experience. The second time, I went with my editor (it was work-related), and we had lots of fun going on a tour of the acting-school and stuff.

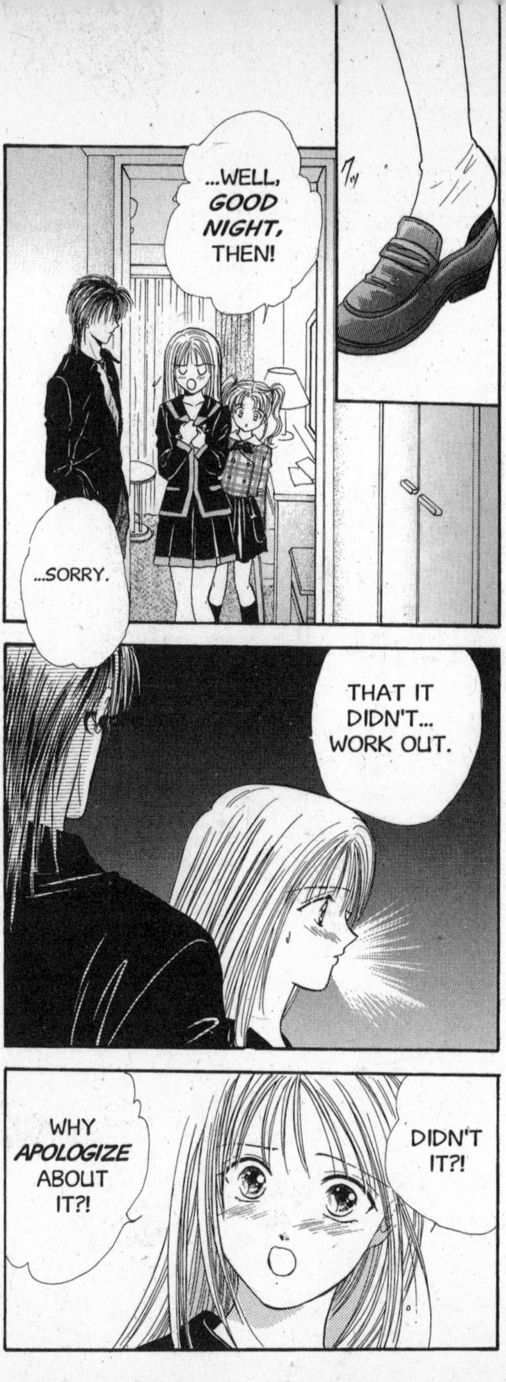
...WELL, GOOD NIGHT, THEN!
...SORRY.
THAT IT DIDN'T... WORK OUT.
DIDN'T IT?!
WHY APOLOGIZE ABOUT IT?!

Can I just say that I think the duo "FEEL" is cool?

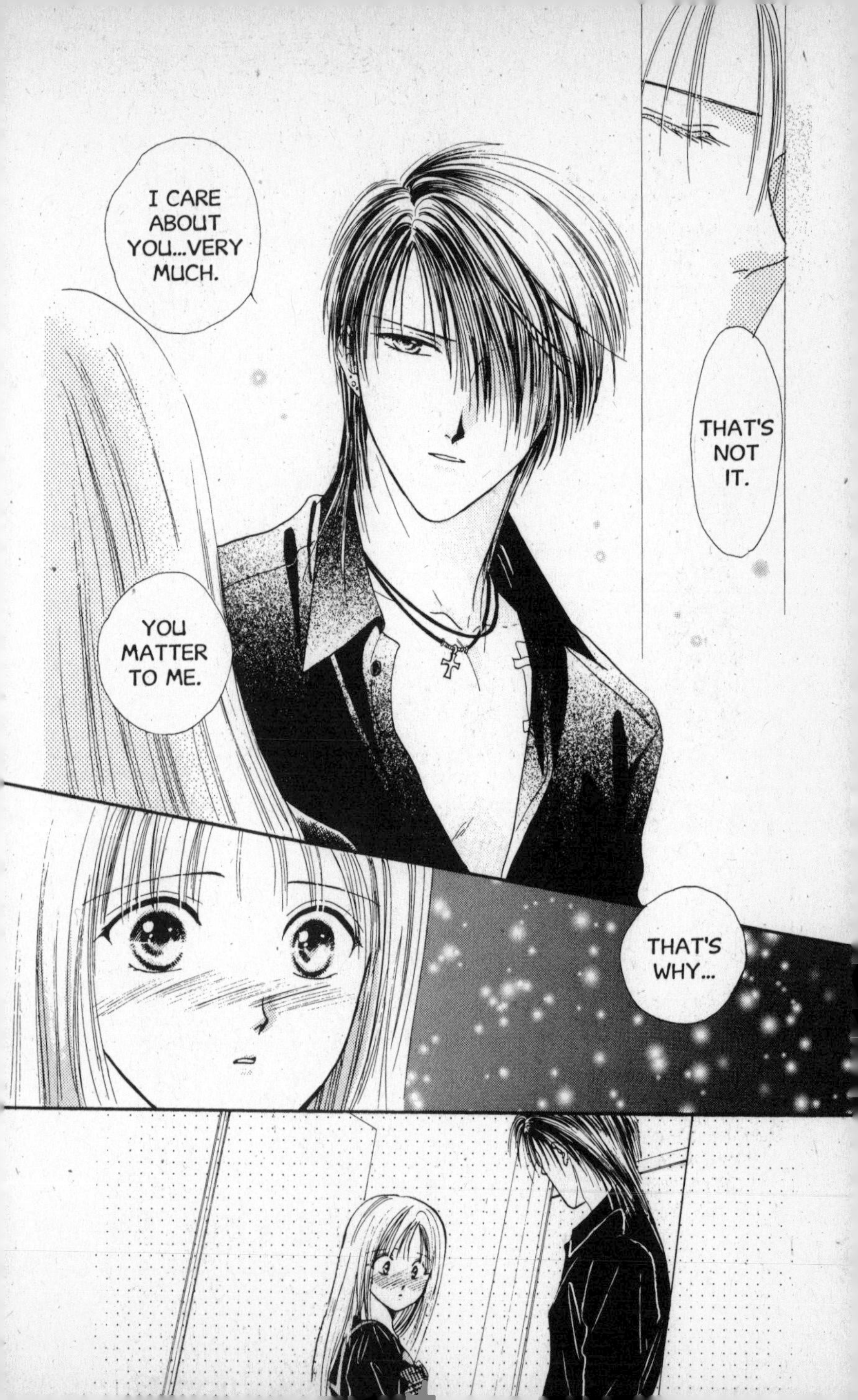

THAT'S NOT IT.
I CARE ABOUT YOU...VERY MUCH.
YOU MATTER TO ME.
THAT'S WHY...

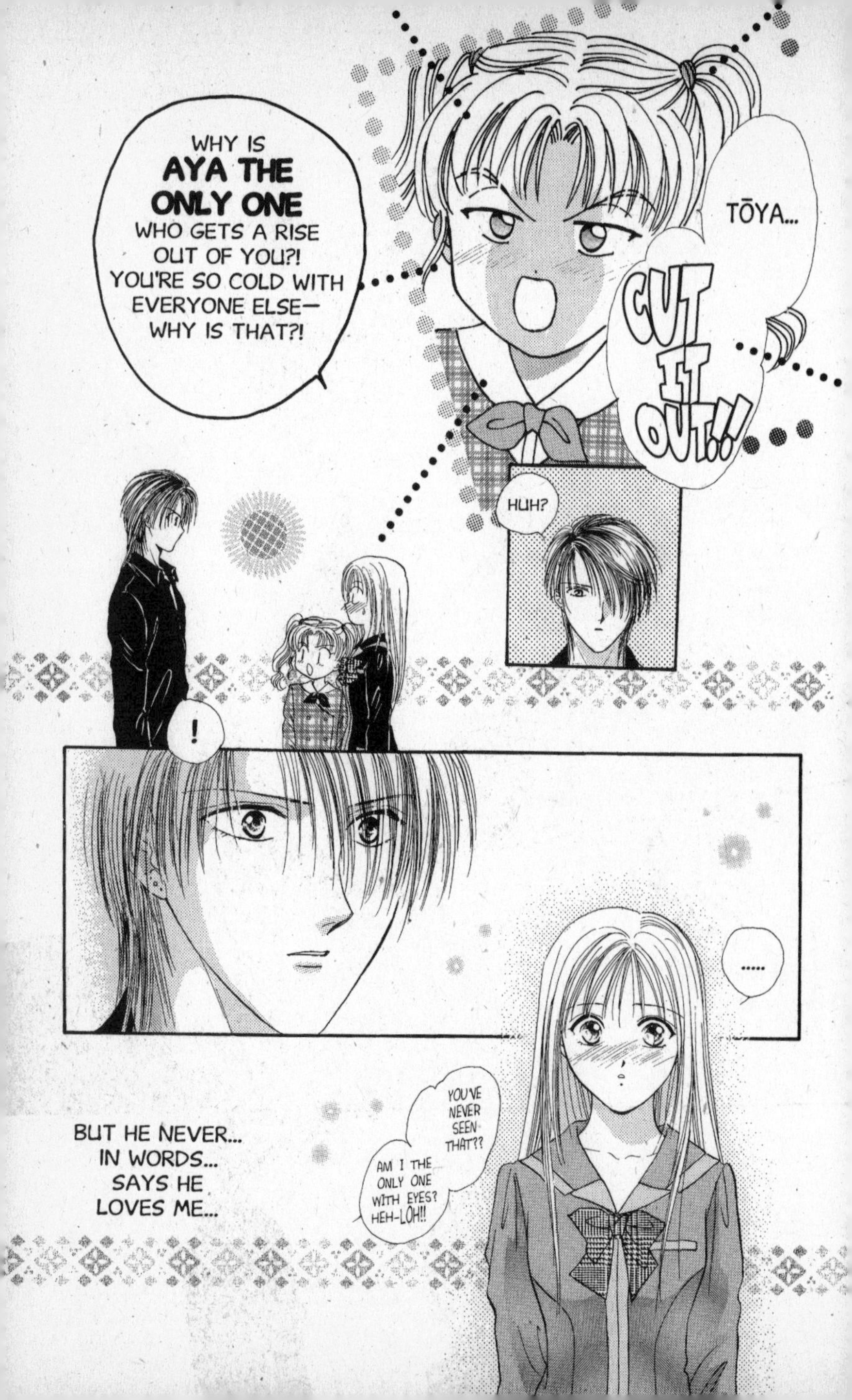
TŌYA...
CUT IT OUT!!
WHY IS AYA THE ONLY ONE WHO GETS A RISE OUT OF YOU?! YOU'RE SO COLD WITH EVERYONE ELSE— WHY IS THAT?!
HUH?
!
.....
YOU'VE NEVER SEEN THAT??
AM I THE ONLY ONE WITH EYES? HEH-LOH!!
BUT HE NEVER... IN WORDS... SAYS HE LOVES ME...

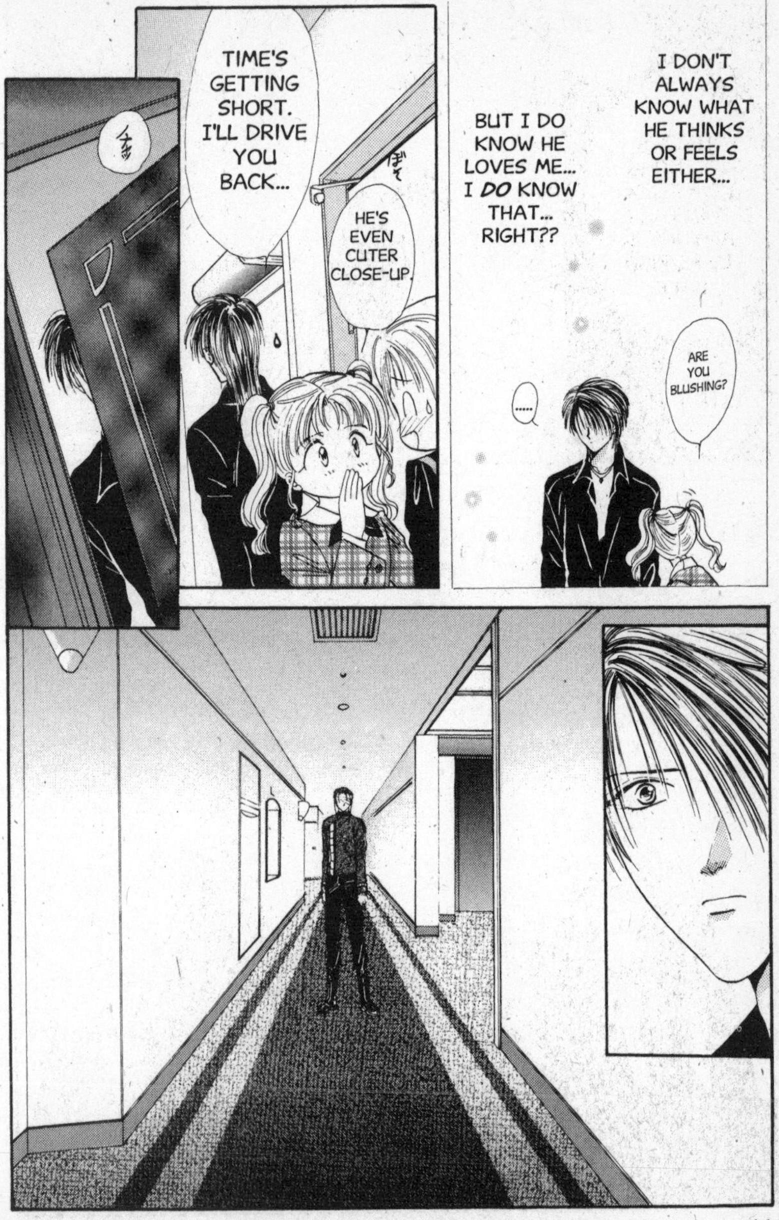
I DON'T ALWAYS KNOW WHAT HE THINKS OR FEELS EITHER...
BUT I DO KNOW HE LOVES ME... I *DO* KNOW THAT... RIGHT??
ARE YOU BLUSHING?
.....
TIME'S GETTING SHORT. I'LL DRIVE YOU BACK...
HE'S EVEN CUTER CLOSE-UP.

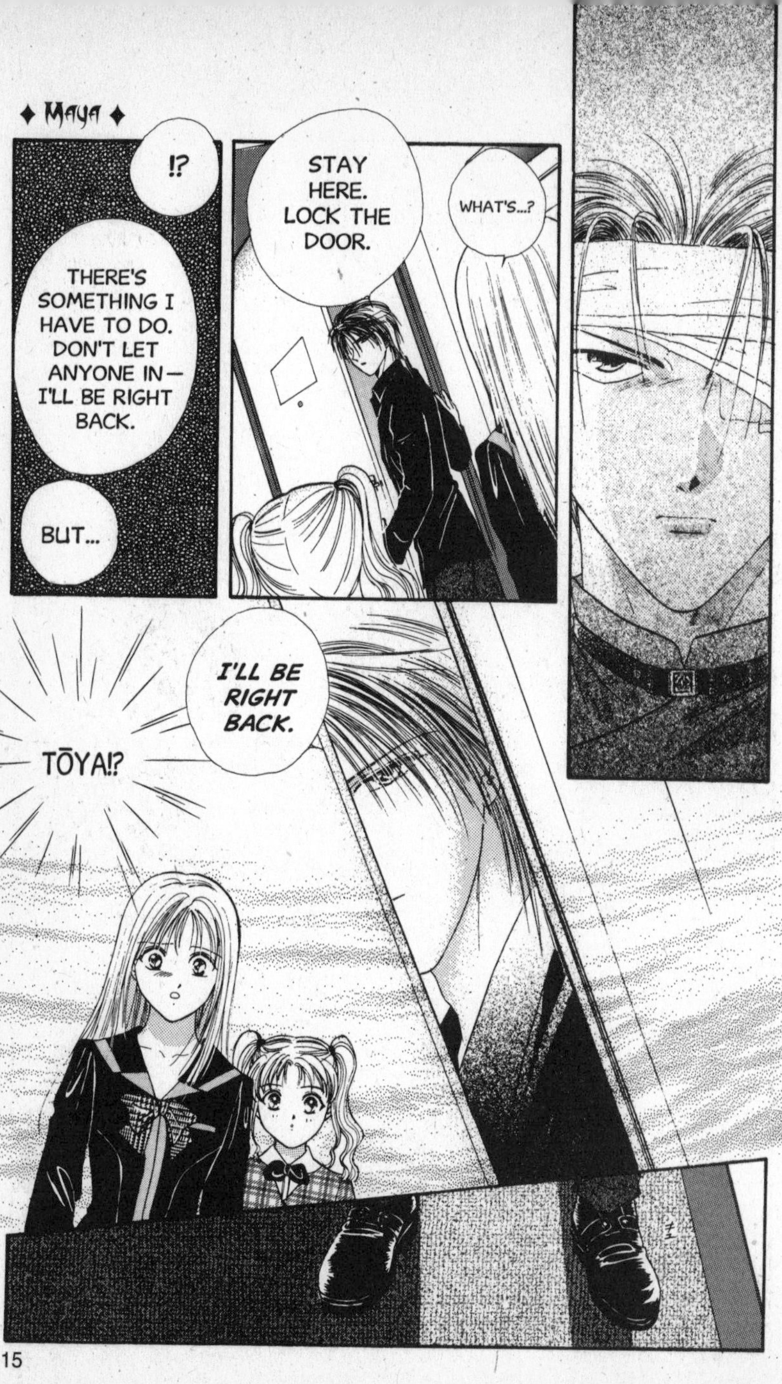
STAY HERE. LOCK THE DOOR.
WHAT'S...?
!?
THERE'S SOMETHING I HAVE TO DO. DON'T LET ANYONE IN— I'LL BE RIGHT BACK.
BUT...
I'LL BE RIGHT BACK.
TŌYA!?

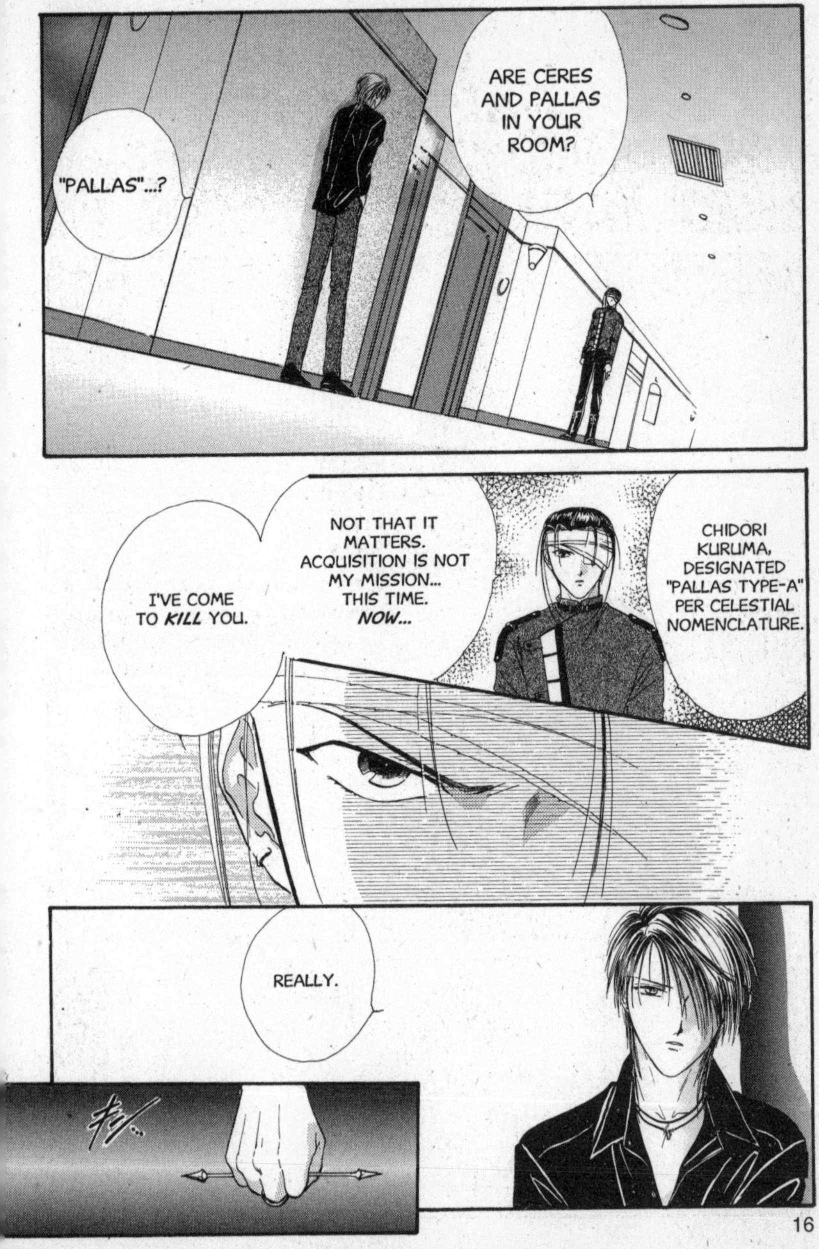
ARE CERES AND PALLAS IN YOUR ROOM?
"PALLAS"...?
CHIDORI KURUMA, DESIGNATED "PALLAS TYPE-A" PER CELESTIAL NOMENCLATURE.
NOT THAT IT MATTERS. ACQUISITION IS NOT MY MISSION... THIS TIME. *NOW...*
I'VE COME TO *KILL* YOU.
REALLY.

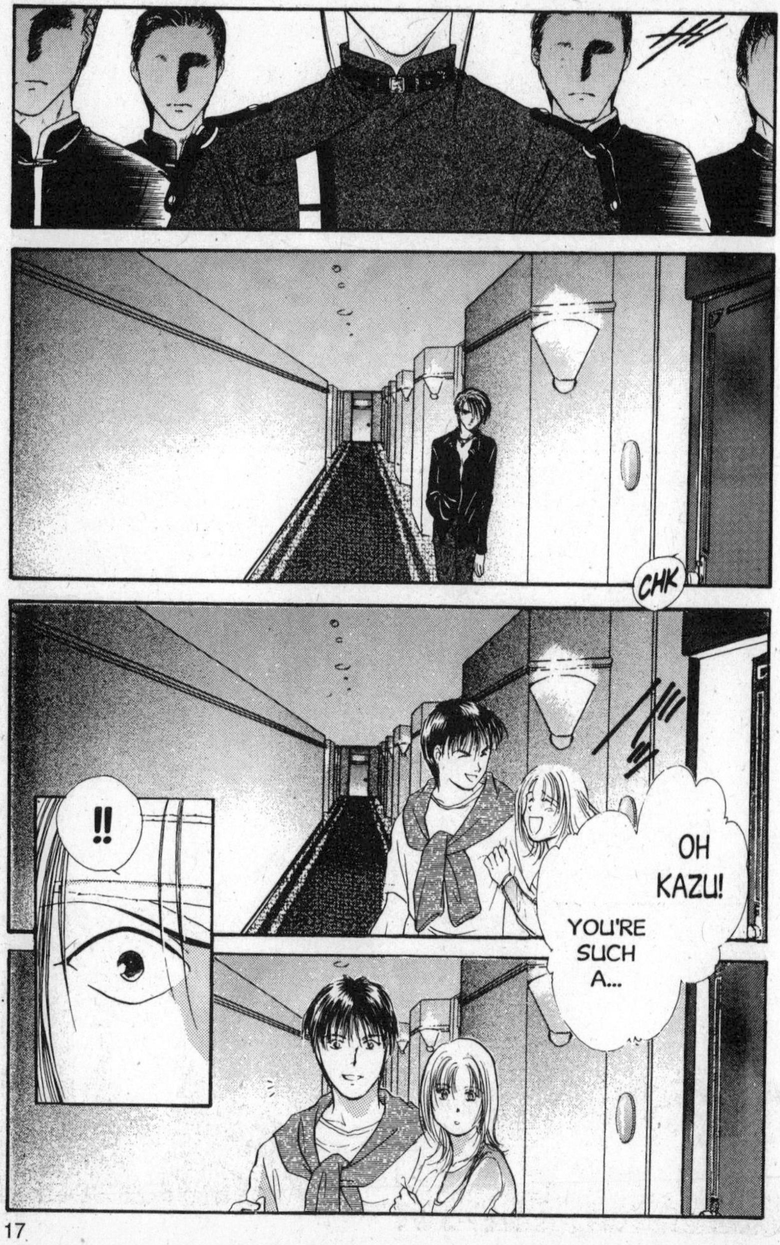
CHK
OH KAZU!
YOU'RE SUCH A...
!!

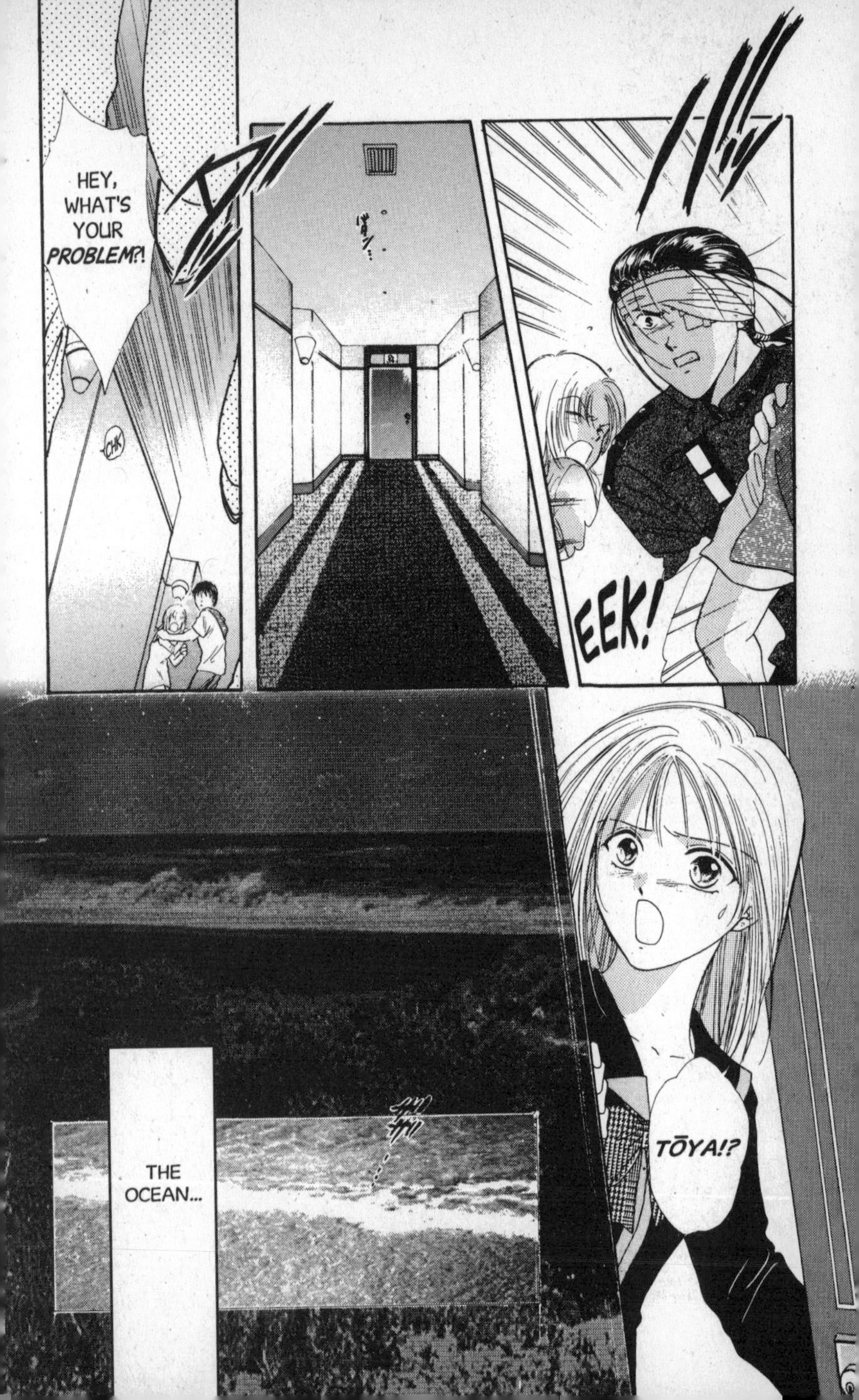
EEK!
HEY, WHAT'S YOUR PROBLEM?!
CHK
TŌYA!?
THE OCEAN...

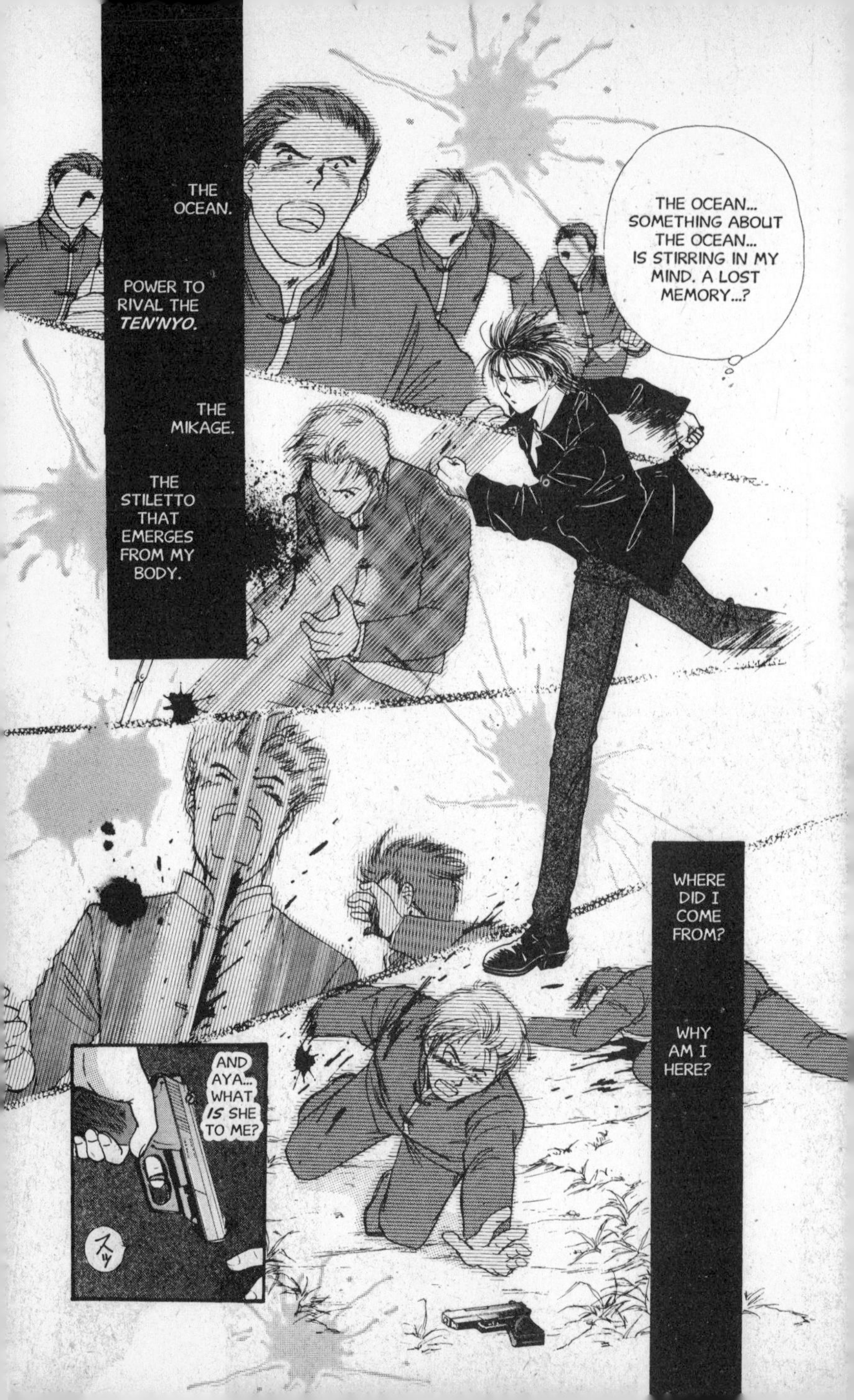
THE OCEAN... SOMETHING ABOUT THE OCEAN... IS STIRRING IN MY MIND. A LOST MEMORY...?
THE OCEAN.
POWER TO RIVAL THE *TEN'NYO.*
THE MIKAGE.
THE STILETTO THAT EMERGES FROM MY BODY.
WHERE DID I COME FROM?
WHY AM I HERE?
AND AYA... WHAT *IS* SHE TO ME?
スッ

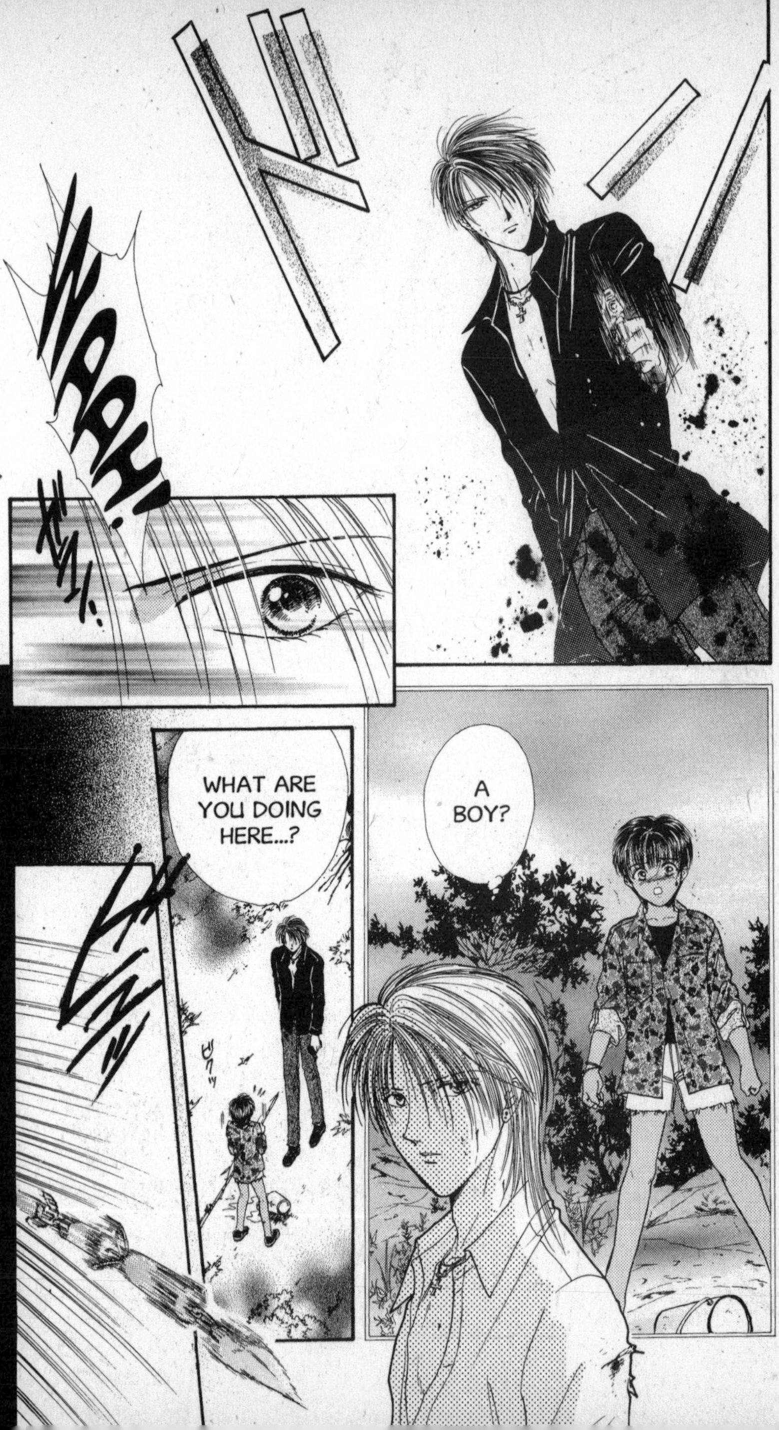
WAAH!
A BOY?
WHAT ARE YOU DOING HERE...?

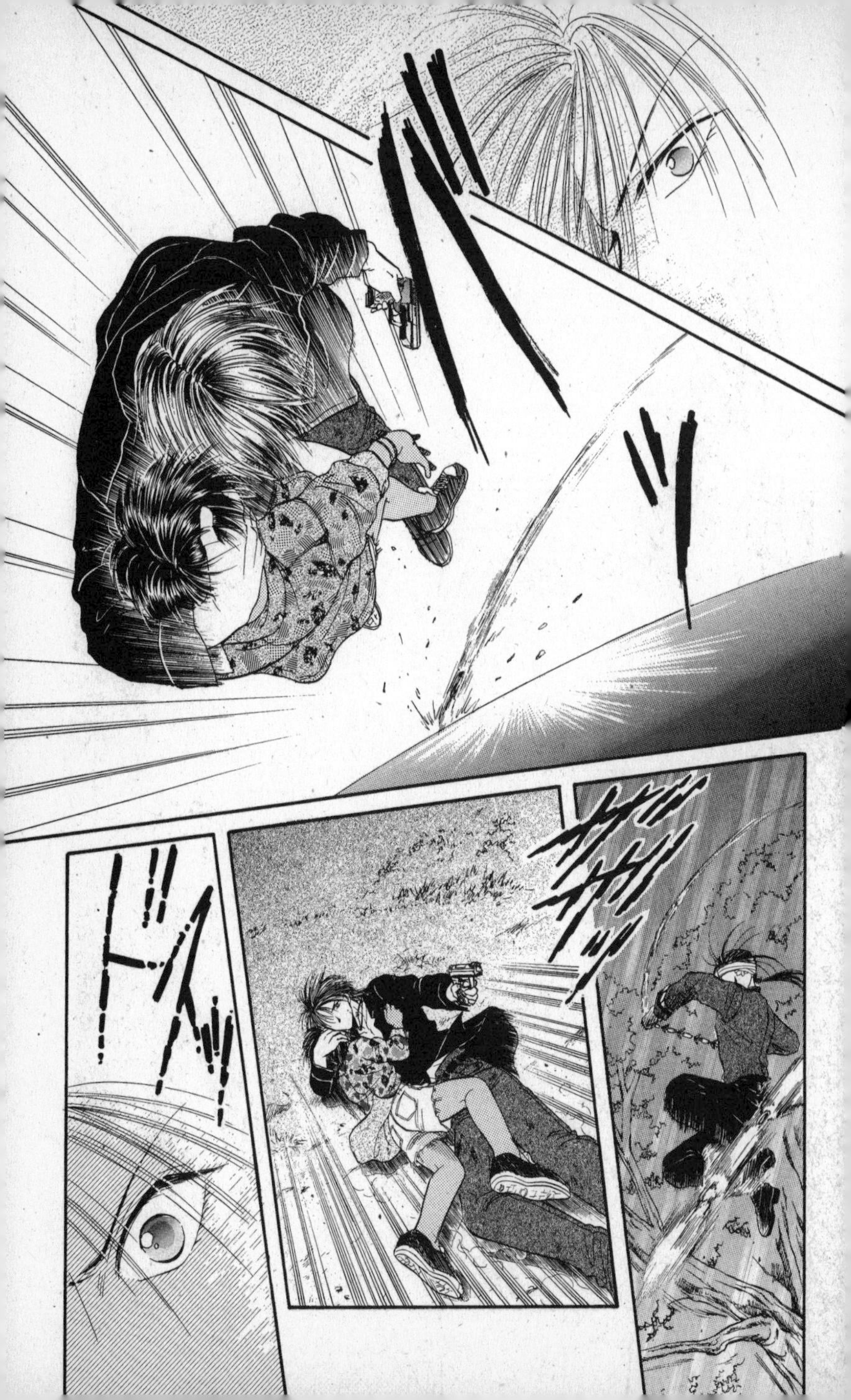
ザザッ
ドス!!

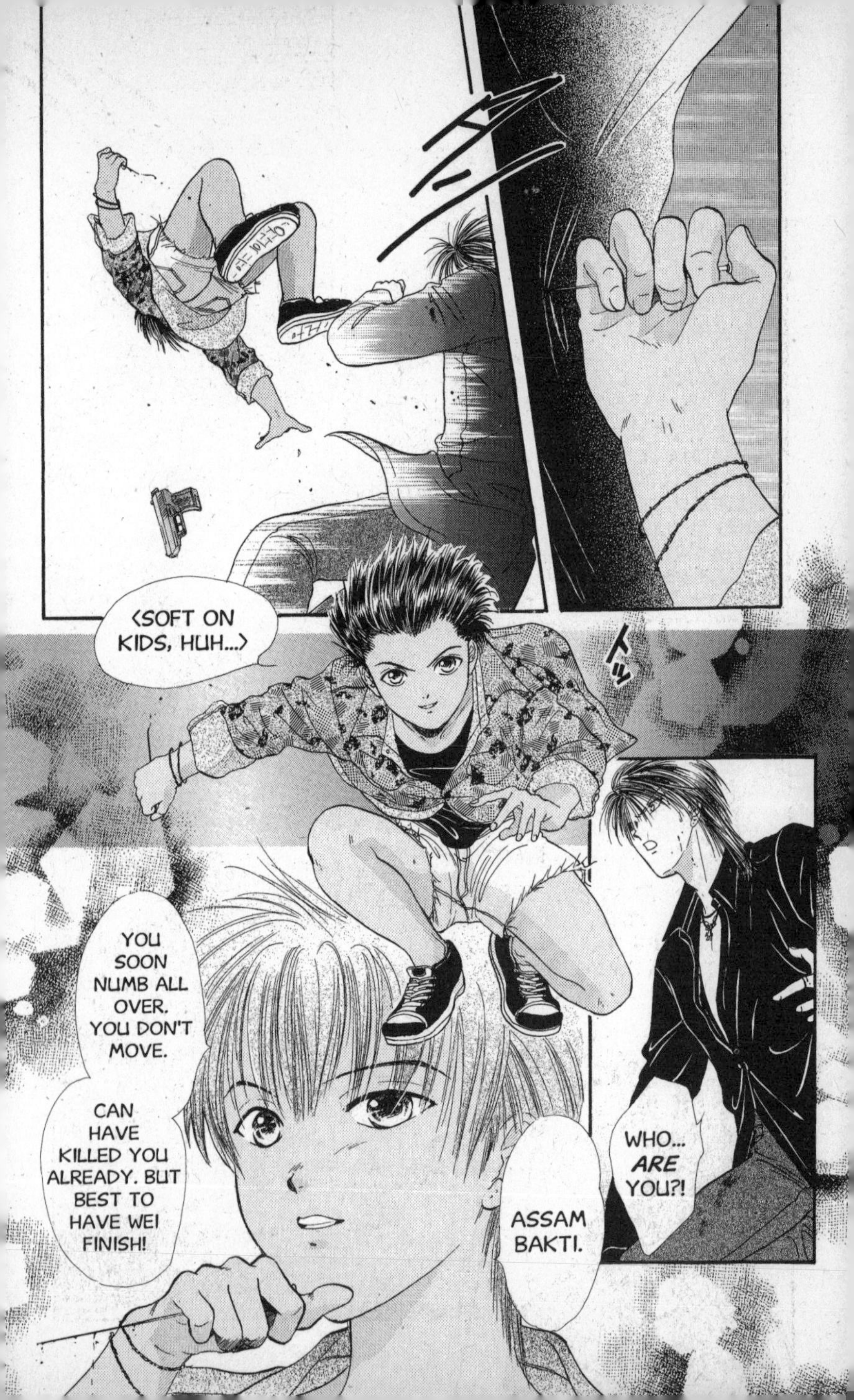
<SOFT ON KIDS, HUH...>
トッ
WHO... ARE YOU?!
ASSAM BAKTI.
YOU SOON NUMB ALL OVER. YOU DON'T MOVE.
CAN HAVE KILLED YOU ALREADY. BUT BEST TO HAVE WEI FINISH!

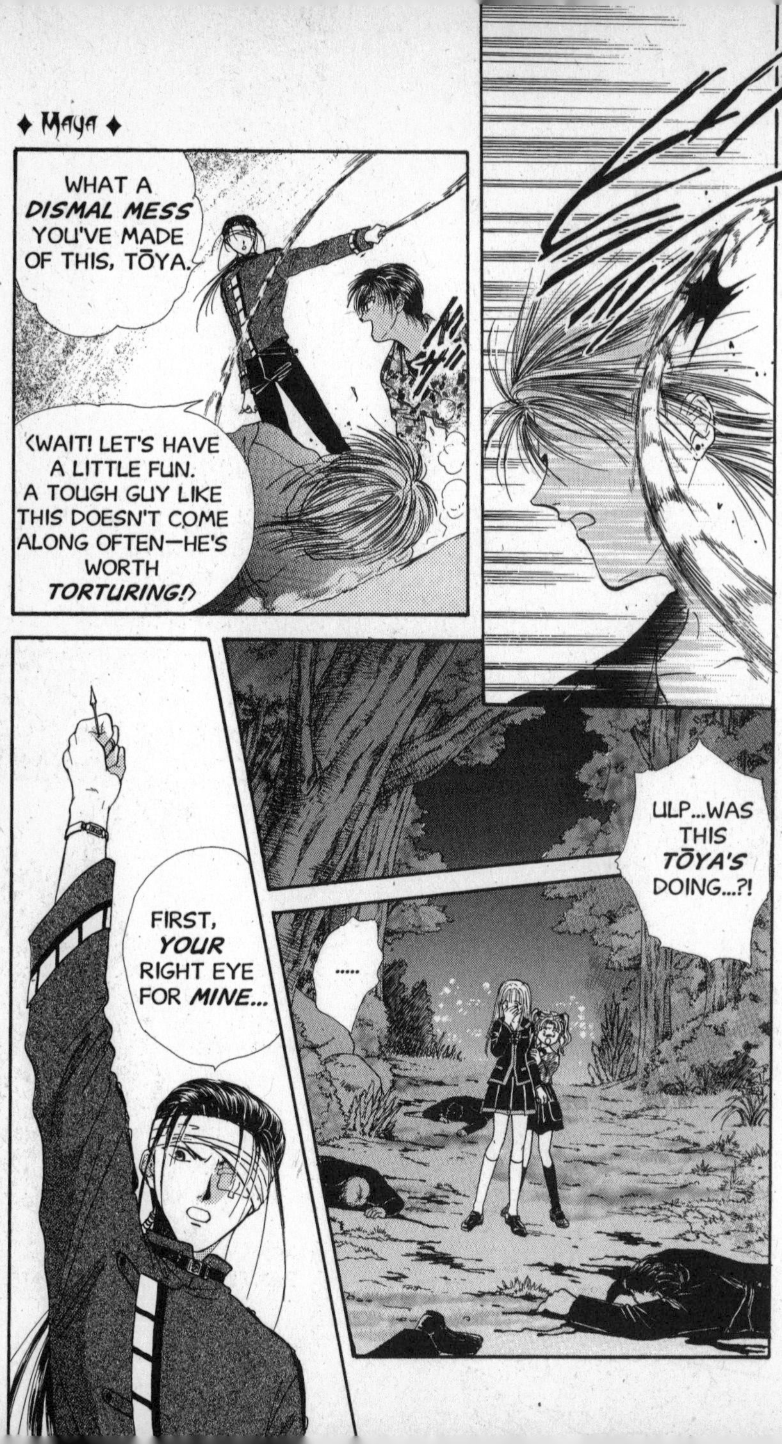
WHAT A *DISMAL MESS* YOU'VE MADE OF THIS, TŌYA.
<WAIT! LET'S HAVE A LITTLE FUN. A TOUGH GUY LIKE THIS DOESN'T COME ALONG OFTEN—HE'S WORTH *TORTURING!*>
ULP...WAS THIS *TŌYA'S* DOING...?!
.....
FIRST, *YOUR* RIGHT EYE FOR *MINE...*

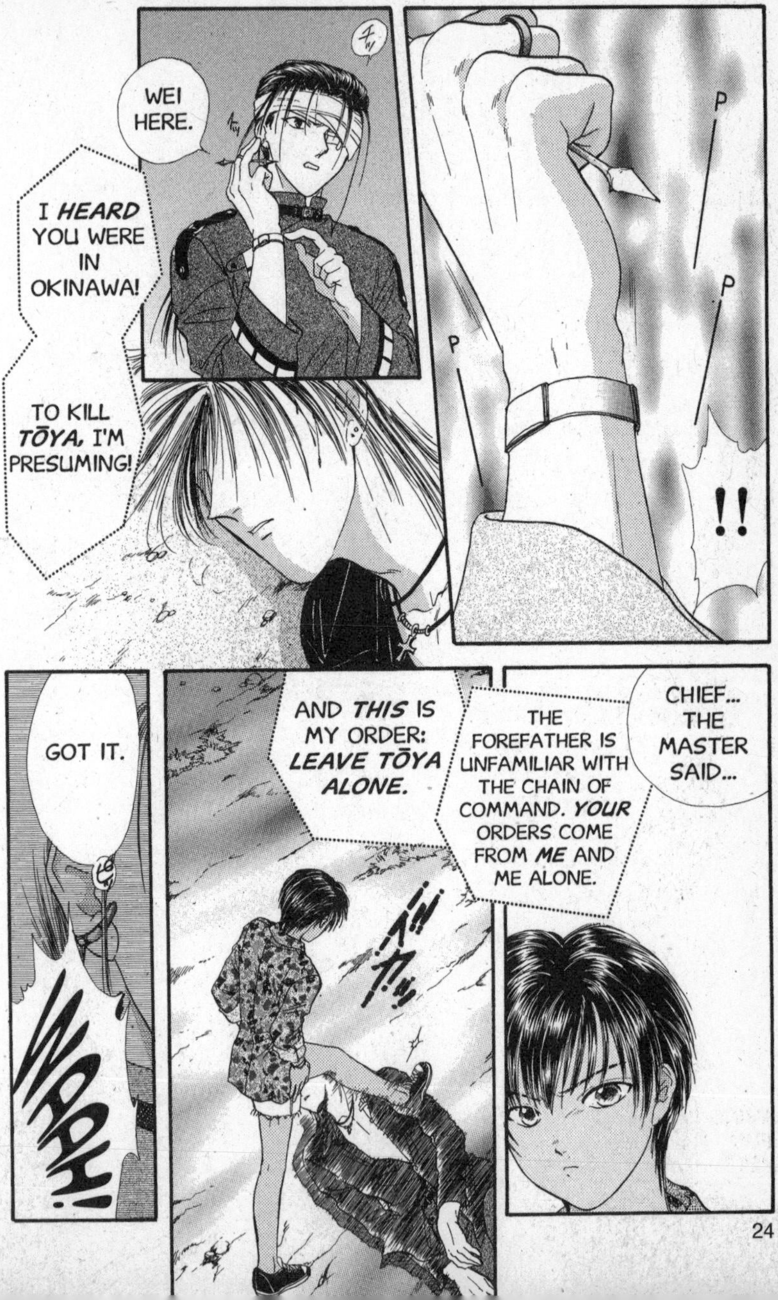

P
P
P
!!
WEI HERE.
I HEARD YOU WERE IN OKINAWA!
TO KILL TŌYA, I'M PRESUMING!
CHIEF... THE MASTER SAID...
THE FOREFATHER IS UNFAMILIAR WITH THE CHAIN OF COMMAND. YOUR ORDERS COME FROM ME AND ME ALONE.
AND THIS IS MY ORDER: LEAVE TŌYA ALONE.
GOT IT.
WAAH!

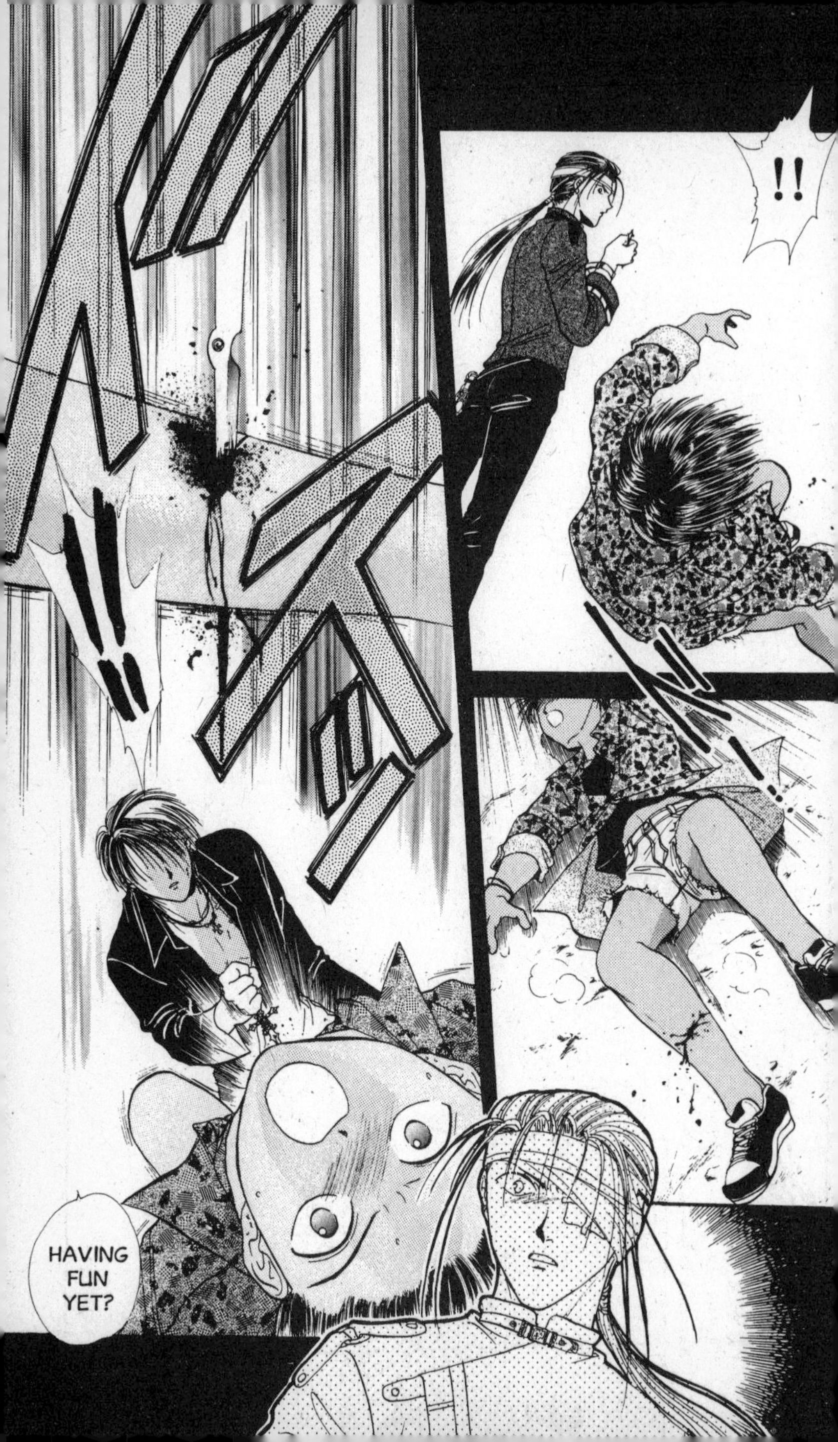
!!
!!
HAVING FUN YET?

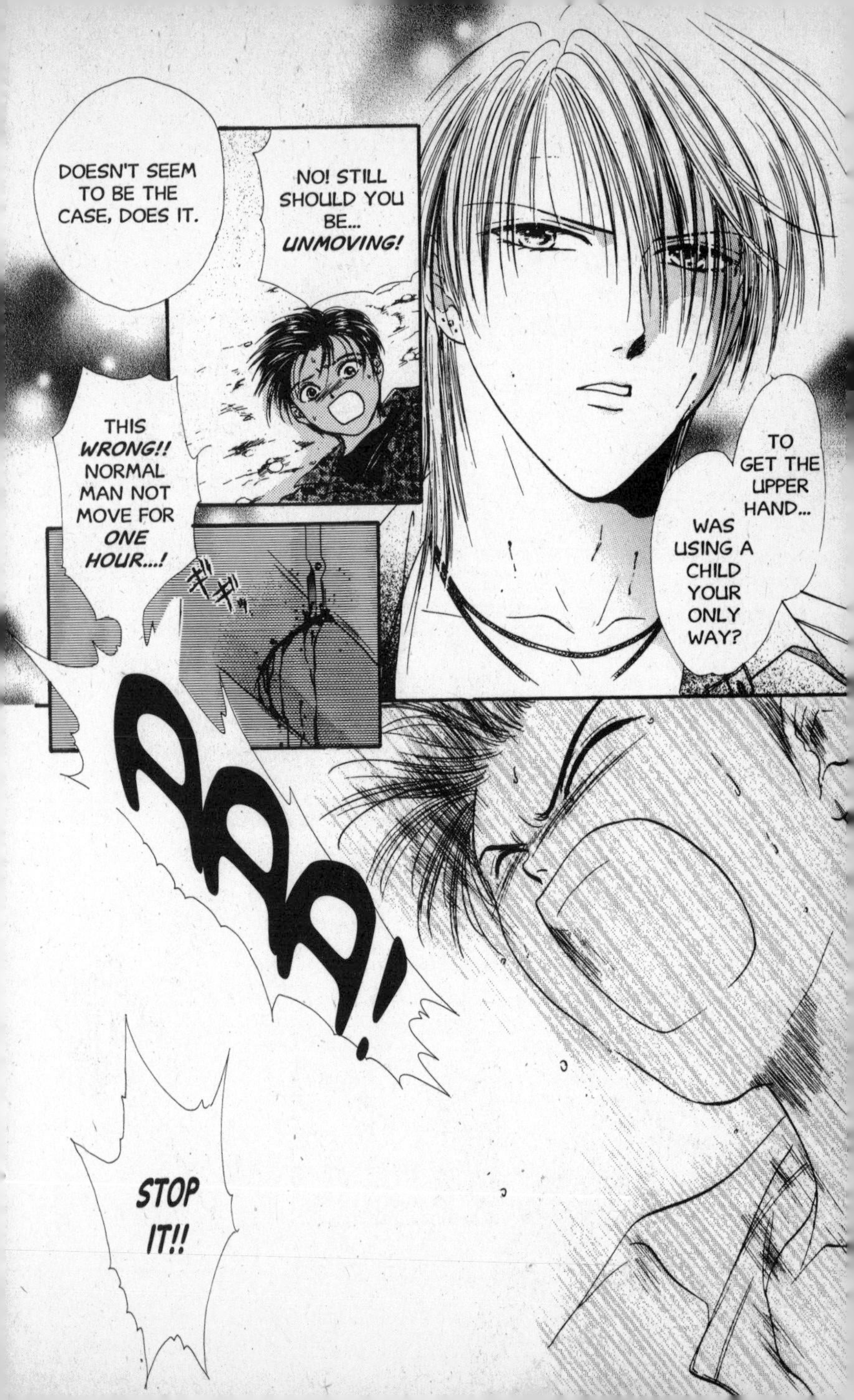
TO GET THE UPPER HAND... WAS USING A CHILD YOUR ONLY WAY?
DOESN'T SEEM TO BE THE CASE, DOES IT.
NO! STILL SHOULD YOU BE... UNMOVING!
THIS WRONG!! NORMAL MAN NOT MOVE FOR ONE HOUR...!
ギギ
STOP IT!!

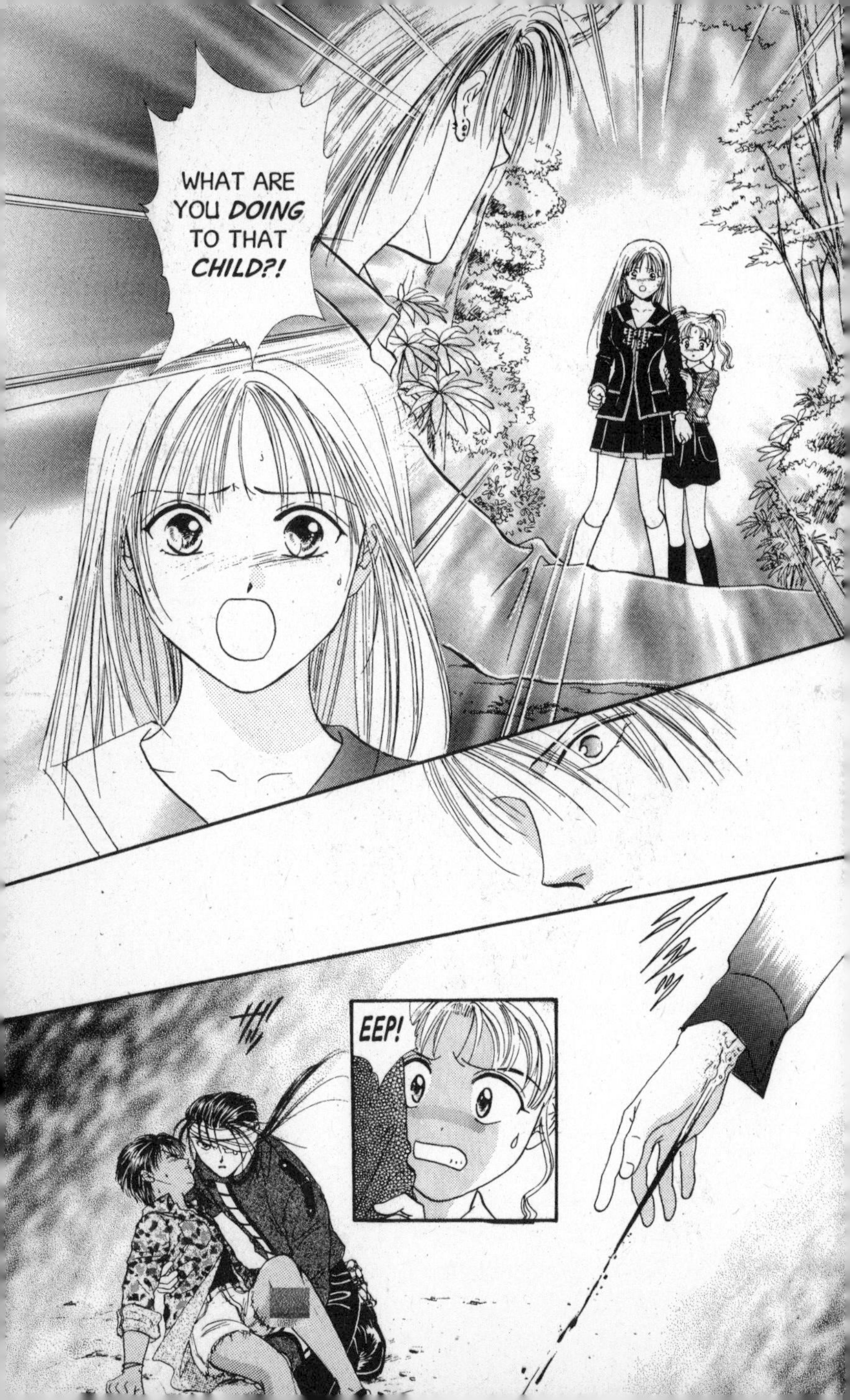
WHAT ARE YOU *DOING* TO THAT *CHILD?!*
EEP!

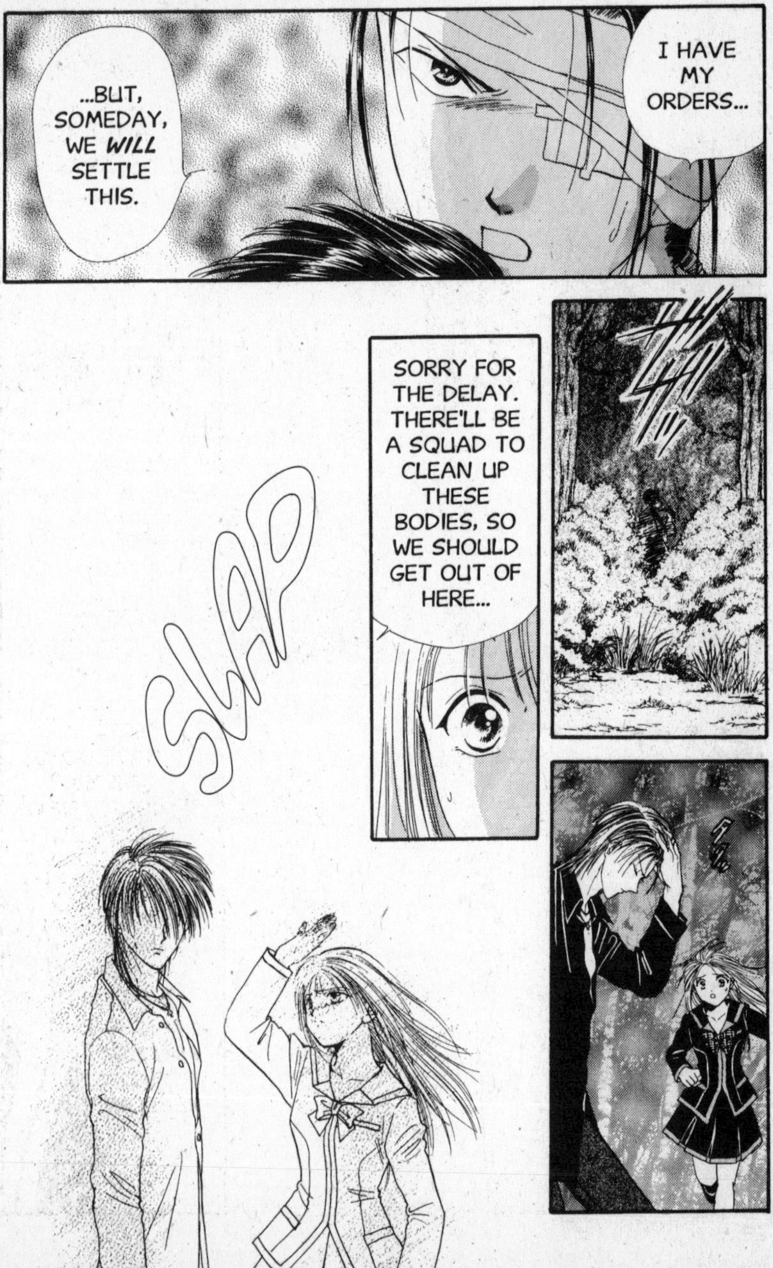
I HAVE MY ORDERS...
...BUT, SOMEDAY, WE *WILL* SETTLE THIS.
SORRY FOR THE DELAY. THERE'LL BE A SQUAD TO CLEAN UP THESE BODIES, SO WE SHOULD GET OUT OF HERE...
SLAP

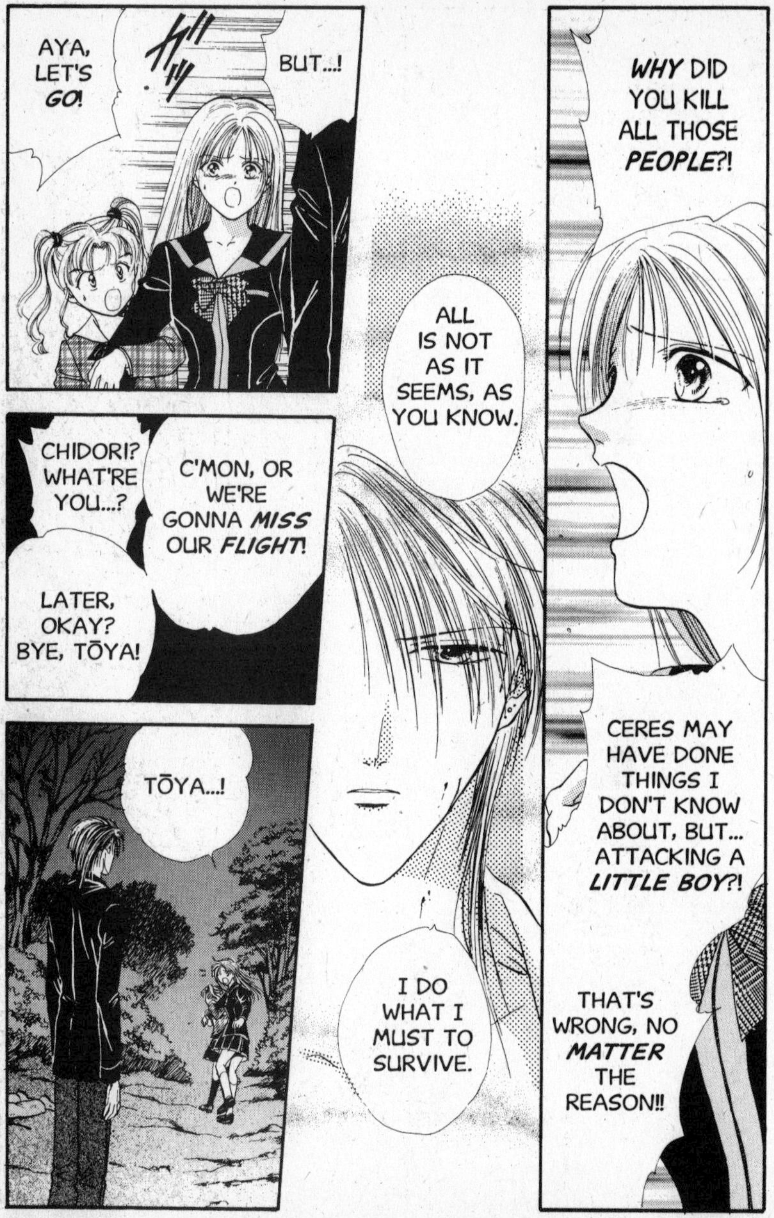
WHY DID YOU KILL ALL THOSE PEOPLE?!
ALL IS NOT AS IT SEEMS, AS YOU KNOW.
CERES MAY HAVE DONE THINGS I DON'T KNOW ABOUT, BUT... ATTACKING A LITTLE BOY?!
THAT'S WRONG, NO MATTER THE REASON!!
I DO WHAT I MUST TO SURVIVE.
BUT...!
AYA, LET'S GO!
C'MON, OR WE'RE GONNA MISS OUR FLIGHT!
CHIDORI? WHAT'RE YOU...?
LATER, OKAY? BYE, TŌYA!
TŌYA...!

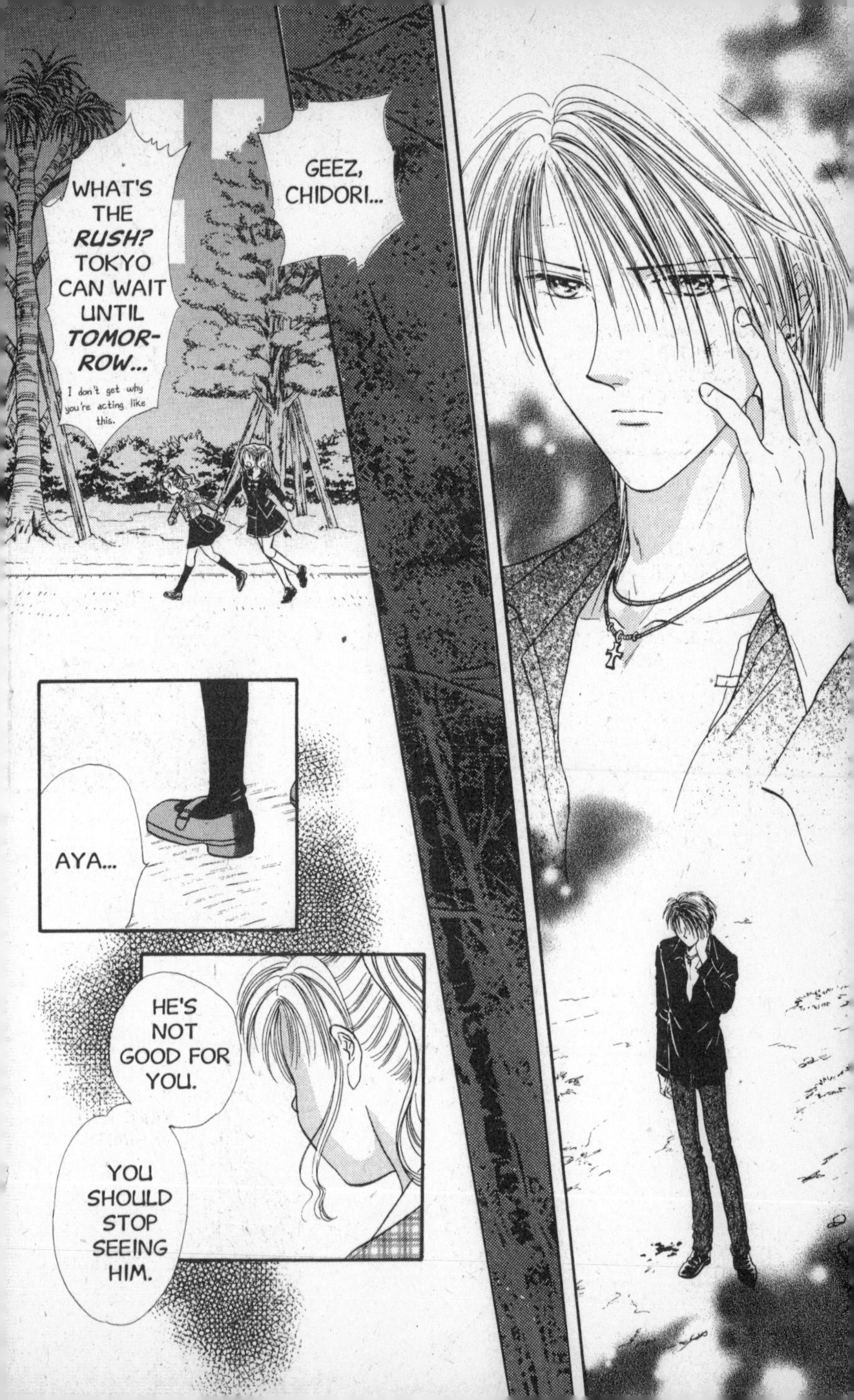
GEEZ, CHIDORI...
WHAT'S THE *RUSH?* TOKYO CAN WAIT UNTIL *TOMORROW...*
I don't get why you're acting like this.
AYA...
HE'S NOT GOOD FOR YOU.
YOU SHOULD STOP SEEING HIM.

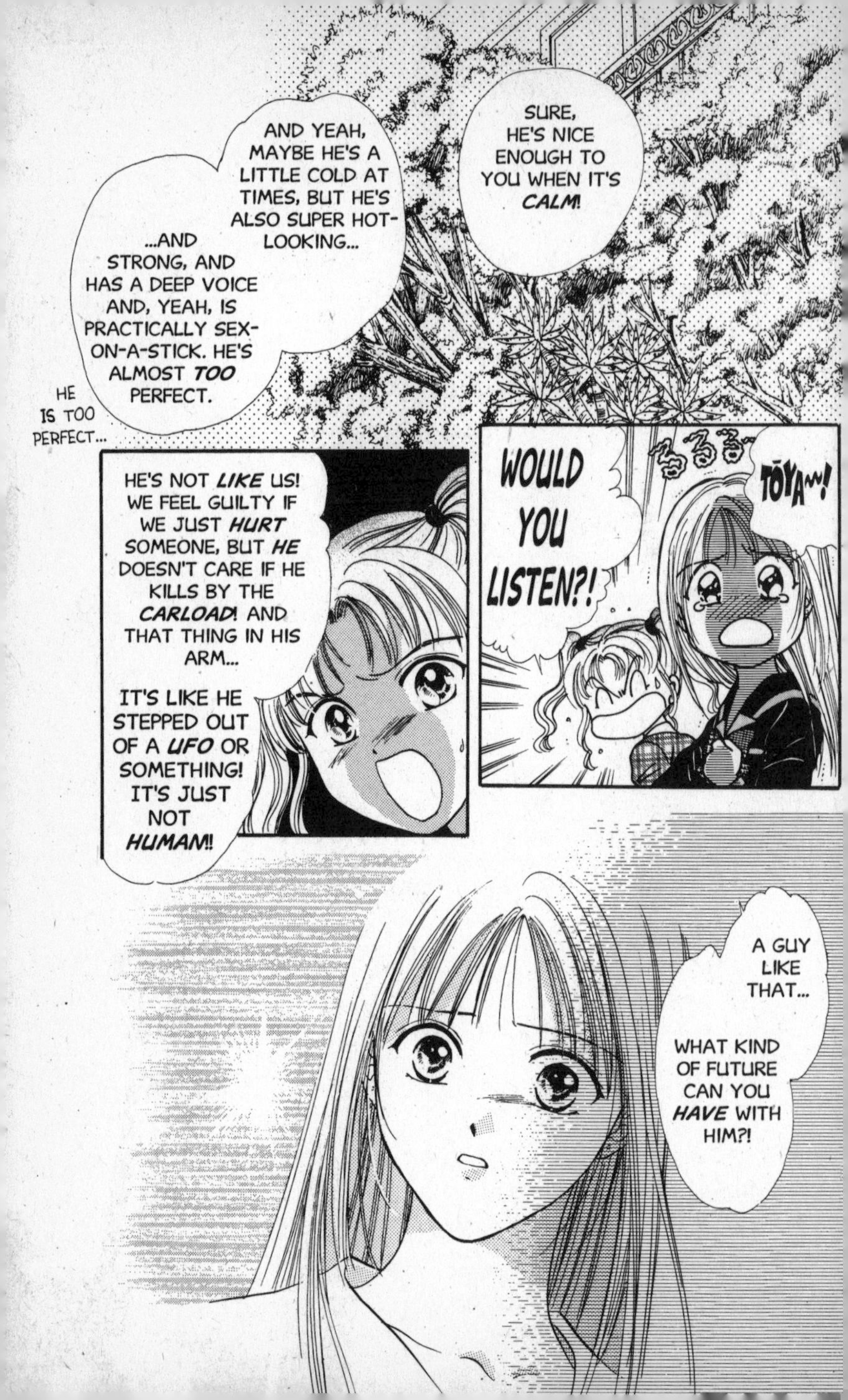
SURE, HE'S NICE ENOUGH TO YOU WHEN IT'S *CALM*!
AND YEAH, MAYBE HE'S A LITTLE COLD AT TIMES, BUT HE'S ALSO SUPER HOT-LOOKING...
...AND STRONG, AND HAS A DEEP VOICE AND, YEAH, IS PRACTICALLY SEX-ON-A-STICK. HE'S ALMOST *TOO* PERFECT.
HE IS TOO PERFECT...
TŌYA~!
WOULD YOU LISTEN?!
HE'S NOT *LIKE* US! WE FEEL GUILTY IF WE JUST *HURT* SOMEONE, BUT *HE* DOESN'T CARE IF HE KILLS BY THE *CARLOAD*! AND THAT THING IN HIS ARM...
IT'S LIKE HE STEPPED OUT OF A *UFO* OR SOMETHING! IT'S JUST NOT *HUMAN*!
A GUY LIKE THAT...
WHAT KIND OF FUTURE CAN YOU *HAVE* WITH HIM?!

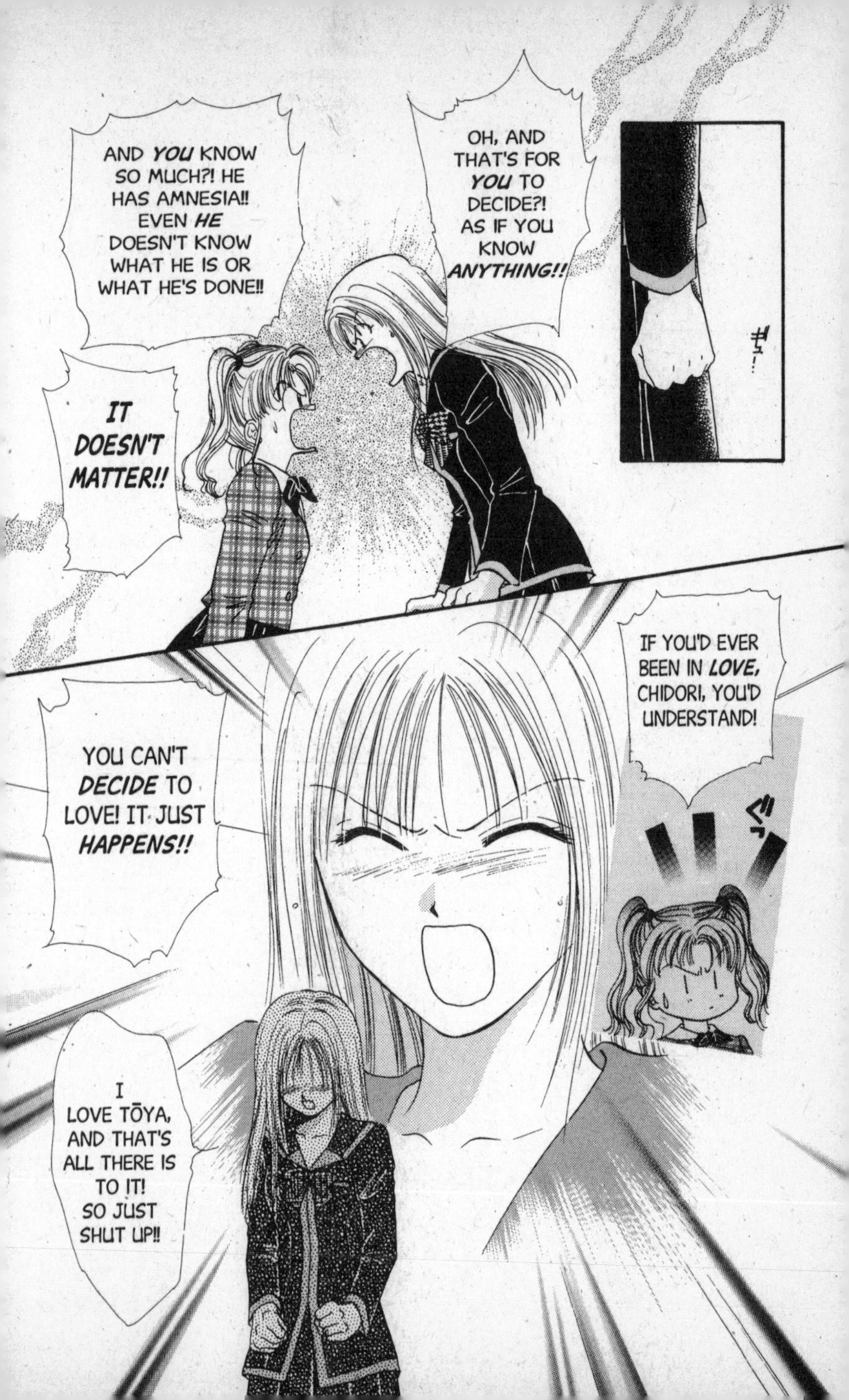
OH, AND THAT'S FOR YOU TO DECIDE?! AS IF YOU KNOW ANYTHING!!
AND YOU KNOW SO MUCH?! HE HAS AMNESIA!! EVEN HE DOESN'T KNOW WHAT HE IS OR WHAT HE'S DONE!!
IT DOESN'T MATTER!!
IF YOU'D EVER BEEN IN LOVE, CHIDORI, YOU'D UNDERSTAND!
YOU CAN'T DECIDE TO LOVE! IT JUST HAPPENS!!
I LOVE TŌYA, AND THAT'S ALL THERE IS TO IT! SO JUST SHUT UP!!

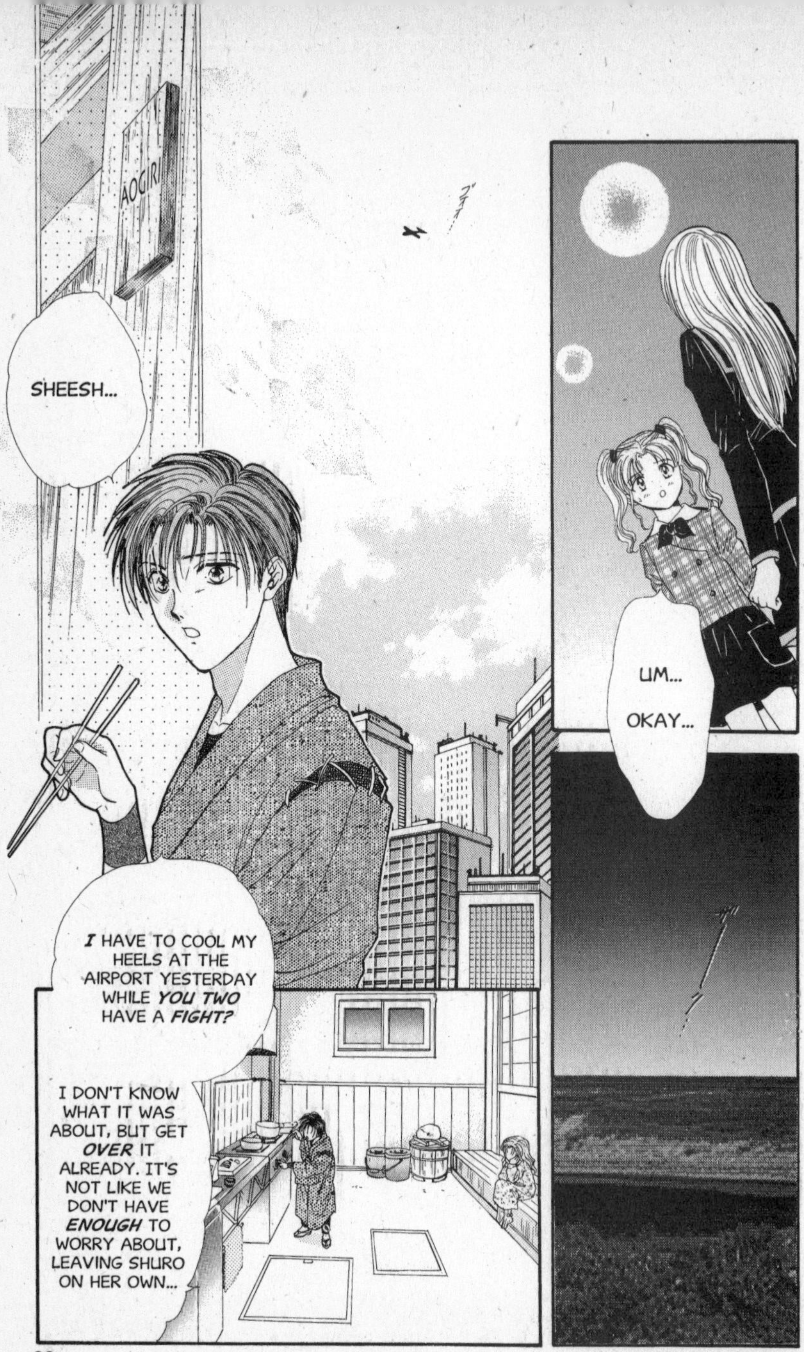
UM... OKAY...
SHEESH...
I HAVE TO COOL MY HEELS AT THE AIRPORT YESTERDAY WHILE YOU TWO HAVE A FIGHT?
I DON'T KNOW WHAT IT WAS ABOUT, BUT GET OVER IT ALREADY. IT'S NOT LIKE WE DON'T HAVE ENOUGH TO WORRY ABOUT, LEAVING SHURO ON HER OWN...

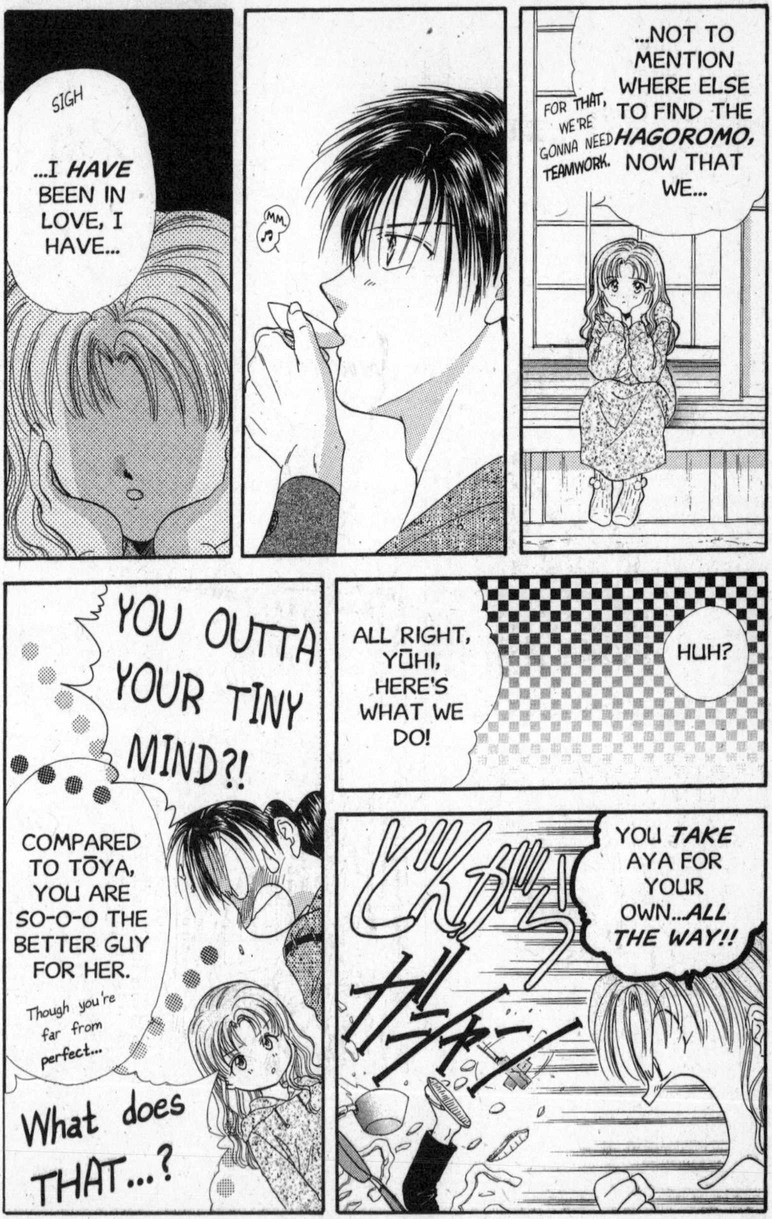
...NOT TO MENTION WHERE ELSE TO FIND THE *HAGOROMO,* NOW THAT WE...
FOR THAT, WE'RE GONNA NEED TEAMWORK.
MM.
SIGH
...I *HAVE* BEEN IN LOVE, I HAVE...
ALL RIGHT, YŪHI, HERE'S WHAT WE DO!
HUH?
YOU *TAKE* AYA FOR YOUR OWN...*ALL THE WAY!!*
YOU OUTTA YOUR TINY MIND?!
COMPARED TO TŌYA, YOU ARE SO-O-O THE BETTER GUY FOR HER.
Though you're far from perfect...
What does THAT...?

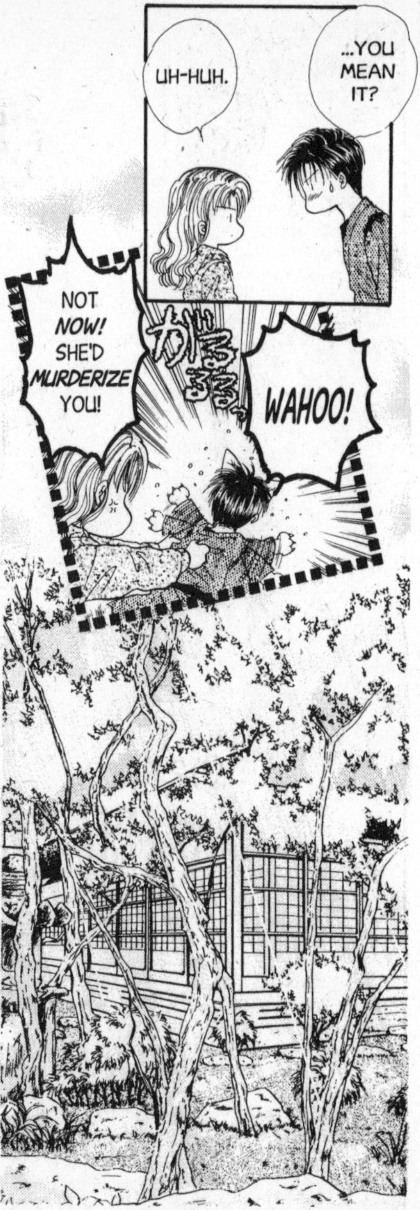
...YOU MEAN IT?
UH-HUH.
WAHOO!
NOT *NOW!* SHE'D *MURDERIZE* YOU!

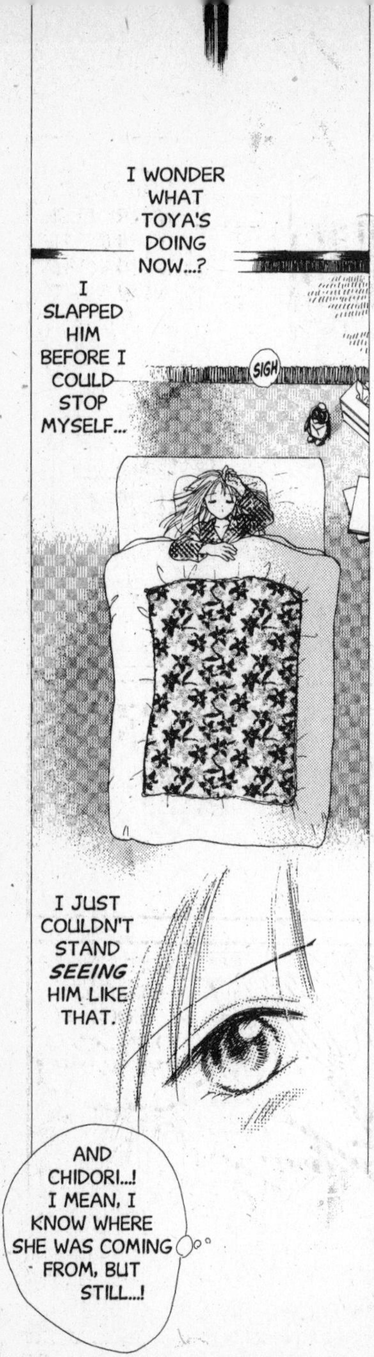
I WONDER WHAT TOYA'S DOING NOW...?
I SLAPPED HIM BEFORE I COULD STOP MYSELF...
SIGH
I JUST COULDN'T STAND *SEEING* HIM LIKE THAT.
AND CHIDORI...! I MEAN, I KNOW WHERE SHE WAS COMING FROM, BUT STILL...!

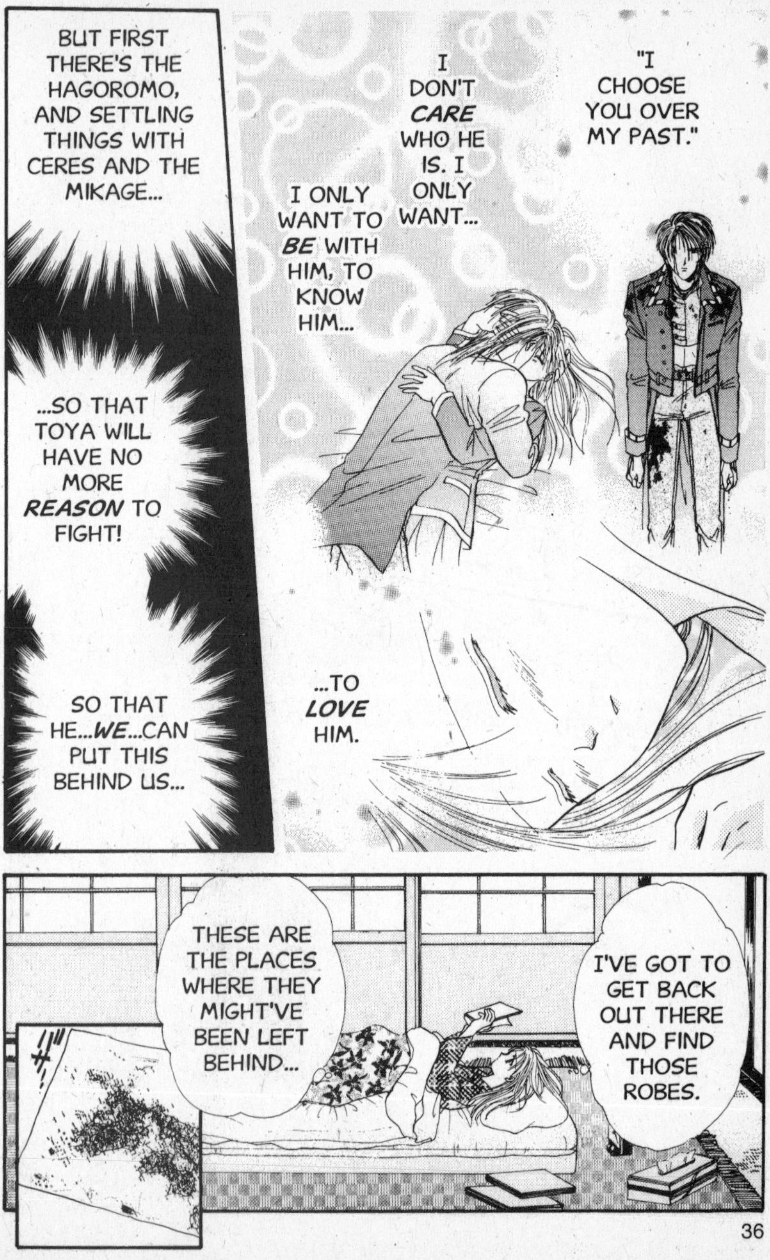
"I CHOOSE YOU OVER MY PAST."
I DON'T CARE WHO HE IS. I ONLY WANT...
I ONLY WANT TO BE WITH HIM, TO KNOW HIM...
...TO LOVE HIM.
BUT FIRST THERE'S THE HAGOROMO, AND SETTLING THINGS WITH CERES AND THE MIKAGE...
...SO THAT TOYA WILL HAVE NO MORE REASON TO FIGHT!
SO THAT HE...WE...CAN PUT THIS BEHIND US...
I'VE GOT TO GET BACK OUT THERE AND FIND THOSE ROBES.
THESE ARE THE PLACES WHERE THEY MIGHT'VE BEEN LEFT BEHIND...

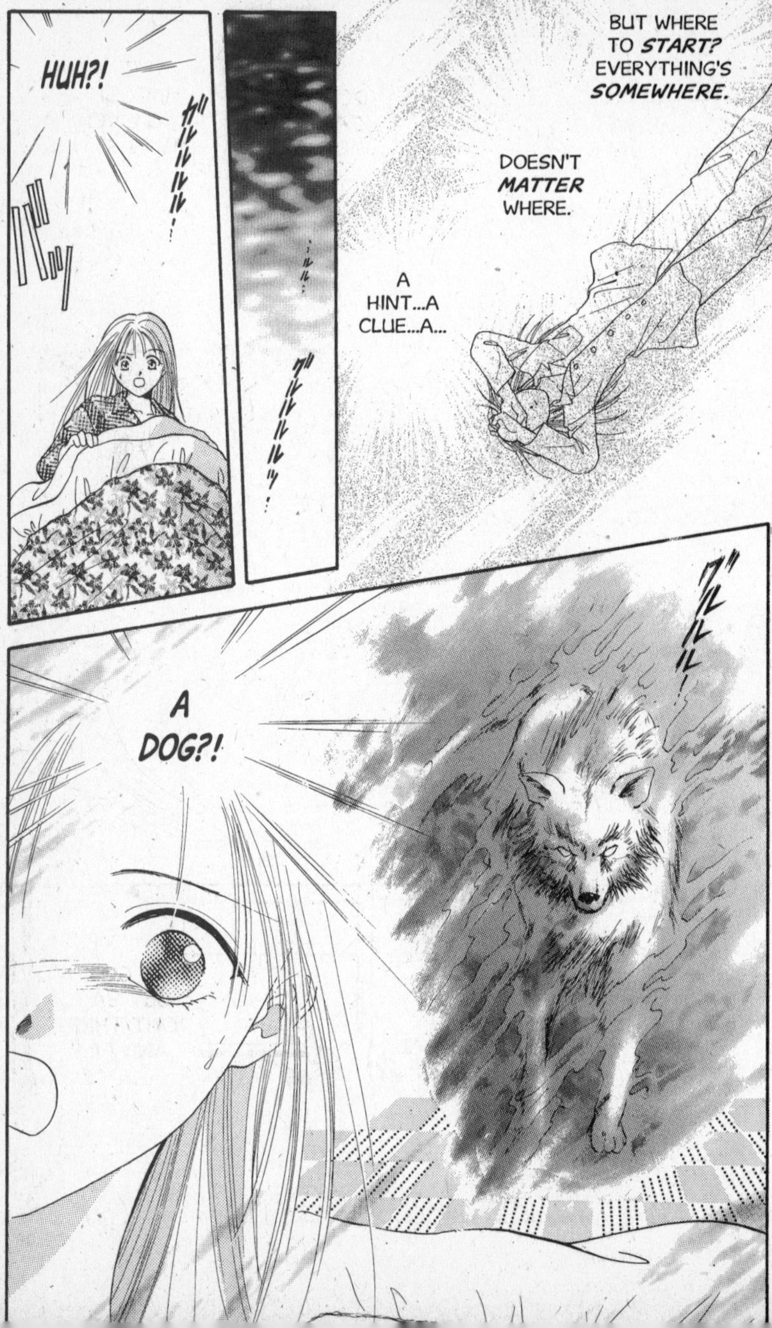
BUT WHERE TO START? EVERYTHING'S SOMEWHERE.
DOESN'T MATTER WHERE.
A HINT...A CLUE...A...
HUH?!
A DOG?!

Special Bonus!! Ta-dah! The Maniac's Guide to "Ceres" (1)

Here's where we take a look back at what's happened so far in "Ceres," as a service to you dedicated fans. Those not interested in the review, feel free to skip ahead (but you may miss some important stuff, so choose carefully!).

In No Particular Order

THE MYSTERIOUS HAND — Mummified hand of Ceres, shown to Aya and Aki by their grandfather. All Mikage girls are shown this object when they reach 16. An ancient tradition intended to prevent Ceres—the long-ago Mikage ancestor who died without regaining her hagoromo—from reincarnating and destroying the Mikage family, only the family's most elder members take the ritual seriously. Most of them consider it an annoyance...all except Kagami, who was acting at the time in his father's stead. Previous to Aya, the last reincarnation to take place was in the 1910s.

YŪHI'S CHOPSTICKS — His primary combat-weapon. Not meant for cooking (and custom-made by Yūhi's father as a junior-high graduation gift), Yūhi's chopsticks are made of steel and are used like nunchucks. For Yūhi, a lover of cooking and martial-arts, the chopsticks help him concentrate, and thus he keeps them with him at all times.

AWAKENING — What happens when the reincarnated Ceres views her mummified body (represented by the hand, above). Upon the change in both appearance and personality, the host's own personality is subsumed. Why the change occurs at age 16 is unknown, but it is theorized that this is the age at which Ceres "awakened" during her first reincarnation. Although Aki also took part in the ritual because they were twins, Aki's response came in a different way.

VISIONS — Images which burst (seemingly from nowhere) into Aya's head, such as the time she fell from the overpass. Since Ceres has been reincarnated several times, the images Aya see include scenes from the lives of her past reincarnations. Not many images of Ceres in her own time remain; mostly what motivates Ceres is bitterness, rage, and sorrow.

CELESTIAL SEAL — Mysterious mark that appears in Aya's visions, and during Ceres' exercises of power. Finally revealed (in Volume 6) to be an unknown substance in her body, the seal is the source of Ceres' abilities and is a shape that holds great power in and of itself...although it's not clear yet how it relates to the "ten'nyo" celestial maidens.

C-PROJECT — Short for "Celestial Project," a top-secret operation of international implications headed by Kagami...more details of which will be revealed in future volumes.

C-GENOME — The "C," of course, is for "Celestial" (see above). A genome, on the other hand, is the genetic information of an organism, and the term signifies the inheritor of celestial genes. Not all Ceres descendants will be C-Genomes; compare to how, in traditional genetics, some traits skip a generation. (Incidentally the Human Genome Project—the transnational effort to map and sequence all DNA in the human genome—is currently underway and is expected to be completed in 2003. This has nothing to do with our story, though.)

VECTOR — Drug containing the aforementioned "unknown substance" extracted from Ceres' body and blood. Not an actual drug per se, the vector is instead an ultra-nanomachine, capable of passing into the bloodstream and forcibly invoking a C-Genome's celestial powers. Note that, in cases where a subject's body is not equal to the vector's power, the vector will be rejected and the subject will die. When the body is equal to the vector's power, the subject will transform into a celestial maiden (presumably from her own ancestry). Most "celestial maidens" are female. (In biology, the term "vector" is used to describe a carrier—such as viral DNA—which delivers genetic material from one organism to another. I've simplified the concept to avoid getting too technical.)

To Continue in (2)!

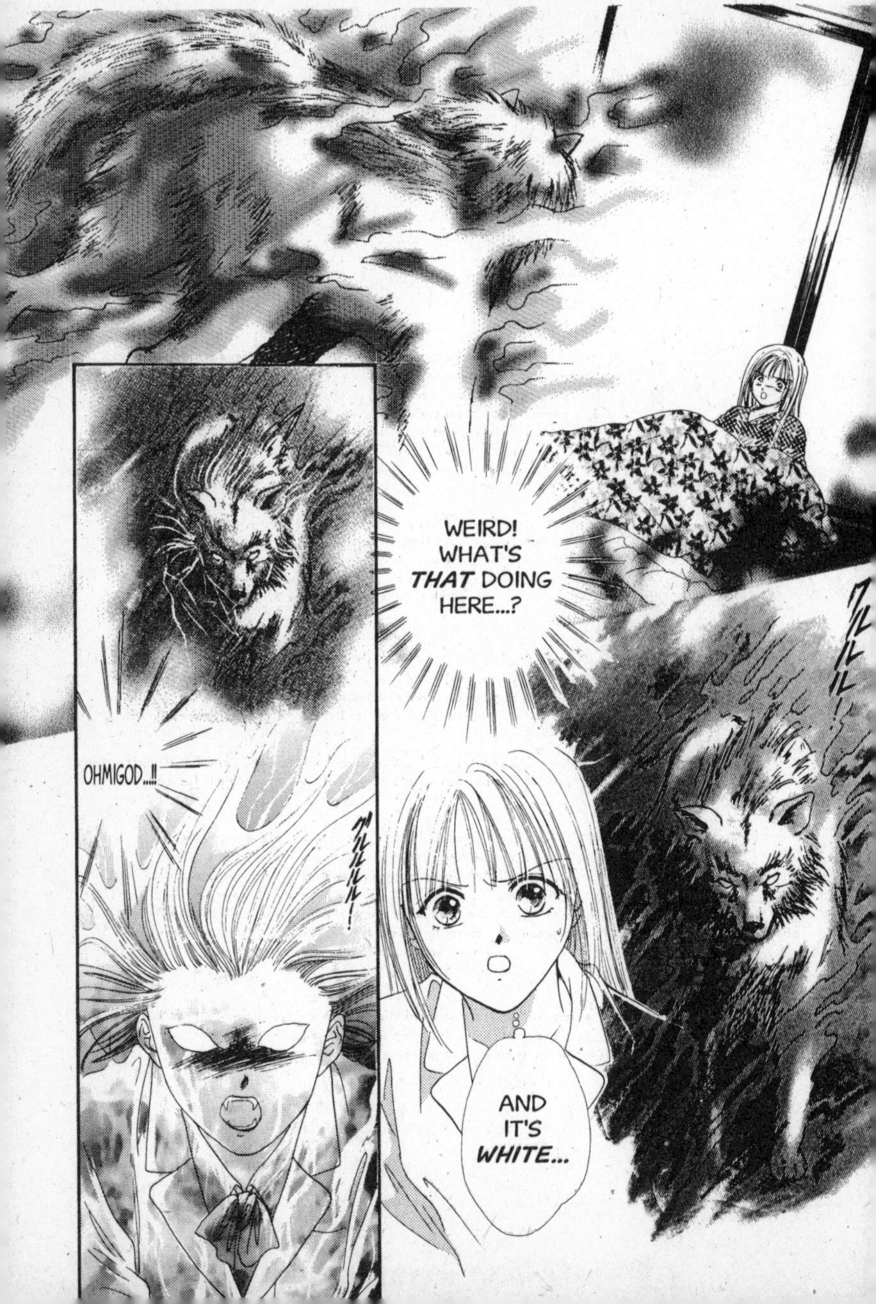
WEIRD! WHAT'S **THAT** DOING HERE...?
ワルルル!
AND IT'S ***WHITE...***
OHMIGOD...!!
グルルルル!

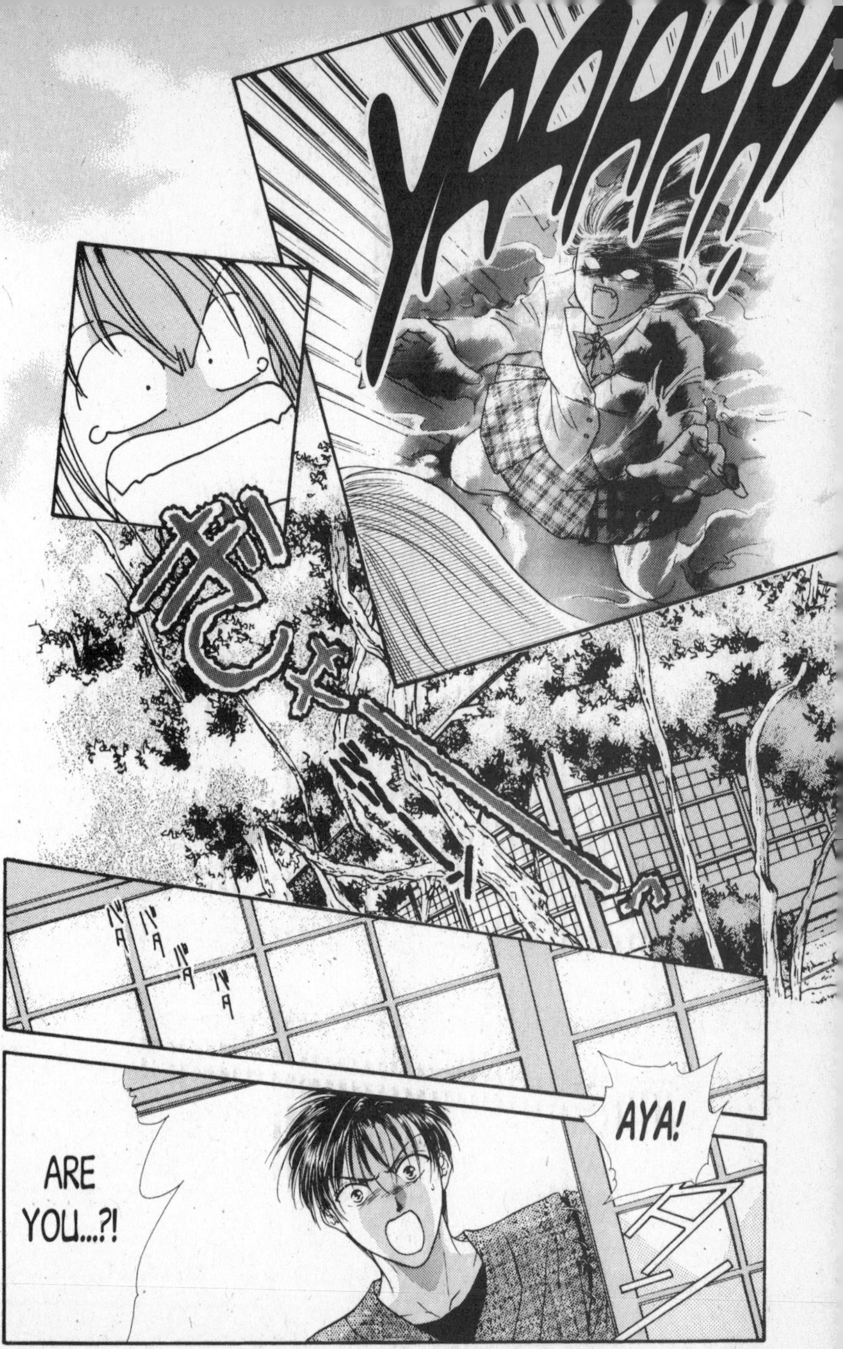
YAAAAH!!
AYA!
ARE YOU...?!

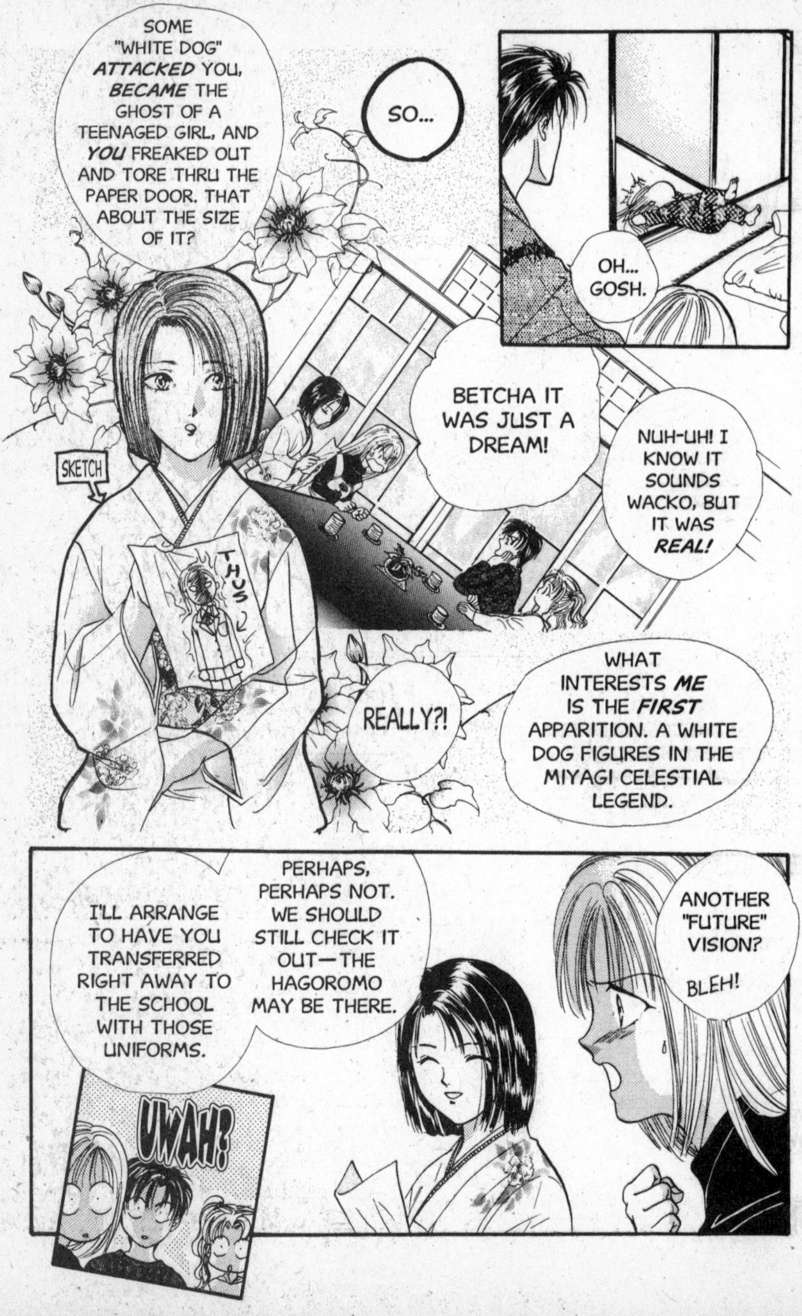
OH... GOSH.
SO...
SOME "WHITE DOG" ATTACKED YOU, BECAME THE GHOST OF A TEENAGED GIRL, AND YOU FREAKED OUT AND TORE THRU THE PAPER DOOR. THAT ABOUT THE SIZE OF IT?
BETCHA IT WAS JUST A DREAM!
NUH-UH! I KNOW IT SOUNDS WACKO, BUT IT WAS REAL!
SKETCH
THUS
WHAT INTERESTS ME IS THE FIRST APPARITION. A WHITE DOG FIGURES IN THE MIYAGI CELESTIAL LEGEND.
REALLY?!
ANOTHER "FUTURE" VISION?
BLEH!
PERHAPS, PERHAPS NOT. WE SHOULD STILL CHECK IT OUT—THE HAGOROMO MAY BE THERE.
I'LL ARRANGE TO HAVE YOU TRANSFERRED RIGHT AWAY TO THE SCHOOL WITH THOSE UNIFORMS.
UWAH?

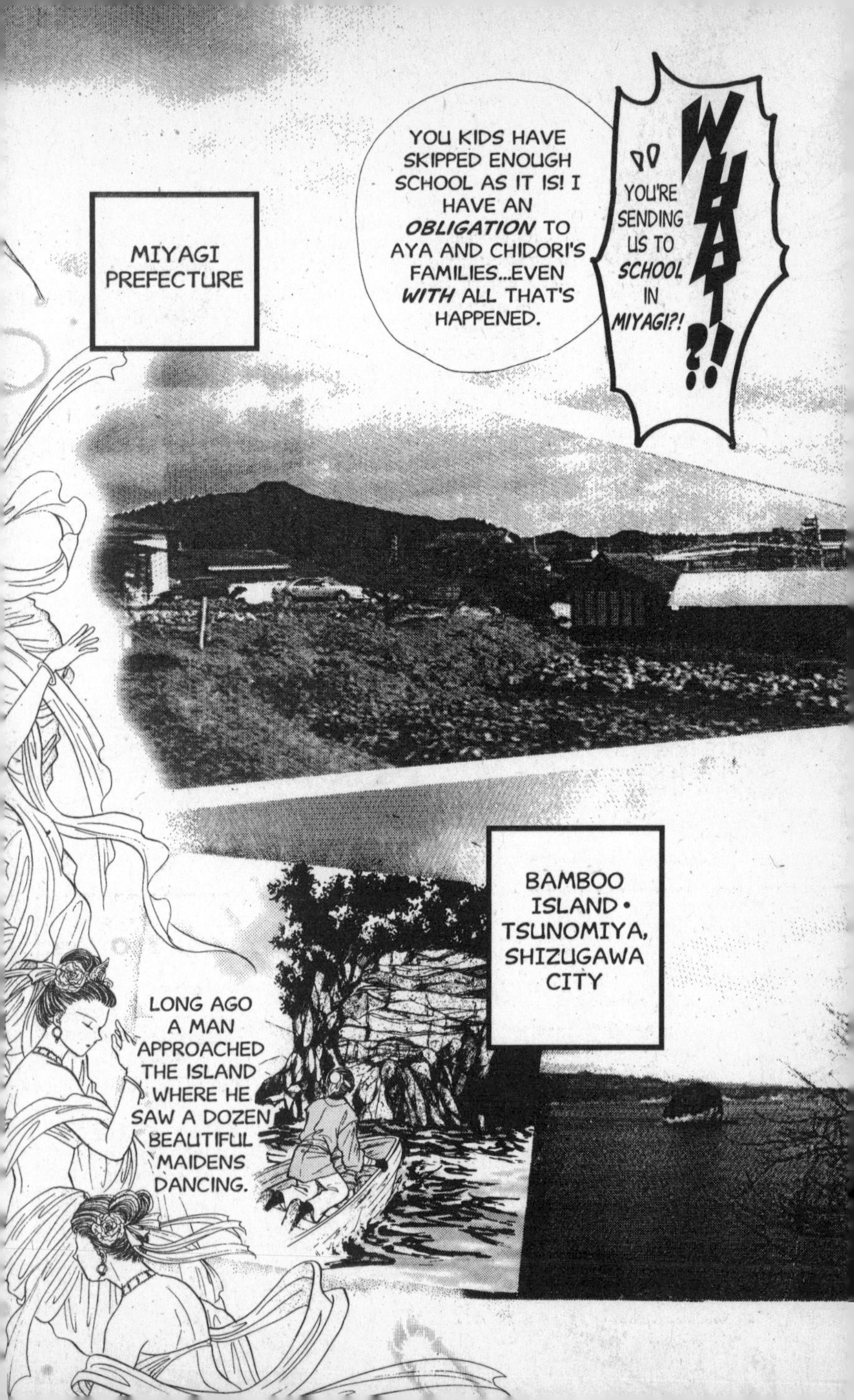
WHAT?!
YOU'RE SENDING US TO SCHOOL IN MIYAGI?!
YOU KIDS HAVE SKIPPED ENOUGH SCHOOL AS IT IS! I HAVE AN OBLIGATION TO AYA AND CHIDORI'S FAMILIES...EVEN WITH ALL THAT'S HAPPENED.
MIYAGI PREFECTURE
BAMBOO ISLAND • TSUNOMIYA, SHIZUGAWA CITY
LONG AGO A MAN APPROACHED THE ISLAND WHERE HE SAW A DOZEN BEAUTIFUL MAIDENS DANCING.

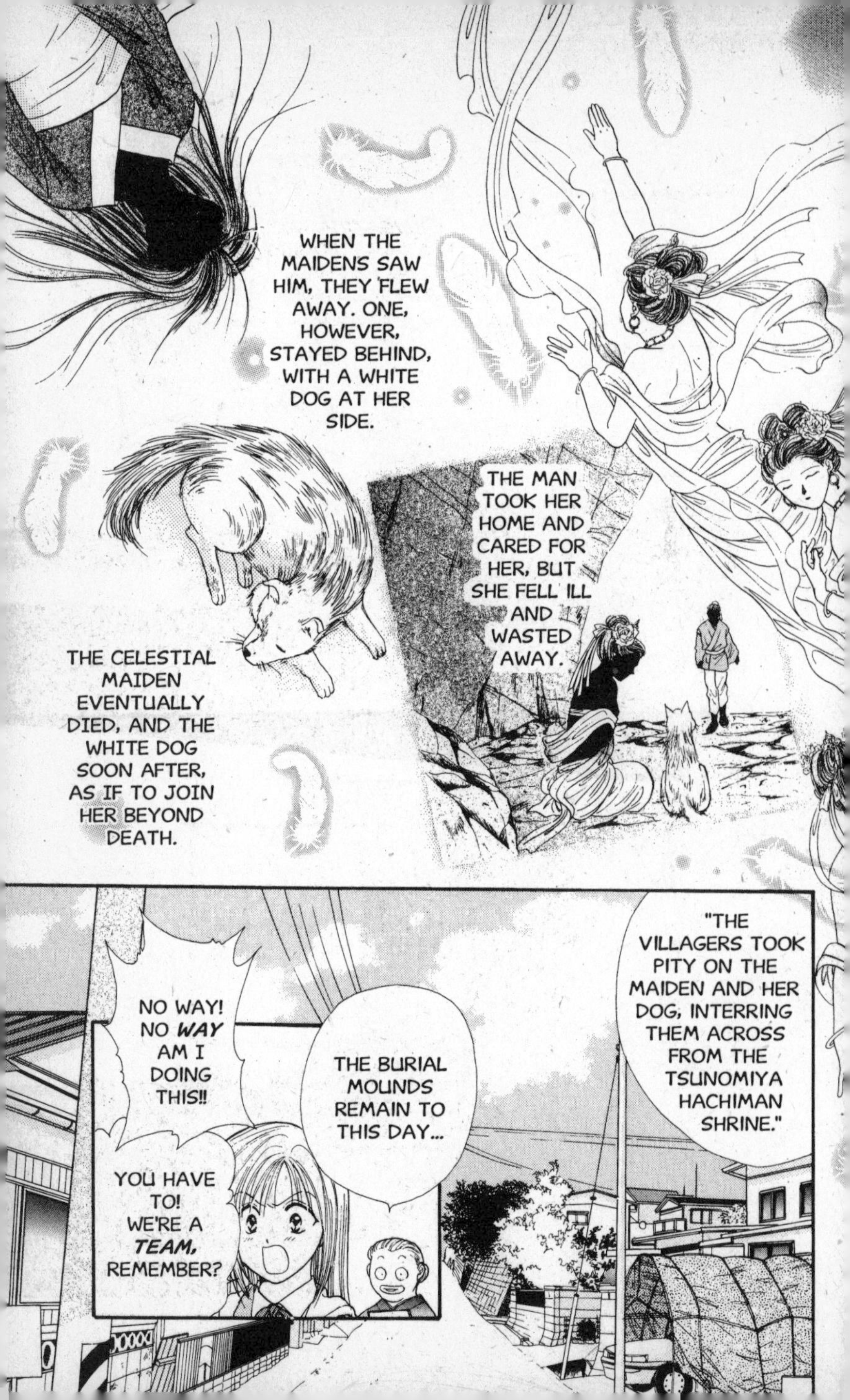
WHEN THE MAIDENS SAW HIM, THEY FLEW AWAY. ONE, HOWEVER, STAYED BEHIND, WITH A WHITE DOG AT HER SIDE.
THE MAN TOOK HER HOME AND CARED FOR HER, BUT SHE FELL ILL AND WASTED AWAY.
THE CELESTIAL MAIDEN EVENTUALLY DIED, AND THE WHITE DOG SOON AFTER, AS IF TO JOIN HER BEYOND DEATH.
"THE VILLAGERS TOOK PITY ON THE MAIDEN AND HER DOG, INTERRING THEM ACROSS FROM THE TSUNOMIYA HACHIMAN SHRINE."
THE BURIAL MOUNDS REMAIN TO THIS DAY...
NO WAY! NO WAY AM I DOING THIS!!
YOU HAVE TO! WE'RE A TEAM, REMEMBER?

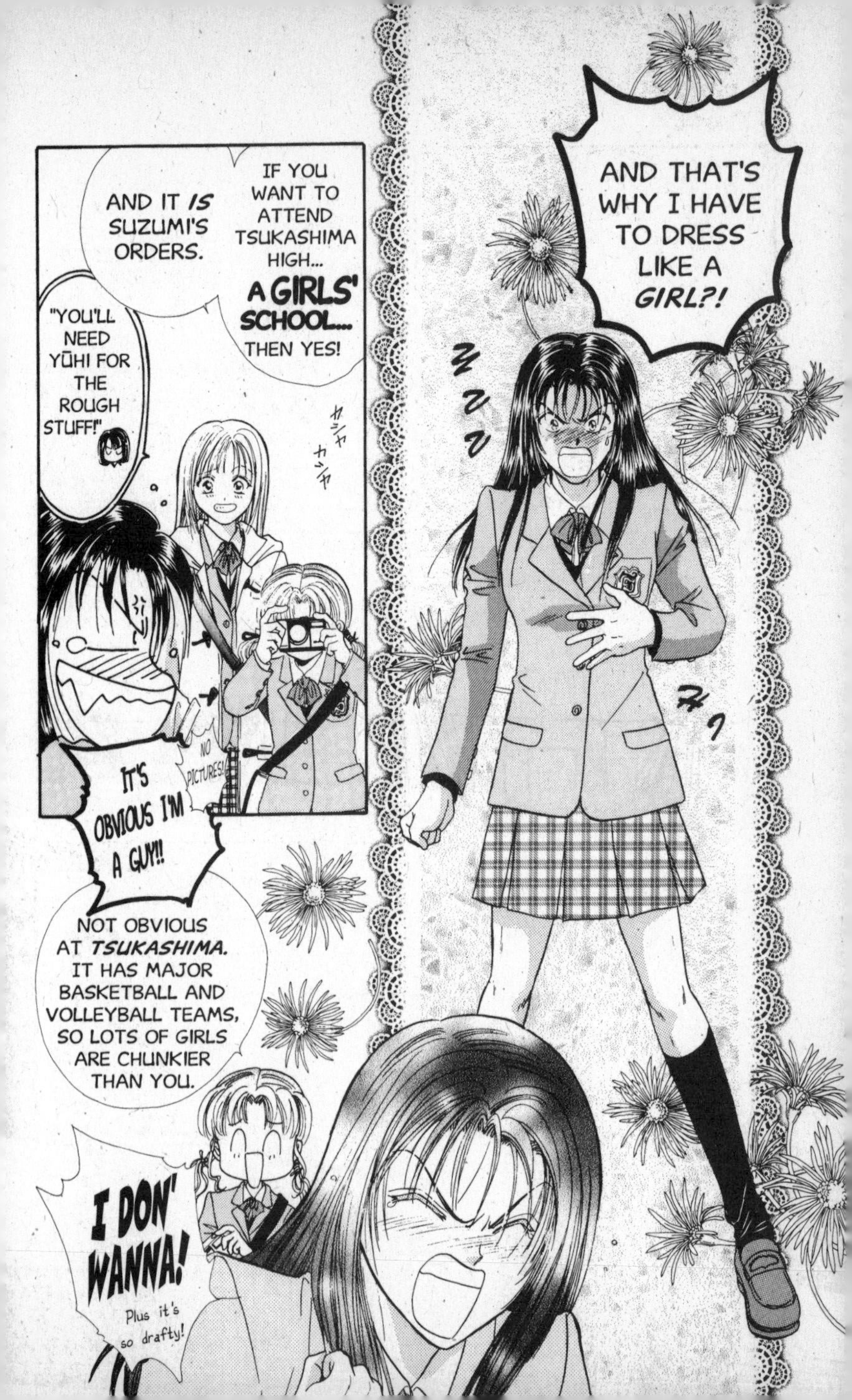

AND THAT'S WHY I HAVE TO DRESS LIKE A *GIRL?!*
IF YOU WANT TO ATTEND TSUKASHIMA HIGH... **A GIRLS' SCHOOL...** THEN YES!
AND IT *IS* SUZUMI'S ORDERS.
"YOU'LL NEED YŪHI FOR THE ROUGH STUFF!"
カシャ カシャ
NO PICTURES!
IT'S OBVIOUS I'M A GUY!!
NOT OBVIOUS AT *TSUKASHIMA.* IT HAS MAJOR BASKETBALL AND VOLLEYBALL TEAMS, SO LOTS OF GIRLS ARE CHUNKIER THAN YOU.
I DON' WANNA!
Plus it's so drafty!

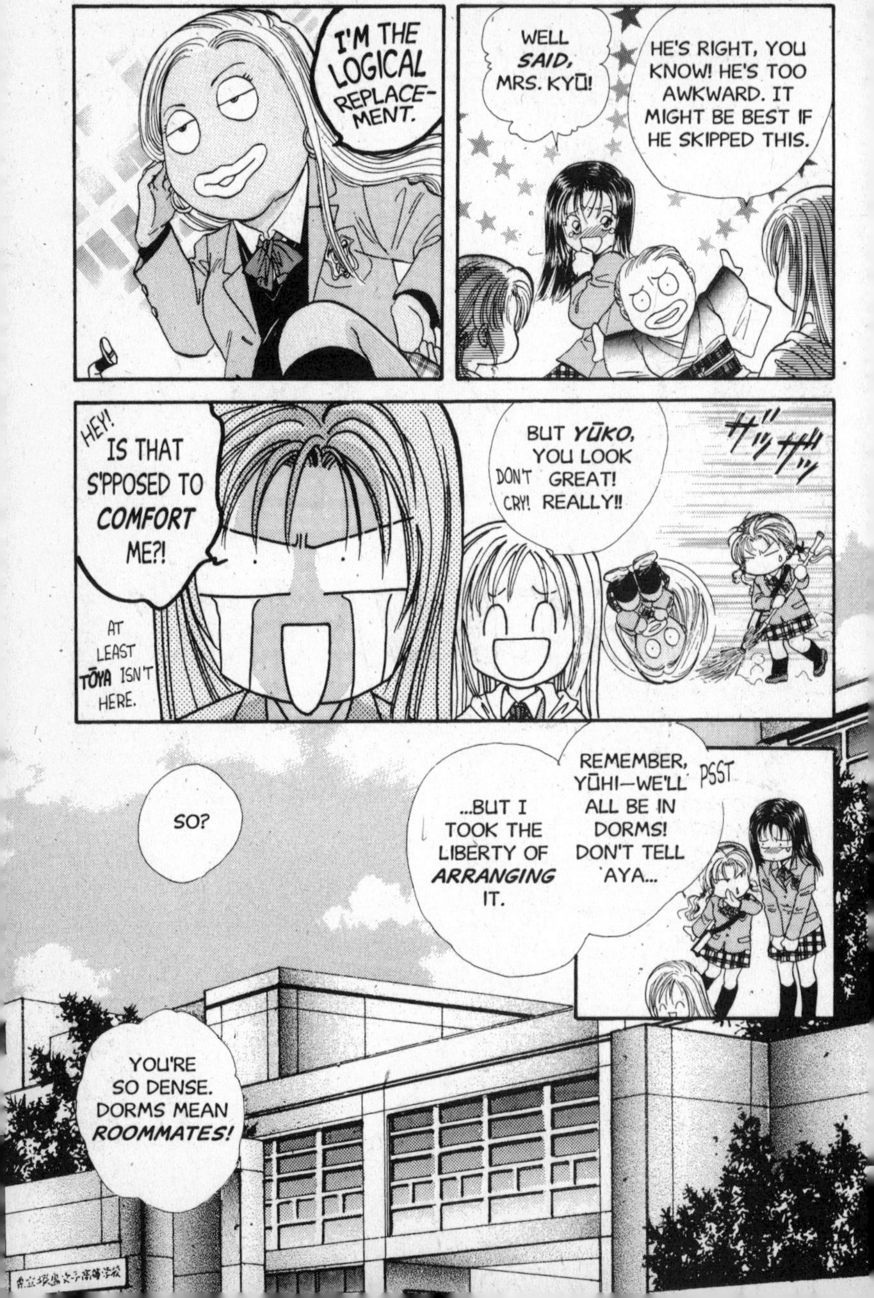
HE'S RIGHT, YOU KNOW! HE'S TOO AWKWARD. IT MIGHT BE BEST IF HE SKIPPED THIS.
WELL SAID, MRS. KYŪ!
I'M THE LOGICAL REPLACEMENT.
ザッザッ
BUT YŪKO, YOU LOOK GREAT! REALLY!!
DON'T CRY!
HEY!
IS THAT S'PPOSED TO COMFORT ME?!
AT LEAST TŌYA ISN'T HERE.
PSST
REMEMBER, YŪHI—WE'LL ALL BE IN DORMS! DON'T TELL `AYA...
...BUT I TOOK THE LIBERTY OF ARRANGING IT.
SO?
YOU'RE SO DENSE. DORMS MEAN ROOMMATES!

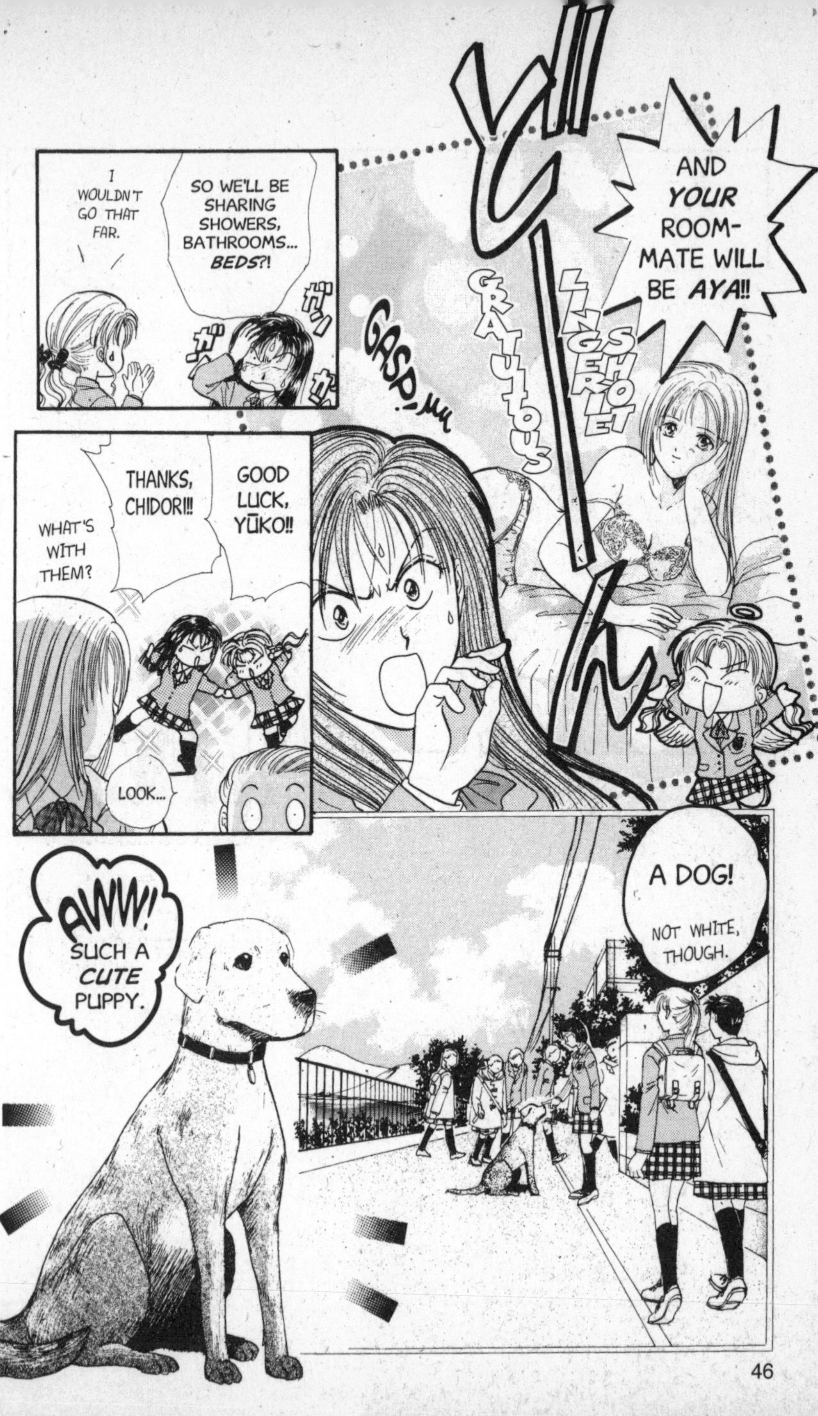
AND YOUR ROOMMATE WILL BE AYA!!
GRATUITOUS LINGERIE SHOT
GASP!
SO WE'LL BE SHARING SHOWERS, BATHROOMS... BEDS?!
I WOULDN'T GO THAT FAR.
GOOD LUCK, YŪKO!!
THANKS, CHIDORI!!
WHAT'S WITH THEM?
LOOK...
A DOG!
NOT WHITE, THOUGH.
AWW! SUCH A CUTE PUPPY.

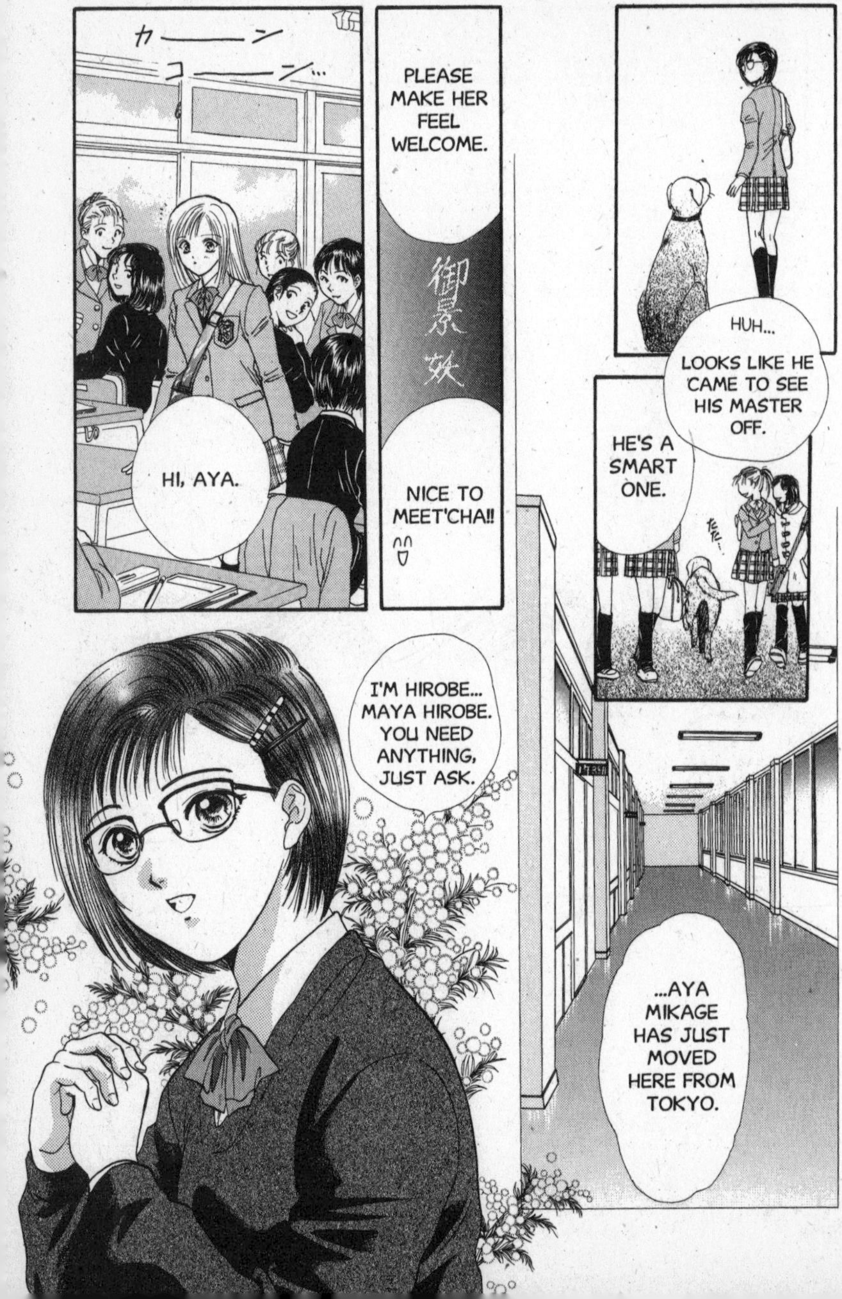
HUH...
LOOKS LIKE HE CAME TO SEE HIS MASTER OFF.
HE'S A SMART ONE.
...AYA MIKAGE HAS JUST MOVED HERE FROM TOKYO.
PLEASE MAKE HER FEEL WELCOME.
御影妖
NICE TO MEET'CHA!!
カーン
コーン...
HI, AYA.
I'M HIROBE... MAYA HIROBE. YOU NEED ANYTHING, JUST ASK.

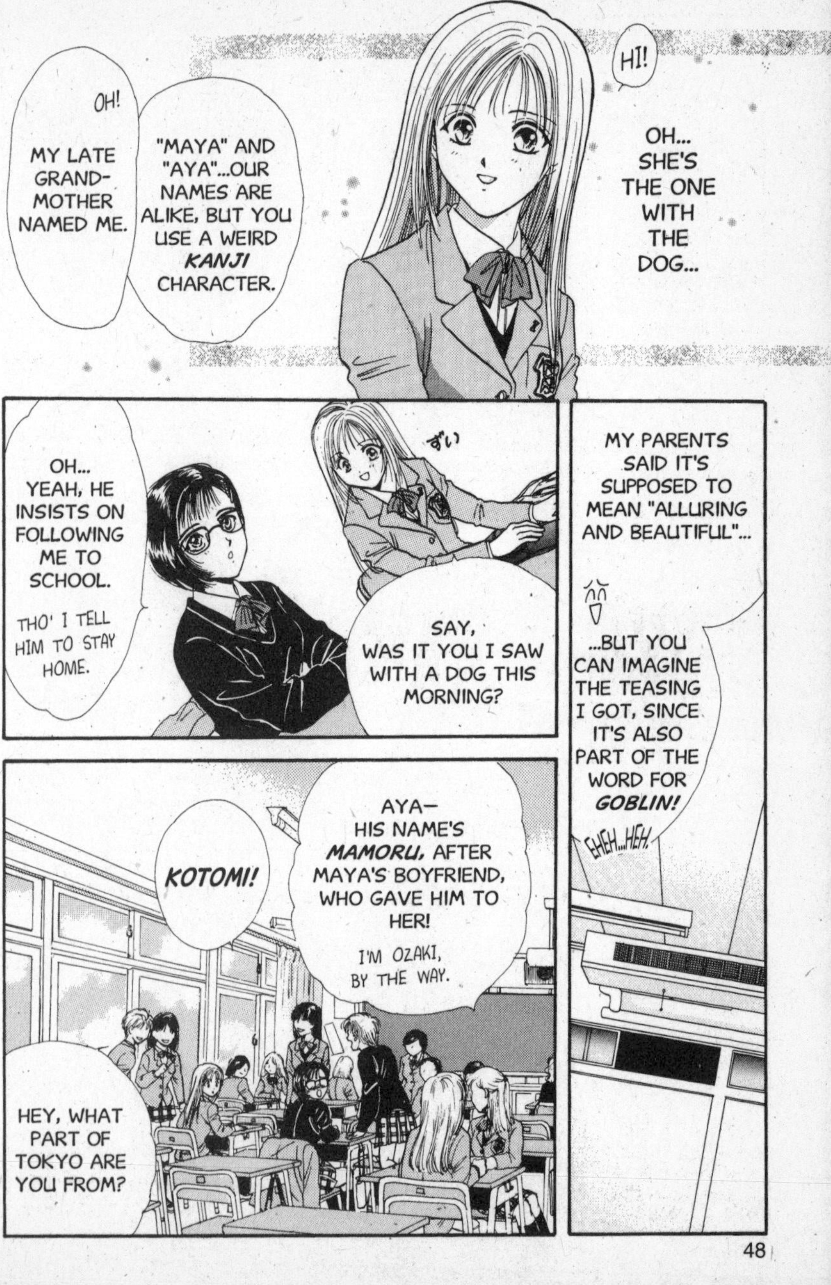
HI!
OH... SHE'S THE ONE WITH THE DOG...
"MAYA" AND "AYA"...OUR NAMES ARE ALIKE, BUT YOU USE A WEIRD KANJI CHARACTER.
OH!
MY LATE GRANDMOTHER NAMED ME.
MY PARENTS SAID IT'S SUPPOSED TO MEAN "ALLURING AND BEAUTIFUL"...
...BUT YOU CAN IMAGINE THE TEASING I GOT, SINCE IT'S ALSO PART OF THE WORD FOR GOBLIN!
EHEH...HEH.
ずい
SAY, WAS IT YOU I SAW WITH A DOG THIS MORNING?
OH... YEAH, HE INSISTS ON FOLLOWING ME TO SCHOOL.
THO' I TELL HIM TO STAY HOME.
AYA— HIS NAME'S MAMORU, AFTER MAYA'S BOYFRIEND, WHO GAVE HIM TO HER!
I'M OZAKI, BY THE WAY.
KOTOMI!
HEY, WHAT PART OF TOKYO ARE YOU FROM?

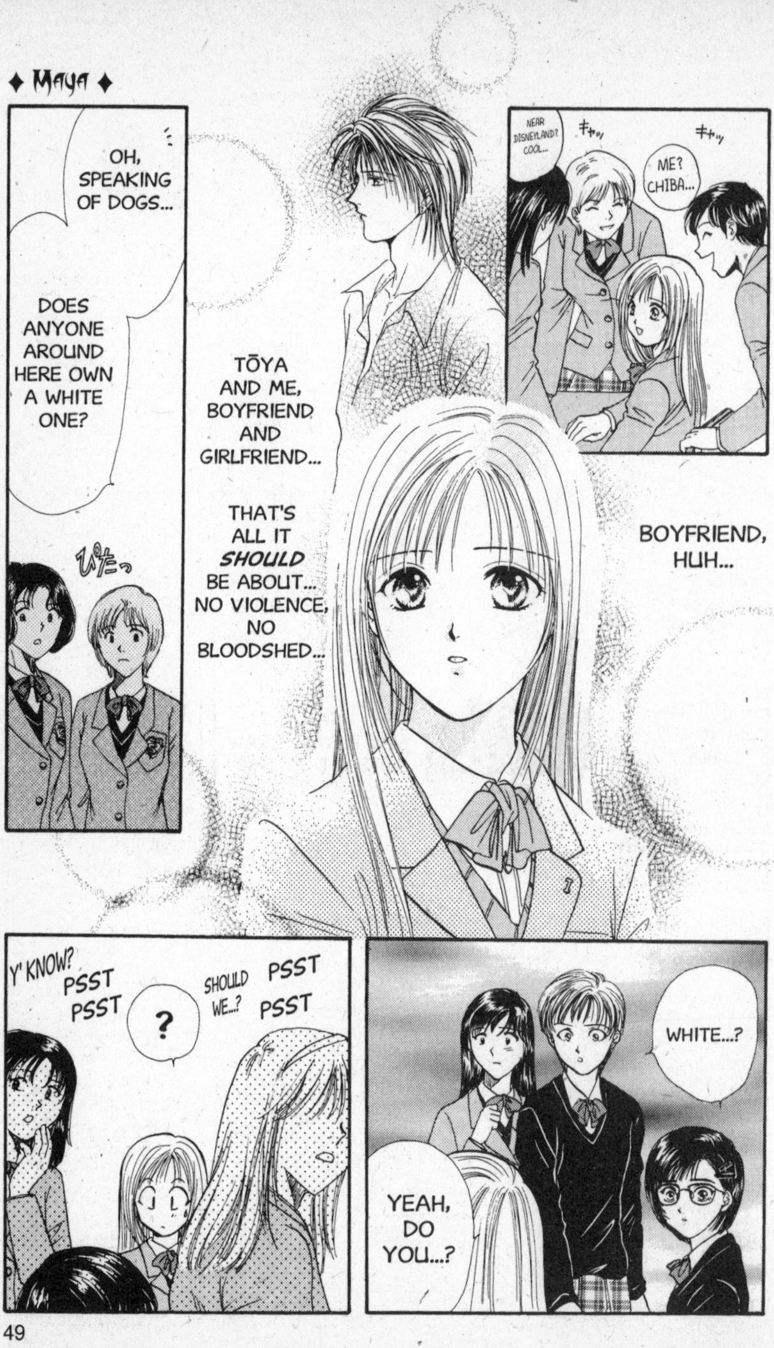
NEAR DISNEYLAND? COOL...
キャッ
キャッ
ME? CHIBA...
BOYFRIEND, HUH...
TŌYA AND ME, BOYFRIEND AND GIRLFRIEND...
THAT'S ALL IT *SHOULD* BE ABOUT... NO VIOLENCE, NO BLOODSHED...
OH, SPEAKING OF DOGS...
DOES ANYONE AROUND HERE OWN A WHITE ONE?
ぴたっ
WHITE...?
YEAH, DO YOU...?
PSST PSST
SHOULD WE...?
?
Y' KNOW?
PSST PSST

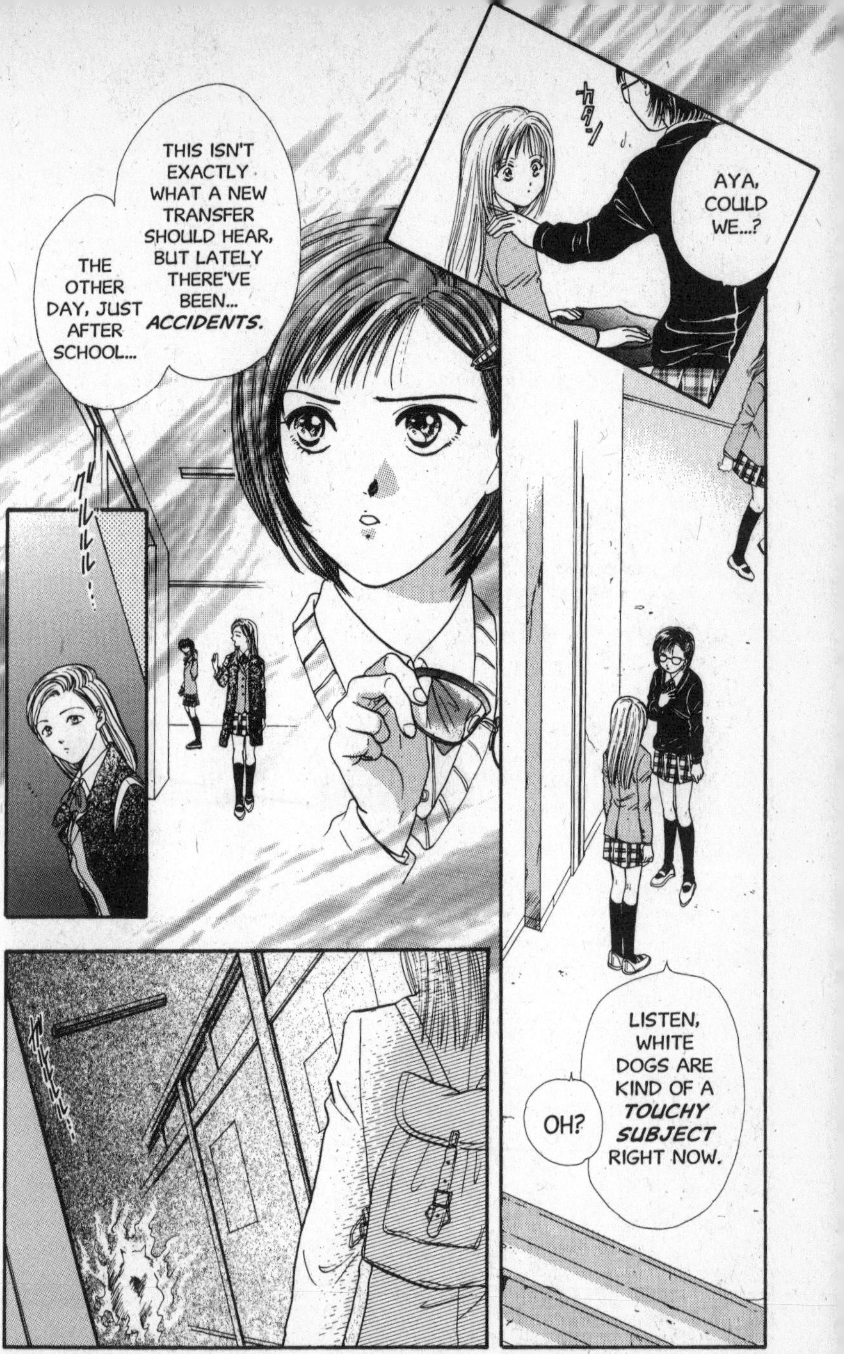
AYA, COULD WE...?
LISTEN, WHITE DOGS ARE KIND OF A *TOUCHY SUBJECT* RIGHT NOW.
OH?
THIS ISN'T EXACTLY WHAT A NEW TRANSFER SHOULD HEAR, BUT LATELY THERE'VE BEEN... ***ACCIDENTS.***
THE OTHER DAY, JUST AFTER SCHOOL...

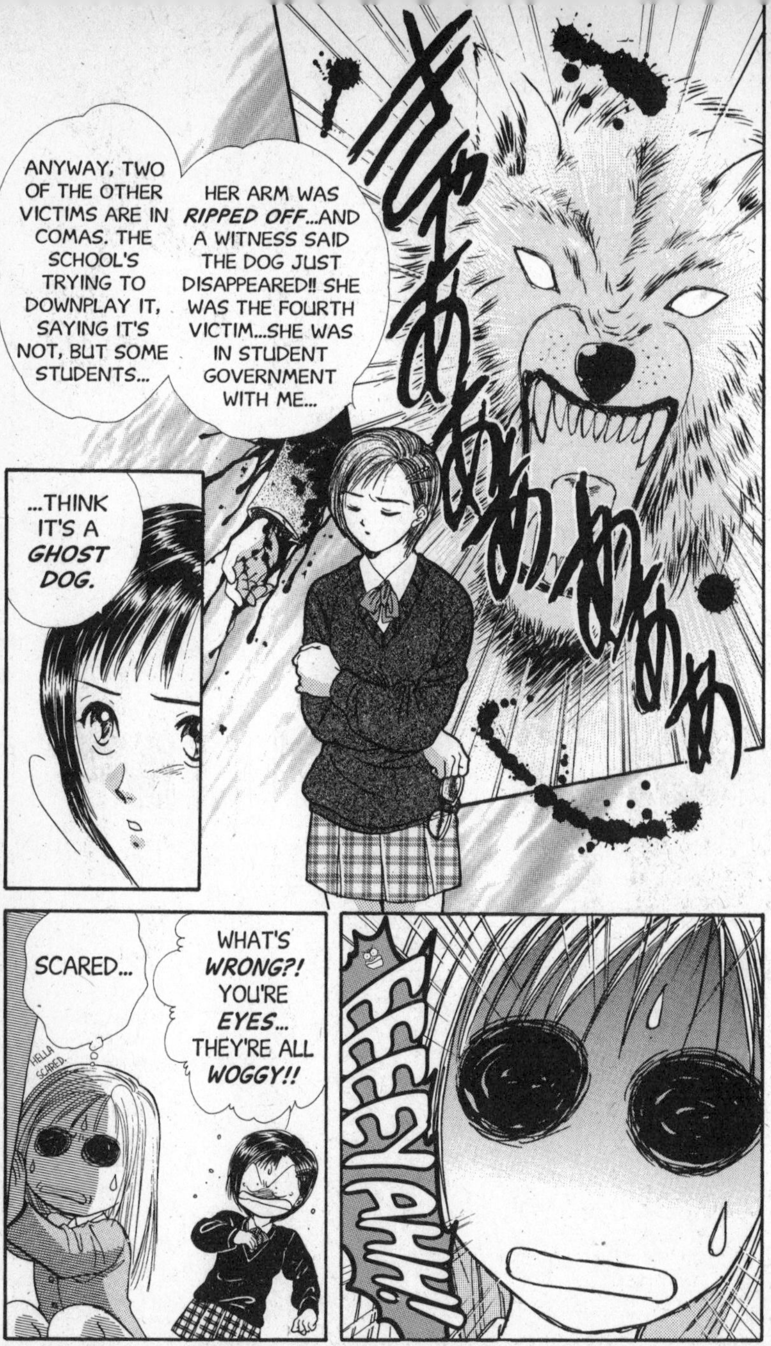
HER ARM WAS *RIPPED OFF*...AND A WITNESS SAID THE DOG JUST DISAPPEARED!! SHE WAS THE FOURTH VICTIM...SHE WAS IN STUDENT GOVERNMENT WITH ME...
ANYWAY, TWO OF THE OTHER VICTIMS ARE IN COMAS. THE SCHOOL'S TRYING TO DOWNPLAY IT, SAYING IT'S NOT, BUT SOME STUDENTS...
...THINK IT'S A *GHOST DOG.*
EEEEYAHH!!
WHAT'S *WRONG?!* YOU'RE *EYES*... THEY'RE ALL *WOGGY!!*
SCARED...
HELLA SCARED.

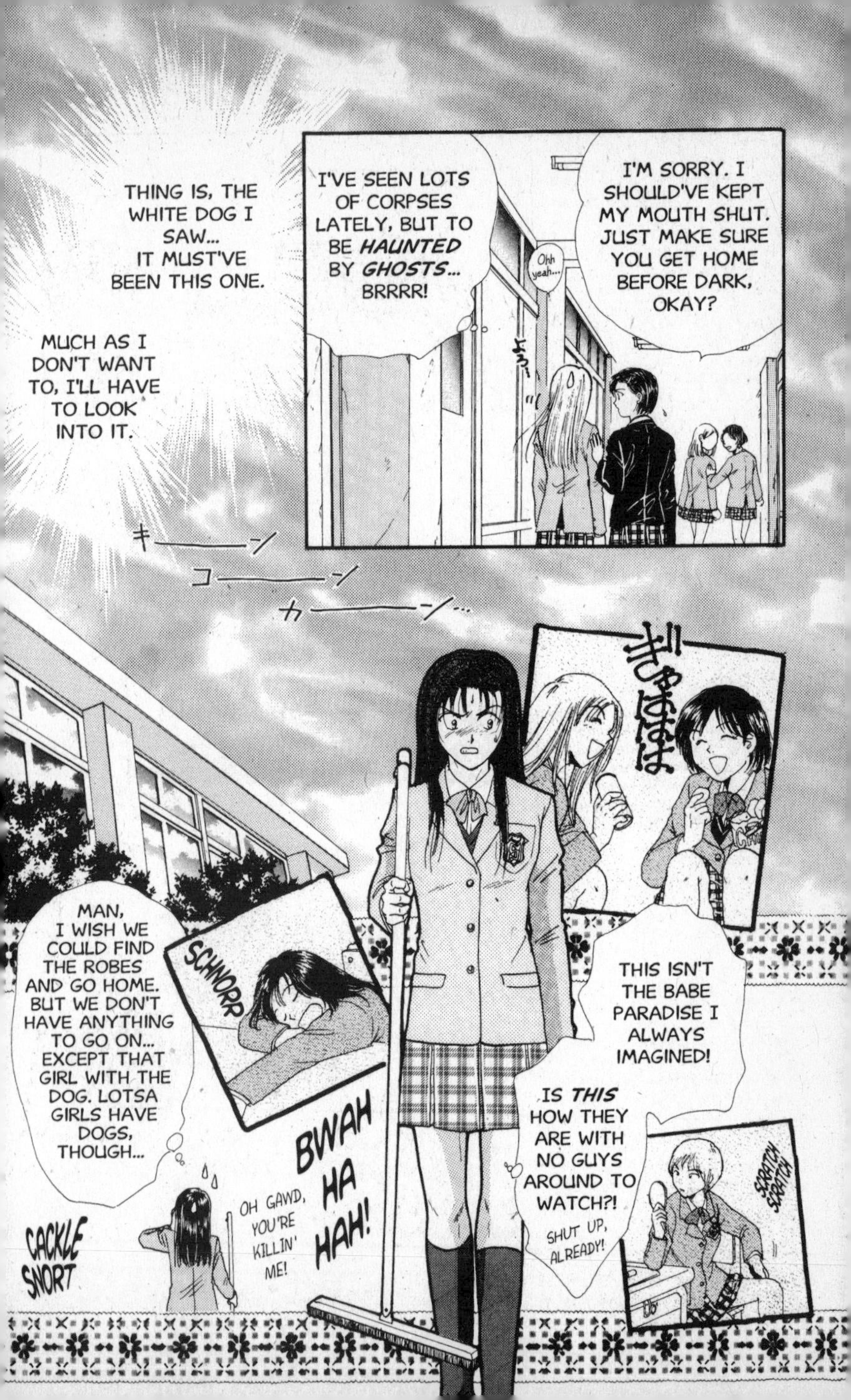
I'M SORRY. I SHOULD'VE KEPT MY MOUTH SHUT. JUST MAKE SURE YOU GET HOME BEFORE DARK, OKAY?
Ohh yeah...
I'VE SEEN LOTS OF CORPSES LATELY, BUT TO BE *HAUNTED* BY *GHOSTS*... BRRRR!
THING IS, THE WHITE DOG I SAW... IT MUST'VE BEEN THIS ONE.
MUCH AS I DON'T WANT TO, I'LL HAVE TO LOOK INTO IT.
キーーーーン
コーーーーン
カーーーーン…
ぎゃははは
THIS ISN'T THE BABE PARADISE I ALWAYS IMAGINED!
IS *THIS* HOW THEY ARE WITH NO GUYS AROUND TO WATCH?!
SHUT UP, ALREADY!
SCRATCH SCRATCH
BWAH HA HAH!
OH GAWD, YOU'RE KILLIN' ME!
MAN, I WISH WE COULD FIND THE ROBES AND GO HOME. BUT WE DON'T HAVE ANYTHING TO GO ON... EXCEPT THAT GIRL WITH THE DOG. LOTSA GIRLS HAVE DOGS, THOUGH...
SCHNORR
CACKLE SNORT

Ceres: 7

On that trip, I visited two sites that were legend-related. One was a well that appears in the musical drama "Mekarushi'i," on the property that was once a foreign residential (military base) housing area. Usually you can't go in there, but our taxi driver kindly negotiated for us (he was so nice, but then I hear all Okinawans are nice in general—wow). We went in and looked around, and it was really densely wooded.... Next was "Okuma Ufuya," also mentioned in the manga. They had a relief-sculpture of a ten'nyo there; it was a pretty famous place. I couldn't detail both these locations in the story, but it **was** interesting.

Among the four "celestial maiden" legends, there actually exists a family descended from ten'nyo whose hagoromo-owner **didn't** go back to heaven. Their name—and even a photo—was in the reference materials. My editor and I were joking that we'd get in big trouble if they read this.... ◡̈ And then, wouldn't you know it—I was reading some fan mail, and came across a familiar-looking name, and...ohmigod! It was from their daughter, and she's a loyal reader! Are you reading this now? (I wonder if she came for the autograph session.) I'm so sorry...! I may have borrowed your family legend to use for Shuro. ◡̈ Her family tree even says "ten'nyo," and they hold a special observance...I was really surprised. 💧 Someone else wrote in from Osaka, and said her ancestors came from Okinawa and that a "ten'nyo" was also in her family tree, but this one doesn't sound quite the same. The ten'nyo had had four girls, and the name "Kanashi" had been kept for four generations... fascinating, isn't it? Others have written in too, to say they may have a legend in their roots as well....

What, so you're **all** C-Genomes?

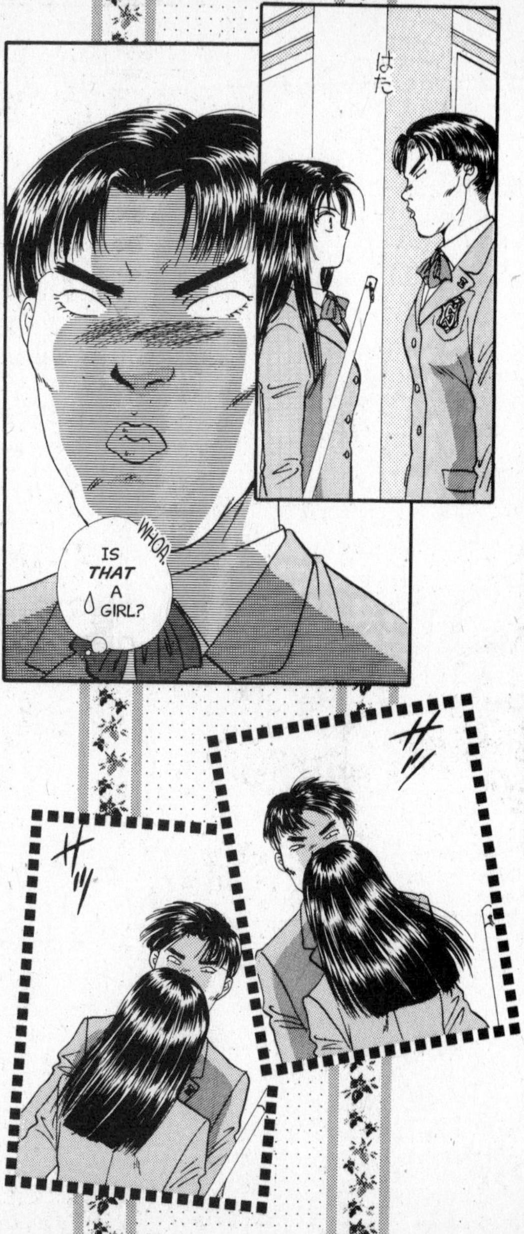
はた
WHOA.
IS *THAT* A GIRL?

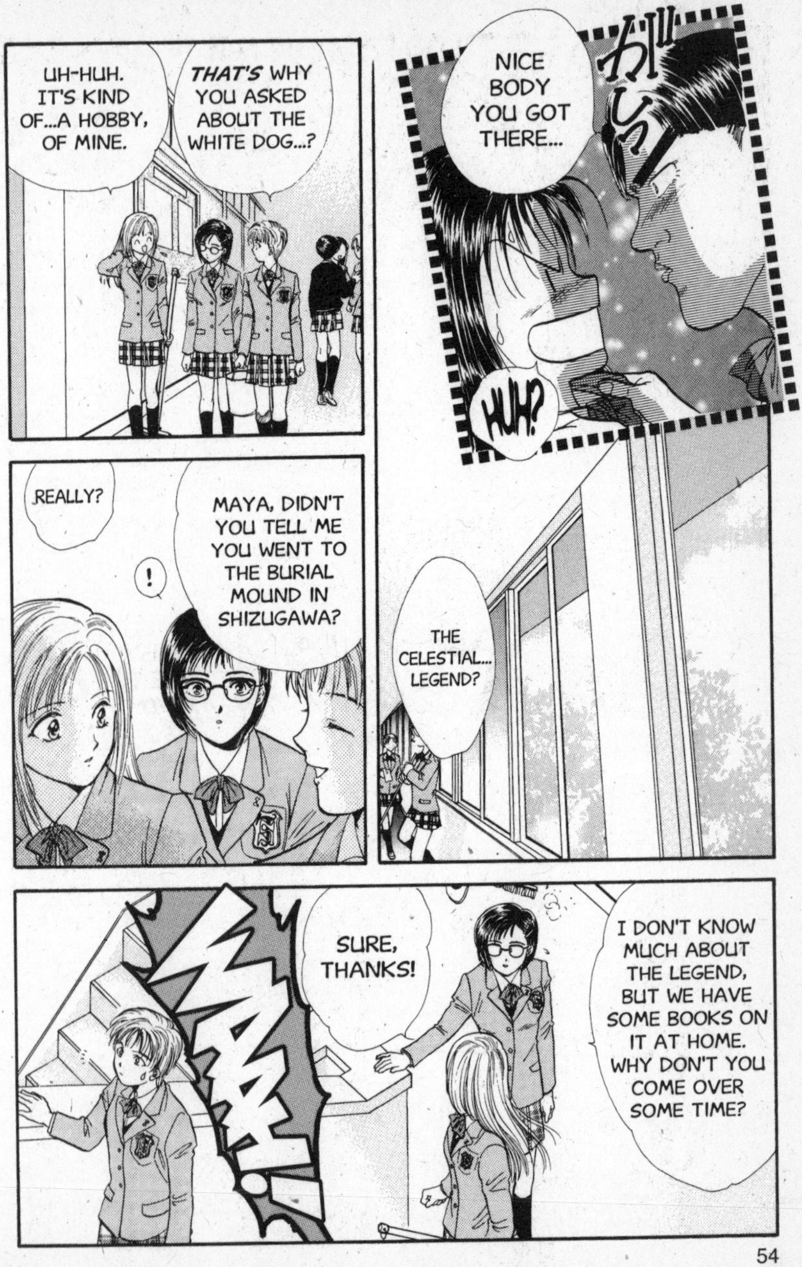
NICE BODY YOU GOT THERE...
HUH?
THAT'S WHY YOU ASKED ABOUT THE WHITE DOG...?
UH-HUH. IT'S KIND OF...A HOBBY, OF MINE.
THE CELESTIAL... LEGEND?
MAYA, DIDN'T YOU TELL ME YOU WENT TO THE BURIAL MOUND IN SHIZUGAWA?
!
REALLY?
I DON'T KNOW MUCH ABOUT THE LEGEND, BUT WE HAVE SOME BOOKS ON IT AT HOME. WHY DON'T YOU COME OVER SOME TIME?
SURE, THANKS!
WAAAH!

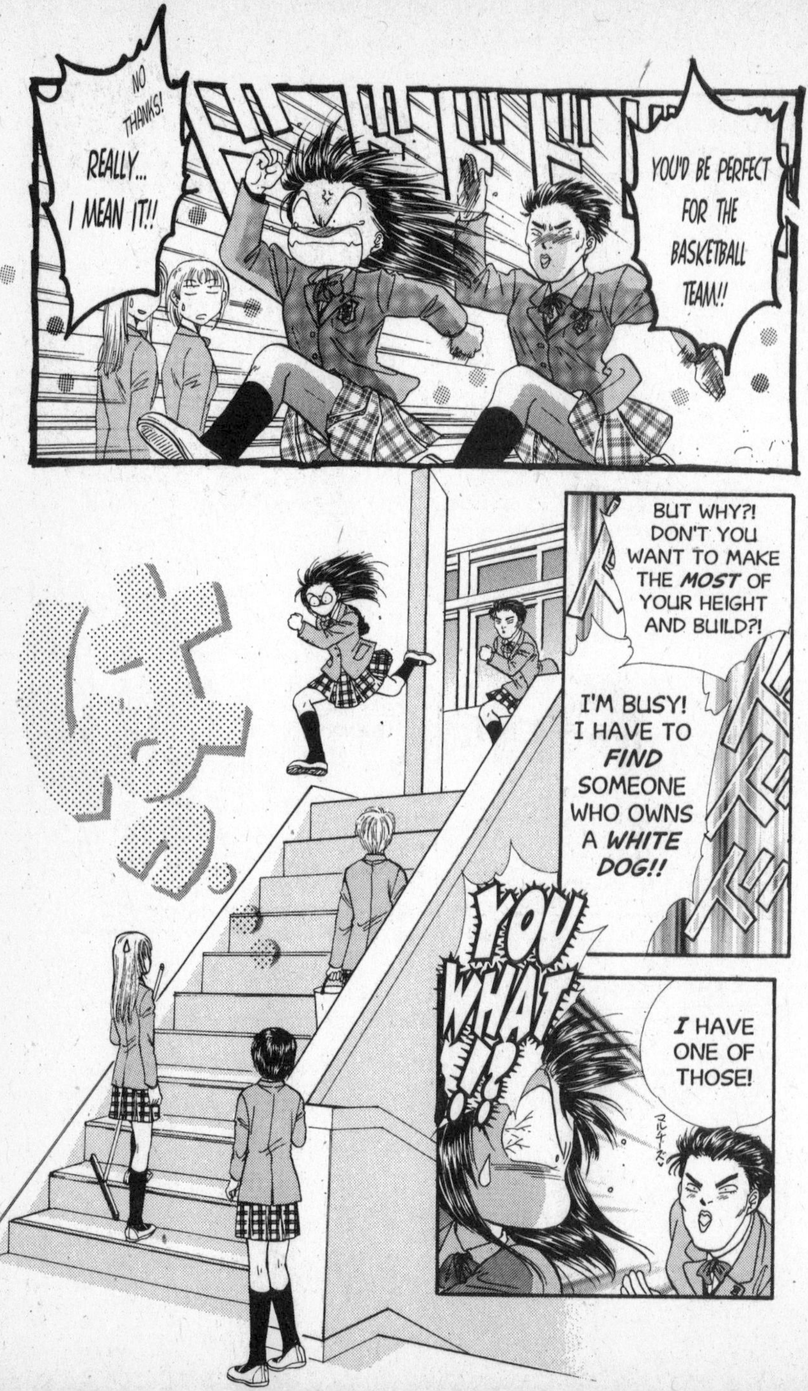
YOU'D BE PERFECT FOR THE BASKETBALL TEAM!!
NO THANKS!
REALLY... I MEAN IT!!
BUT WHY?! DON'T YOU WANT TO MAKE THE MOST OF YOUR HEIGHT AND BUILD?!
I'M BUSY! I HAVE TO FIND SOMEONE WHO OWNS A WHITE DOG!!
I HAVE ONE OF THOSE!
マルチーズ
YOU WHAT!!?

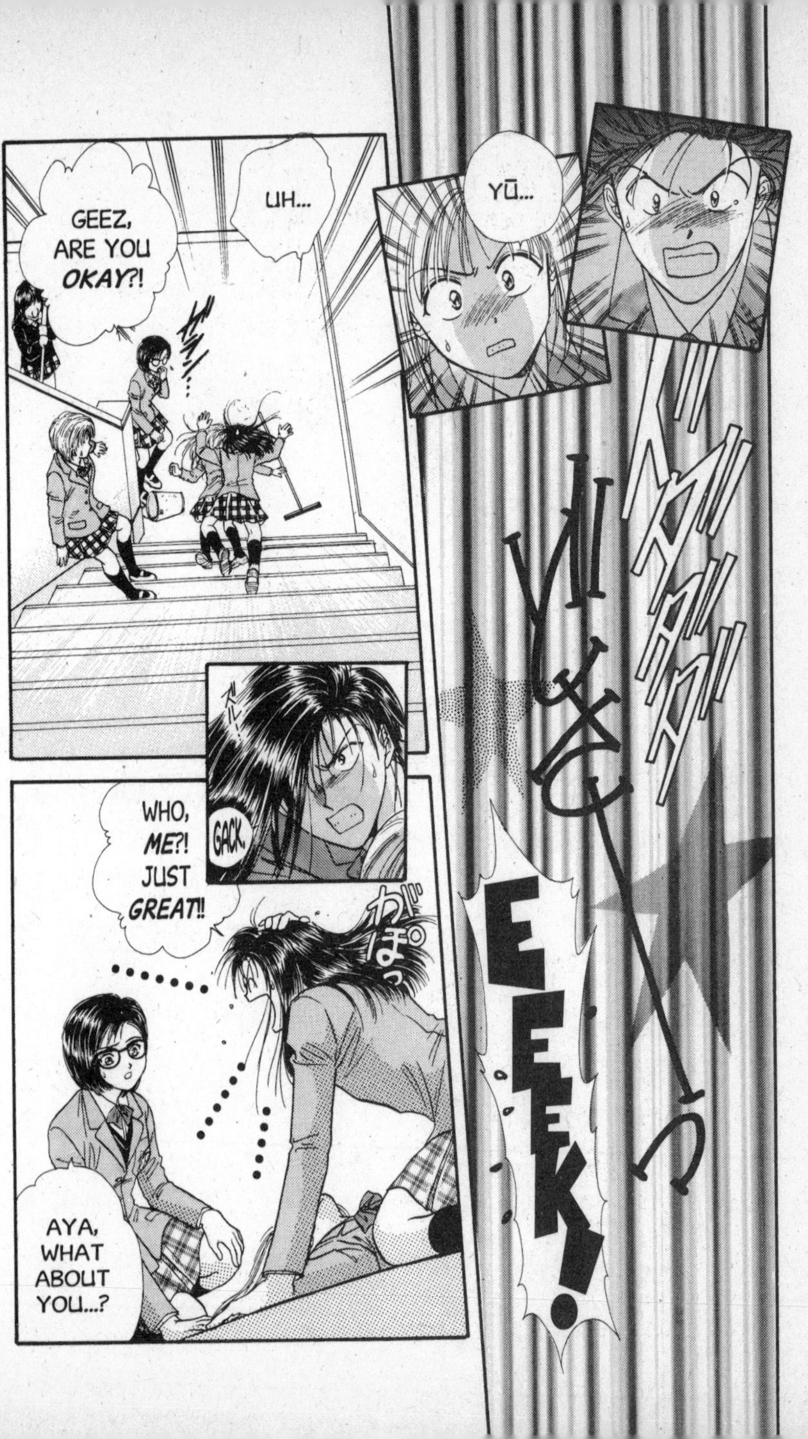
YŪ...
EEEK!
UH...
GEEZ, ARE YOU OKAY?!
GACK.
WHO, ME?! JUST GREAT!!
AYA, WHAT ABOUT YOU...?

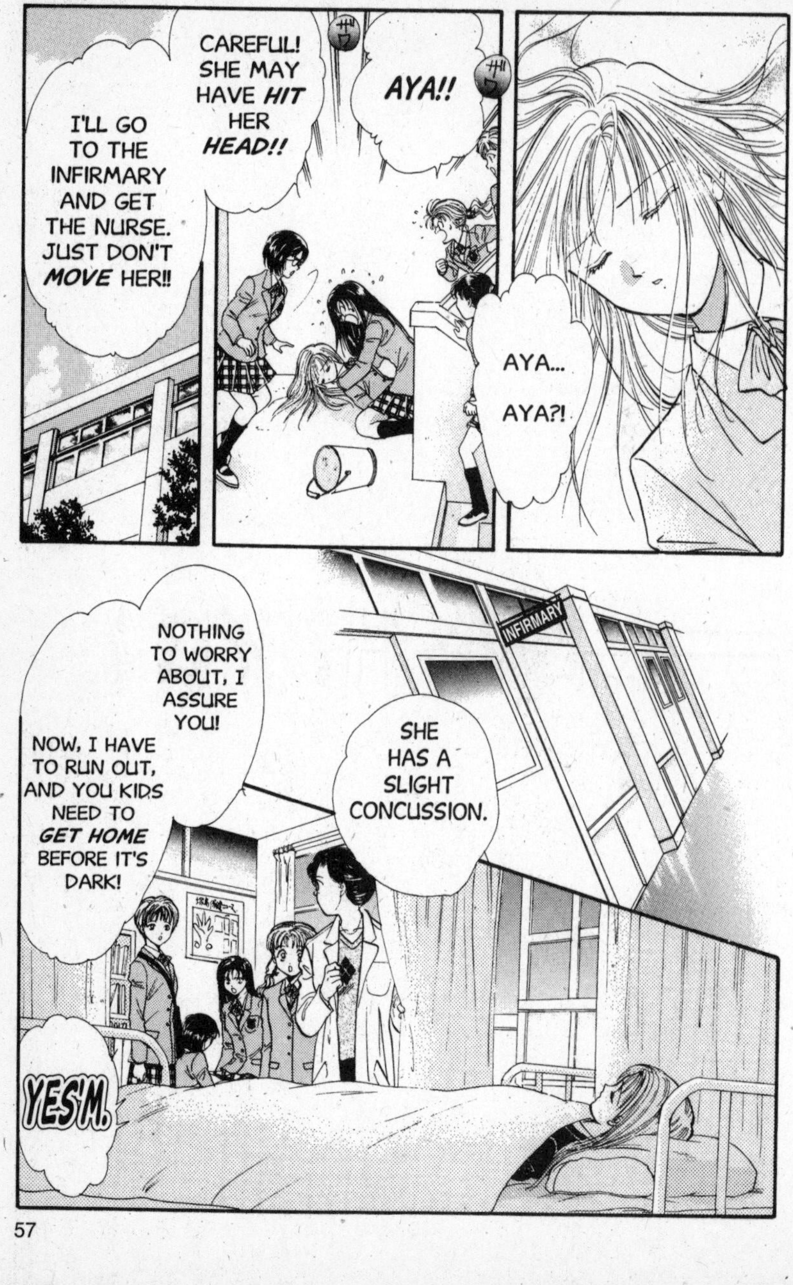
AYA...
AYA?!
AYA!!
CAREFUL! SHE MAY HAVE *HIT* HER *HEAD!!*
I'LL GO TO THE INFIRMARY AND GET THE NURSE. JUST DON'T *MOVE* HER!!
INFIRMARY
SHE HAS A SLIGHT CONCUSSION.
NOTHING TO WORRY ABOUT, I ASSURE YOU!
NOW, I HAVE TO RUN OUT, AND YOU KIDS NEED TO *GET HOME* BEFORE IT'S DARK!
YES'M.

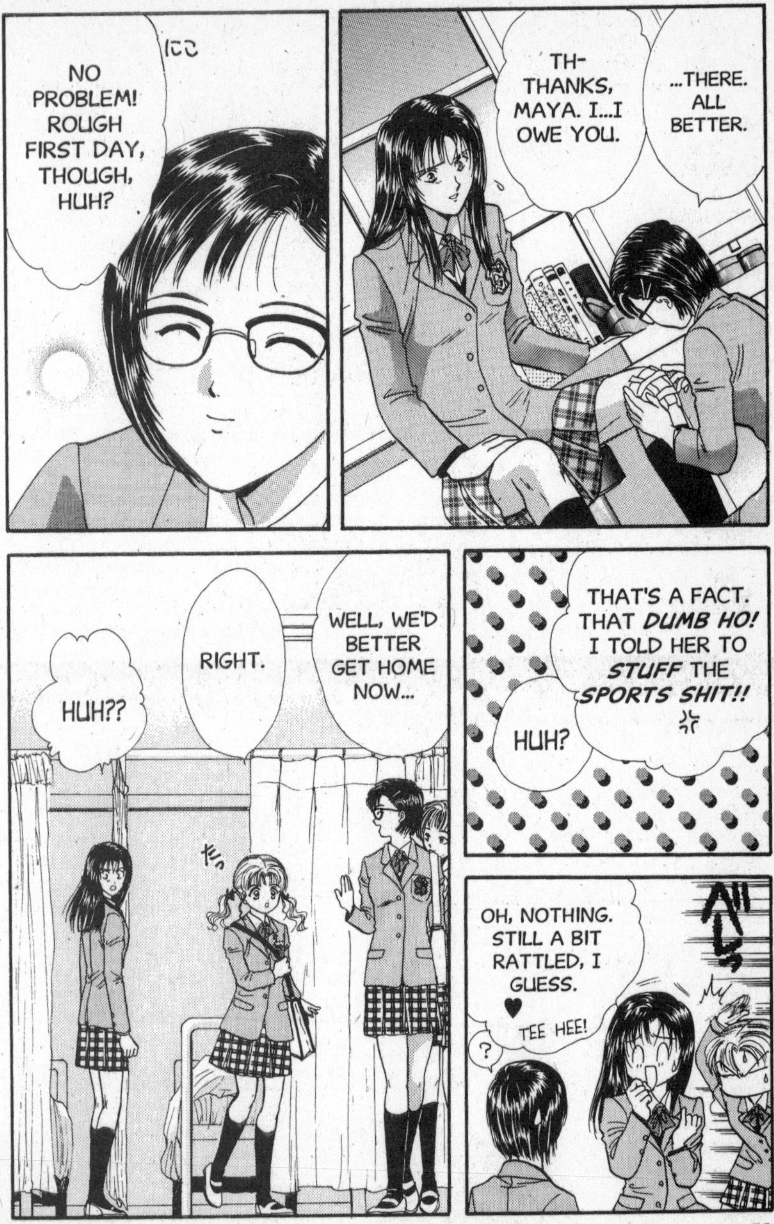
...THERE. ALL BETTER.
TH- THANKS, MAYA. I...I OWE YOU.
にこ
NO PROBLEM! ROUGH FIRST DAY, THOUGH, HUH?
THAT'S A FACT. THAT *DUMB HO!* I TOLD HER TO *STUFF* THE *SPORTS SHIT!!*
HUH?
べしっ
OH, NOTHING. STILL A BIT RATTLED, I GUESS. ♥ TEE HEE!
?
WELL, WE'D BETTER GET HOME NOW...
RIGHT.
HUH??
たっ

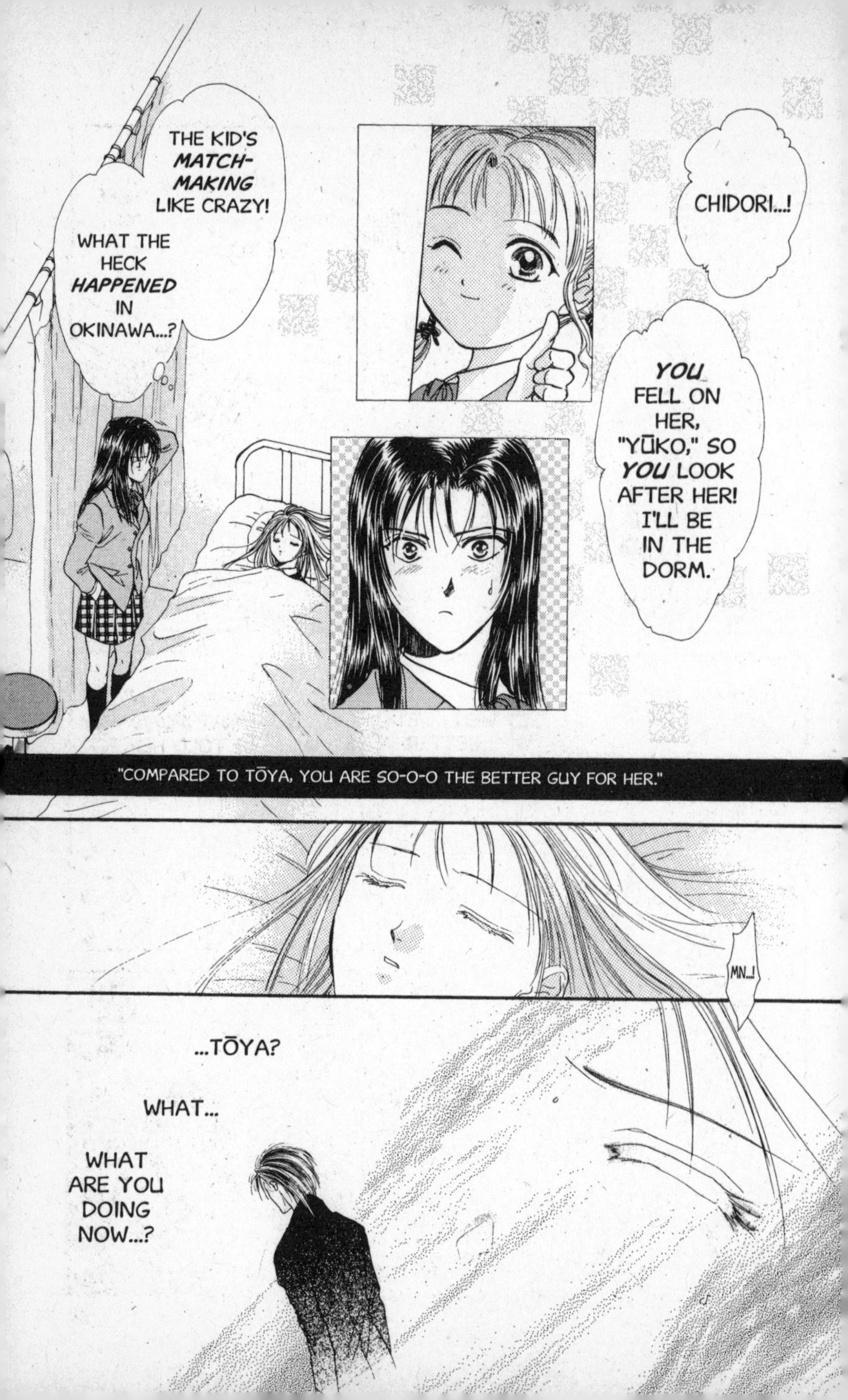
CHIDORI...!
YOU FELL ON HER, "YŪKO," SO YOU LOOK AFTER HER! I'LL BE IN THE DORM.
THE KID'S MATCH-MAKING LIKE CRAZY!
WHAT THE HECK HAPPENED IN OKINAWA...?
"COMPARED TO TŌYA, YOU ARE SO-O-O THE BETTER GUY FOR HER."
MN...!
...TŌYA?
WHAT...
WHAT ARE YOU DOING NOW...?

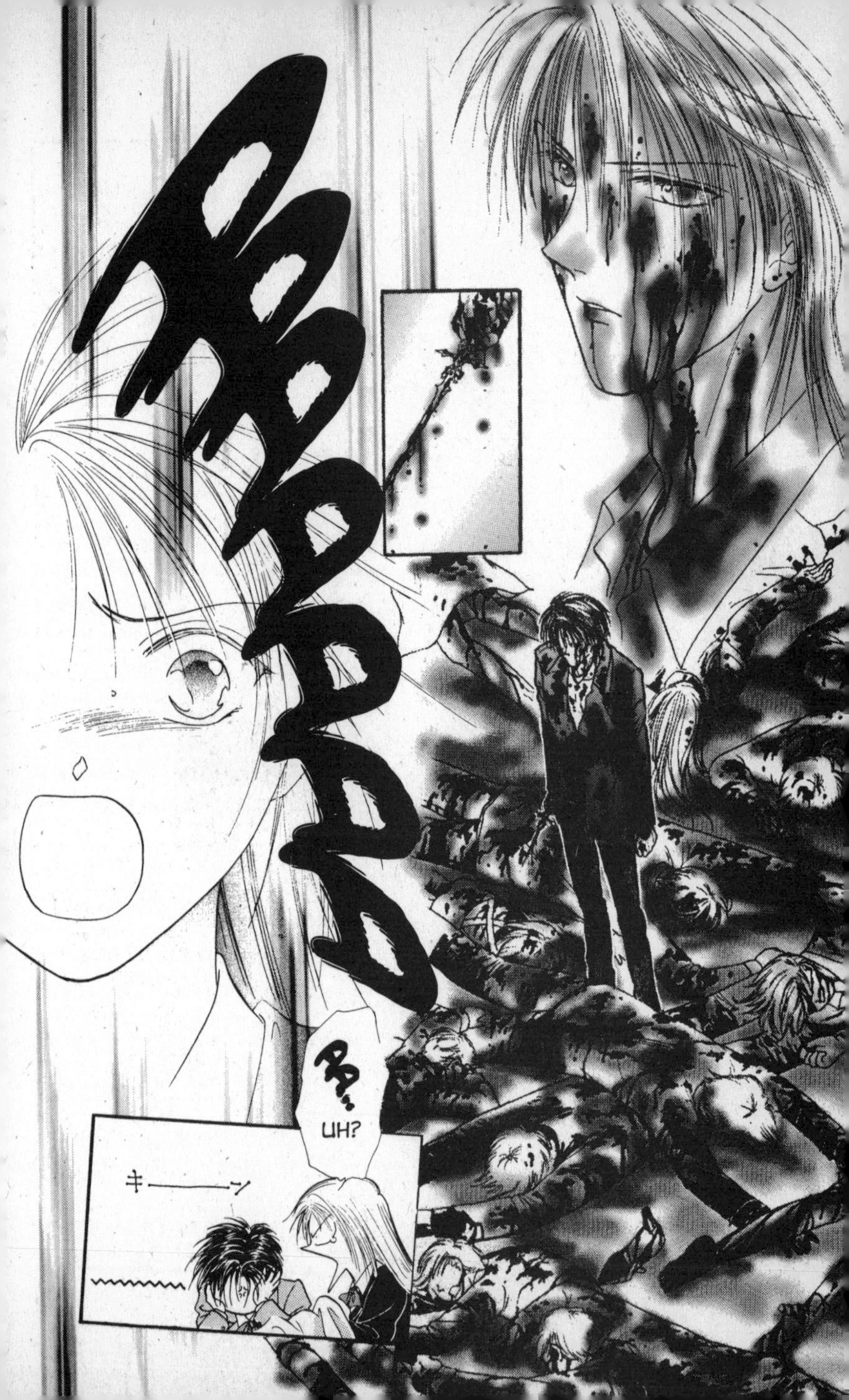
RA..
UH?

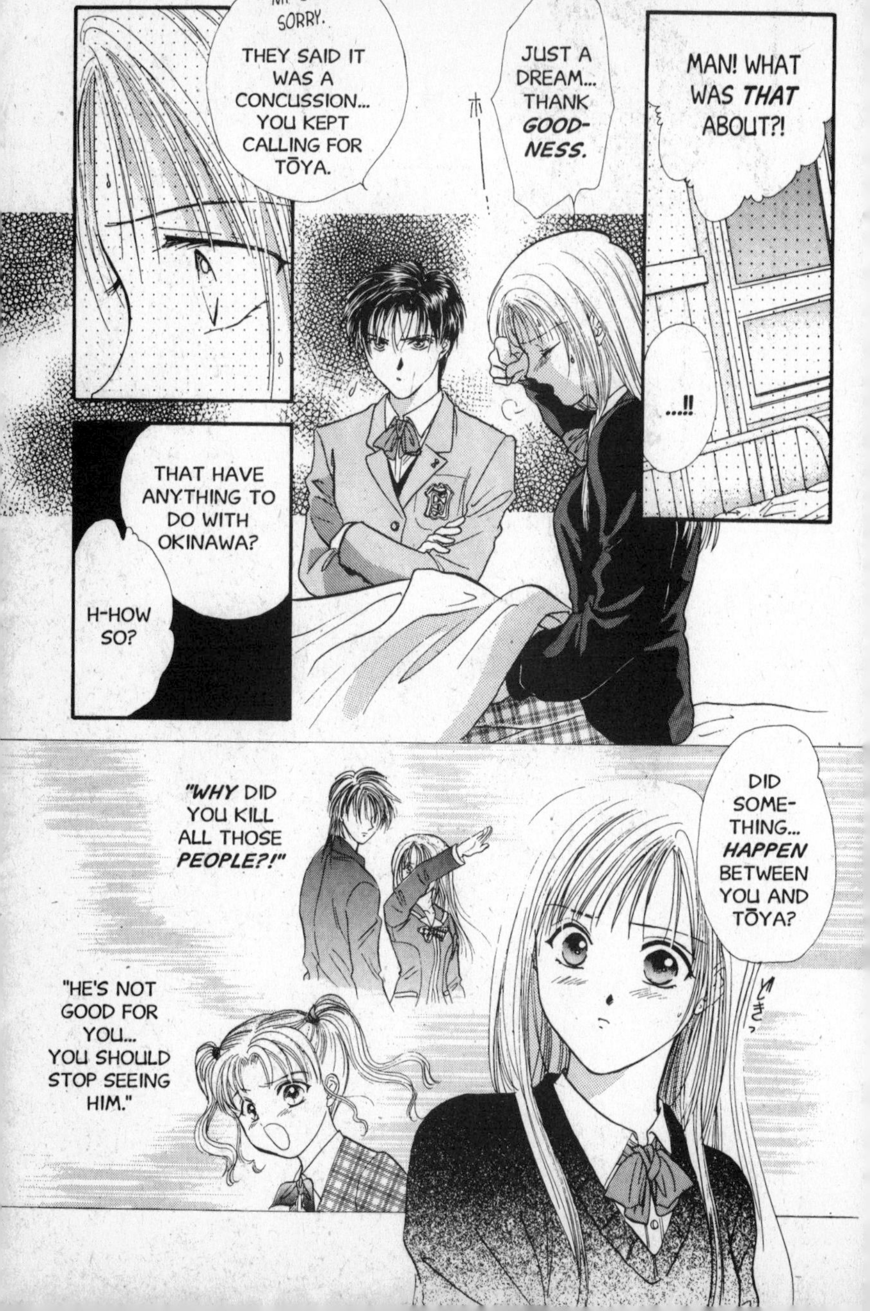
MAN! WHAT WAS THAT ABOUT?!
...!!
JUST A DREAM... THANK GOODNESS.
MY BAD. SORRY.
THEY SAID IT WAS A CONCUSSION... YOU KEPT CALLING FOR TŌYA.
THAT HAVE ANYTHING TO DO WITH OKINAWA?
H-HOW SO?
DID SOMETHING... HAPPEN BETWEEN YOU AND TŌYA?
"WHY DID YOU KILL ALL THOSE PEOPLE?!"
"HE'S NOT GOOD FOR YOU... YOU SHOULD STOP SEEING HIM."

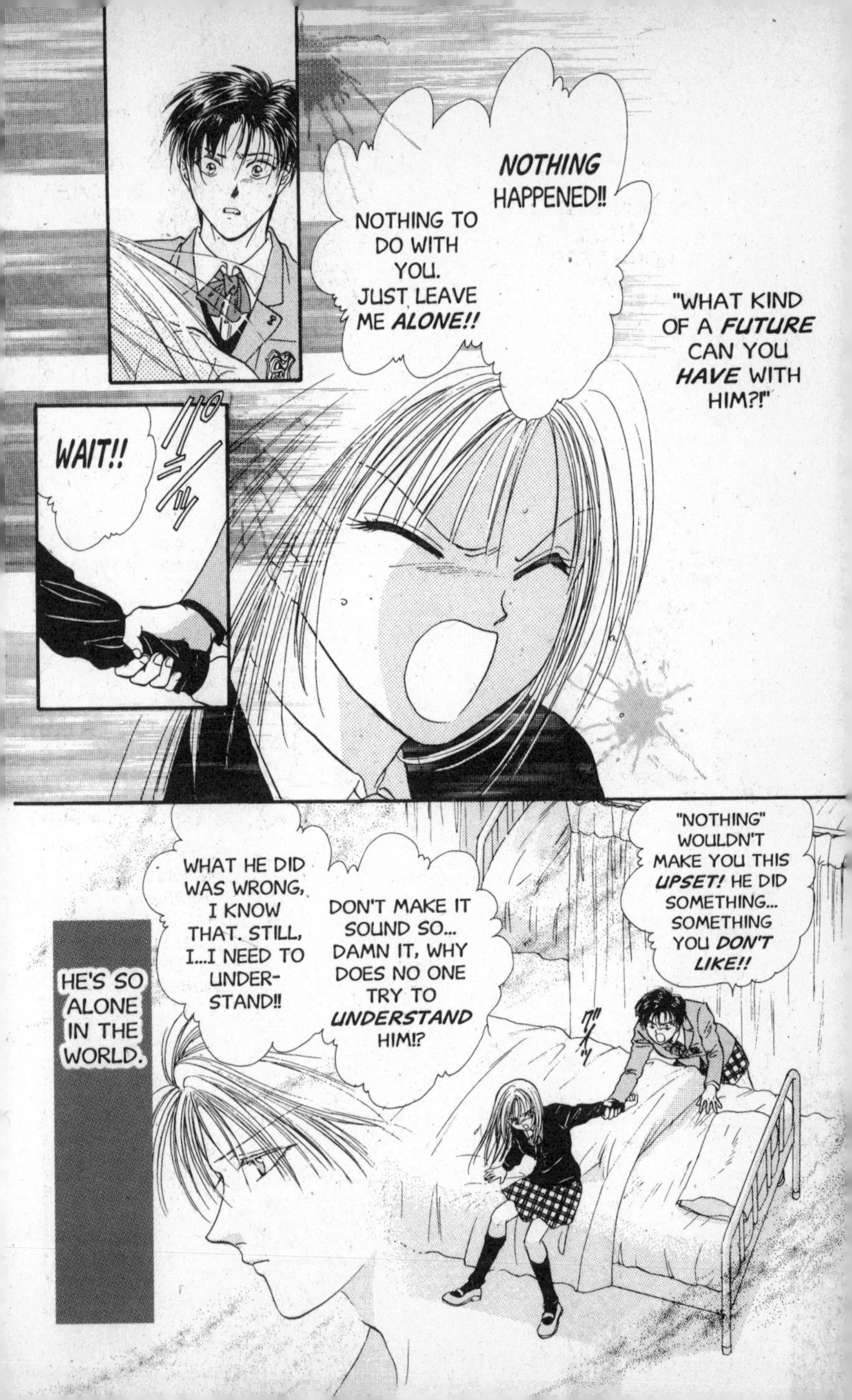
"WHAT KIND OF A FUTURE CAN YOU HAVE WITH HIM?!"
NOTHING HAPPENED!!
NOTHING TO DO WITH YOU. JUST LEAVE ME ALONE!!
WAIT!!
"NOTHING" WOULDN'T MAKE YOU THIS UPSET! HE DID SOMETHING... SOMETHING YOU DON'T LIKE!!
DON'T MAKE IT SOUND SO... DAMN IT, WHY DOES NO ONE TRY TO UNDERSTAND HIM!?
WHAT HE DID WAS WRONG, I KNOW THAT. STILL, I...I NEED TO UNDER-STAND!!
HE'S SO ALONE IN THE WORLD.

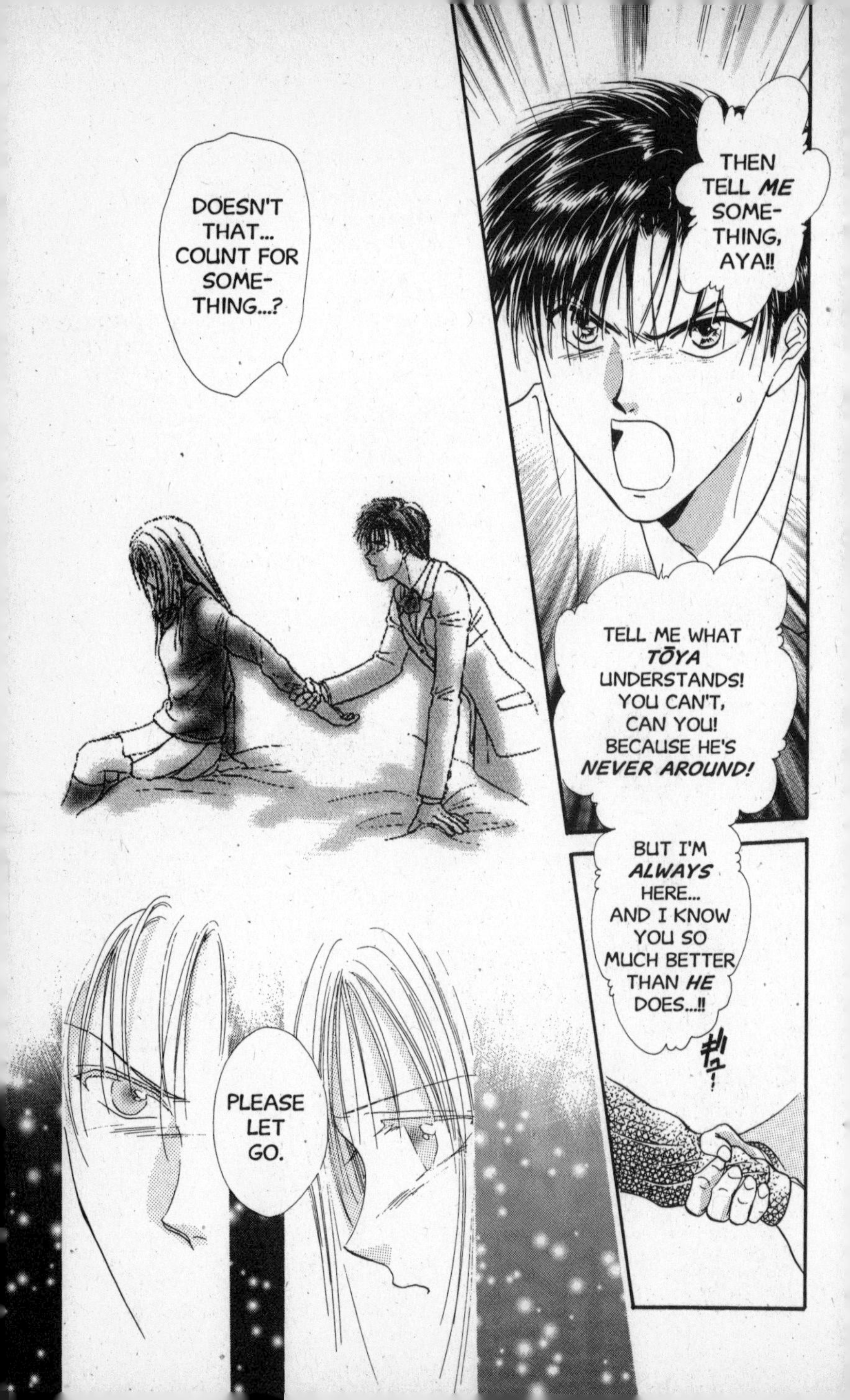
THEN TELL *ME* SOME-THING, AYA!!
TELL ME WHAT *TŌYA* UNDERSTANDS! YOU CAN'T, CAN YOU! BECAUSE HE'S *NEVER AROUND!*
BUT I'M *ALWAYS* HERE... AND I KNOW YOU SO MUCH BETTER THAN *HE* DOES...!!
DOESN'T THAT... COUNT FOR SOME-THING...?
PLEASE LET GO.

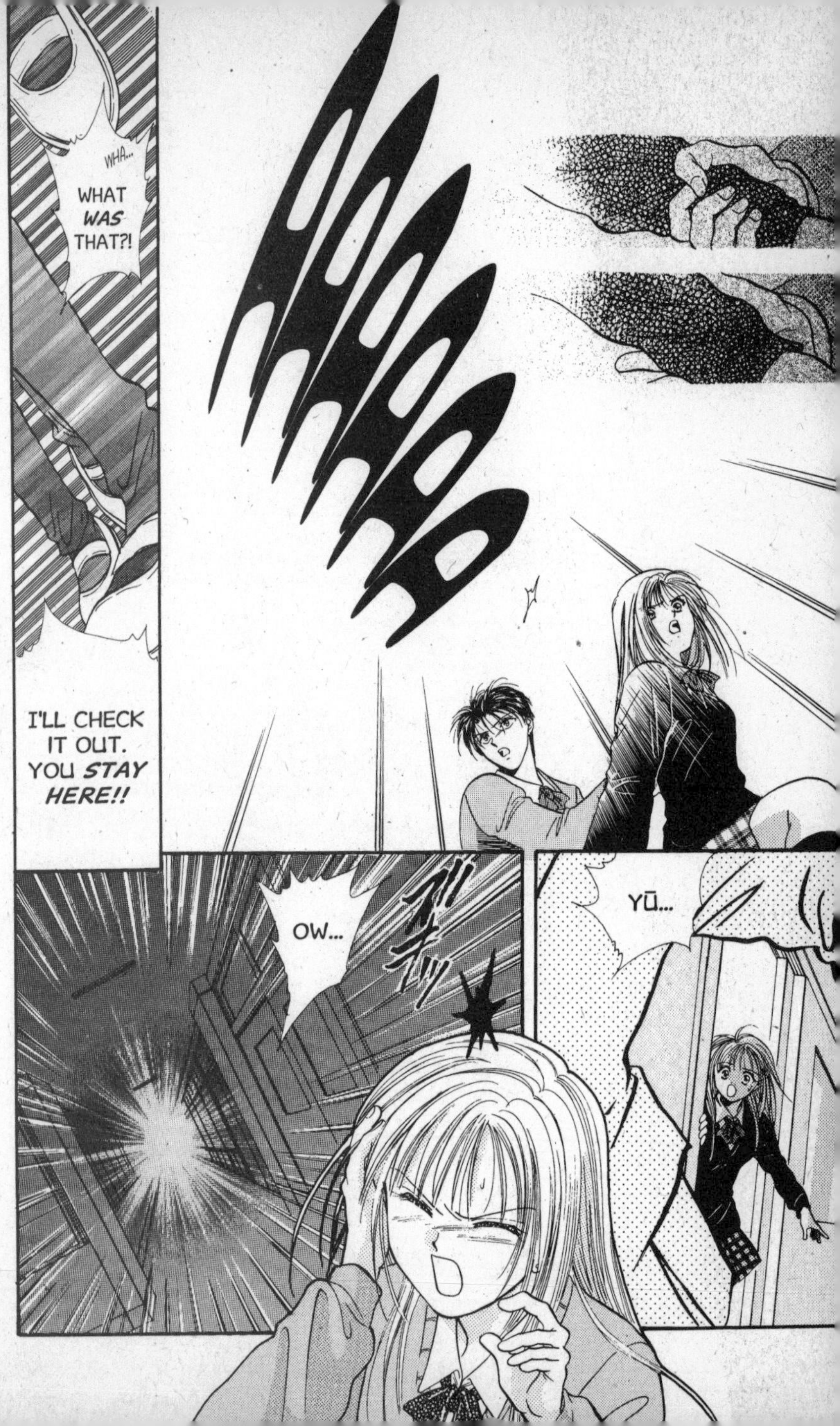
WHA...
WHAT WAS THAT?!
I'LL CHECK IT OUT. YOU STAY HERE!!
YŪ...
OW...

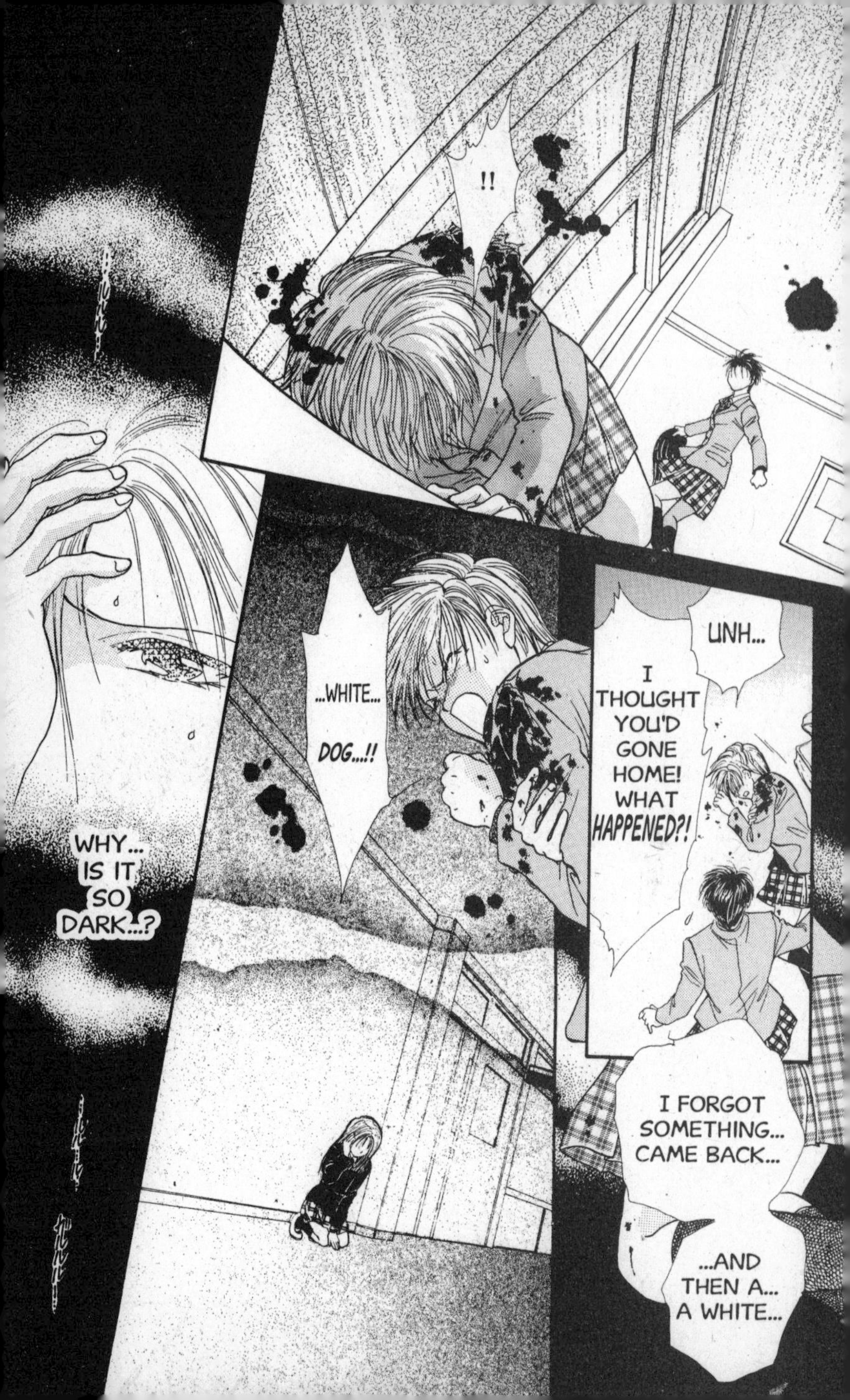
!!
UNH...
I THOUGHT YOU'D GONE HOME! WHAT HAPPENED?!
I FORGOT SOMETHING... CAME BACK...
...AND THEN A... A WHITE...
...WHITE...
DOG...!!
WHY... IS IT SO DARK...?

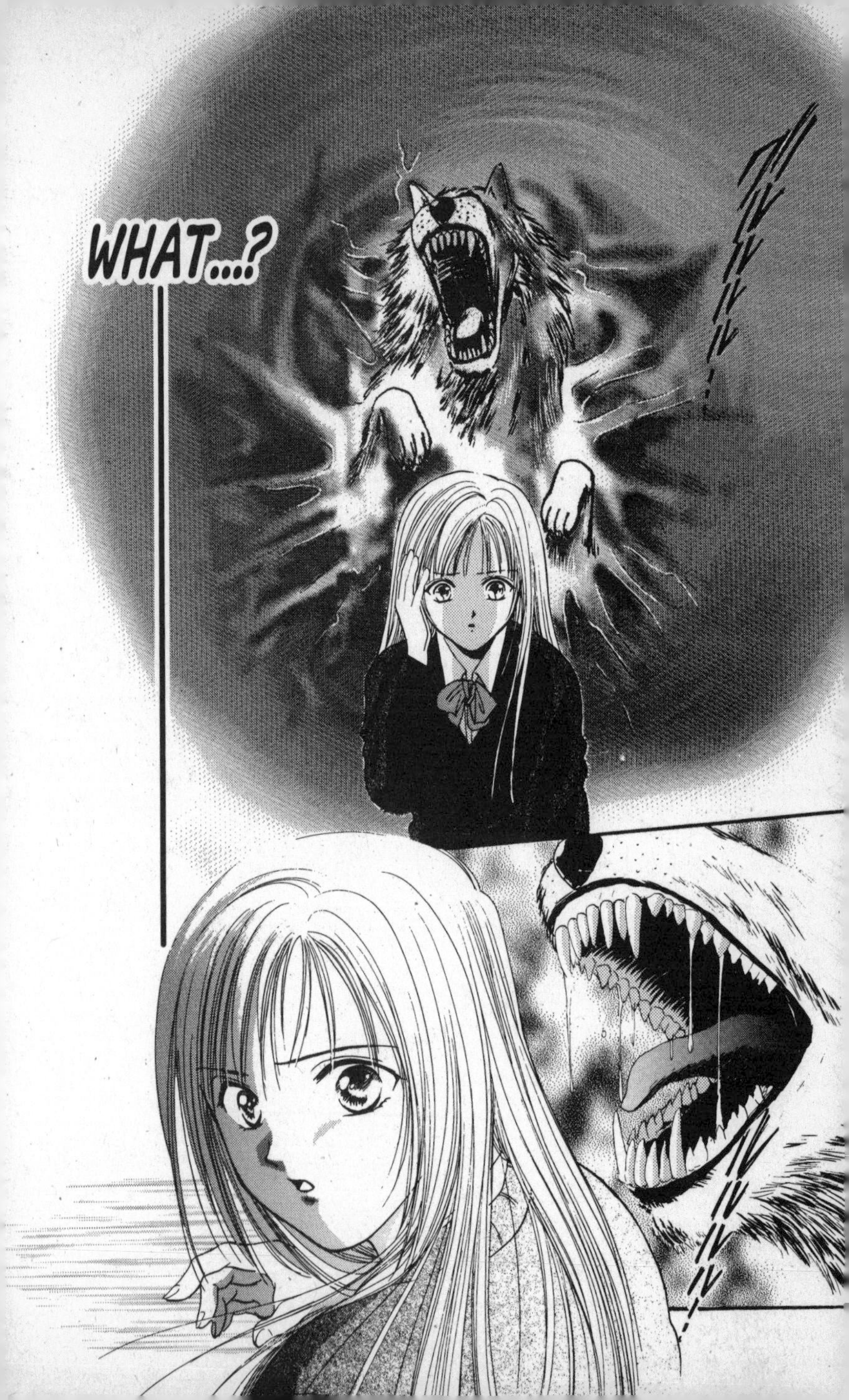
WHAT...?

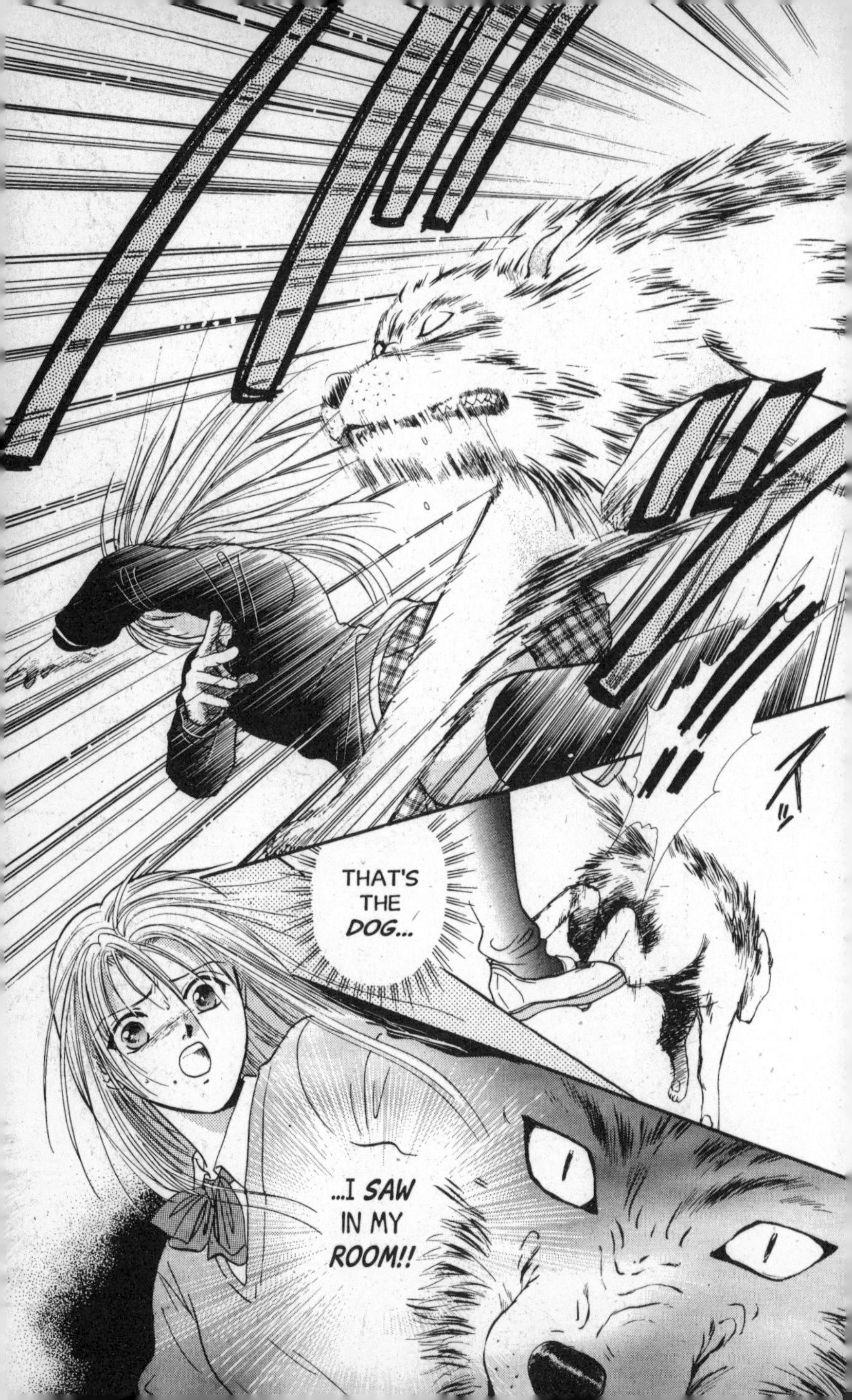
THAT'S THE *DOG...*
...I *SAW* IN MY *ROOM!!*

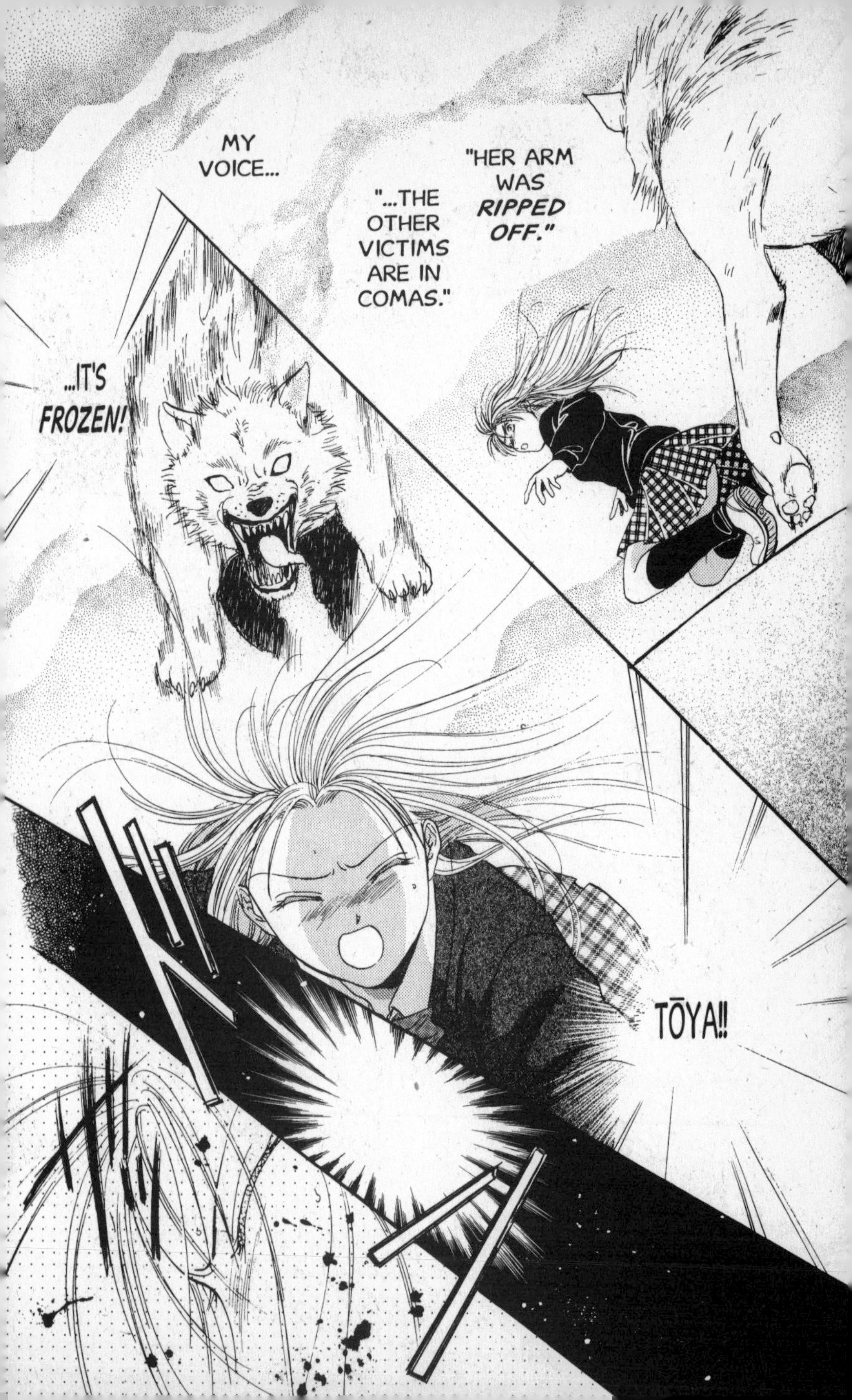
"HER ARM WAS *RIPPED OFF.*"
"...THE OTHER VICTIMS ARE IN COMAS."
MY VOICE...
...IT'S *FROZEN!*
TŌYA!!

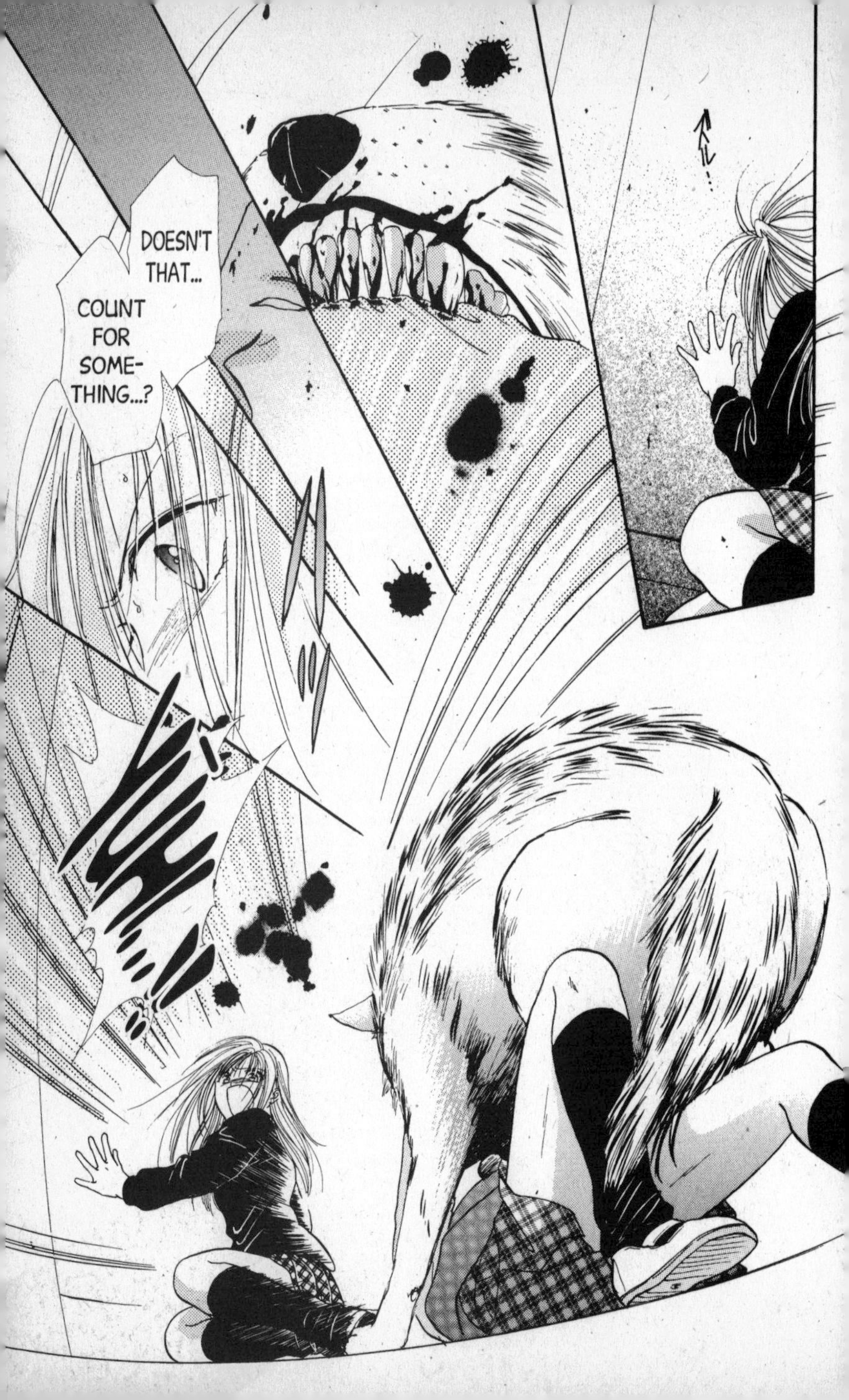
DOESN'T THAT...
COUNT FOR SOME-THING...?

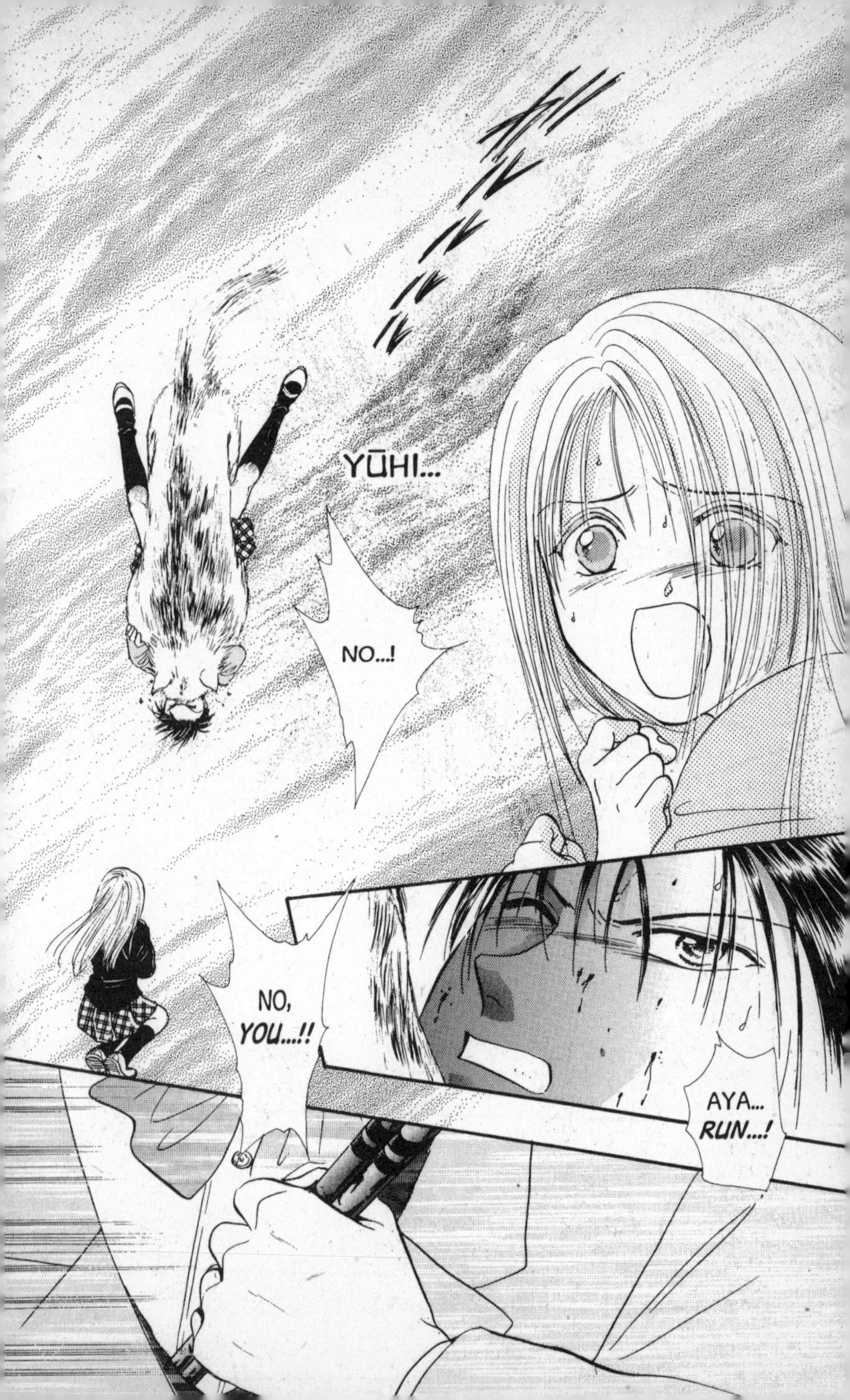
YŪHI...
NO...!
AYA... RUN...!
NO, YOU...!!

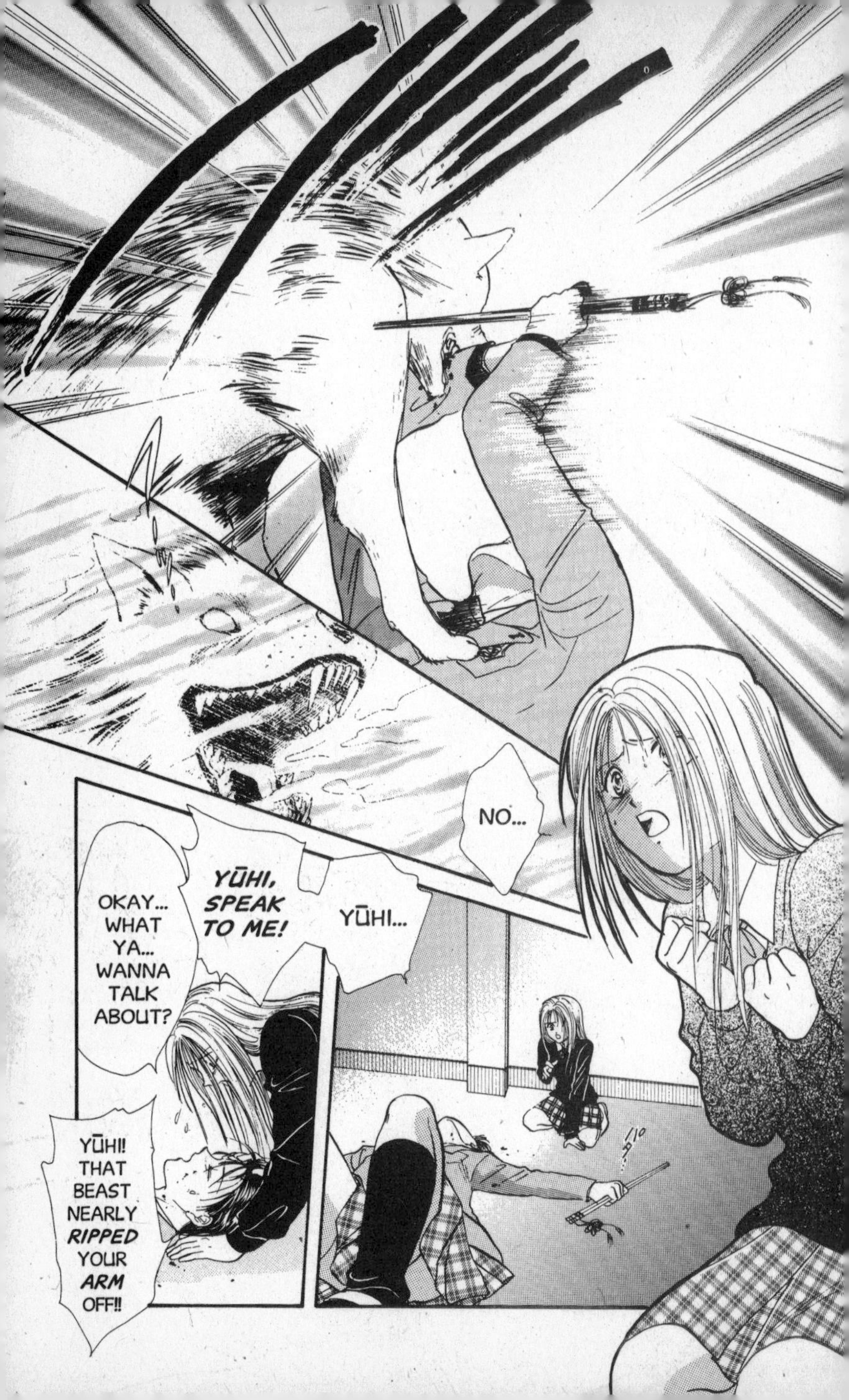
NO...
YŪHI...
YŪHI, SPEAK TO ME!
OKAY... WHAT YA... WANNA TALK ABOUT?
YŪHI! THAT BEAST NEARLY *RIPPED* YOUR *ARM* OFF!!

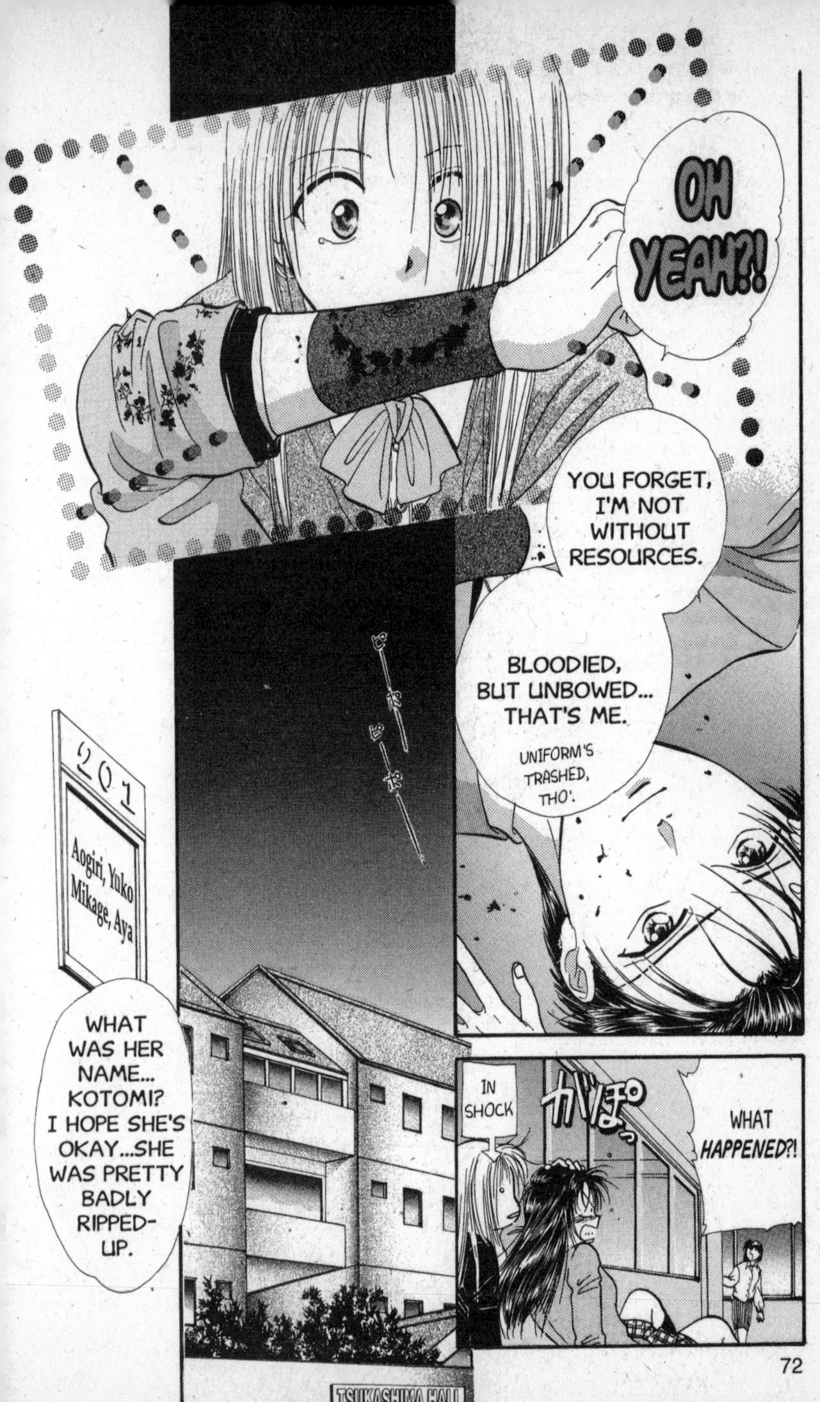
OH YEAH?!
YOU FORGET, I'M NOT WITHOUT RESOURCES.
BLOODIED, BUT UNBOWED... THAT'S ME.
UNIFORM'S TRASHED, THO'.
WHAT HAPPENED?!
IN SHOCK
201
Aogiri, Yuko
Mikage, Aya
WHAT WAS HER NAME... KOTOMI? I HOPE SHE'S OKAY...SHE WAS PRETTY BADLY RIPPED-UP.
TSUKASHIMA HALL

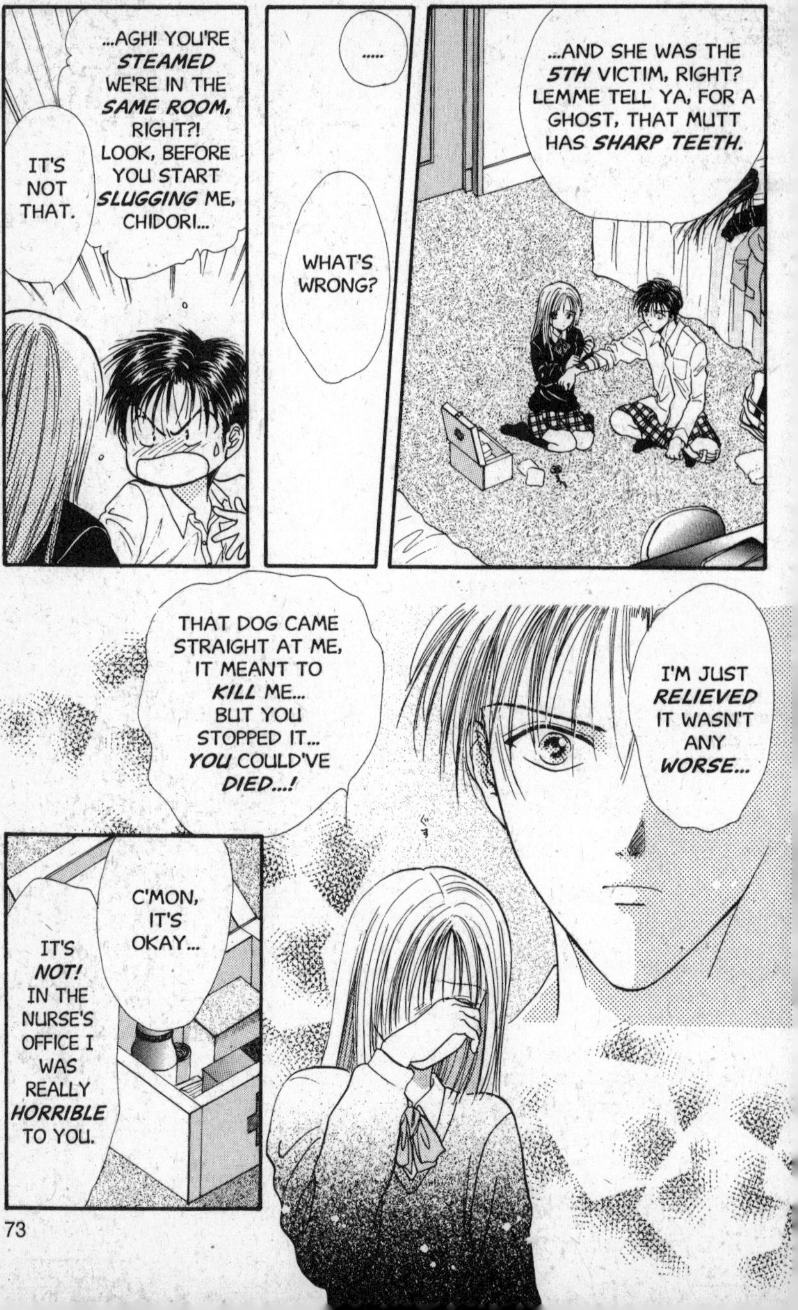
...AND SHE WAS THE 5TH VICTIM, RIGHT? LEMME TELL YA, FOR A GHOST, THAT MUTT HAS SHARP TEETH.
.....
WHAT'S WRONG?
...AGH! YOU'RE STEAMED WE'RE IN THE SAME ROOM, RIGHT?! LOOK, BEFORE YOU START SLUGGING ME, CHIDORI...
IT'S NOT THAT.
I'M JUST RELIEVED IT WASN'T ANY WORSE...
THAT DOG CAME STRAIGHT AT ME, IT MEANT TO KILL ME... BUT YOU STOPPED IT... YOU COULD'VE DIED...!
C'MON, IT'S OKAY...
IT'S NOT! IN THE NURSE'S OFFICE I WAS REALLY HORRIBLE TO YOU.

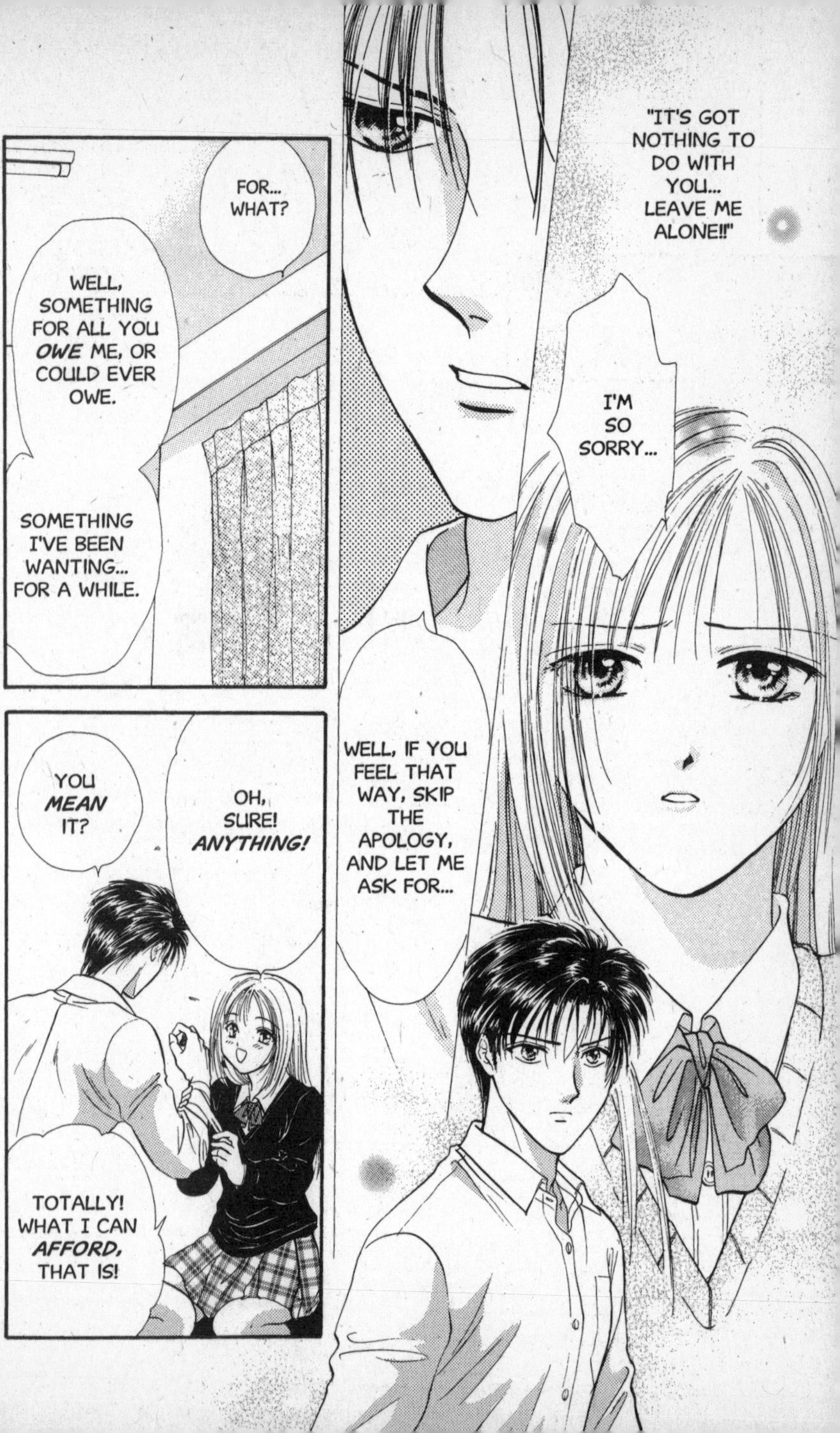
"IT'S GOT NOTHING TO DO WITH YOU... LEAVE ME ALONE!!"
I'M SO SORRY...
WELL, IF YOU FEEL THAT WAY, SKIP THE APOLOGY, AND LET ME ASK FOR...
FOR... WHAT?
WELL, SOMETHING FOR ALL YOU *OWE* ME, OR COULD EVER OWE.
SOMETHING I'VE BEEN WANTING... FOR A WHILE.
OH, SURE! *ANYTHING!*
YOU *MEAN* IT?
TOTALLY! WHAT I CAN *AFFORD,* THAT IS!

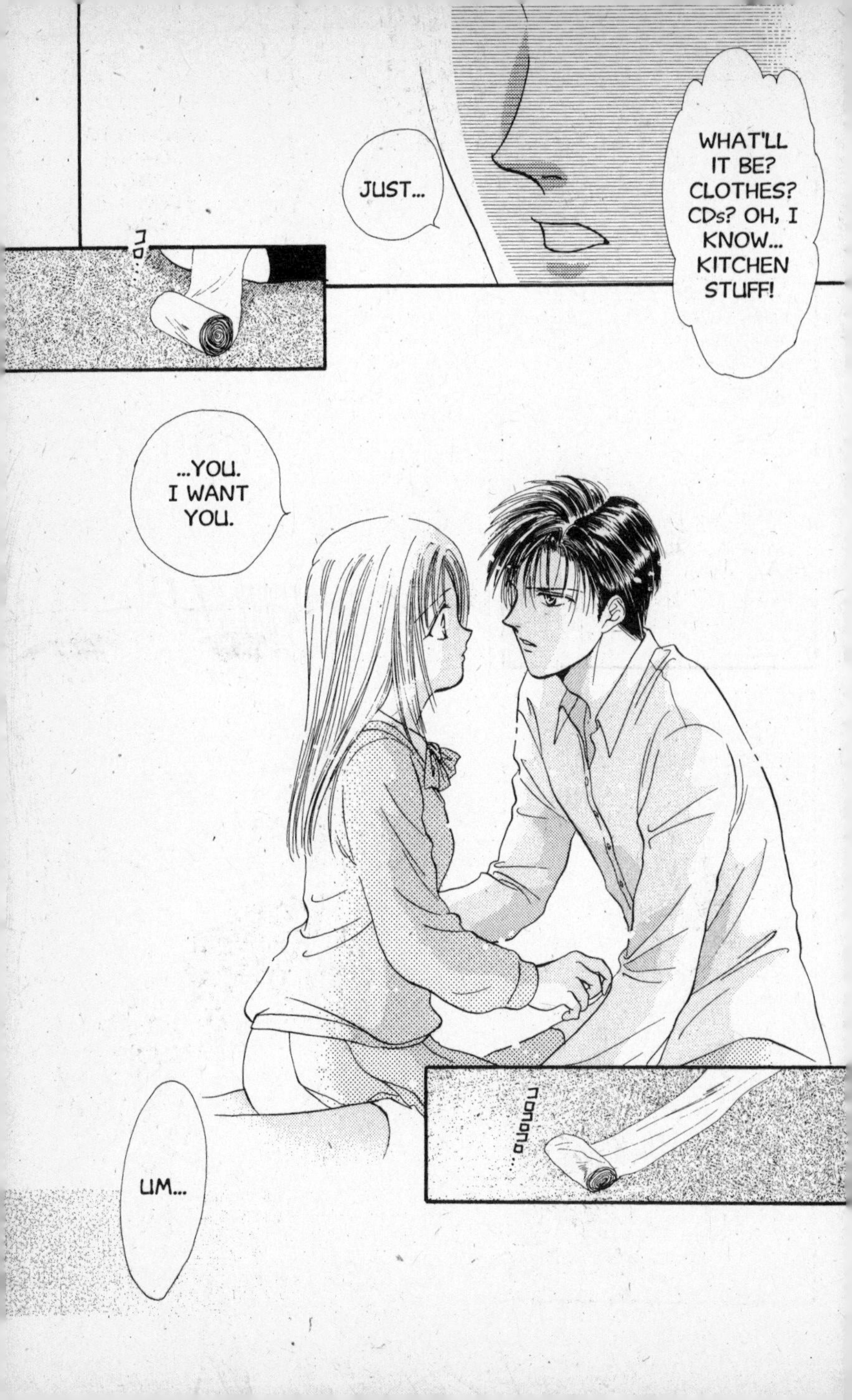
WHAT'LL IT BE? CLOTHES? CDs? OH, I KNOW... KITCHEN STUFF!
JUST...
...YOU. I WANT YOU.
UM...

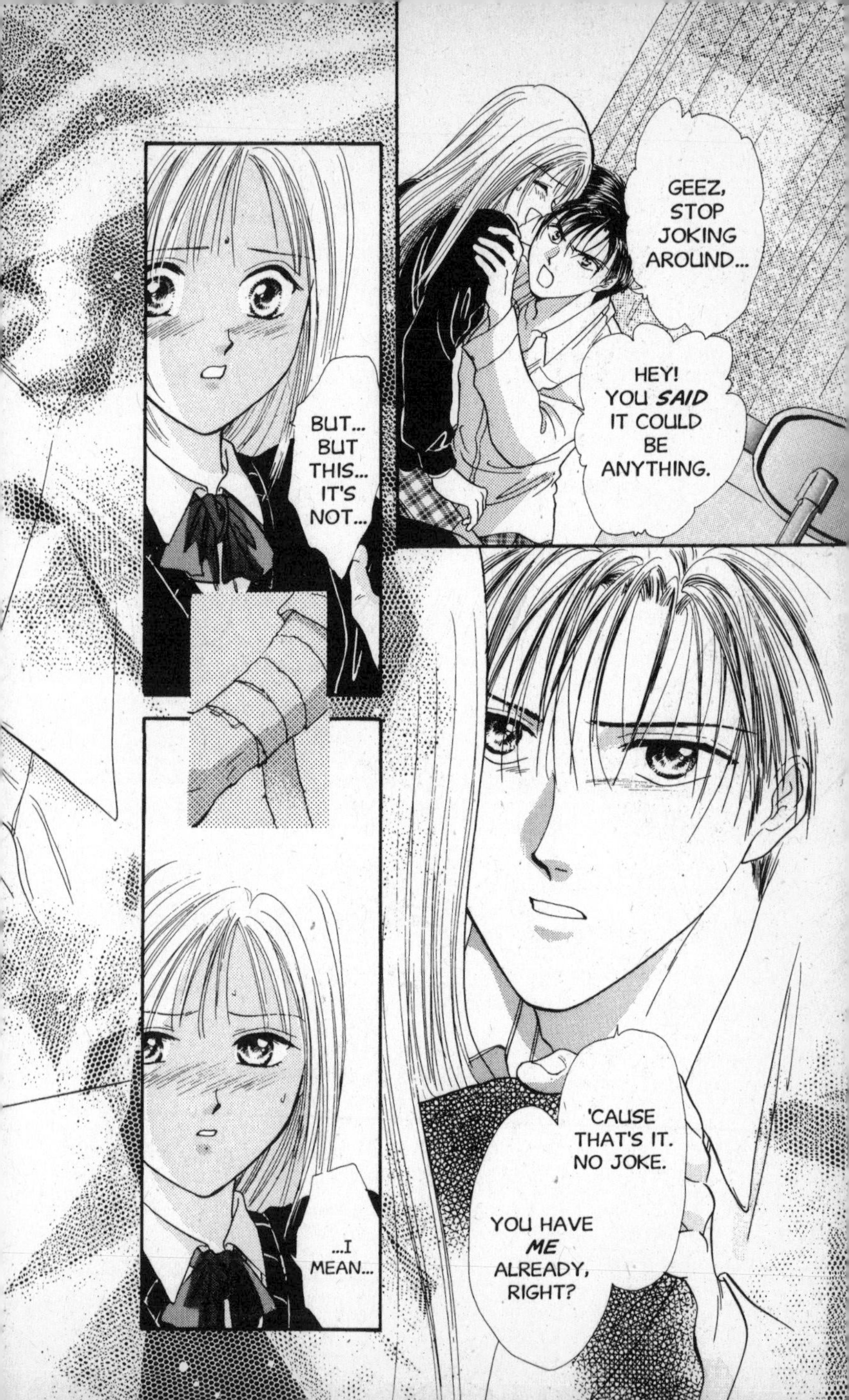
GEEZ, STOP JOKING AROUND...
HEY! YOU *SAID* IT COULD BE ANYTHING.
BUT... BUT THIS... IT'S NOT...
'CAUSE THAT'S IT. NO JOKE.
YOU HAVE *ME* ALREADY, RIGHT?
...I MEAN...

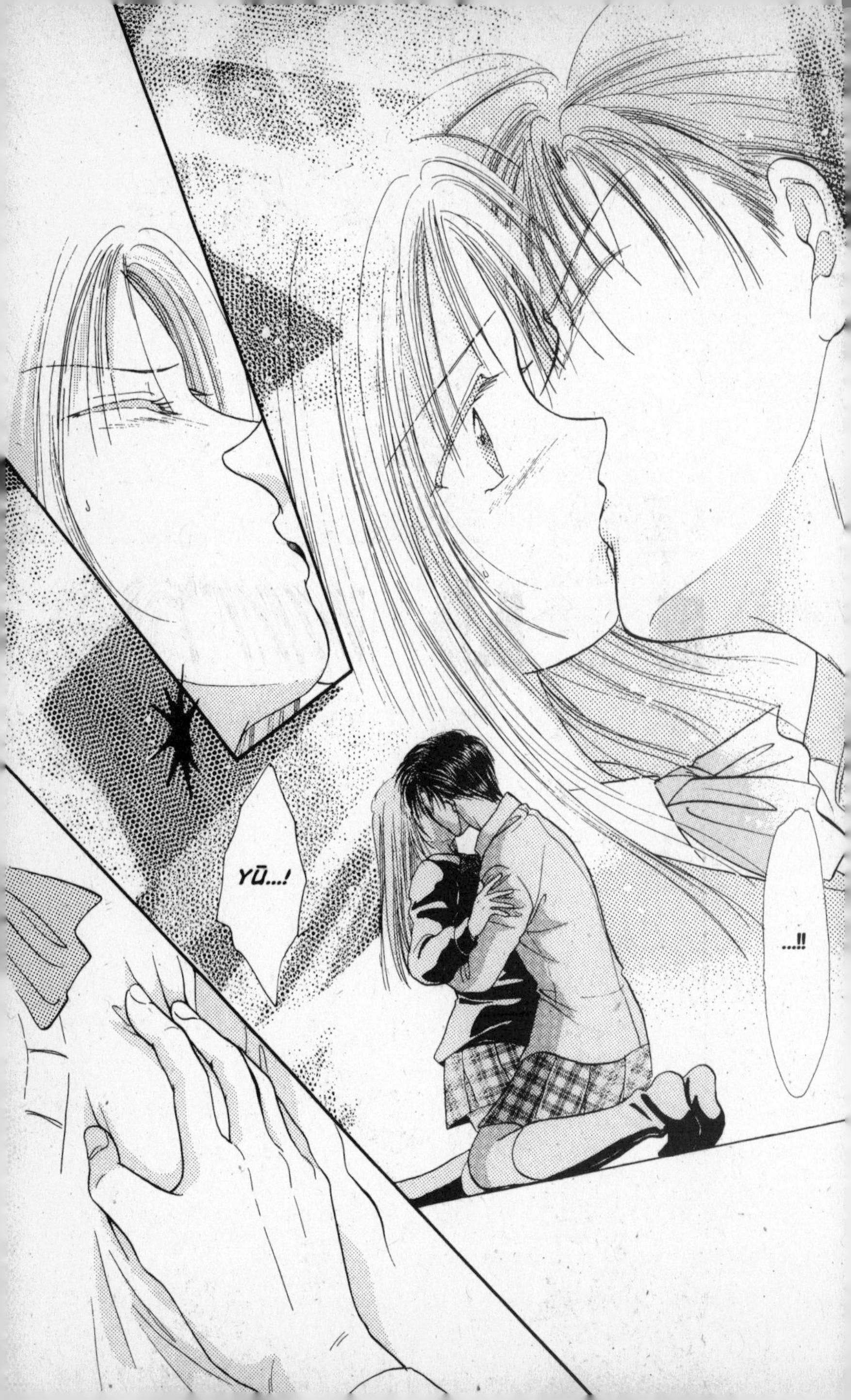
...!!
YŪ...!

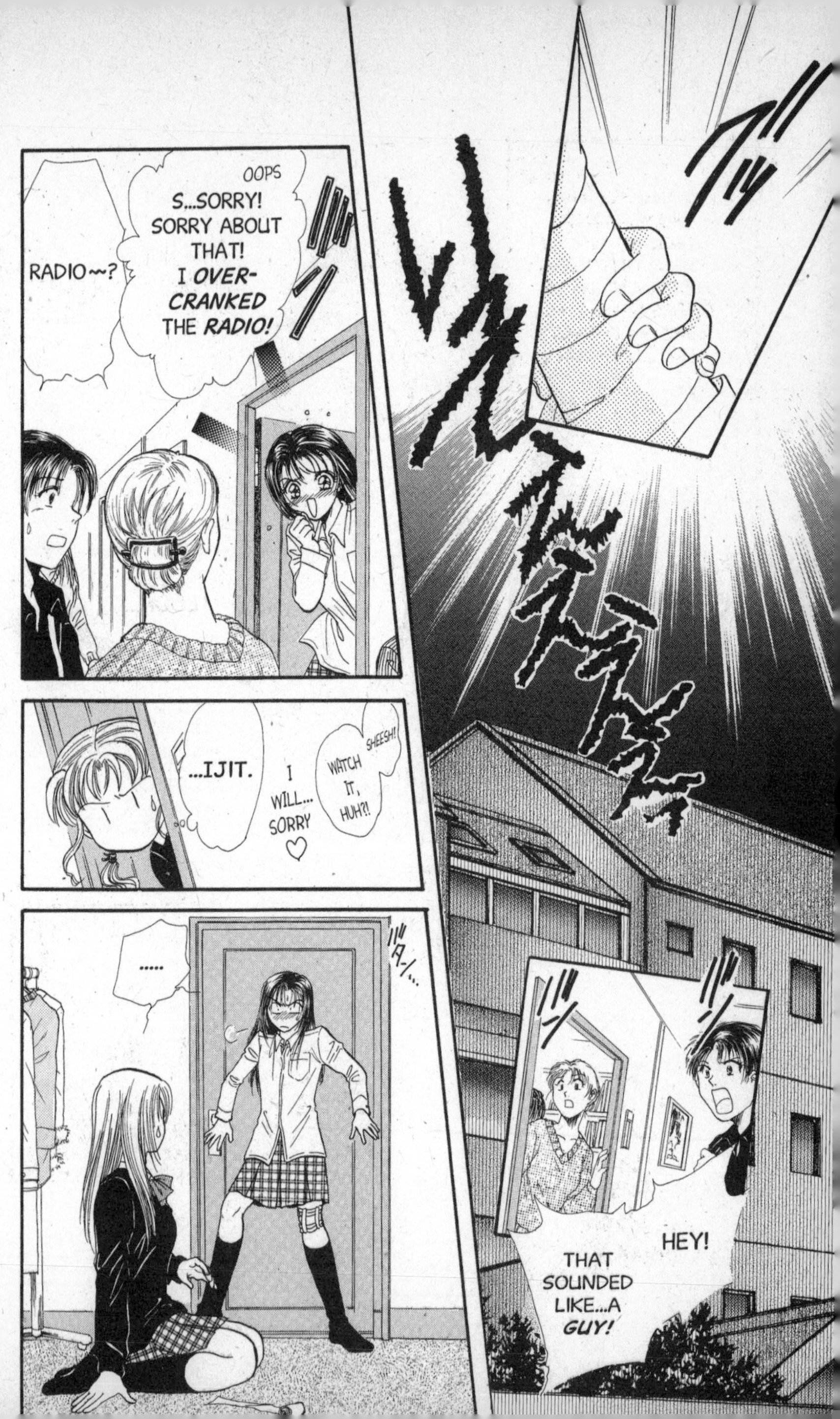
HEY!
THAT SOUNDED LIKE...A GUY!
OOPS
S...SORRY! SORRY ABOUT THAT! I OVER-CRANKED THE RADIO!
RADIO~~?
SHEESH!
WATCH IT, HUH?!
I WILL... SORRY ♡
...IJIT.
......

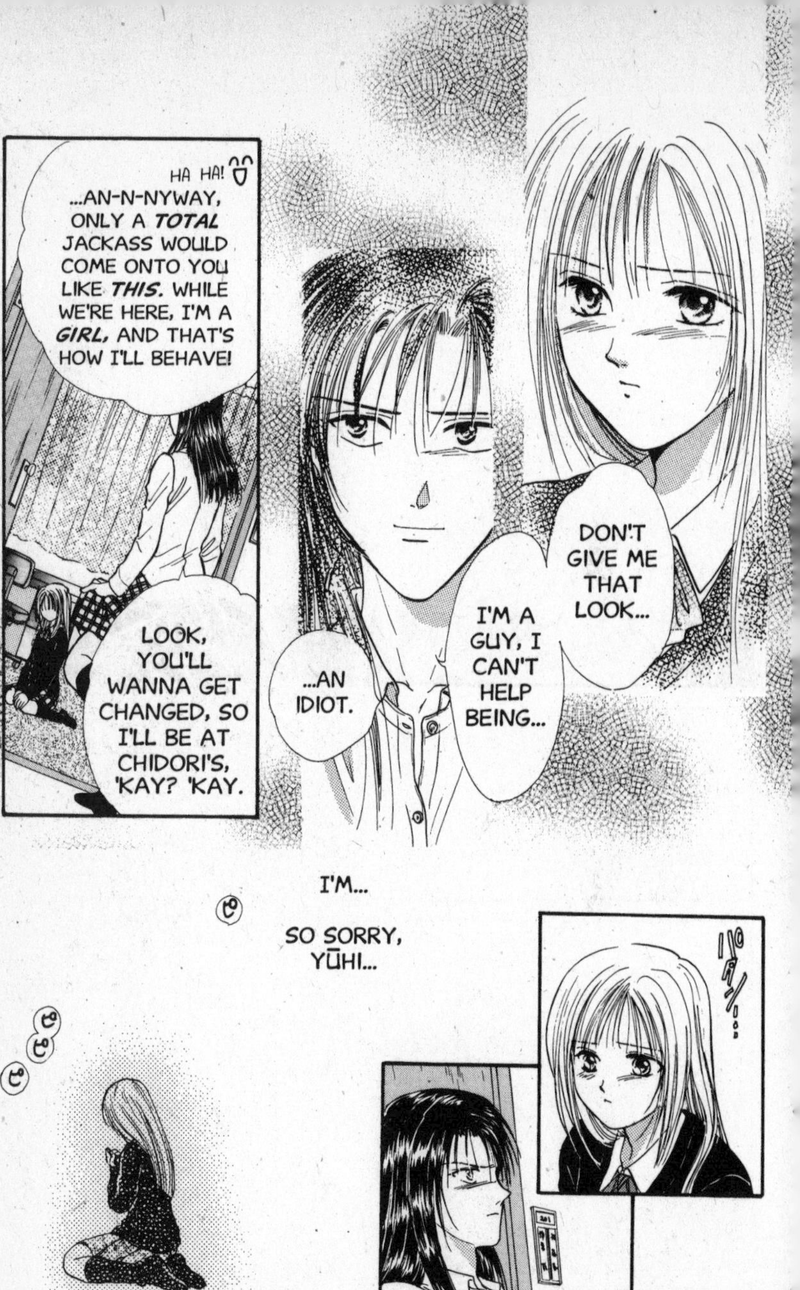
DON'T GIVE ME THAT LOOK...
I'M A GUY, I CAN'T HELP BEING...
...AN IDIOT.
HA HA!
...AN-N-NYWAY, ONLY A *TOTAL* JACKASS WOULD COME ONTO YOU LIKE *THIS.* WHILE WE'RE HERE, I'M A *GIRL,* AND THAT'S HOW I'LL BEHAVE!
LOOK, YOU'LL WANNA GET CHANGED, SO I'LL BE AT CHIDORI'S, 'KAY? 'KAY.
I'M...
SO SORRY, YŪHI...

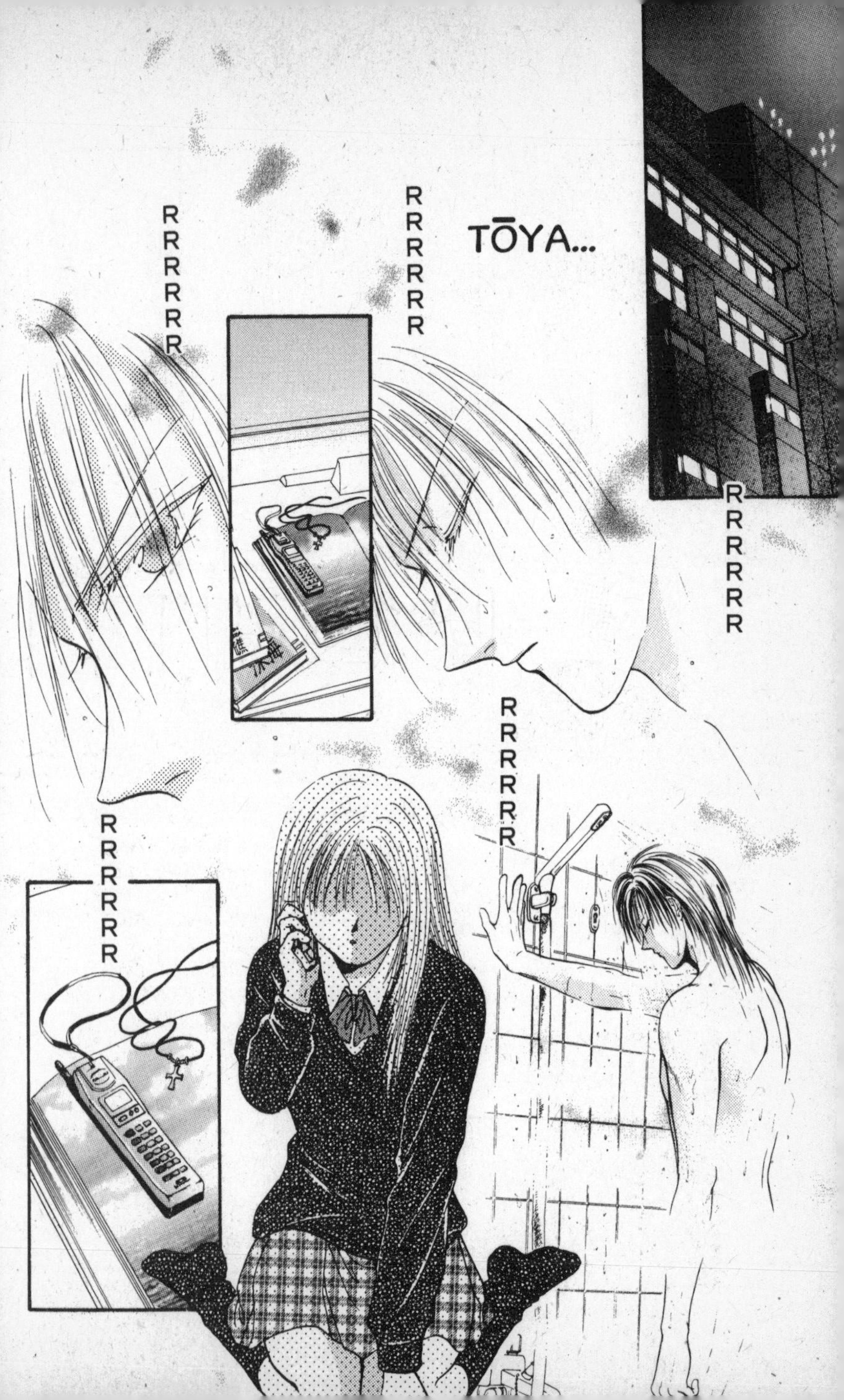
RRRRRR
TŌYA...
RRRRRR
RRRRRR
RRRRRR
RRRRRR

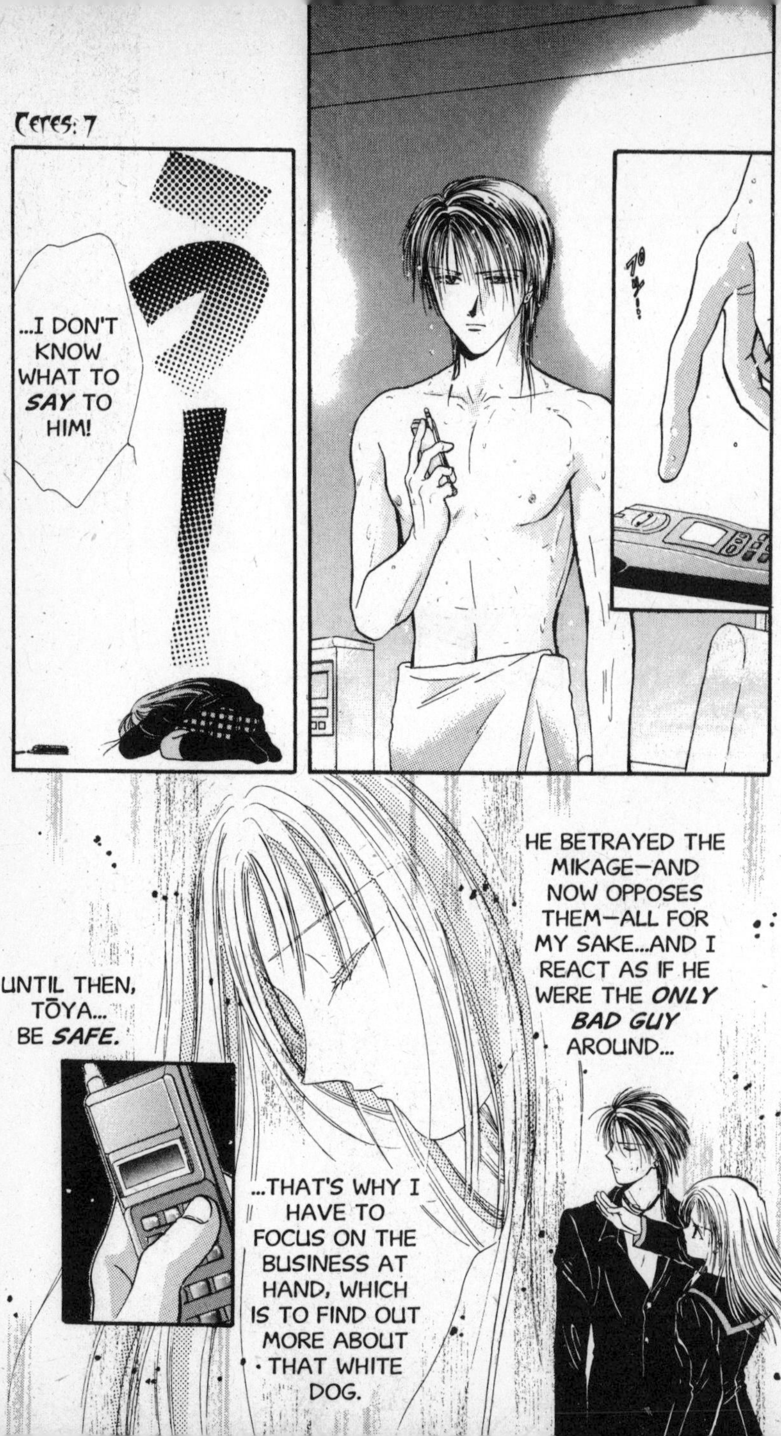
...I DON'T KNOW WHAT TO *SAY* TO HIM!
HE BETRAYED THE MIKAGE—AND NOW OPPOSES THEM—ALL FOR MY SAKE...AND I REACT AS IF HE WERE THE *ONLY BAD GUY* AROUND...
...THAT'S WHY I HAVE TO FOCUS ON THE BUSINESS AT HAND, WHICH IS TO FIND OUT MORE ABOUT THAT WHITE DOG.
UNTIL THEN, TŌYA... BE *SAFE.*

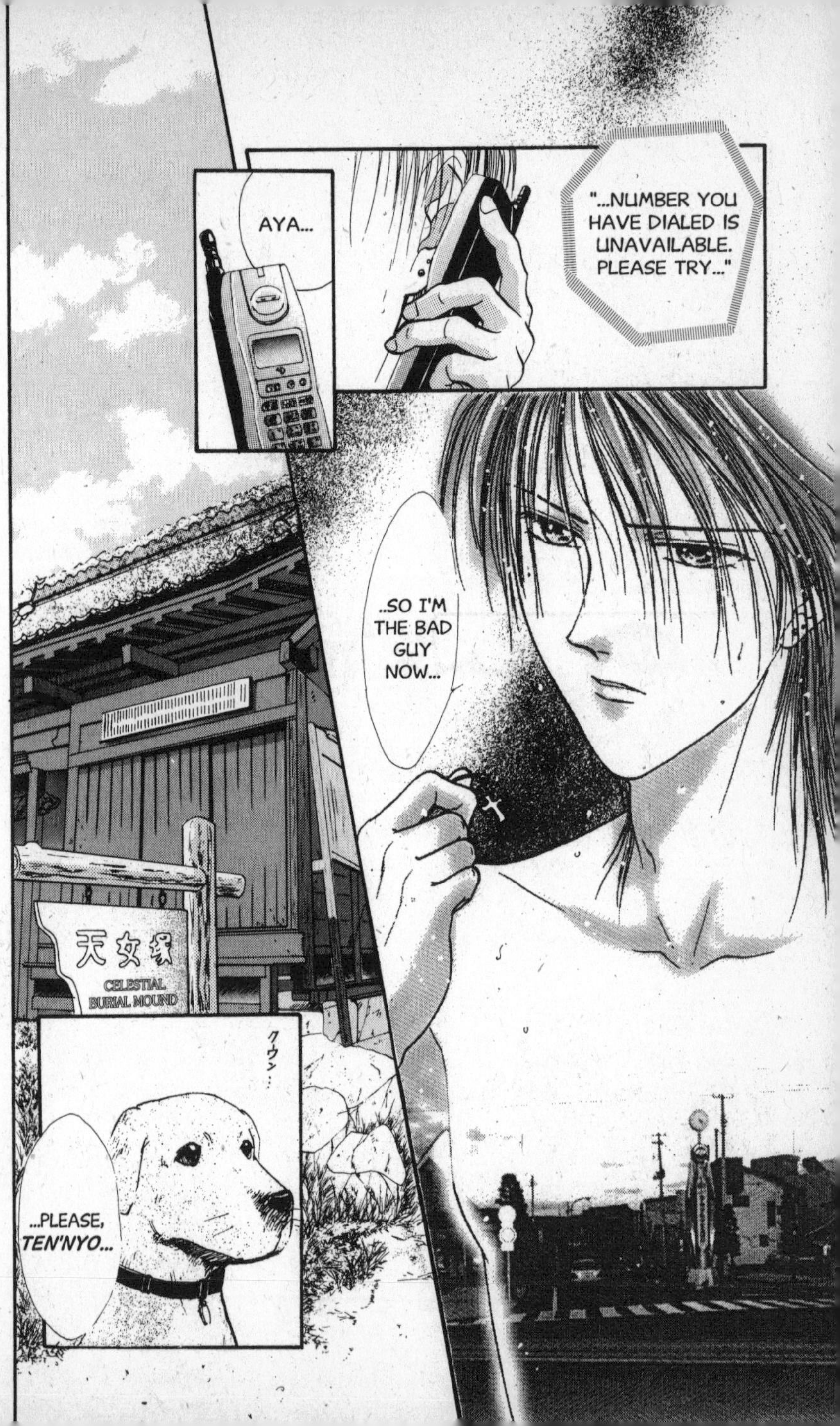
"...NUMBER YOU HAVE DIALED IS UNAVAILABLE. PLEASE TRY..."
AYA...
..SO I'M THE BAD GUY NOW...
天女塚
CELESTIAL BURIAL MOUND
クウン…
...PLEASE, TEN'NYO...

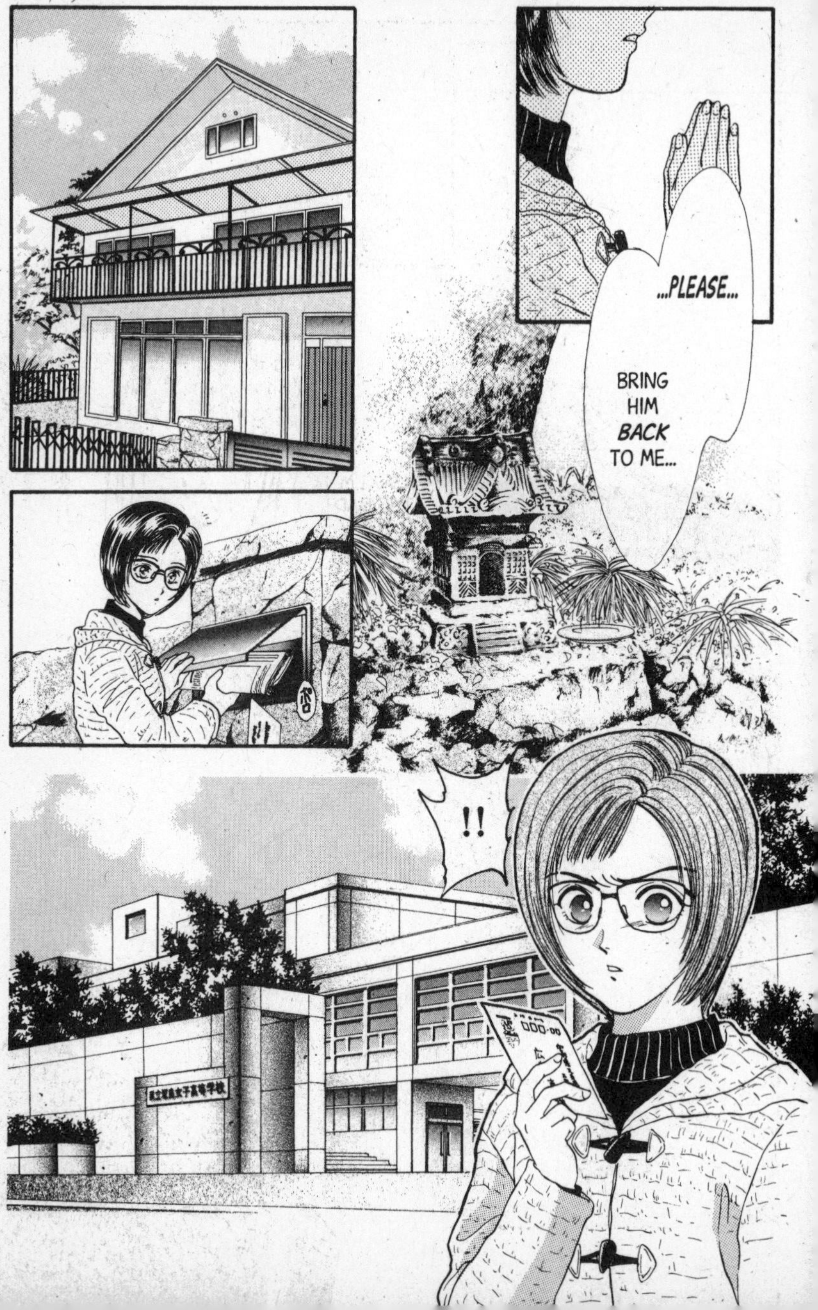
...PLEASE...
BRING HIM BACK TO ME...
!!

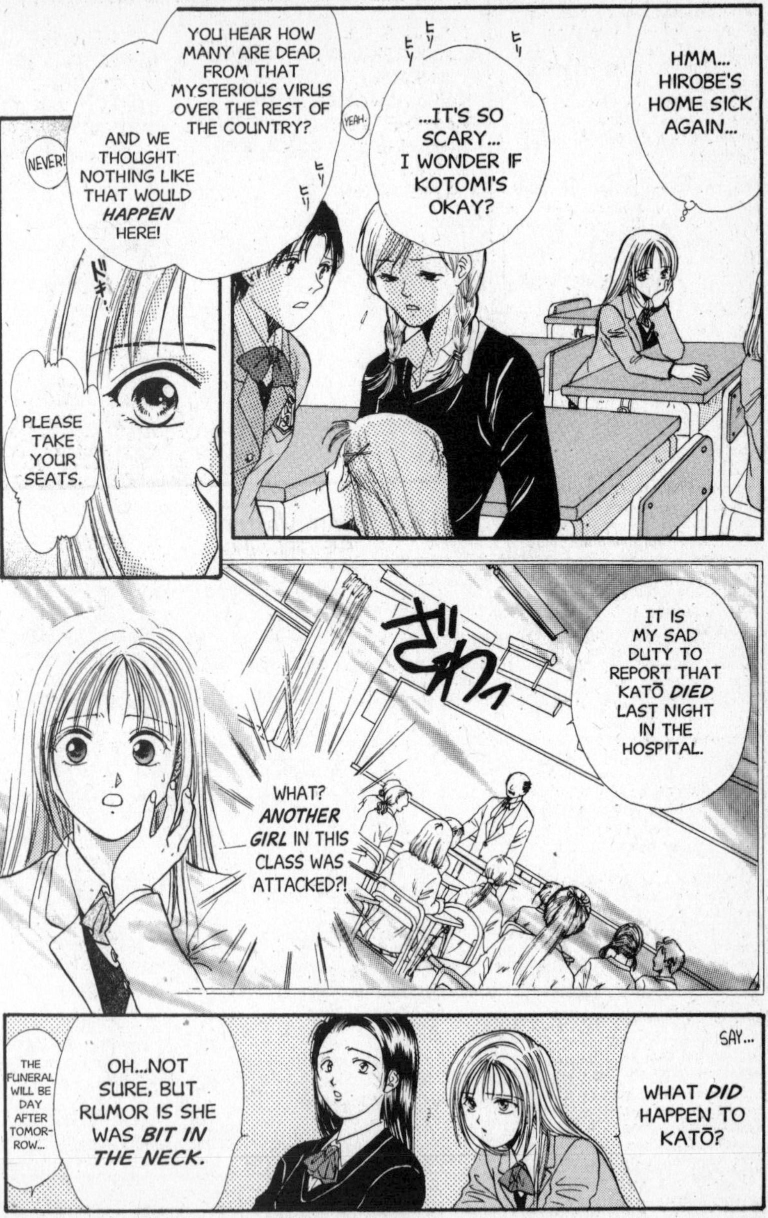
HMM... HIROBE'S HOME SICK AGAIN...
ヒソ ヒソ
...IT'S SO SCARY... I WONDER IF KOTOMI'S OKAY?
YEAH.
YOU HEAR HOW MANY ARE DEAD FROM THAT MYSTERIOUS VIRUS OVER THE REST OF THE COUNTRY?
ヒソ ヒソ
AND WE THOUGHT NOTHING LIKE THAT WOULD *HAPPEN* HERE!
NEVER!
ドキ...
PLEASE TAKE YOUR SEATS.
IT IS MY SAD DUTY TO REPORT THAT KATŌ *DIED* LAST NIGHT IN THE HOSPITAL.
ざわっ
WHAT? ***ANOTHER GIRL*** IN THIS CLASS WAS ATTACKED?!
SAY...
WHAT *DID* HAPPEN TO KATŌ?
OH...NOT SURE, BUT RUMOR IS SHE WAS ***BIT IN THE NECK.***
THE FUNERAL WILL BE DAY AFTER TOMOR-ROW...

I hardly went anywhere during this trip, but the "Hotel Alivila" was something else. I took a walk down the beach, bathed in the moonlight... Hee hee.
I fell asleep to the sound of waves gently breaking on shore—the hotel faced the East China Sea.

Oh, and I went on the submarine tour "Moglyn," a hundred feet under the sea! The ocean floor was amazing—the fish were so cute, like the Okinawan prefectural fish, **gurukun** (a type of sea bass). I'll definitely be going back to Okinawa again...oh-h-h, yeah!

So now—we're in Miyagi. I went on another research trip, but we couldn't get to the Bamboo Island 'cause of high-tide. (We did go up to it by boat, tho'.) That's why the island will only make a cameo. You **can** go ashore at low-tide. Shizugawa was also a quiet, nice place, although I was disappointed that the "*ten'nyo* burial mound" was smack in the middle of a residential complex. (Some people had mentioned that in their fan letters before the episode appeared in print, but I'd already started work on it by that point. Something similar happened during the "Okinawa chapter"—fascinating.) Anyway, the "celestial legend" exists all over Japan—all over the **world**—and Aya can't possibly get to all of it. But there **are** a limited number of places where hagoromo remained on Earth, so it's not impossible that she may visit **your** hometown, next!

Incidentally, this volume was the first time for Aya to talk about her name. Yes, that particular *kanji* is almost always used in a "bad" way (such as in "goblin"), but its true meaning according to the *kanji* dictionary is "(1) alluring; beautiful." Aya's grandmother meant it in the "bewitching, voluptuous" sense, and I chose it because I wanted her name to link to the series title, and also because a distinctive name for your main character is always easier to remember. I'll admit it felt a little weird at first. What I noticed later, though, was that—

To Be Continued

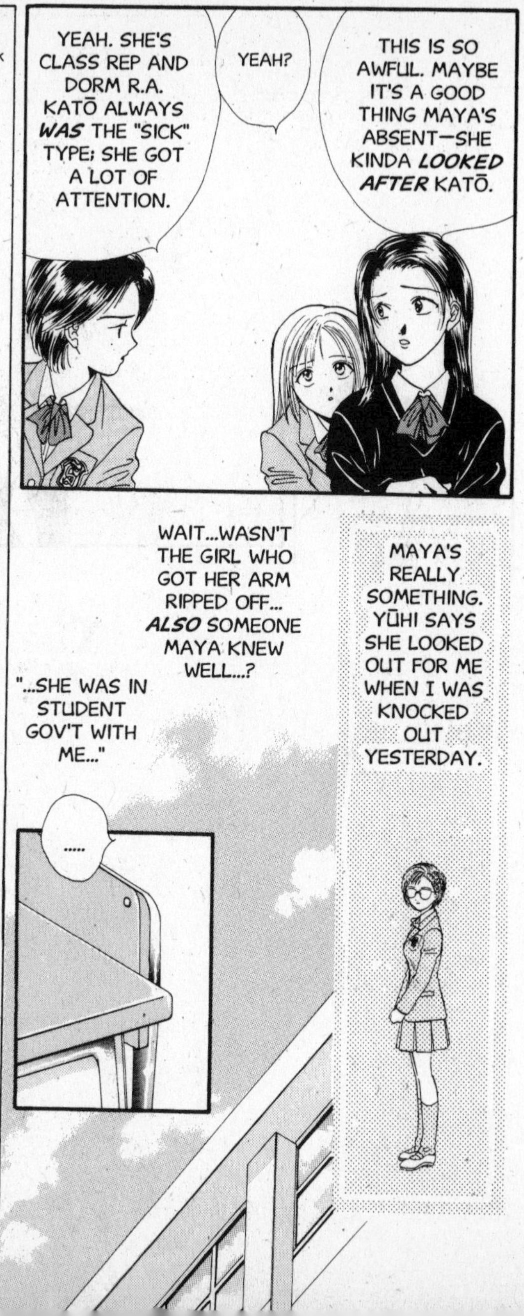
THIS IS SO AWFUL. MAYBE IT'S A GOOD THING MAYA'S ABSENT—SHE KINDA *LOOKED AFTER* KATŌ.
YEAH?
YEAH. SHE'S CLASS REP AND DORM R.A. KATŌ ALWAYS *WAS* THE "SICK" TYPE; SHE GOT A LOT OF ATTENTION.
MAYA'S REALLY SOMETHING. YŪHI SAYS SHE LOOKED OUT FOR ME WHEN I WAS KNOCKED OUT YESTERDAY.
WAIT...WASN'T THE GIRL WHO GOT HER ARM RIPPED OFF... *ALSO* SOMEONE MAYA KNEW WELL...?
"...SHE WAS IN STUDENT GOV'T WITH ME..."
.....

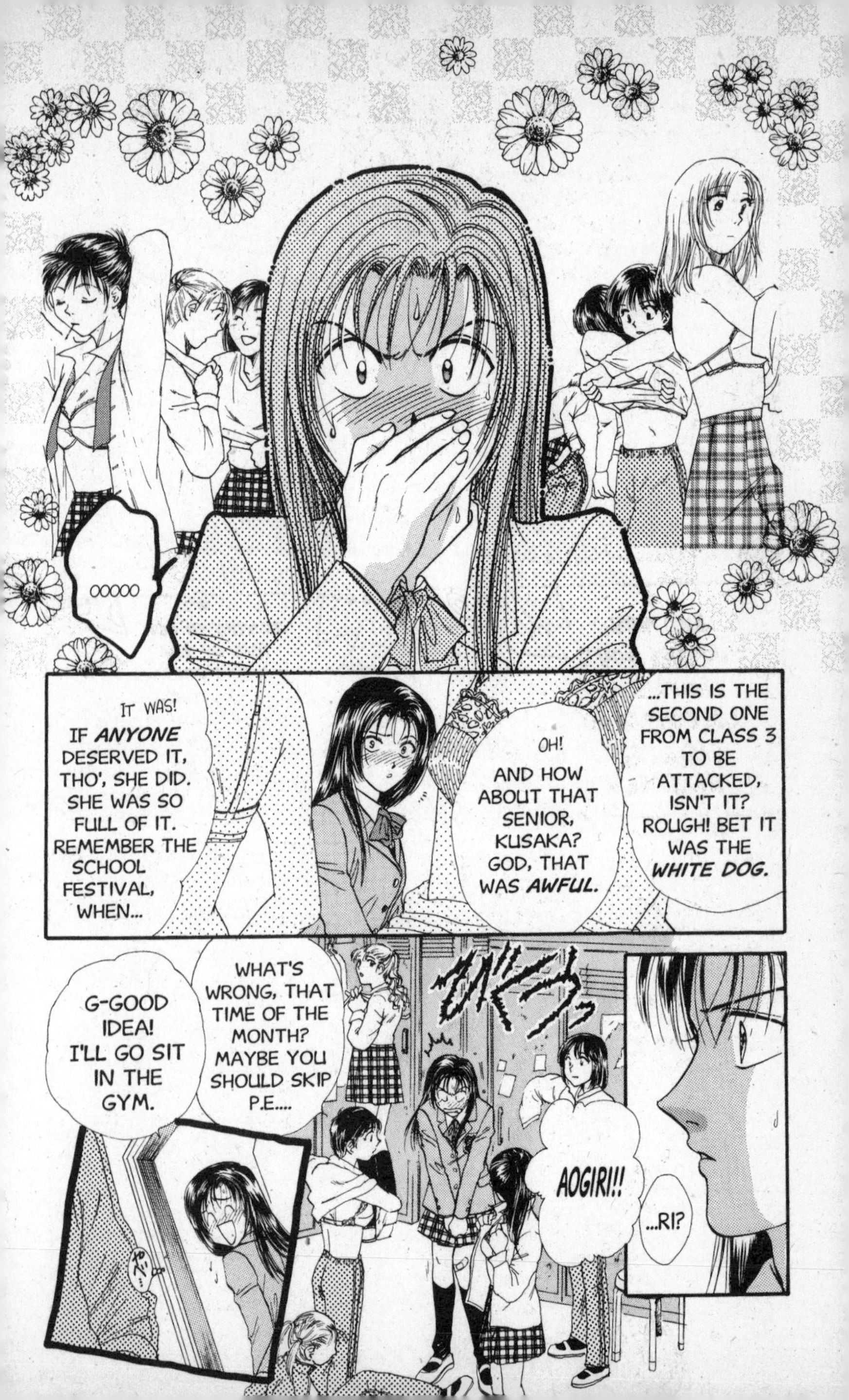
OOOOO
...THIS IS THE SECOND ONE FROM CLASS 3 TO BE ATTACKED, ISN'T IT? ROUGH! BET IT WAS THE WHITE DOG.
OH! AND HOW ABOUT THAT SENIOR, KUSAKA? GOD, THAT WAS AWFUL.
IT WAS! IF ANYONE DESERVED IT, THO', SHE DID. SHE WAS SO FULL OF IT. REMEMBER THE SCHOOL FESTIVAL, WHEN...
AOGIRI!!
...RI?
WHAT'S WRONG, THAT TIME OF THE MONTH? MAYBE YOU SHOULD SKIP P.E....
G-GOOD IDEA! I'LL GO SIT IN THE GYM.

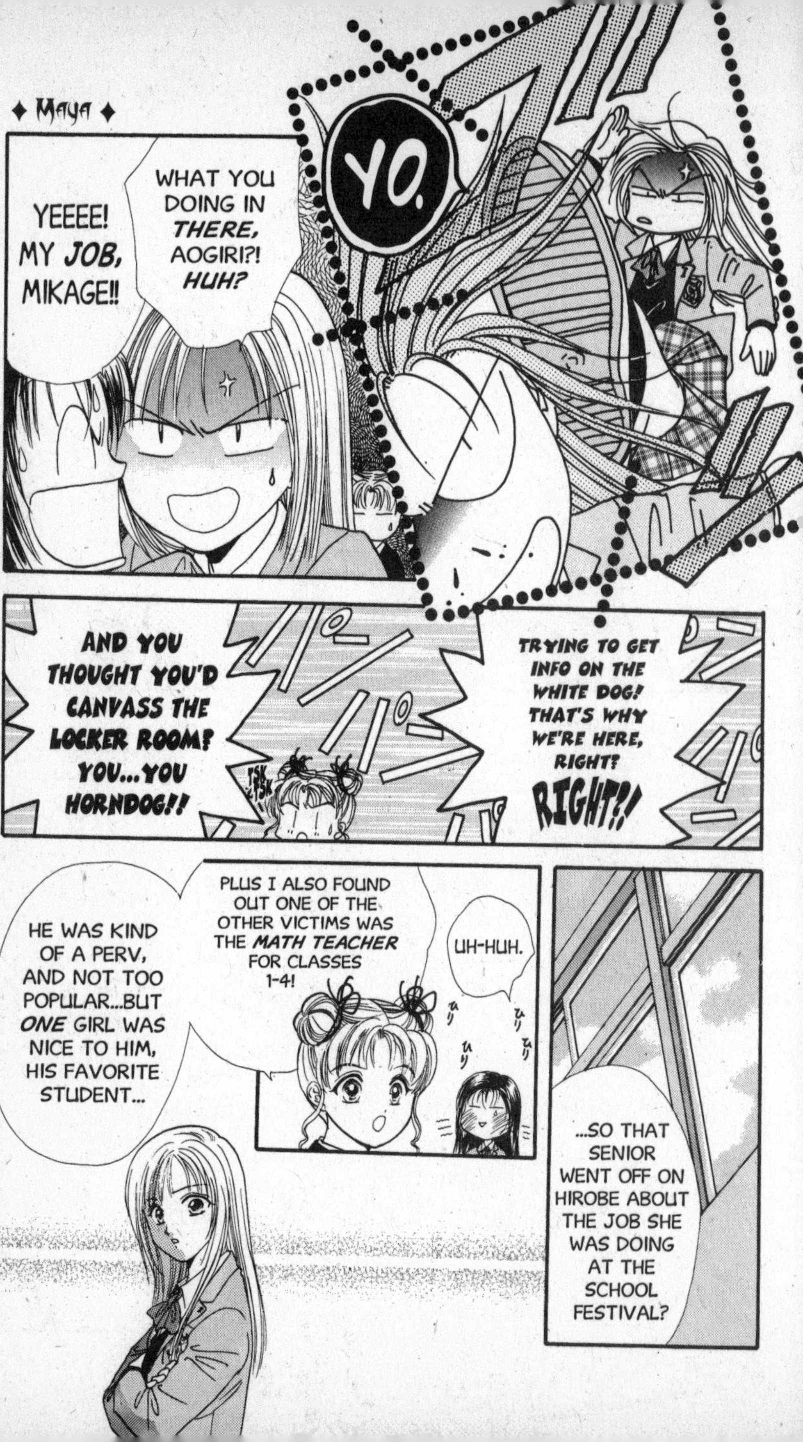
YO.
WHAT YOU DOING IN THERE, AOGIRI?! HUH?
YEEEE! MY JOB, MIKAGE!!
TRYING TO GET INFO ON THE WHITE DOG! THAT'S WHY WE'RE HERE, RIGHT? RIGHT?!
AND YOU THOUGHT YOU'D CANVASS THE LOCKER ROOM? YOU...YOU HORNDOG!!
TSK TSK
...SO THAT SENIOR WENT OFF ON HIROBE ABOUT THE JOB SHE WAS DOING AT THE SCHOOL FESTIVAL?
UH-HUH.
PLUS I ALSO FOUND OUT ONE OF THE OTHER VICTIMS WAS THE MATH TEACHER FOR CLASSES 1-4!
HE WAS KIND OF A PERV, AND NOT TOO POPULAR...BUT ONE GIRL WAS NICE TO HIM, HIS FAVORITE STUDENT...

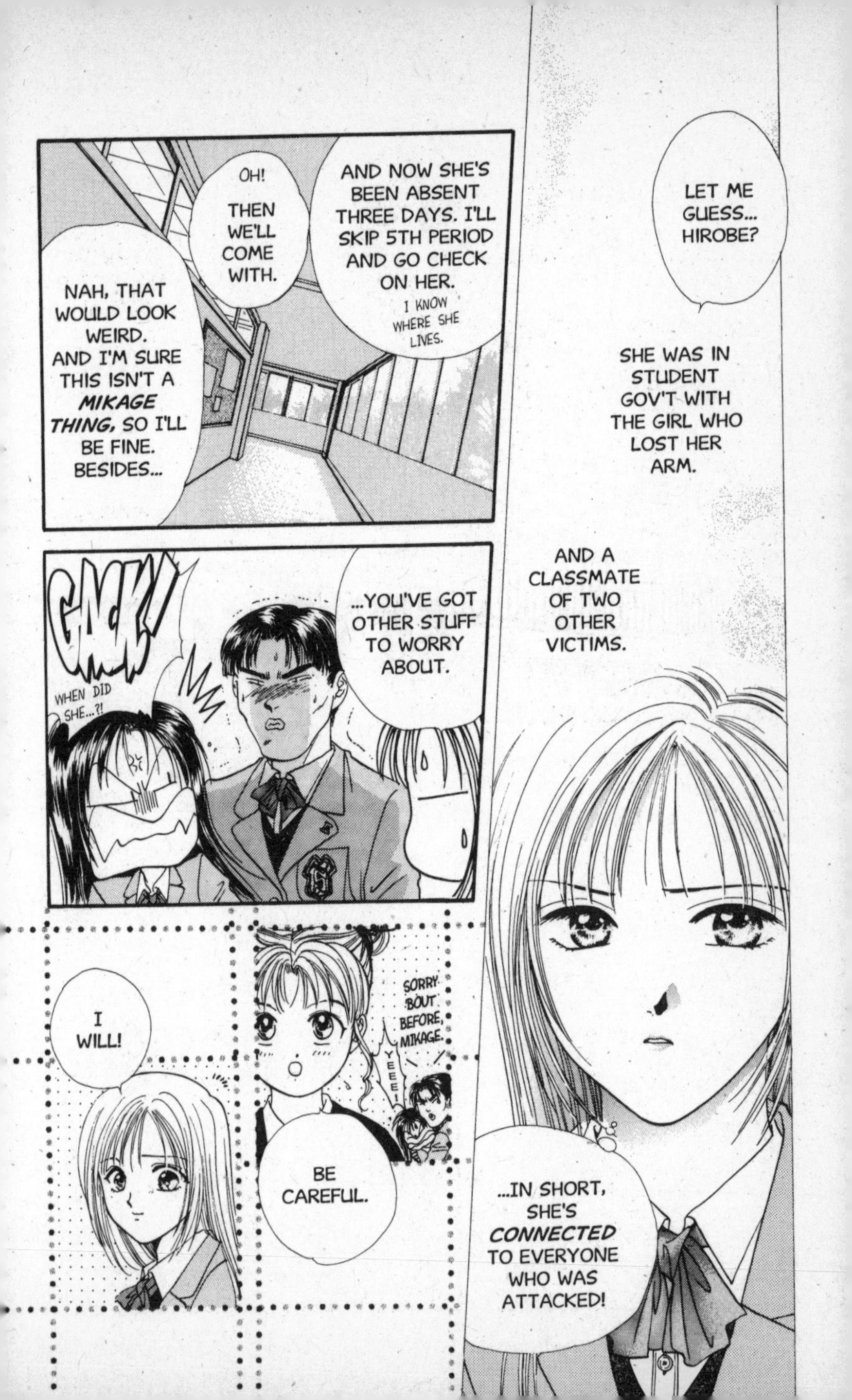
LET ME GUESS... HIROBE?
SHE WAS IN STUDENT GOV'T WITH THE GIRL WHO LOST HER ARM.
AND A CLASSMATE OF TWO OTHER VICTIMS.
...IN SHORT, SHE'S *CONNECTED* TO EVERYONE WHO WAS ATTACKED!
AND NOW SHE'S BEEN ABSENT THREE DAYS. I'LL SKIP 5TH PERIOD AND GO CHECK ON HER.
I KNOW WHERE SHE LIVES.
OH!
THEN WE'LL COME WITH.
NAH, THAT WOULD LOOK WEIRD. AND I'M SURE THIS ISN'T A *MIKAGE THING,* SO I'LL BE FINE. BESIDES...
...YOU'VE GOT OTHER STUFF TO WORRY ABOUT.
GACK!
WHEN DID SHE...?!
SORRY 'BOUT BEFORE, MIKAGE.
YEEE!
BE CAREFUL.
I WILL!

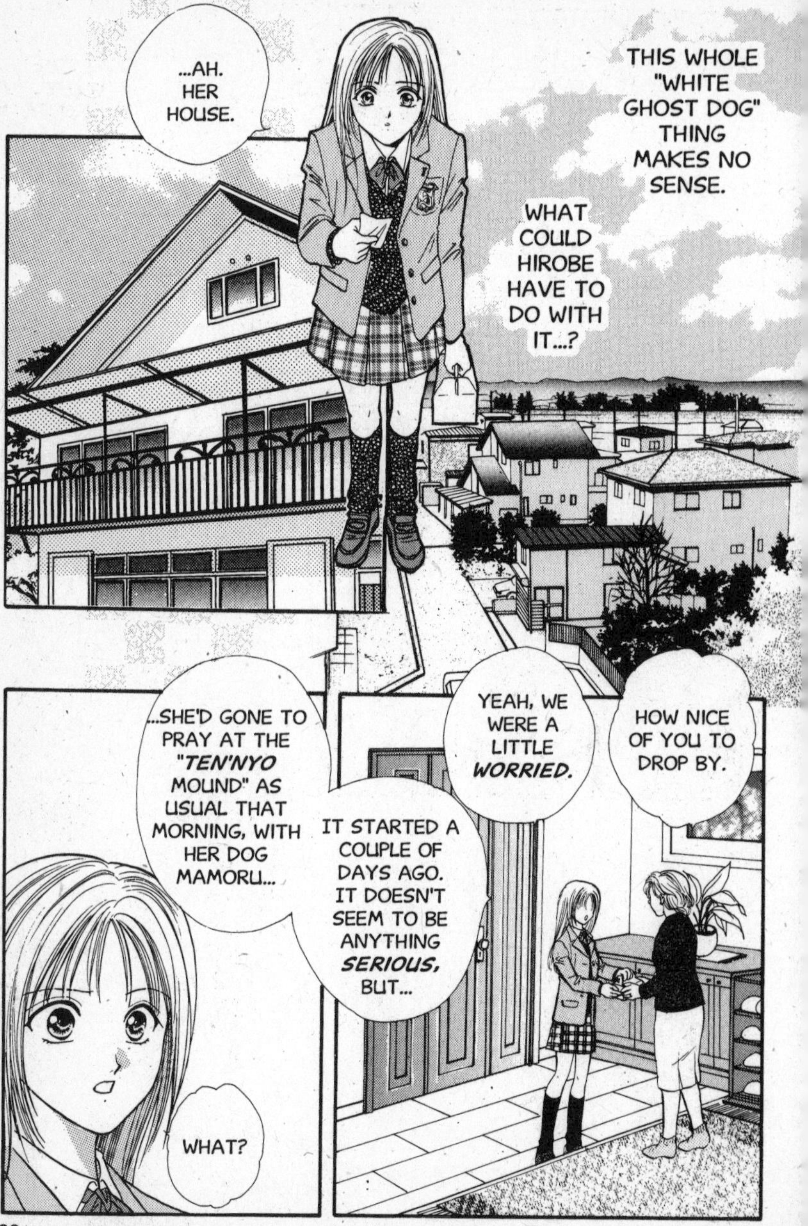
THIS WHOLE "WHITE GHOST DOG" THING MAKES NO SENSE.
WHAT COULD HIROBE HAVE TO DO WITH IT...?
...AH. HER HOUSE.
HOW NICE OF YOU TO DROP BY.
YEAH, WE WERE A LITTLE ***WORRIED.***
IT STARTED A COUPLE OF DAYS AGO. IT DOESN'T SEEM TO BE ANYTHING ***SERIOUS,*** BUT...
...SHE'D GONE TO PRAY AT THE "***TEN'NYO*** MOUND" AS USUAL THAT MORNING, WITH HER DOG MAMORU...
WHAT?

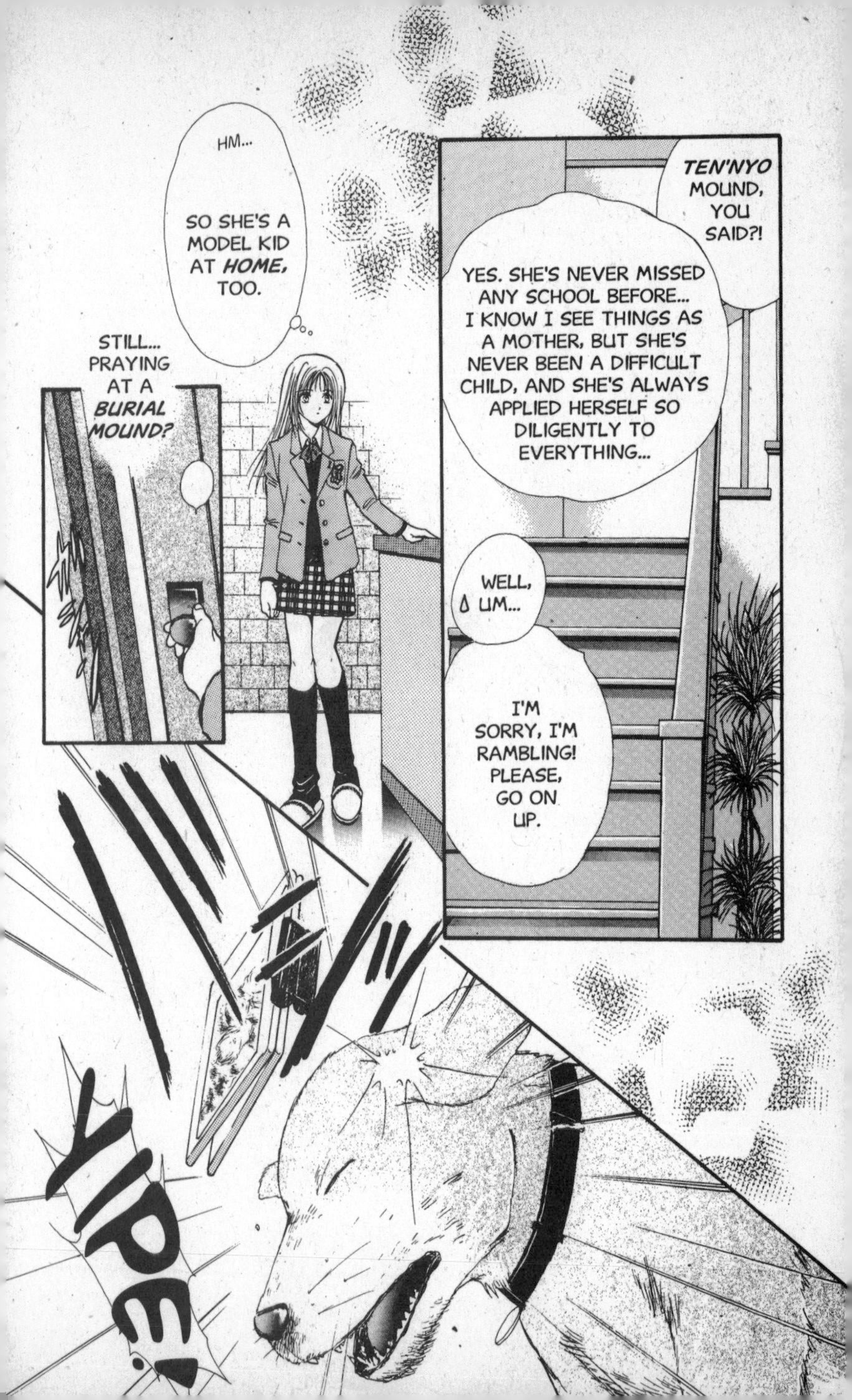
TEN'NYO MOUND, YOU SAID?!
YES. SHE'S NEVER MISSED ANY SCHOOL BEFORE... I KNOW I SEE THINGS AS A MOTHER, BUT SHE'S NEVER BEEN A DIFFICULT CHILD, AND SHE'S ALWAYS APPLIED HERSELF SO DILIGENTLY TO EVERYTHING...
WELL, UM...
I'M SORRY, I'M RAMBLING! PLEASE, GO ON UP.
HM...
SO SHE'S A MODEL KID AT HOME, TOO.
STILL... PRAYING AT A BURIAL MOUND?
YIPE!

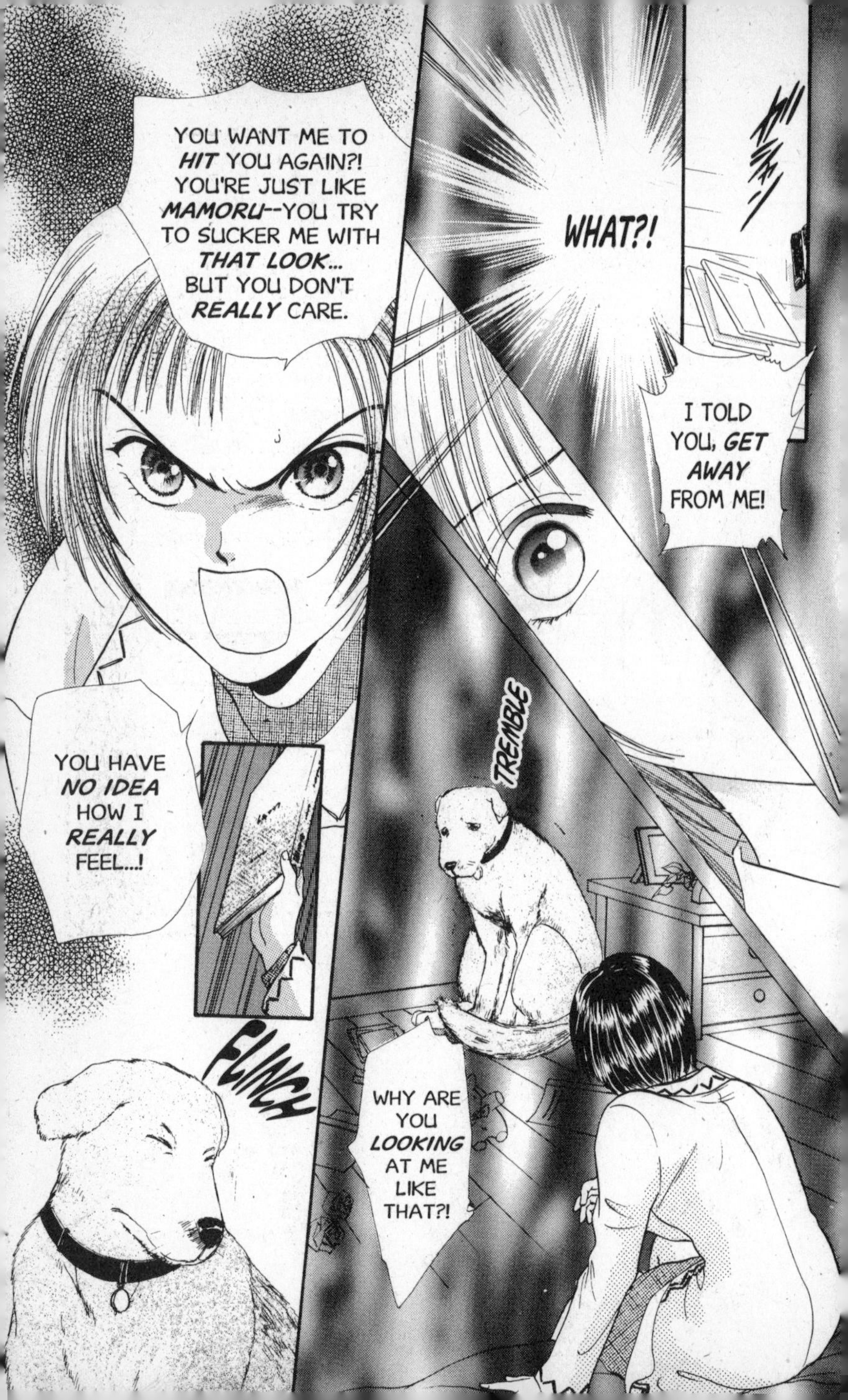
WHAT?!
I TOLD YOU, GET AWAY FROM ME!
TREMBLE
WHY ARE YOU LOOKING AT ME LIKE THAT?!
YOU WANT ME TO HIT YOU AGAIN?! YOU'RE JUST LIKE MAMORU--YOU TRY TO SUCKER ME WITH THAT LOOK... BUT YOU DON'T REALLY CARE.
YOU HAVE NO IDEA HOW I REALLY FEEL...!
FLINCH

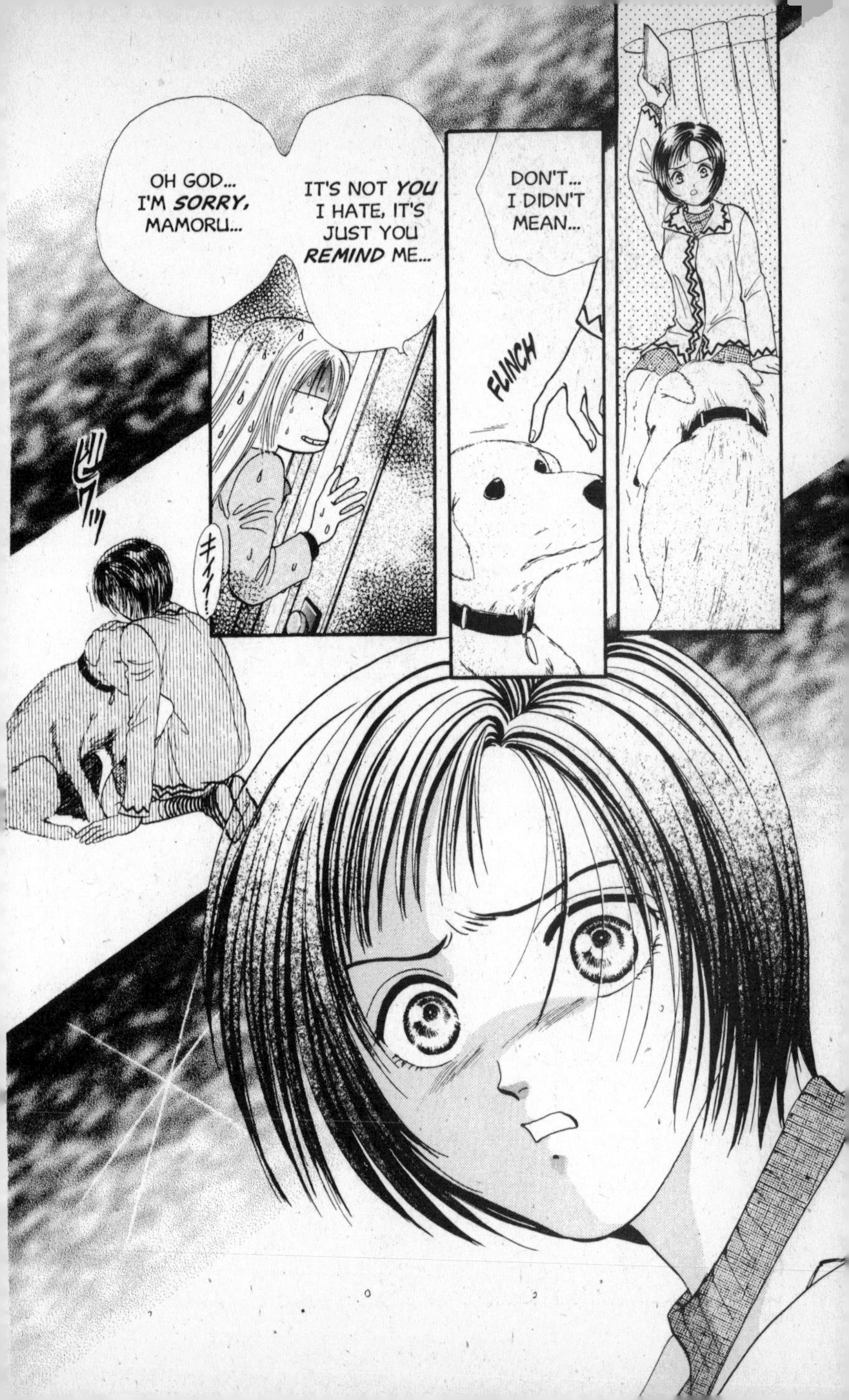
DON'T... I DIDN'T MEAN...
FLINCH
IT'S NOT YOU I HATE, IT'S JUST YOU REMIND ME...
OH GOD... I'M SORRY, MAMORU...

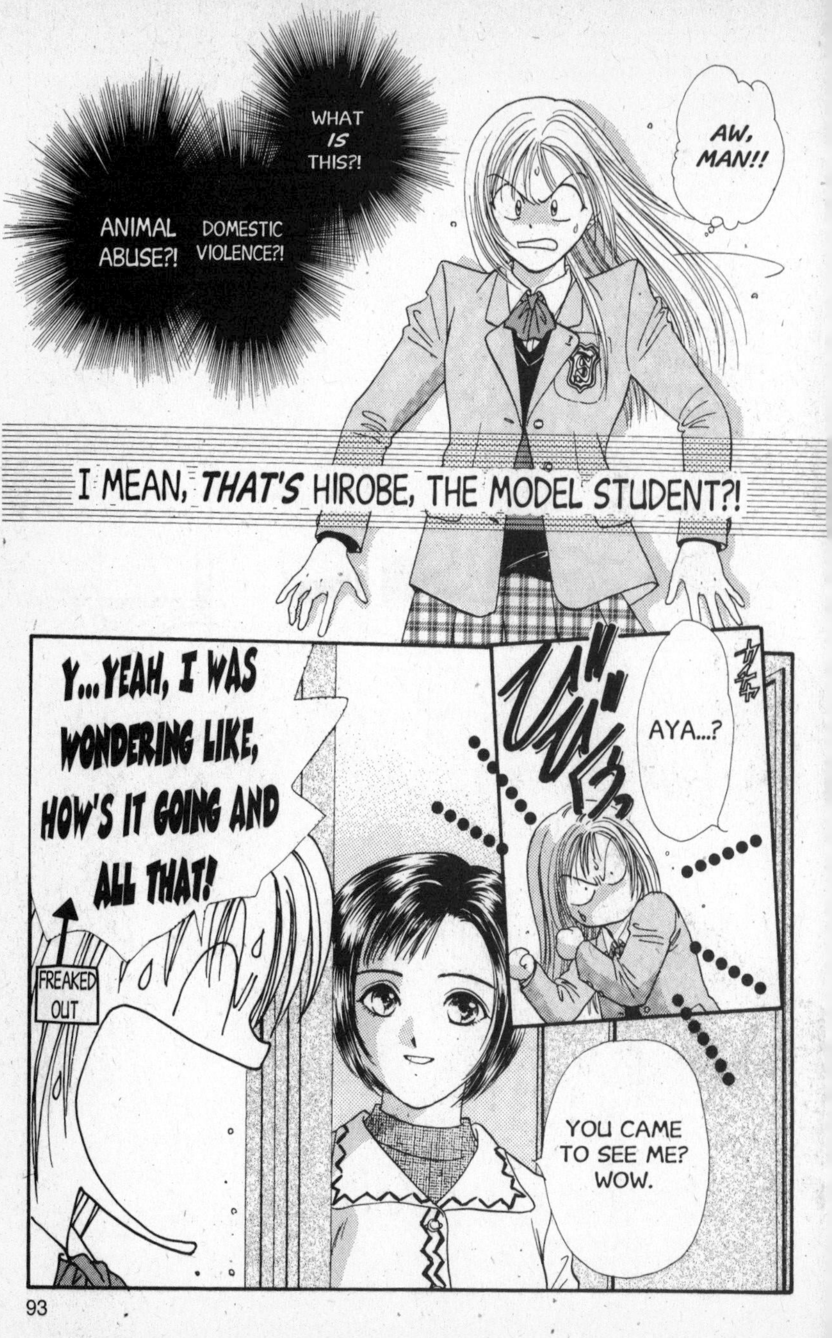
AW, MAN!!
WHAT *IS* THIS?!
DOMESTIC VIOLENCE?!
ANIMAL ABUSE?!
I MEAN, *THAT'S* HIROBE, THE MODEL STUDENT?!
AYA...?
YOU CAME TO SEE ME? WOW.
Y...YEAH, I WAS WONDERING LIKE, HOW'S IT GOING AND ALL THAT!
FREAKED OUT

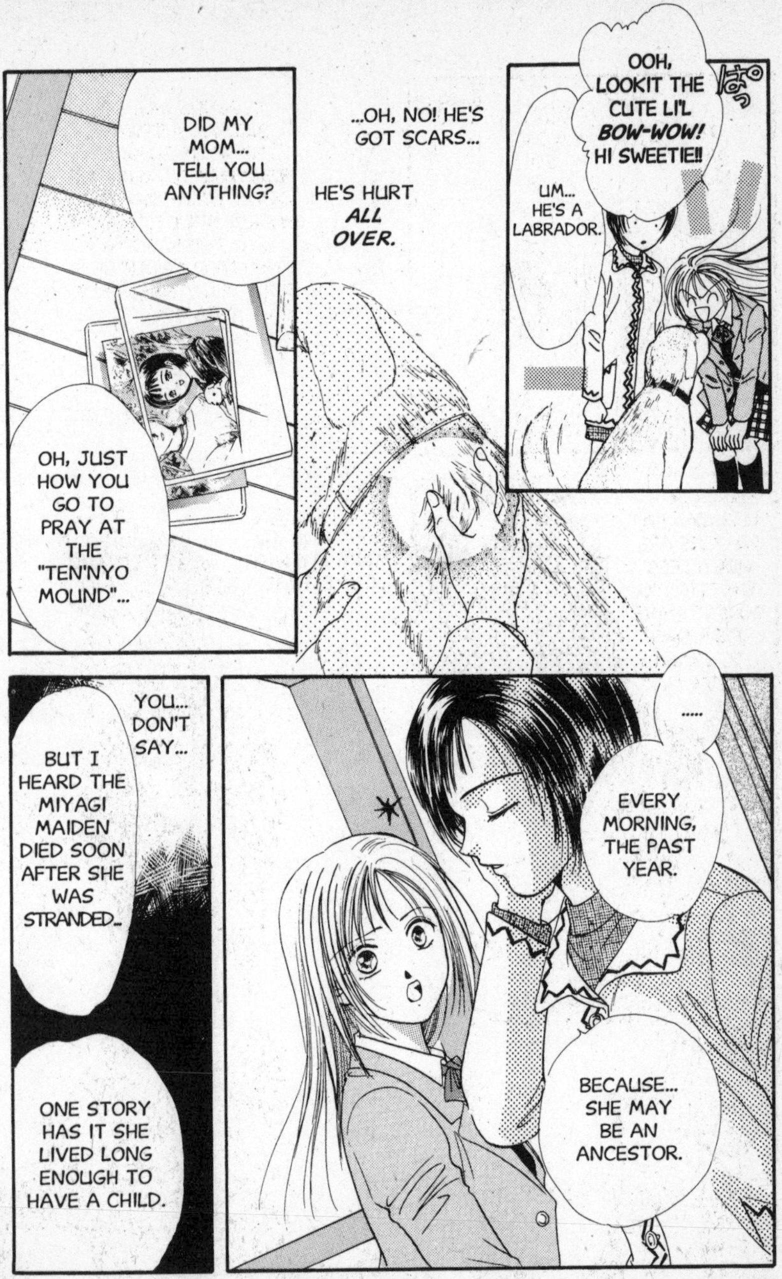
OOH, LOOKIT THE CUTE LI'L **BOW-WOW!** HI SWEETIE!!
ぱっ
UM... HE'S A LABRADOR.
...OH, NO! HE'S GOT SCARS...
HE'S HURT **ALL OVER.**
DID MY MOM... TELL YOU ANYTHING?
OH, JUST HOW YOU GO TO PRAY AT THE "TEN'NYO MOUND"...
.....
EVERY MORNING, THE PAST YEAR.
BECAUSE... SHE MAY BE AN ANCESTOR.
YOU... DON'T SAY...
BUT I HEARD THE MIYAGI MAIDEN DIED SOON AFTER SHE WAS STRANDED..
ONE STORY HAS IT SHE LIVED LONG ENOUGH TO HAVE A CHILD.

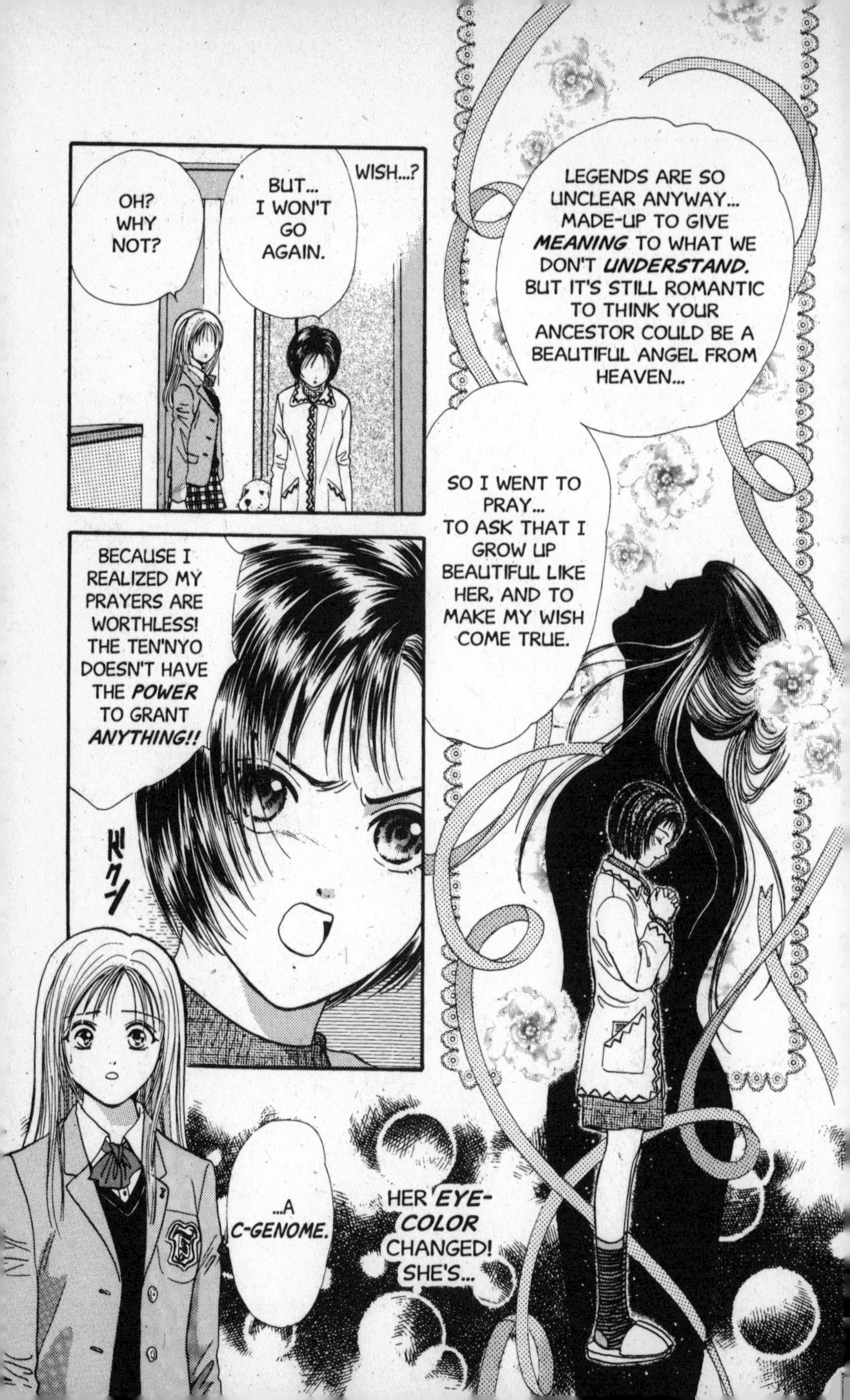

LEGENDS ARE SO UNCLEAR ANYWAY... MADE-UP TO GIVE *MEANING* TO WHAT WE DON'T *UNDERSTAND.* BUT IT'S STILL ROMANTIC TO THINK YOUR ANCESTOR COULD BE A BEAUTIFUL ANGEL FROM HEAVEN...
SO I WENT TO PRAY... TO ASK THAT I GROW UP BEAUTIFUL LIKE HER, AND TO MAKE MY WISH COME TRUE.
WISH...?
BUT... I WON'T GO AGAIN.
OH? WHY NOT?
BECAUSE I REALIZED MY PRAYERS ARE WORTHLESS! THE TEN'NYO DOESN'T HAVE THE *POWER* TO GRANT *ANYTHING!!*
ドクン
HER *EYE-COLOR* CHANGED! SHE'S...
...A C-GENOME.

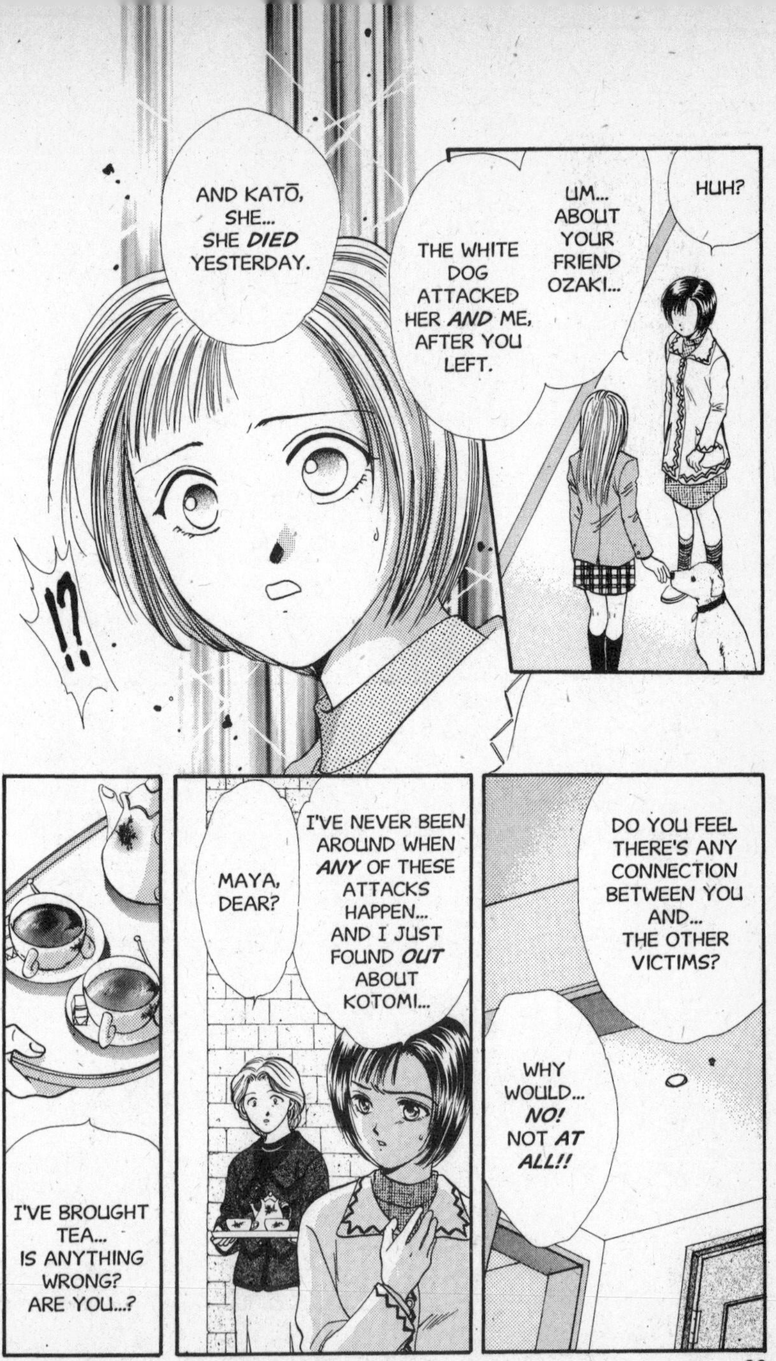
HUH?
UM... ABOUT YOUR FRIEND OZAKI...
THE WHITE DOG ATTACKED HER *AND* ME, AFTER YOU LEFT.
AND KATŌ, SHE... SHE *DIED* YESTERDAY.
!?
DO YOU FEEL THERE'S ANY CONNECTION BETWEEN YOU AND... THE OTHER VICTIMS?
WHY WOULD... *NO!* NOT *AT ALL!!*
I'VE NEVER BEEN AROUND WHEN *ANY* OF THESE ATTACKS HAPPEN... AND I JUST FOUND *OUT* ABOUT KOTOMI...
MAYA, DEAR?
I'VE BROUGHT TEA... IS ANYTHING WRONG? ARE YOU...?

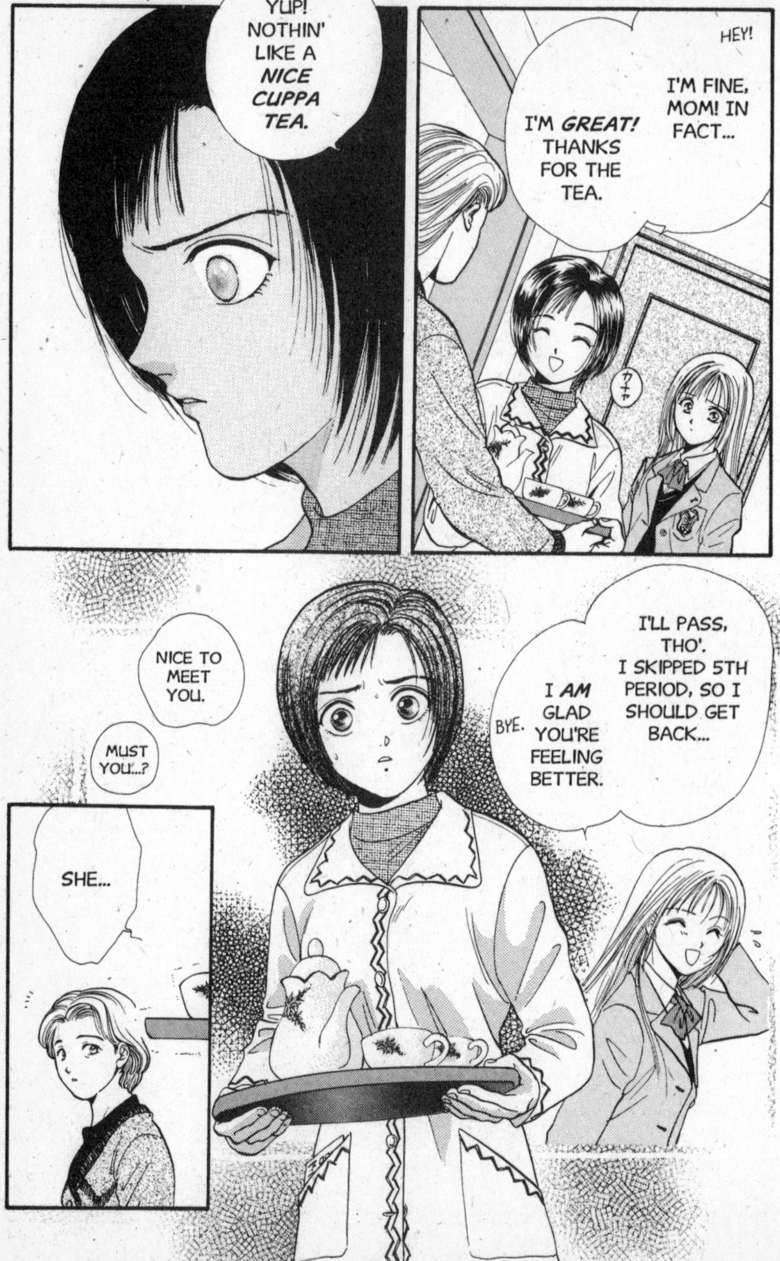
HEY!
I'M FINE, MOM! IN FACT...
I'M *GREAT!* THANKS FOR THE TEA.
YUP! NOTHIN' LIKE A *NICE CUPPA TEA.*
I'LL PASS, THO'. I SKIPPED 5TH PERIOD, SO I SHOULD GET BACK...
I *AM* GLAD YOU'RE FEELING BETTER.
BYE.
NICE TO MEET YOU.
MUST YOU...?
SHE...

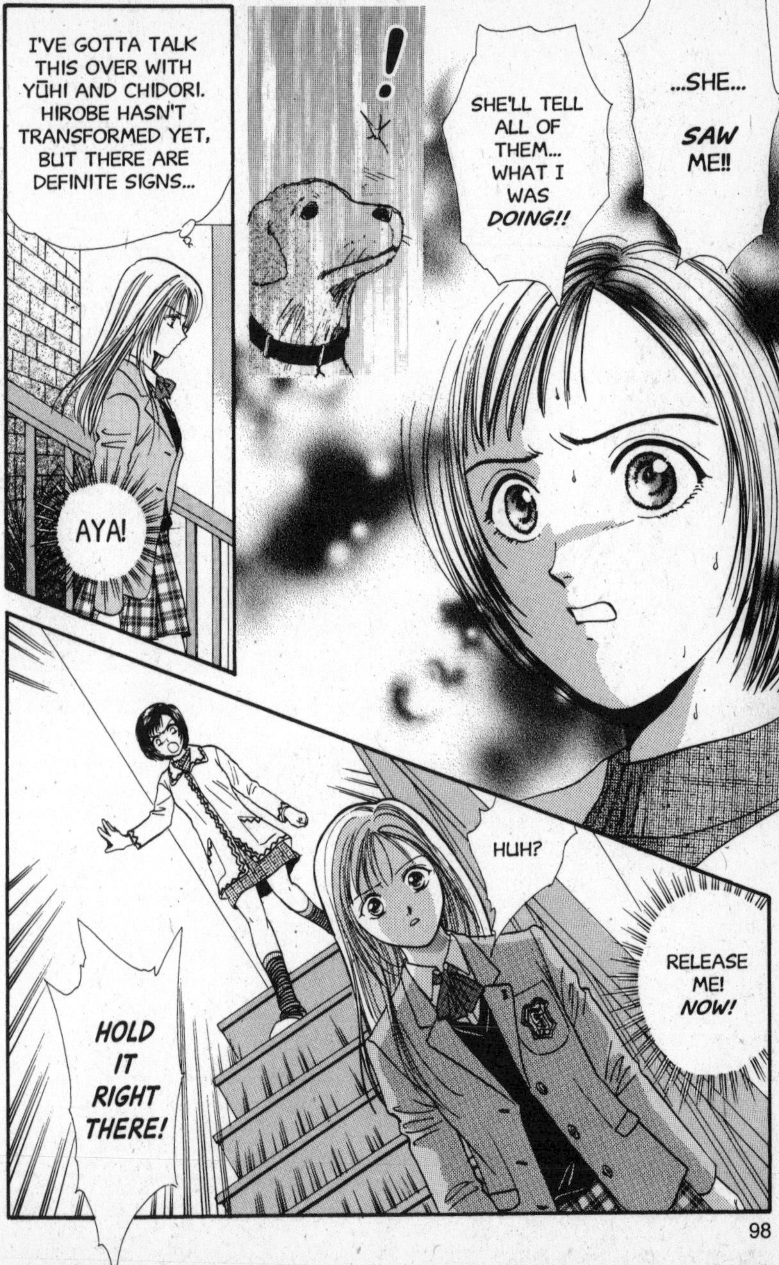
...SHE...
SAW ME!!
SHE'LL TELL ALL OF THEM... WHAT I WAS DOING!!
!
I'VE GOTTA TALK THIS OVER WITH YŪHI AND CHIDORI. HIROBE HASN'T TRANSFORMED YET, BUT THERE ARE DEFINITE SIGNS...
AYA!
HUH?
RELEASE ME! NOW!
HOLD IT RIGHT THERE!

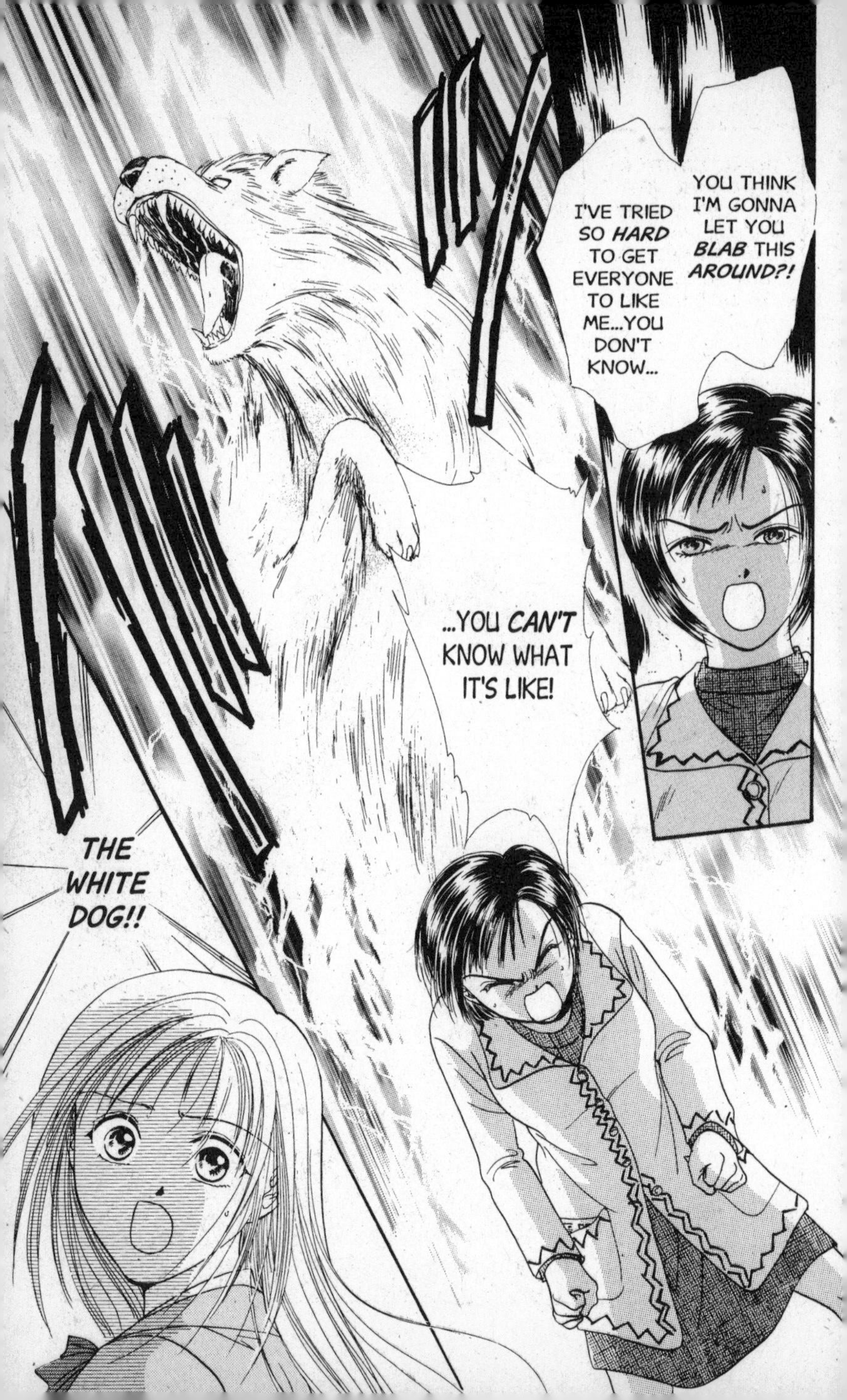
YOU THINK I'M GONNA LET YOU BLAB THIS AROUND?!
I'VE TRIED SO HARD TO GET EVERYONE TO LIKE ME...YOU DON'T KNOW...
...YOU CAN'T KNOW WHAT IT'S LIKE!
THE WHITE DOG!!

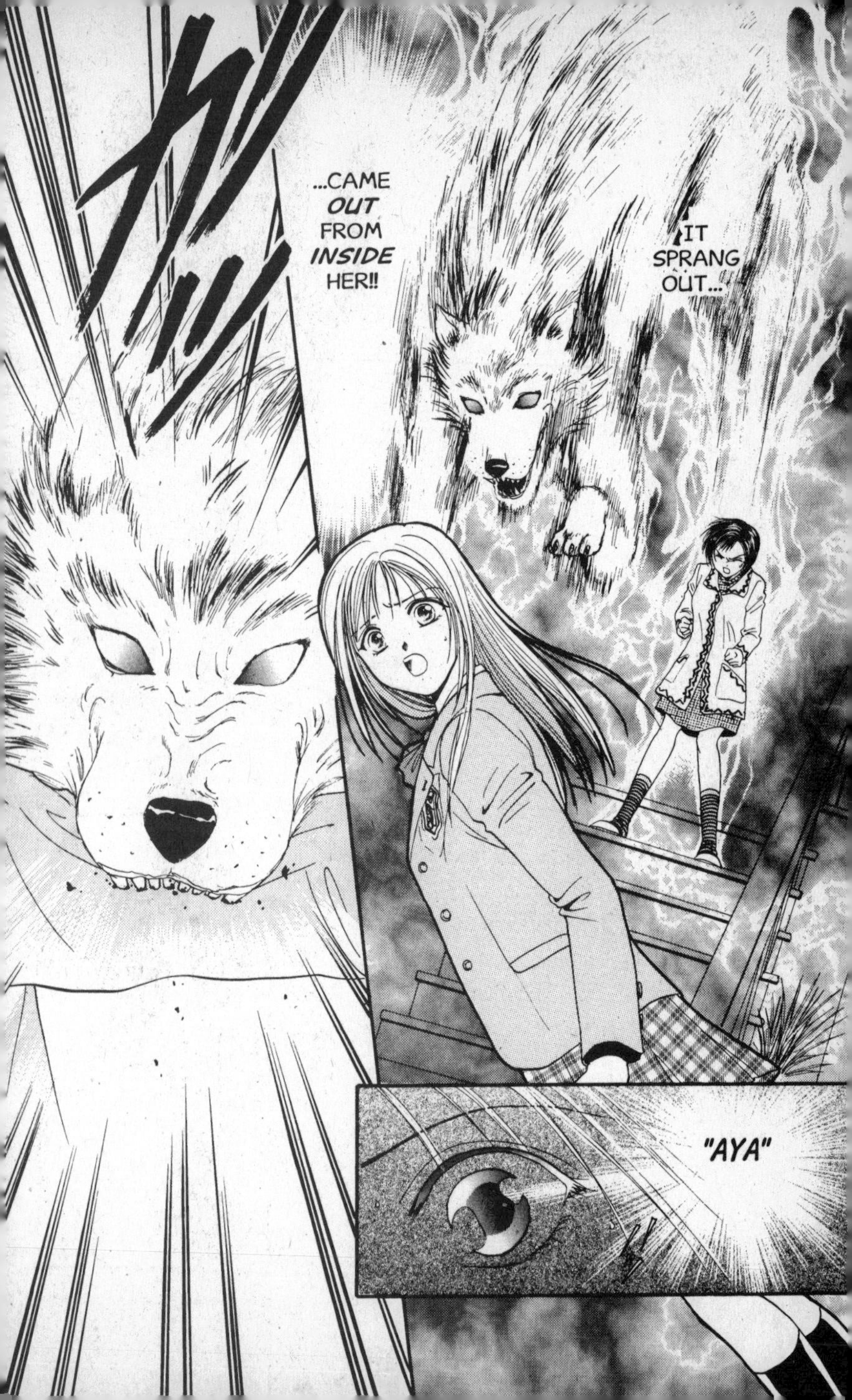
IT SPRANG OUT...
...CAME *OUT* FROM *INSIDE* HER!!
"AYA"

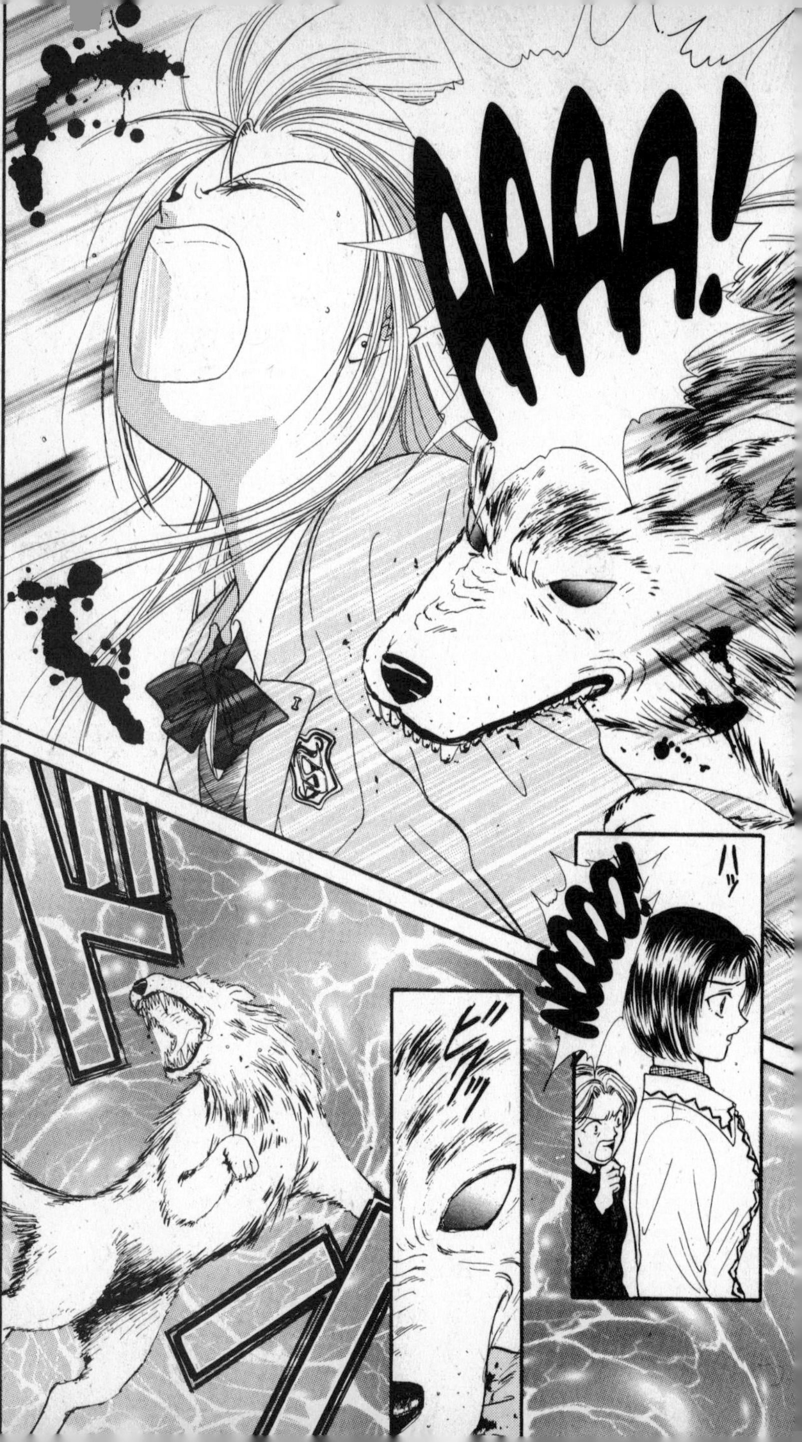
AAAA!
ハッ
WOOO!
ビクッ

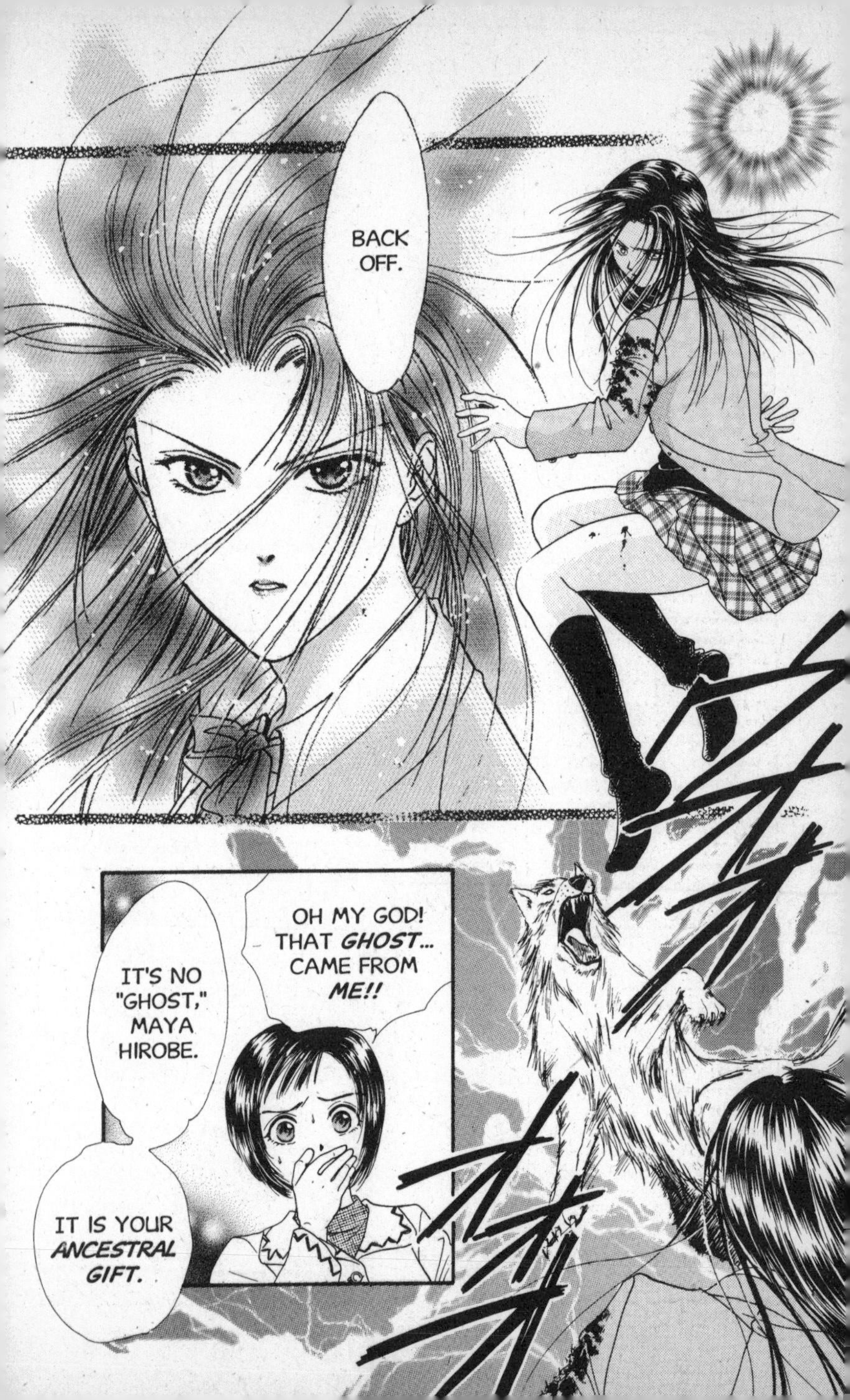
BACK OFF.
OH MY GOD! THAT *GHOST*... CAME FROM *ME!!*
IT'S NO "GHOST," MAYA HIROBE.
IT IS YOUR *ANCESTRAL GIFT*.

If you were to split the *kanji* for "Aya" into its two components and flip those around, wouldn't it then look more like the *kanji* for "ten'nyo"...? (Too much of a stretch? Yeah, thought so.)
But "*aya*"—aside from the other meanings mentioned elsewhere—also means "calamity." Hm.... 💧
Kanji can be so deep, huh? The second part of Aya's *kanji*, though, can also mean "young and beautiful," or "free spirit." Then again, it still could be "calamity," or "dying young." Uh~ 💧💧💧
Ah, well, so what, right?! A name's supposed to stand out. Aki, now—that name is normal. It's like Aya's grandma knew their fate, and named them accordingly. (Uh-**huh**.)

So! I started this "writing-about-the-characters'-names" thing last time, so now's Yūhi's turn. Yūhi fans and Tōya fans have totally opposite opinions—Yūhi is popular 'cause people feel sorry for him (Aya doesn't like him back), or 'cause he tries so hard that it's almost sad. Guys, on average, tend to be Yūhi fans (no surprise there). My assistants have pointed out, though, that girls would totally back off a guy if he were to actually keep macking on Aya like Yūhi has. ◡̈ Yūhi's also at a disadvantage for being always around—meaning he's more like "family." He really is a nice guy, though. He's still a kid, so it's cute how he can't control himself. Tōya fans say, "He's obnoxious! Guys should be mature and always keep their cool," or "I don't like him 'cause he's such a horndog." Now all of you, look here: **Yūhi is not a horndog**. He's just a normal guy! People have said in the past that **FY**'s "Tamahome" is too horny, but that's kinda harsh. You girls, you have this unrealistic expectation about guys. Teenage boys think about sex like, once every five minutes—seriously! Maybe even once a **minute**. Plus, they You-Know-What almost every **night**. (Gasp!)

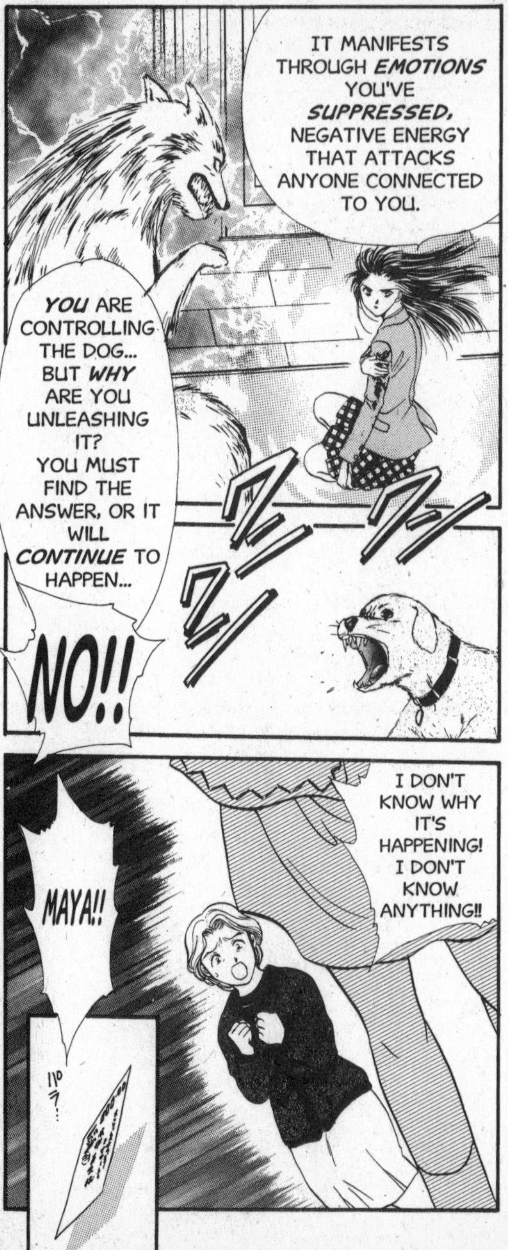
IT MANIFESTS THROUGH *EMOTIONS* YOU'VE *SUPPRESSED,* NEGATIVE ENERGY THAT ATTACKS ANYONE CONNECTED TO YOU.
YOU ARE CONTROLLING THE DOG... BUT *WHY* ARE YOU UNLEASHING IT? YOU MUST FIND THE ANSWER, OR IT WILL *CONTINUE* TO HAPPEN...
NO!!
I DON'T KNOW WHY IT'S HAPPENING! I DON'T KNOW ANYTHING!!
MAYA!!

 Sorry, kids...but them's the facts.

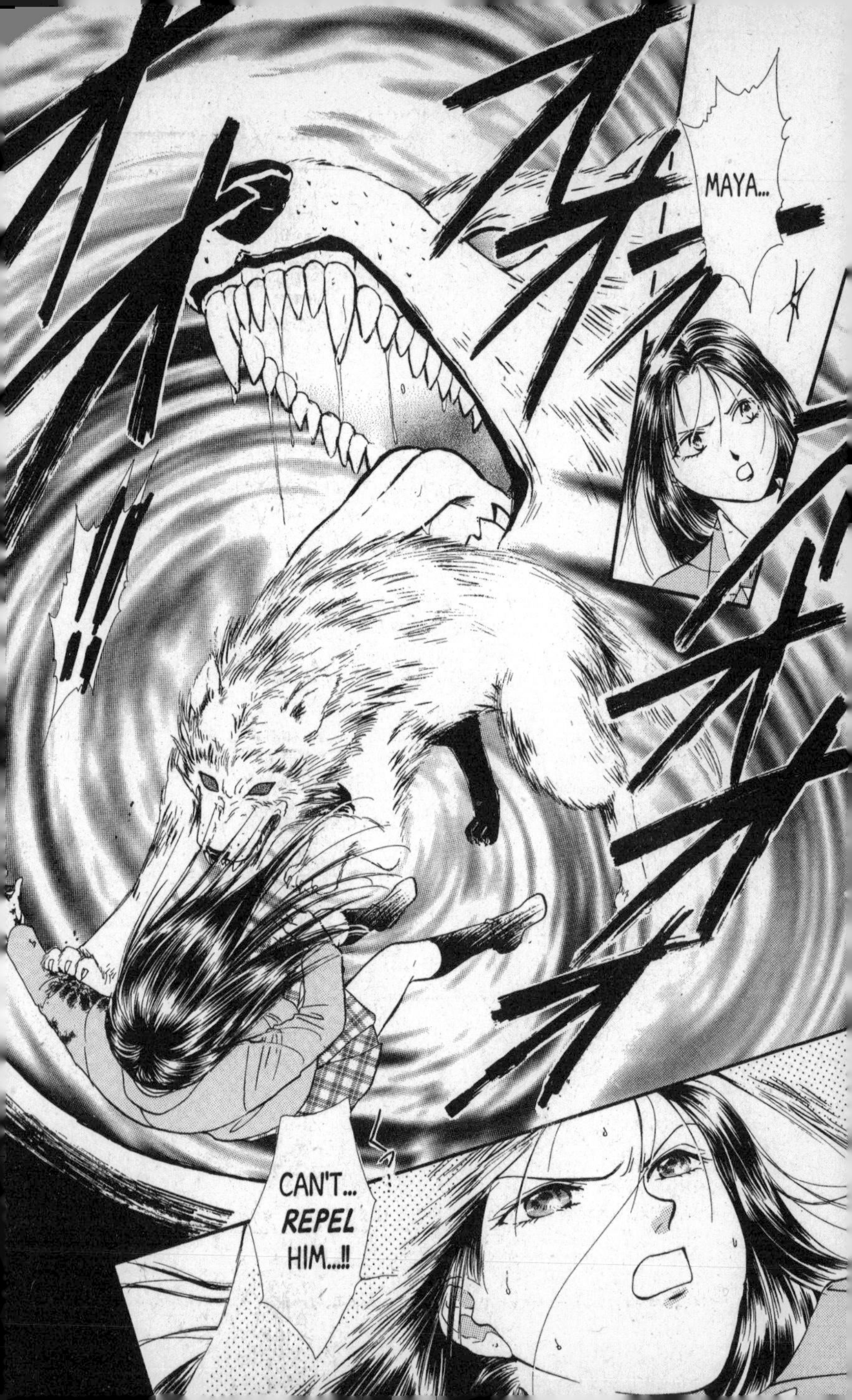
MAYA...
CAN'T... *REPEL* HIM...!!

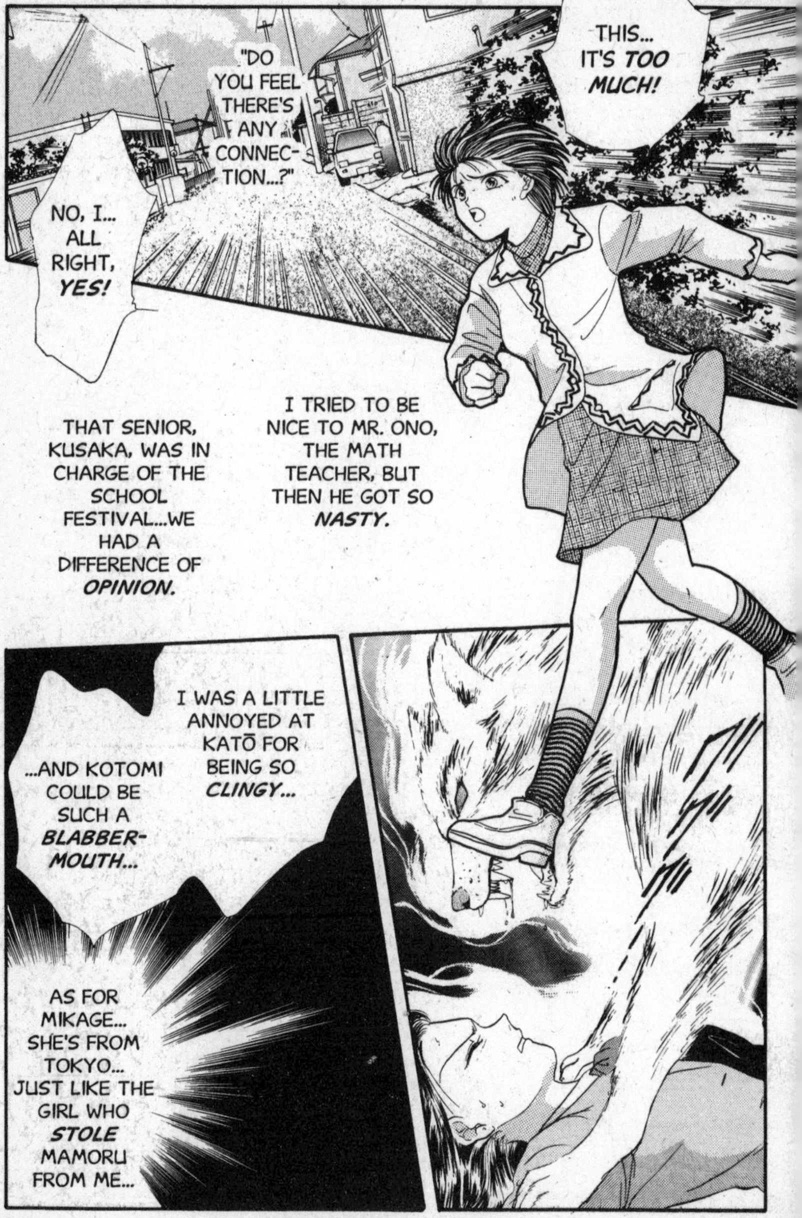
THIS... IT'S *TOO MUCH!*
"DO YOU FEEL THERE'S ANY CONNECTION...?"
NO, I... ALL RIGHT, *YES!*
I TRIED TO BE NICE TO MR. ONO, THE MATH TEACHER, BUT THEN HE GOT SO *NASTY.*
THAT SENIOR, KUSAKA, WAS IN CHARGE OF THE SCHOOL FESTIVAL...WE HAD A DIFFERENCE OF *OPINION.*
I WAS A LITTLE ANNOYED AT KATŌ FOR BEING SO *CLINGY...*
...AND KOTOMI COULD BE SUCH A *BLABBERMOUTH...*
AS FOR MIKAGE... SHE'S FROM TOKYO... JUST LIKE THE GIRL WHO *STOLE* MAMORU FROM ME...

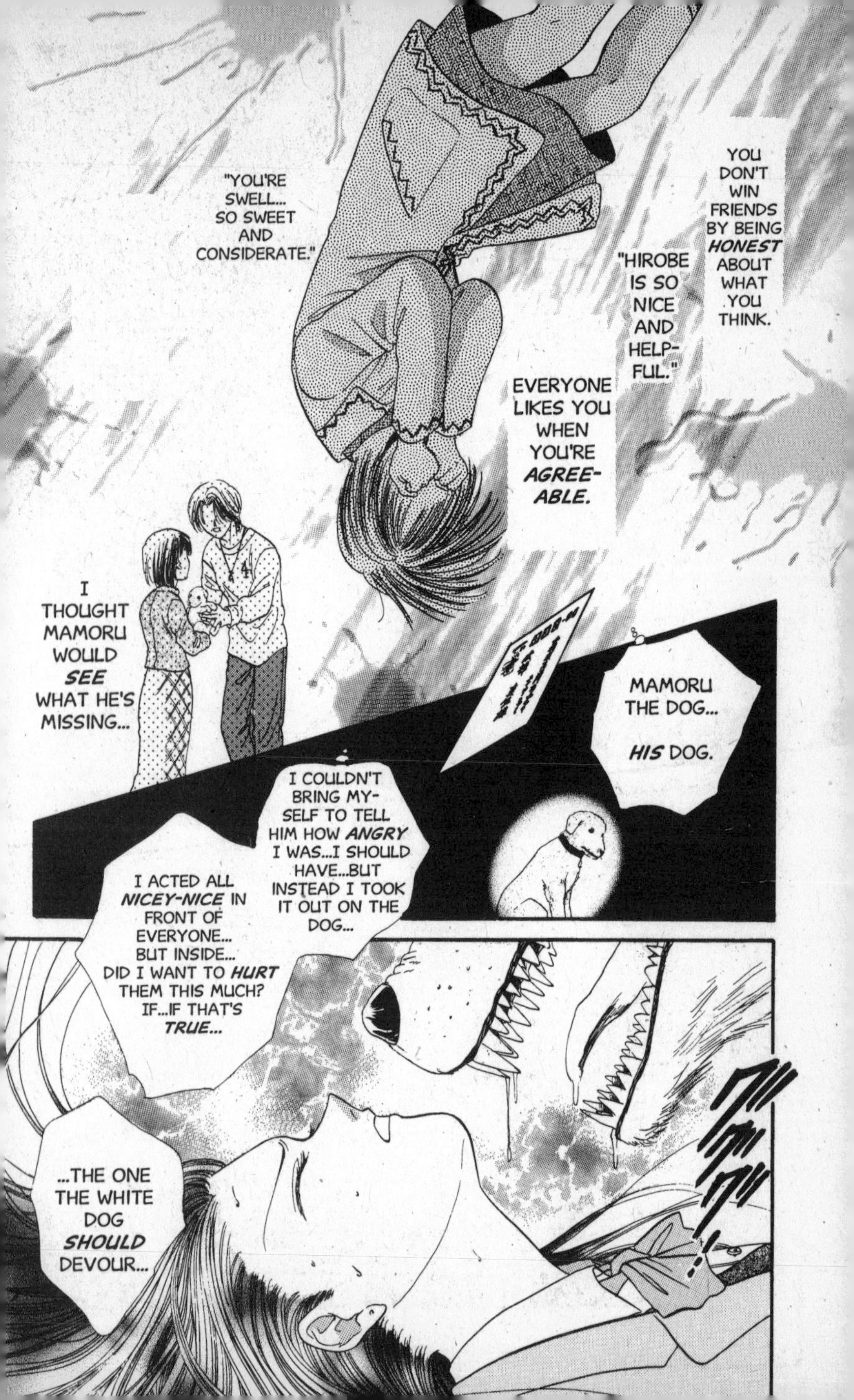
YOU DON'T WIN FRIENDS BY BEING HONEST ABOUT WHAT YOU THINK.
"HIROBE IS SO NICE AND HELP-FUL."
EVERYONE LIKES YOU WHEN YOU'RE AGREE-ABLE.
"YOU'RE SWELL... SO SWEET AND CONSIDERATE."
I THOUGHT MAMORU WOULD SEE WHAT HE'S MISSING...
MAMORU THE DOG...
HIS DOG.
I COULDN'T BRING MY-SELF TO TELL HIM HOW ANGRY I WAS...I SHOULD HAVE...BUT INSTEAD I TOOK IT OUT ON THE DOG...
I ACTED ALL NICEY-NICE IN FRONT OF EVERYONE... BUT INSIDE... DID I WANT TO HURT THEM THIS MUCH? IF...IF THAT'S TRUE...
...THE ONE THE WHITE DOG SHOULD DEVOUR...

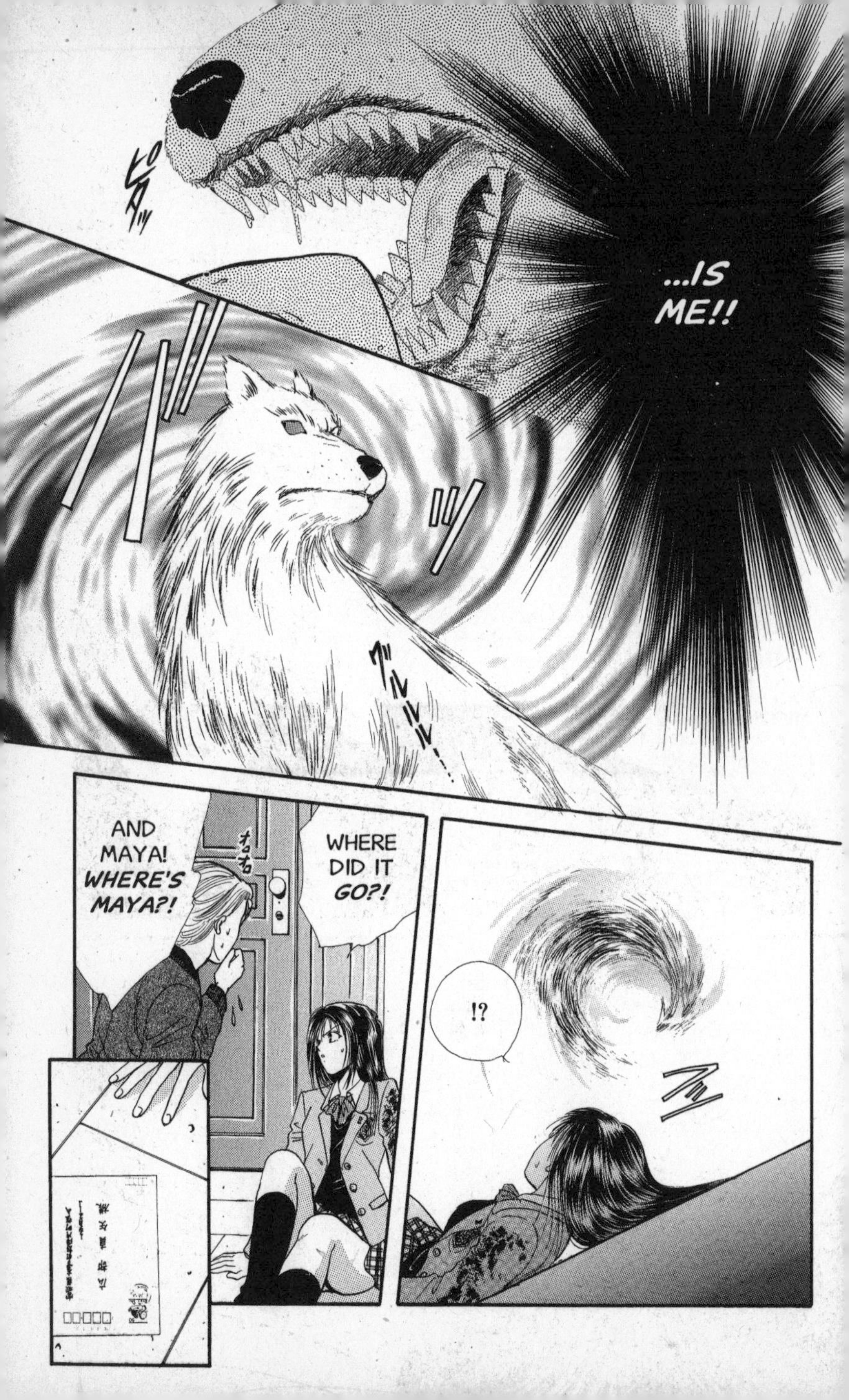
...IS ME!!
WHERE DID IT GO?!
AND MAYA! WHERE'S MAYA?!
!?

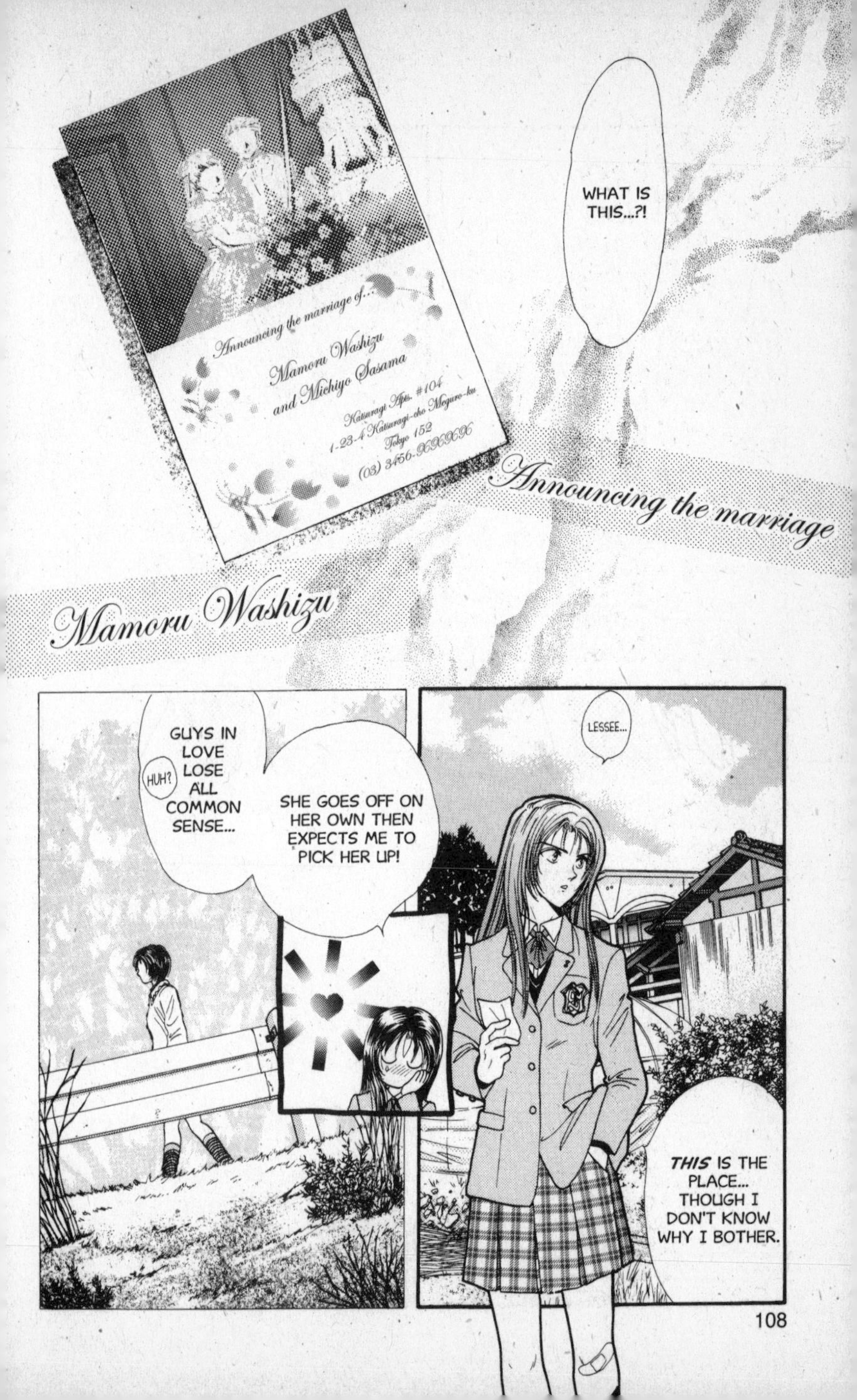
WHAT IS THIS...?!
Announcing the marriage of...
Mamoru Washizu
and Michiyo Sasama
Katsuragi Apts. #104
1-23-4 Katsuragi-cho Meguro-ku
Tokyo 152
(03) 3456-96969696
Announcing the marriage
Mamoru Washizu
LESSEE...
THIS IS THE PLACE... THOUGH I DON'T KNOW WHY I BOTHER.
GUYS IN LOVE LOSE ALL COMMON SENSE...
HUH?
SHE GOES OFF ON HER OWN THEN EXPECTS ME TO PICK HER UP!

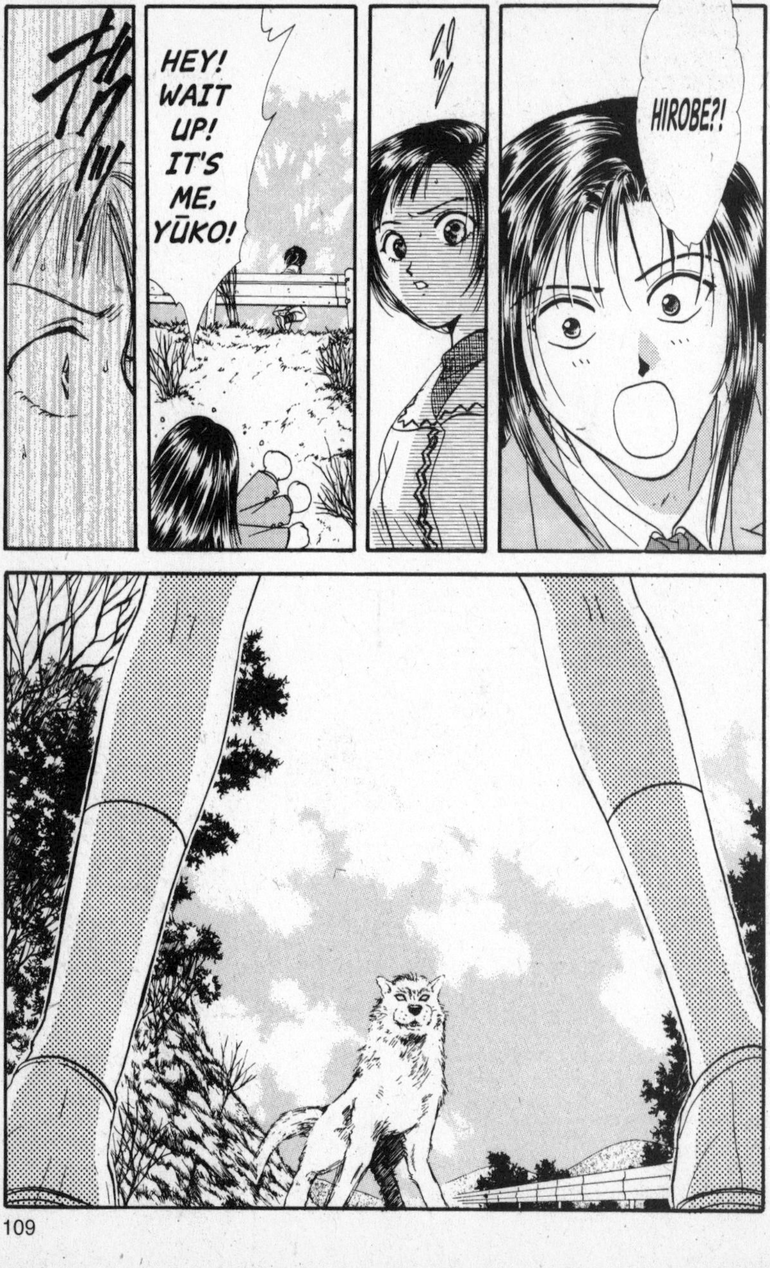
HIROBE?!
HEY! WAIT UP! IT'S ME, YŪKO!

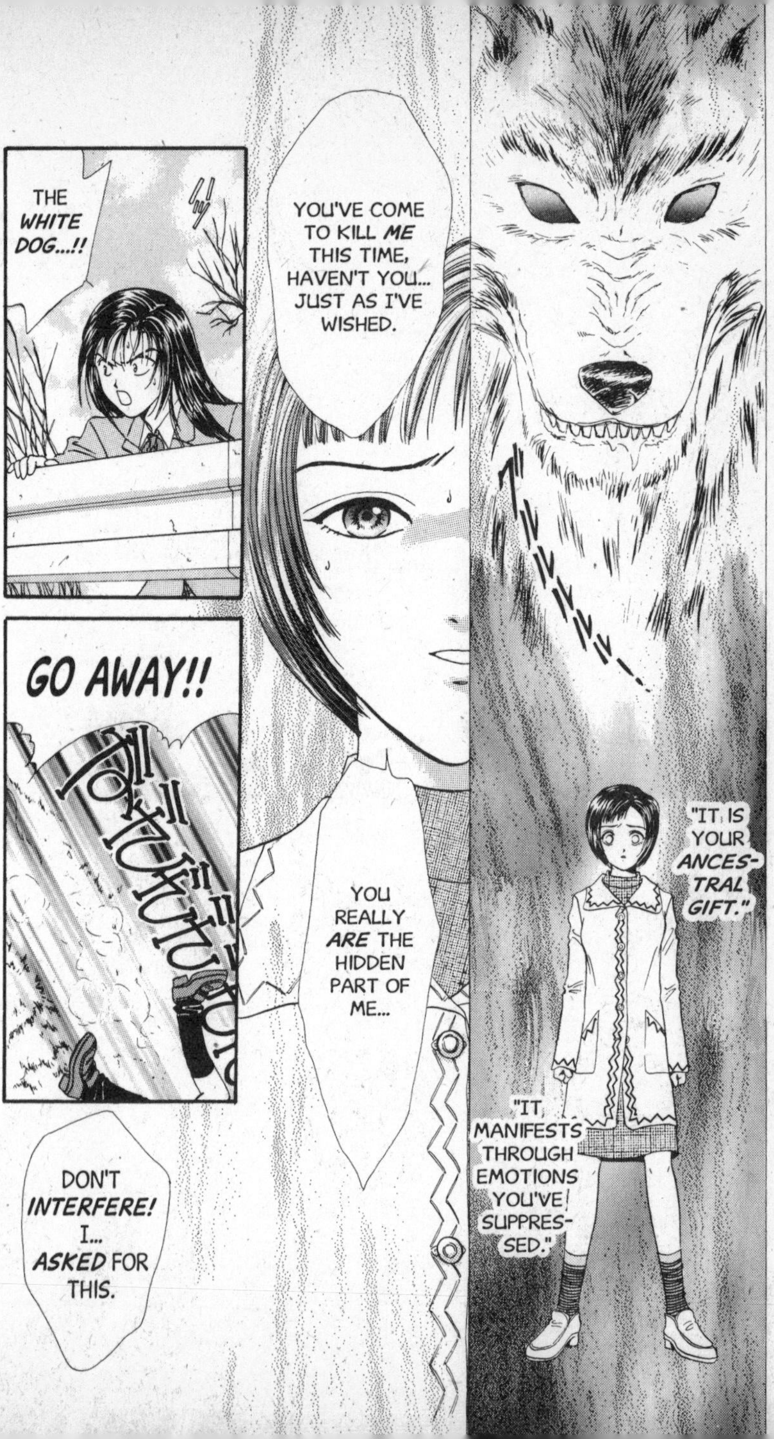
"IT IS YOUR ANCES-TRAL GIFT."
"IT MANIFESTS THROUGH EMOTIONS YOU'VE SUPPRES-SED."
YOU'VE COME TO KILL ME THIS TIME, HAVEN'T YOU... JUST AS I'VE WISHED.
YOU REALLY ARE THE HIDDEN PART OF ME...
THE WHITE DOG...!!
GO AWAY!!
DON'T INTERFERE! I... ASKED FOR THIS.

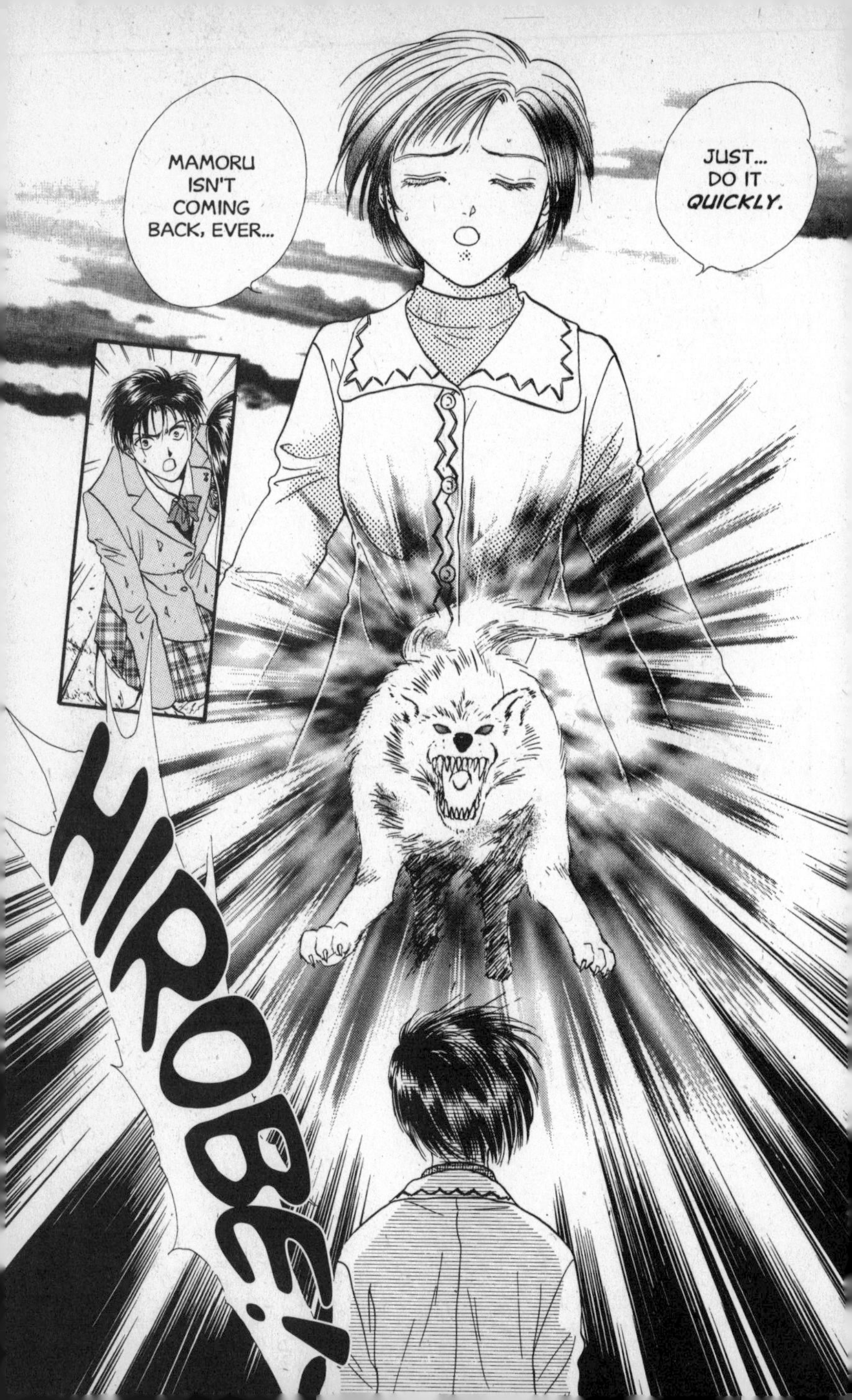
JUST... DO IT *QUICKLY.*
MAMORU ISN'T COMING BACK, EVER...
HIROBE!!

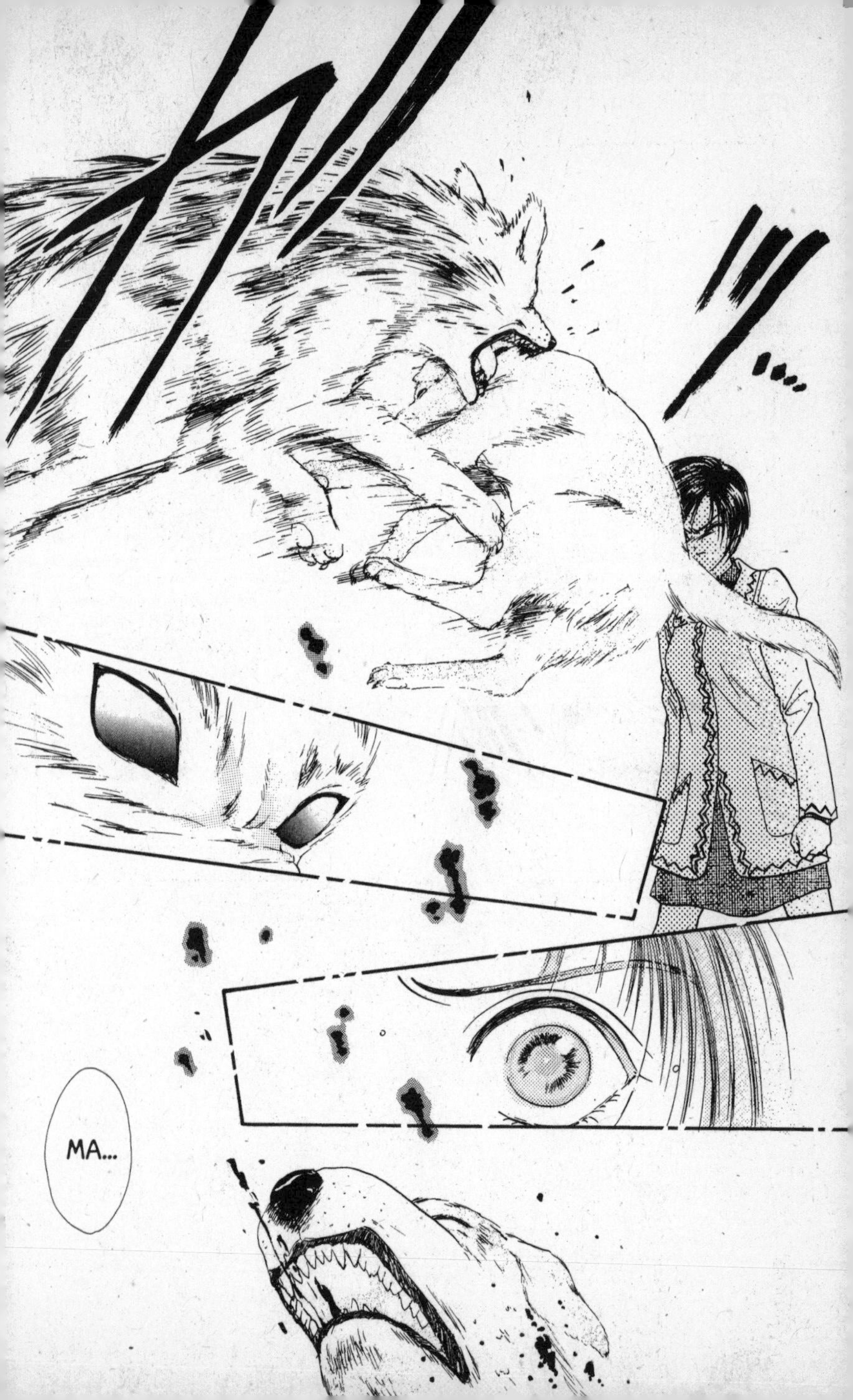
!...
MA...

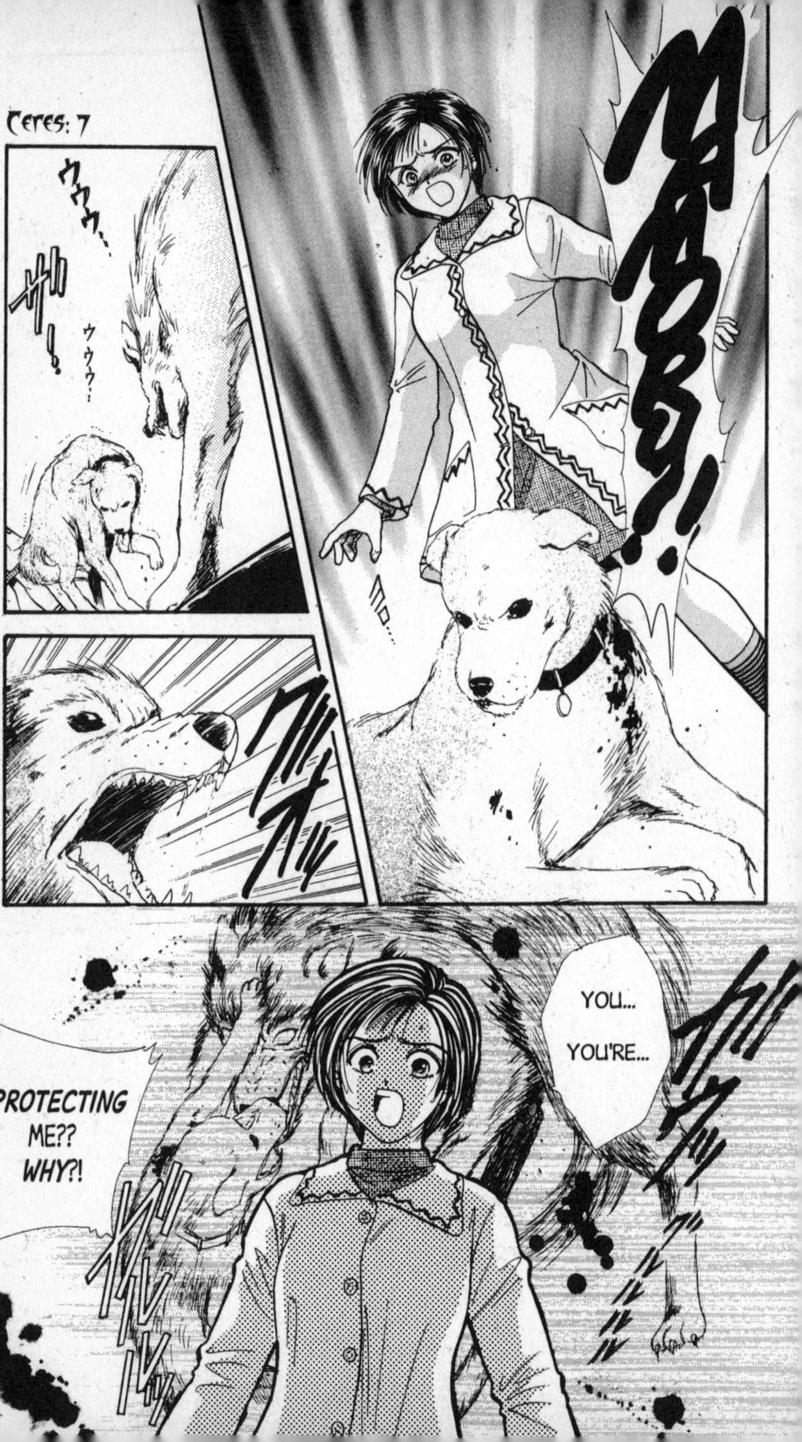
ウウウ‥
ウウウ!
YOU...
YOU'RE...
...PROTECTING
ME??
WHY?!

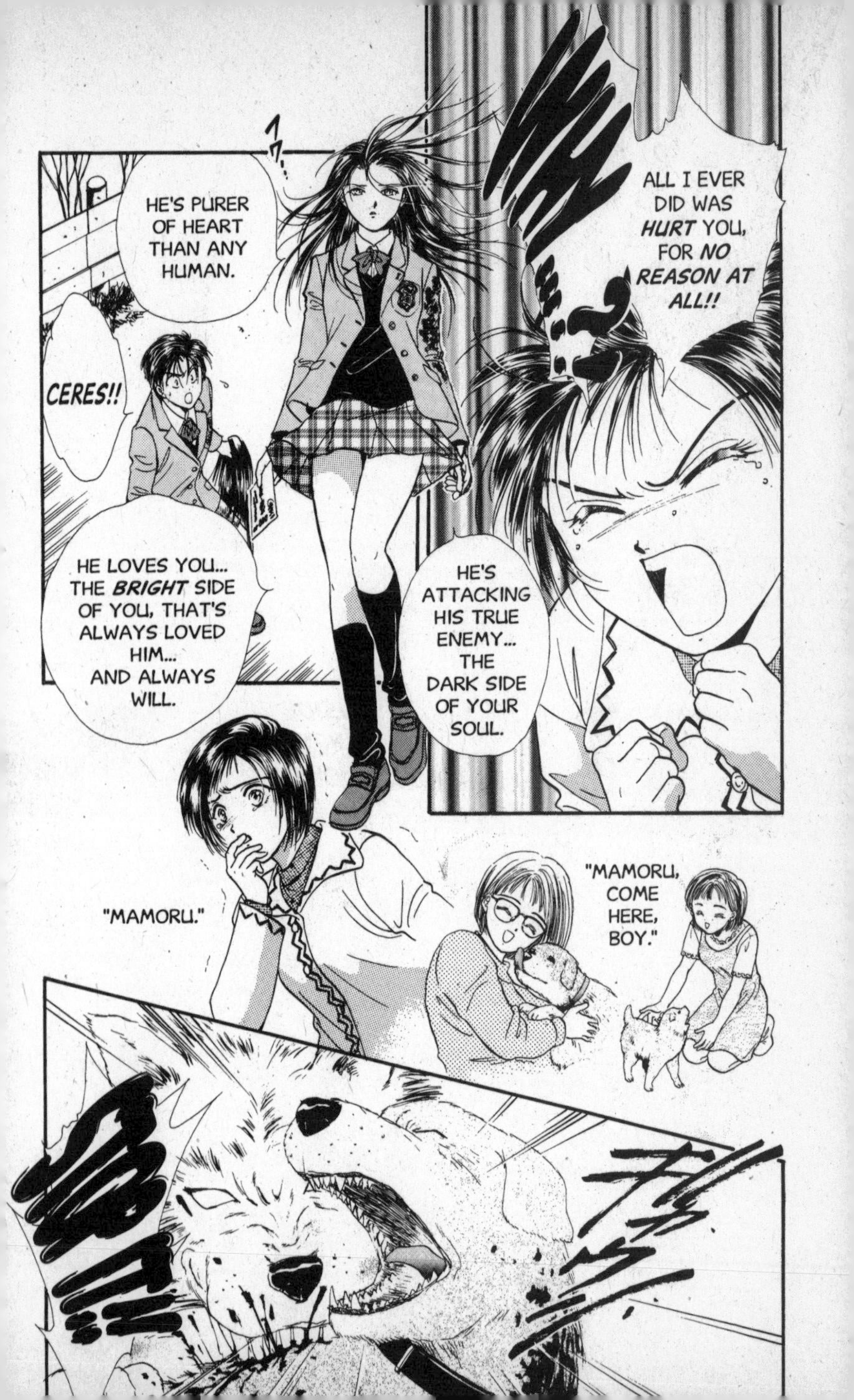
ALL I EVER DID WAS *HURT* YOU, FOR *NO REASON AT ALL!!*
HE'S PURER OF HEART THAN ANY HUMAN.
CERES!!
HE'S ATTACKING HIS TRUE ENEMY... THE DARK SIDE OF YOUR SOUL.
HE LOVES YOU... THE *BRIGHT* SIDE OF YOU, THAT'S ALWAYS LOVED HIM... AND ALWAYS WILL.
"MAMORU, COME HERE, BOY."
"MAMORU."

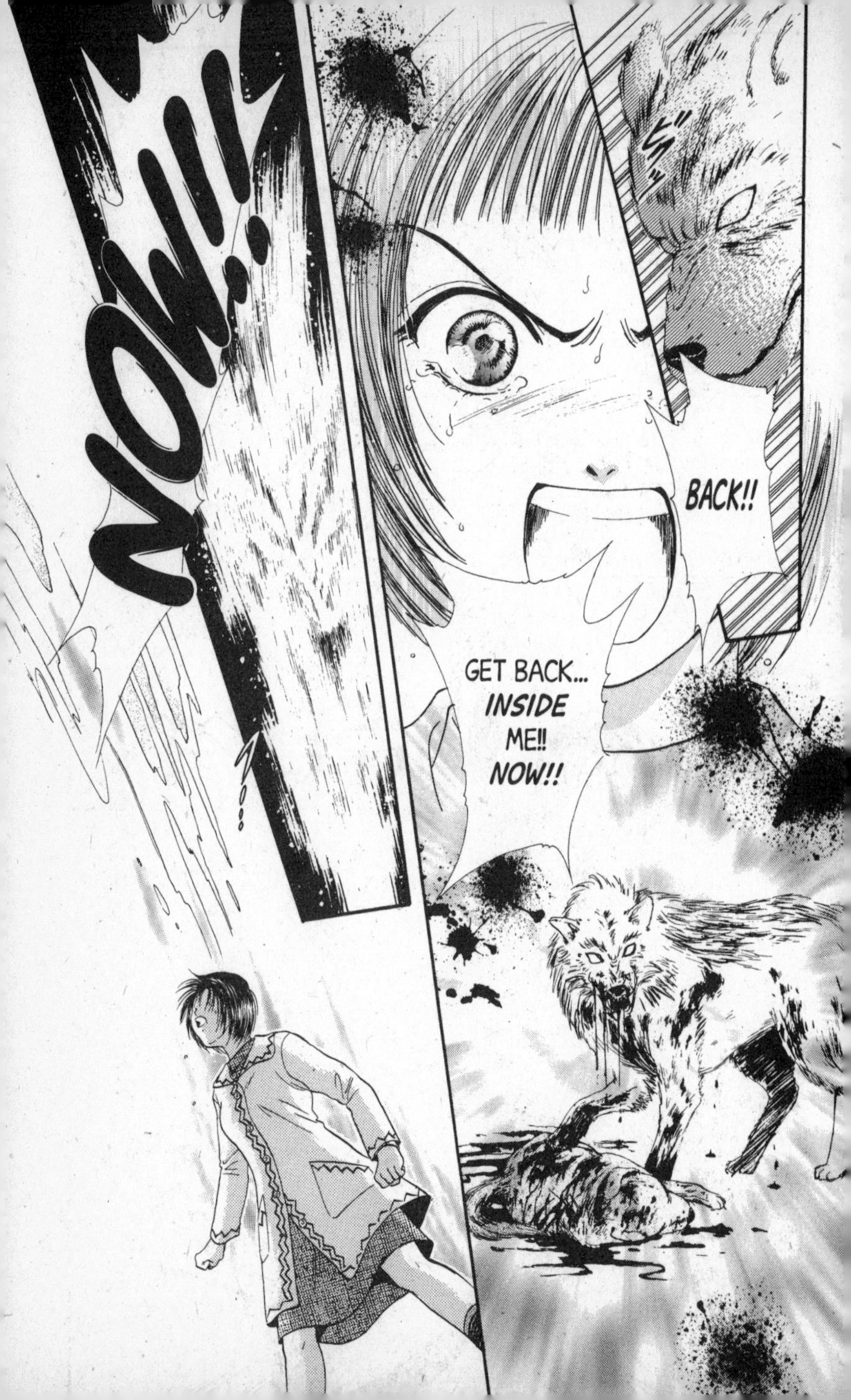
BACK!!
GET BACK... INSIDE ME!! NOW!!
NOW!!

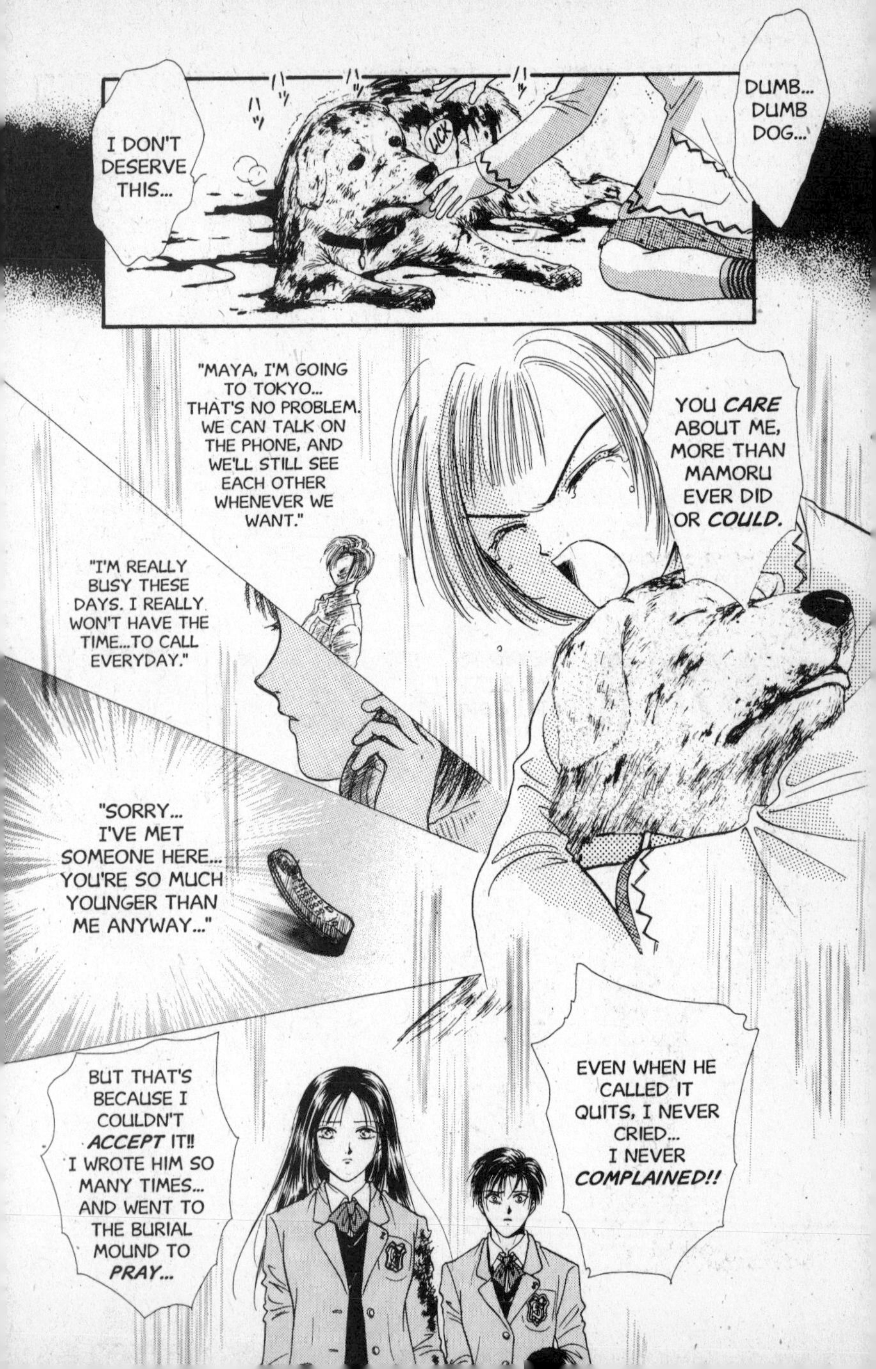
DUMB... DUMB DOG...
LICK
I DON'T DESERVE THIS...
YOU *CARE* ABOUT ME, MORE THAN MAMORU EVER DID OR *COULD.*
"MAYA, I'M GOING TO TOKYO... THAT'S NO PROBLEM. WE CAN TALK ON THE PHONE, AND WE'LL STILL SEE EACH OTHER WHENEVER WE WANT."
"I'M REALLY BUSY THESE DAYS. I REALLY WON'T HAVE THE TIME...TO CALL EVERYDAY."
"SORRY... I'VE MET SOMEONE HERE... YOU'RE SO MUCH YOUNGER THAN ME ANYWAY..."
EVEN WHEN HE CALLED IT QUITS, I NEVER CRIED... I NEVER *COMPLAINED!!*
BUT THAT'S BECAUSE I COULDN'T *ACCEPT* IT!! I WROTE HIM SO MANY TIMES... AND WENT TO THE BURIAL MOUND TO *PRAY...*

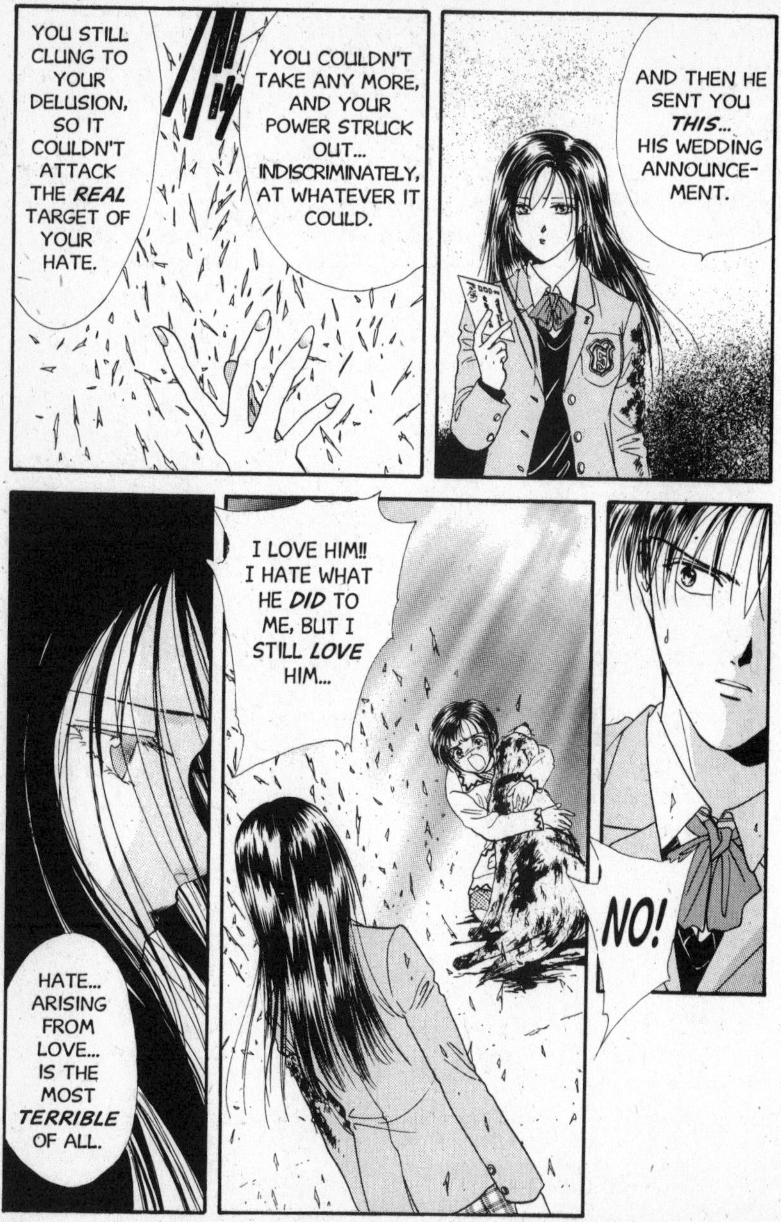
AND THEN HE SENT YOU *THIS*... HIS WEDDING ANNOUNCEMENT.
YOU COULDN'T TAKE ANY MORE, AND YOUR POWER STRUCK OUT... INDISCRIMINATELY, AT WHATEVER IT COULD.
YOU STILL CLUNG TO YOUR DELUSION, SO IT COULDN'T ATTACK THE *REAL* TARGET OF YOUR HATE.
NO!
I LOVE HIM!! I HATE WHAT HE *DID* TO ME, BUT I STILL *LOVE* HIM...
HATE... ARISING FROM LOVE... IS THE MOST *TERRIBLE* OF ALL.

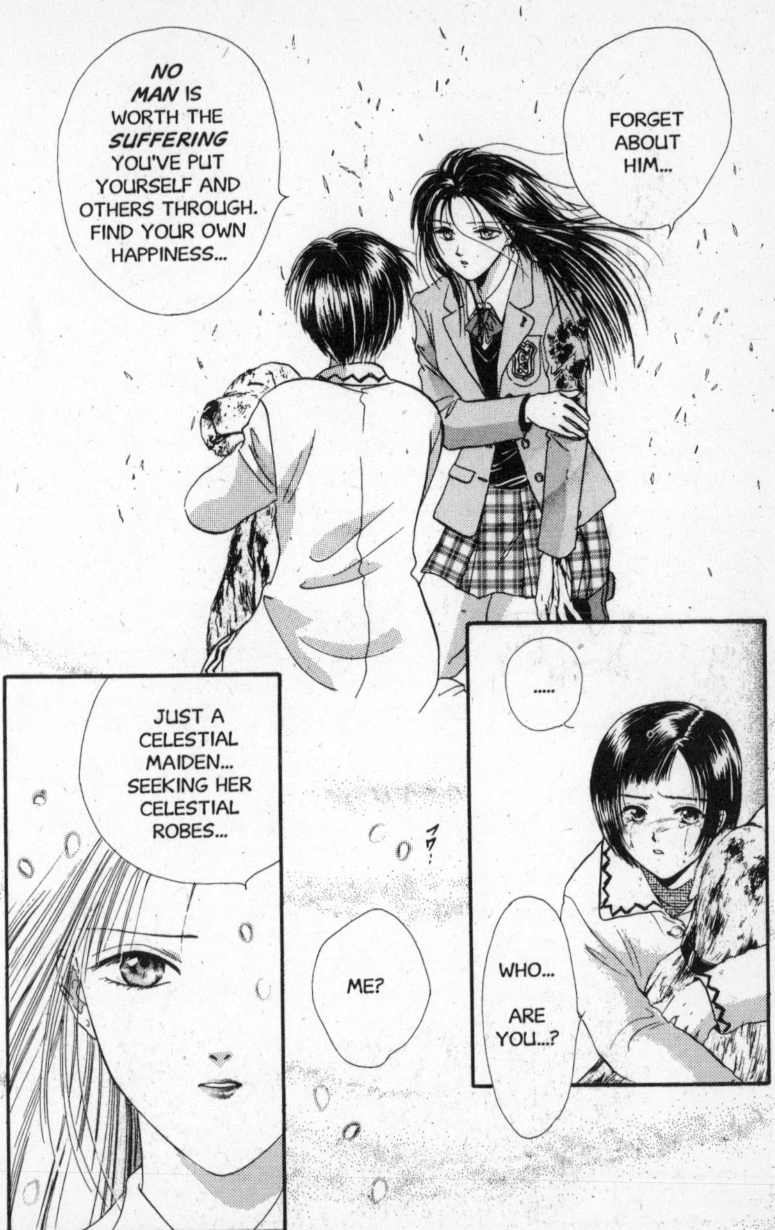
FORGET ABOUT HIM...
NO MAN IS WORTH THE ***SUFFERING*** YOU'VE PUT YOURSELF AND OTHERS THROUGH. FIND YOUR OWN HAPPINESS...
.....
WHO... ARE YOU...?
ME?
JUST A CELESTIAL MAIDEN... SEEKING HER CELESTIAL ROBES...

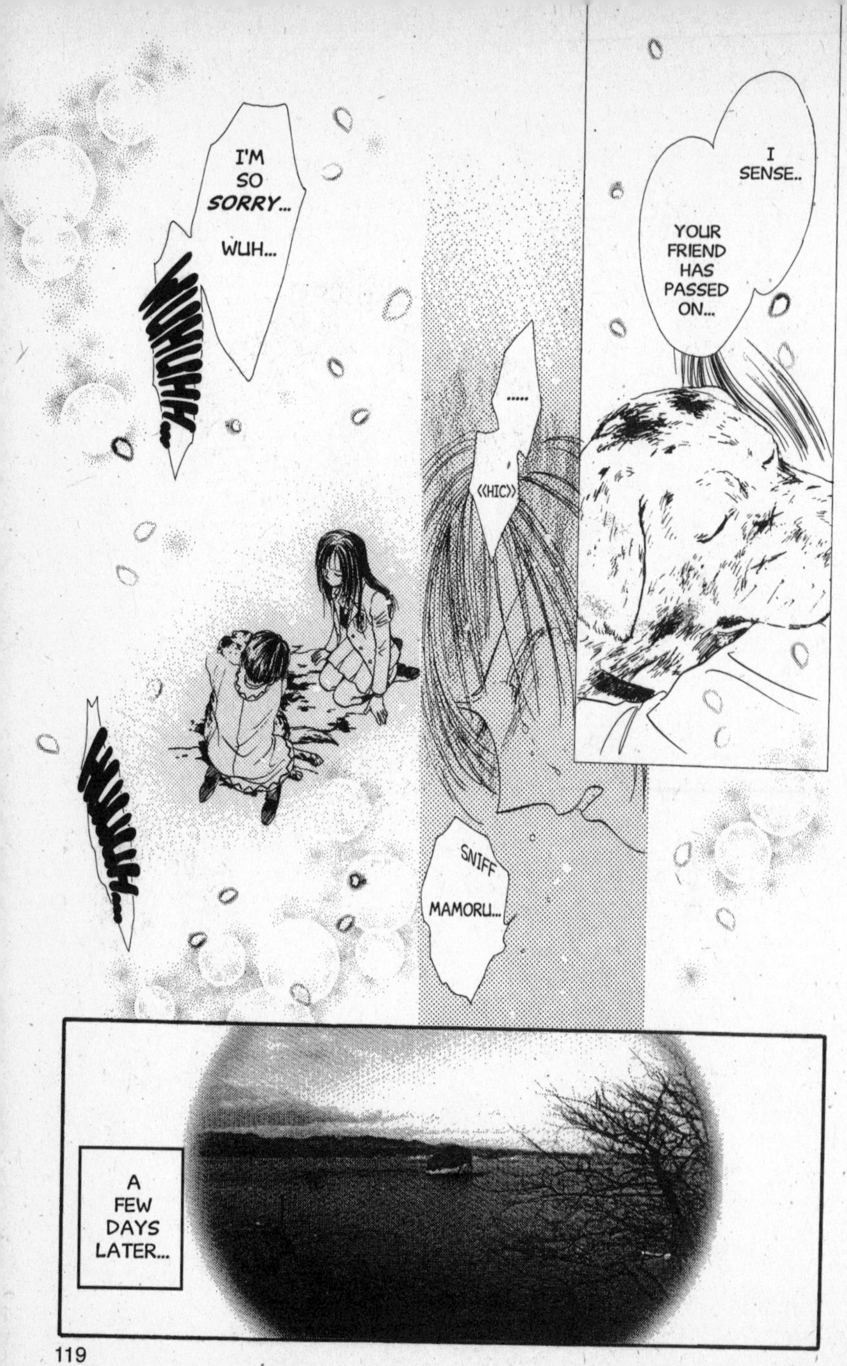
I SENSE..
YOUR FRIEND HAS PASSED ON...
.....
<<HIC>>
SNIFF
MAMORU...
I'M SO SORRY...
WUH...
WUHUHH...
WHUUUH...
A FEW DAYS LATER...

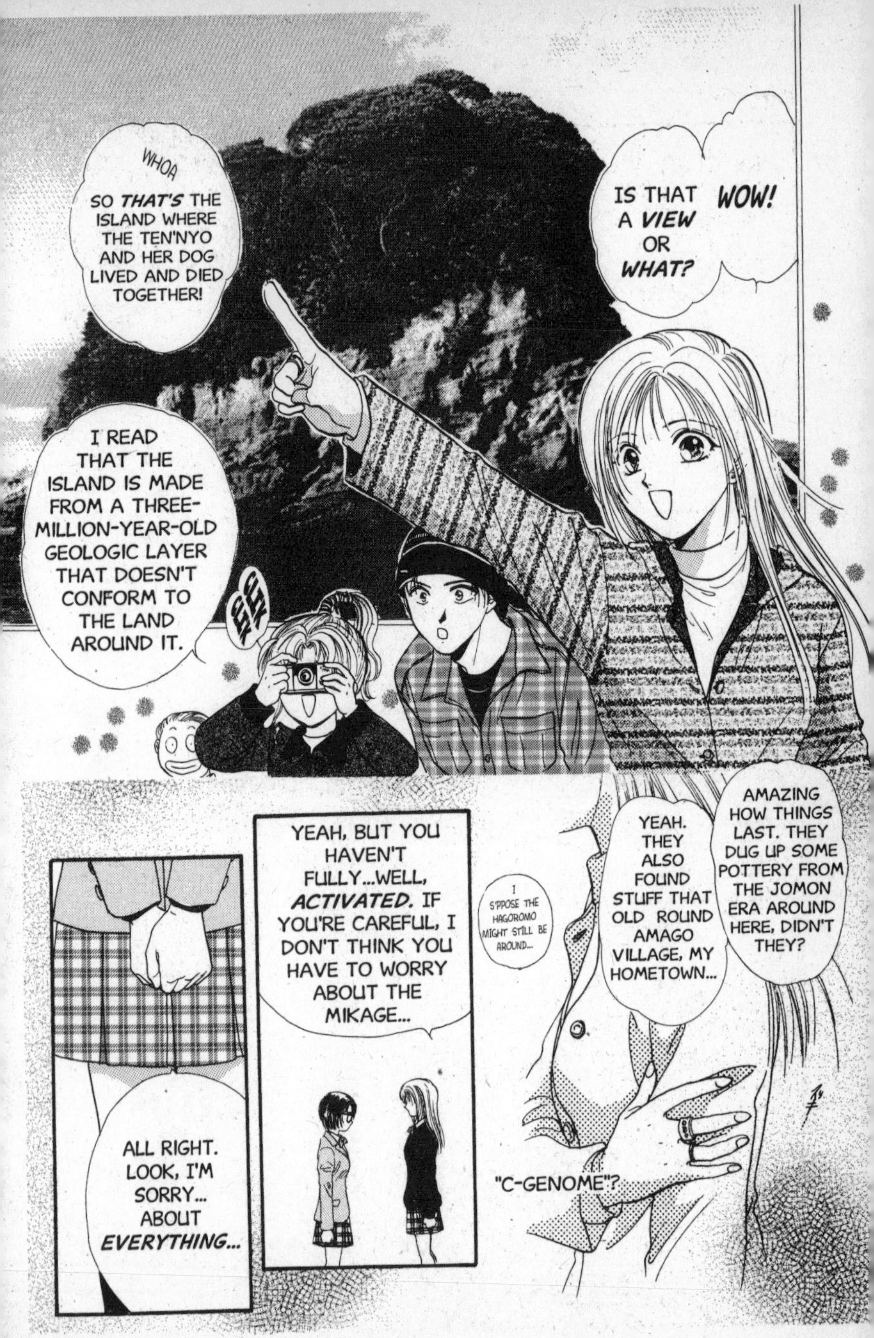

WOW!
IS THAT A *VIEW* OR *WHAT?*
WHOA
SO *THAT'S* THE ISLAND WHERE THE TEN'NYO AND HER DOG LIVED AND DIED TOGETHER!
I READ THAT THE ISLAND IS MADE FROM A THREE-MILLION-YEAR-OLD GEOLOGIC LAYER THAT DOESN'T CONFORM TO THE LAND AROUND IT.
CLIK CLIK
AMAZING HOW THINGS LAST. THEY DUG UP SOME POTTERY FROM THE JOMON ERA AROUND HERE, DIDN'T THEY?
YEAH. THEY ALSO FOUND STUFF THAT OLD ROUND AMAGO VILLAGE, MY HOMETOWN...
I S'POSE THE HAGOROMO MIGHT STILL BE AROUND...
"C-GENOME"?
YEAH, BUT YOU HAVEN'T FULLY...WELL, *ACTIVATED.* IF YOU'RE CAREFUL, I DON'T THINK YOU HAVE TO WORRY ABOUT THE MIKAGE...
ALL RIGHT. LOOK, I'M SORRY... ABOUT *EVERYTHING...*

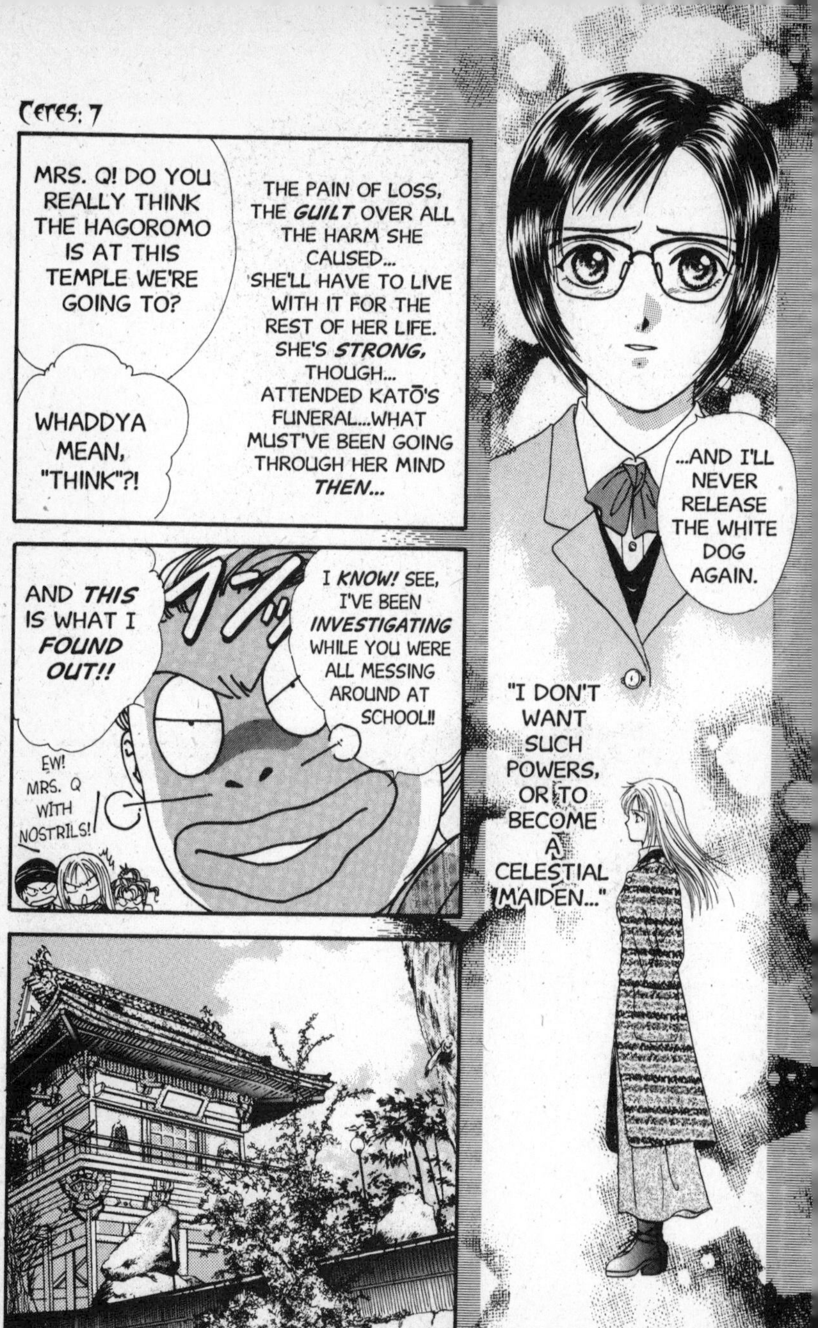
...AND I'LL NEVER RELEASE THE WHITE DOG AGAIN.
"I DON'T WANT SUCH POWERS, OR TO BECOME A CELESTIAL MAIDEN..."
THE PAIN OF LOSS, THE *GUILT* OVER ALL THE HARM SHE CAUSED... SHE'LL HAVE TO LIVE WITH IT FOR THE REST OF HER LIFE. SHE'S *STRONG,* THOUGH... ATTENDED KATŌ'S FUNERAL...WHAT MUST'VE BEEN GOING THROUGH HER MIND *THEN...*
MRS. Q! DO YOU REALLY THINK THE HAGOROMO IS AT THIS TEMPLE WE'RE GOING TO?
WHADDYA MEAN, "THINK"?!
I *KNOW!* SEE, I'VE BEEN *INVESTIGATING* WHILE YOU WERE ALL MESSING AROUND AT SCHOOL!!
AND *THIS* IS WHAT I *FOUND OUT!!*
EW! MRS. Q WITH NOSTRILS!

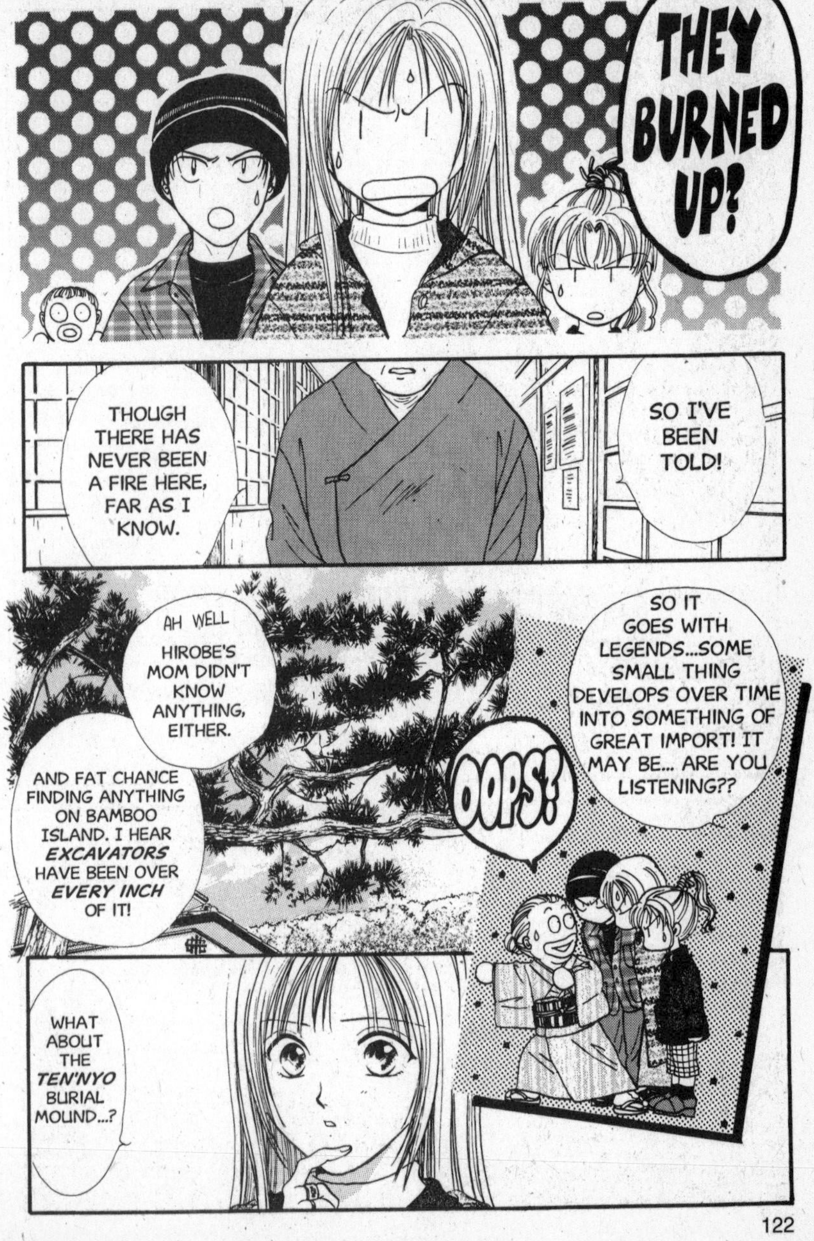
THEY BURNED UP?
SO I'VE BEEN TOLD!
THOUGH THERE HAS NEVER BEEN A FIRE HERE, FAR AS I KNOW.
SO IT GOES WITH LEGENDS...SOME SMALL THING DEVELOPS OVER TIME INTO SOMETHING OF GREAT IMPORT! IT MAY BE... ARE YOU LISTENING??
OOPS?
AH WELL
HIROBE'S MOM DIDN'T KNOW ANYTHING, EITHER.
AND FAT CHANCE FINDING ANYTHING ON BAMBOO ISLAND. I HEAR ***EXCAVATORS*** HAVE BEEN OVER ***EVERY INCH*** OF IT!
WHAT ABOUT THE ***TEN'NYO*** BURIAL MOUND...?

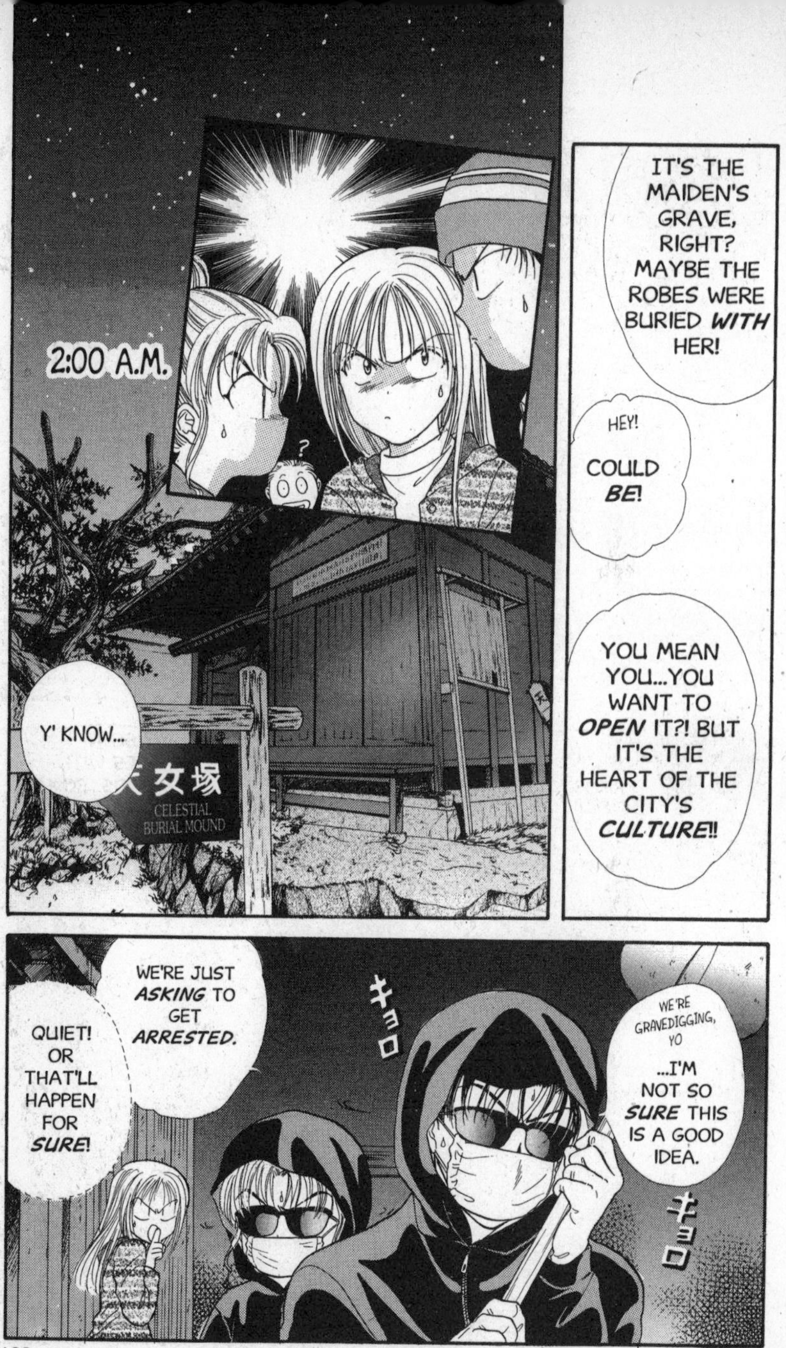
IT'S THE MAIDEN'S GRAVE, RIGHT? MAYBE THE ROBES WERE BURIED *WITH* HER!
HEY!
COULD *BE*!
YOU MEAN YOU...YOU WANT TO *OPEN* IT?! BUT IT'S THE HEART OF THE CITY'S *CULTURE*!!
2:00 A.M.
Y' KNOW...
CELESTIAL BURIAL MOUND
WE'RE GRAVEDIGGING, YO
...I'M NOT SO *SURE* THIS IS A GOOD IDEA.
キョロ
キョロ
WE'RE JUST *ASKING* TO GET *ARRESTED.*
QUIET! OR THAT'LL HAPPEN FOR *SURE*!

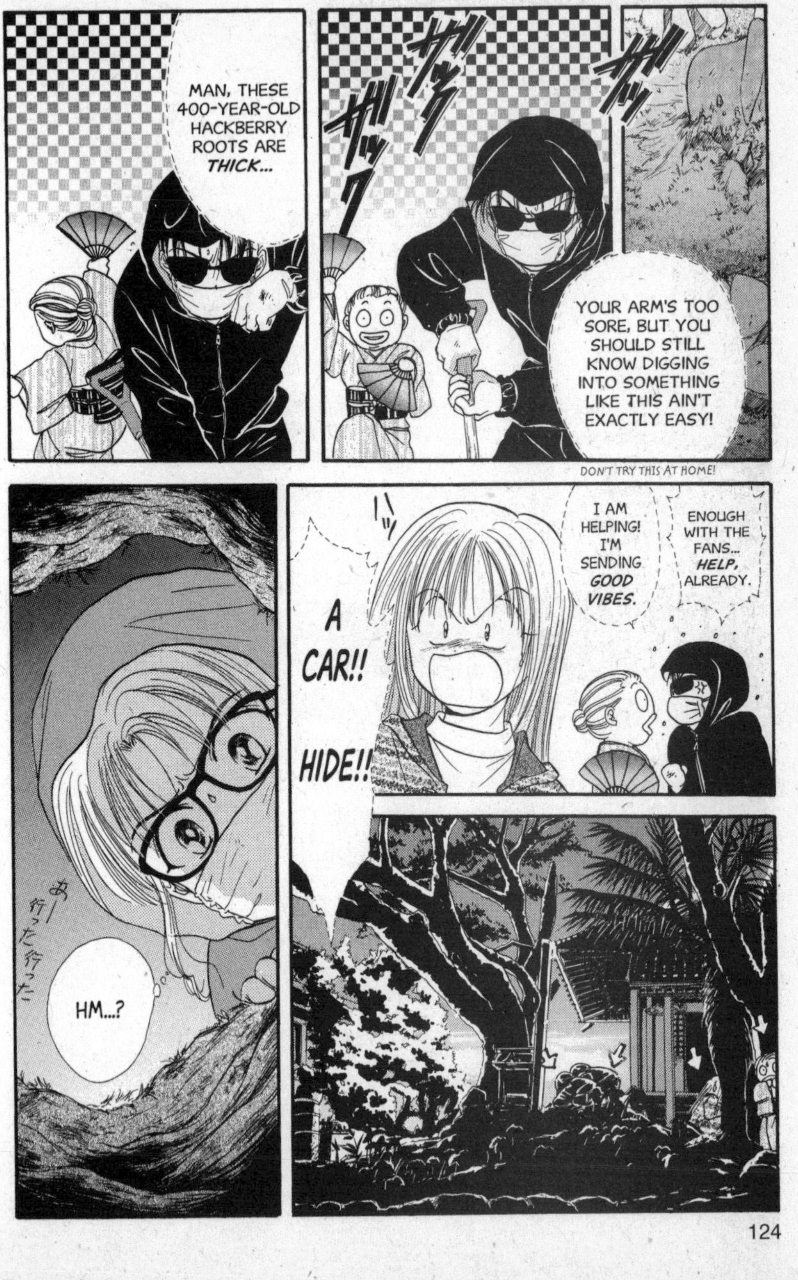
YOUR ARM'S TOO SORE, BUT YOU SHOULD STILL KNOW DIGGING INTO SOMETHING LIKE THIS AIN'T EXACTLY EASY!
DON'T TRY THIS AT HOME!
MAN, THESE 400-YEAR-OLD HACKBERRY ROOTS ARE *THICK*...
ENOUGH WITH THE FANS... *HELP,* ALREADY.
I AM HELPING! I'M SENDING *GOOD VIBES.*
A CAR!!
HIDE!!
あー行った行った
HM...?

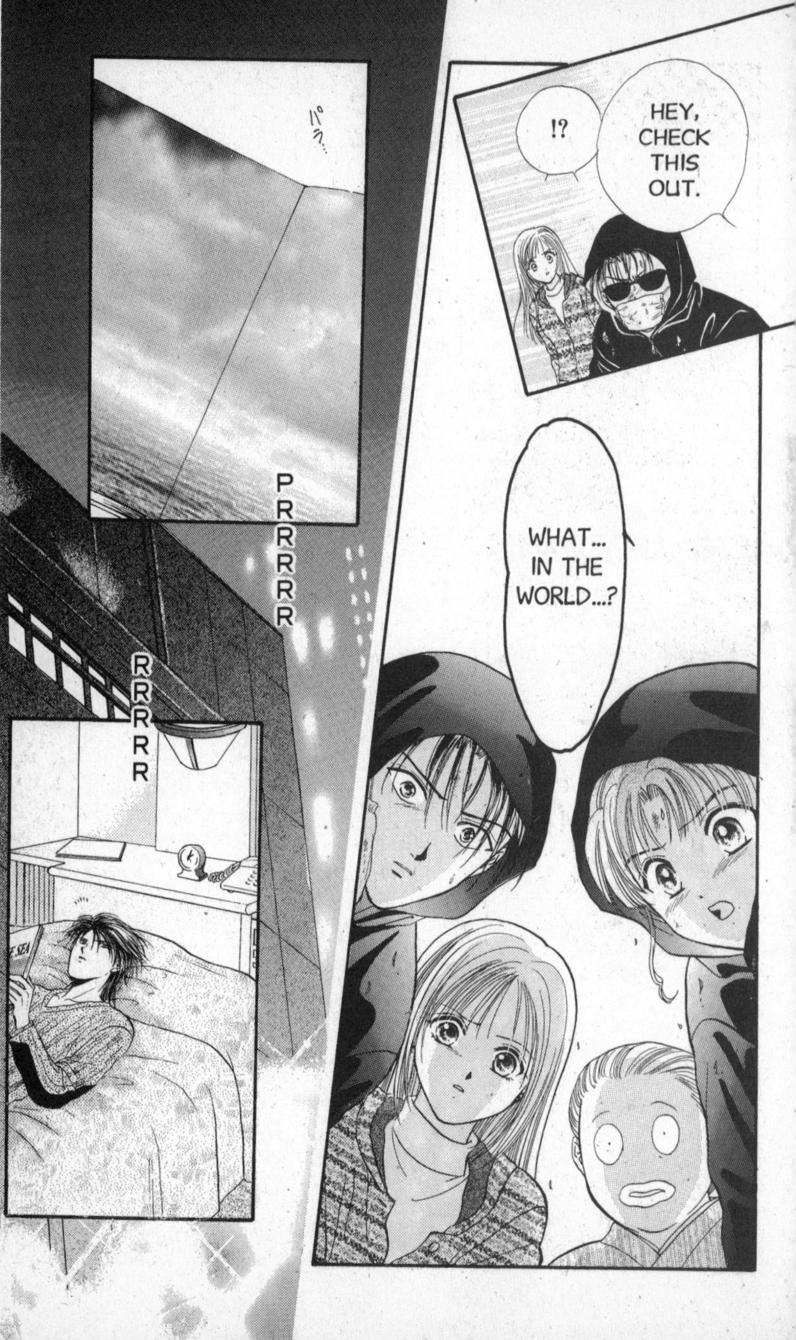
HEY, CHECK THIS OUT.
!?
WHAT... IN THE WORLD...?
パラ…
PRRRRR
RRRRR

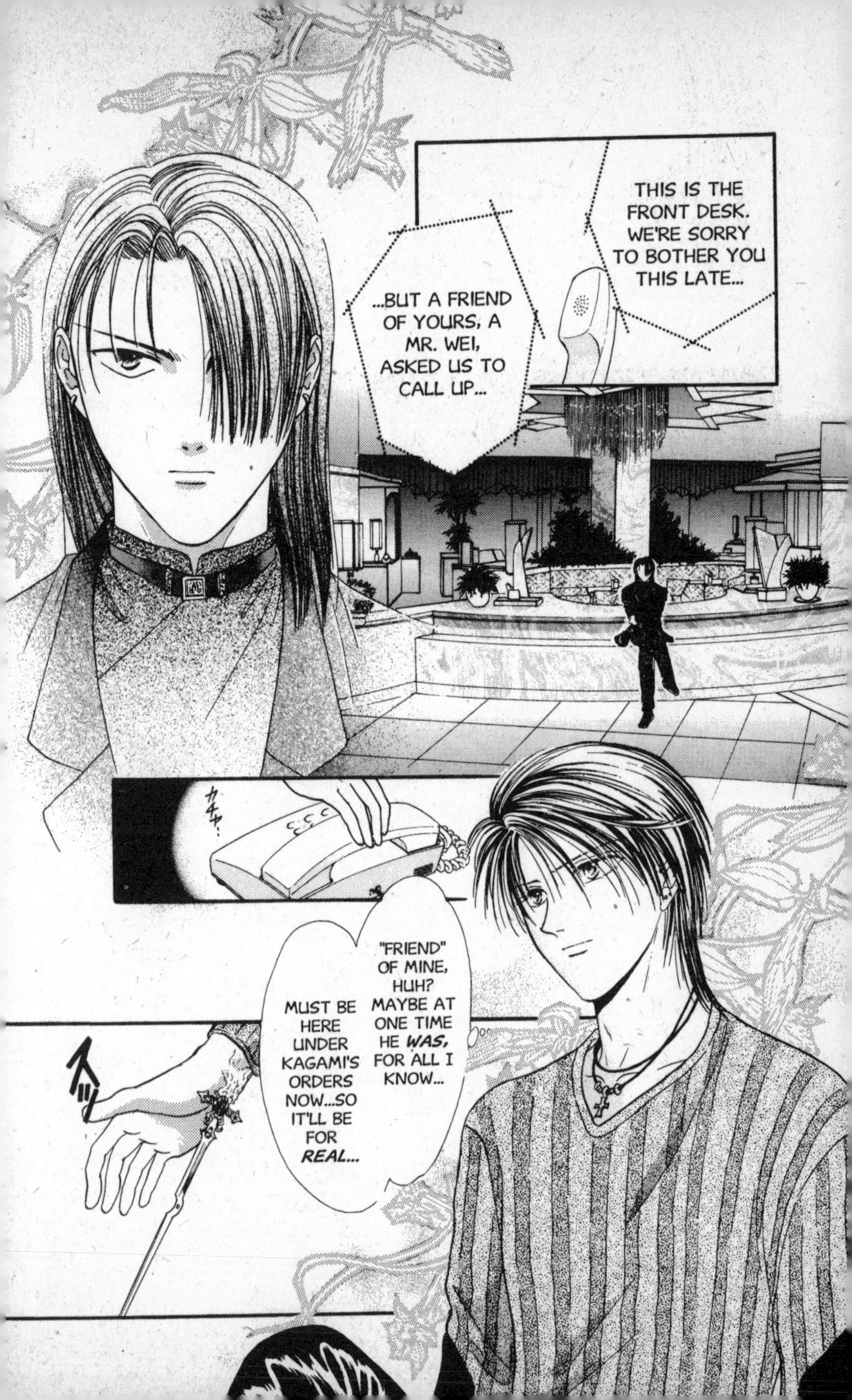
THIS IS THE FRONT DESK. WE'RE SORRY TO BOTHER YOU THIS LATE...
...BUT A FRIEND OF YOURS, A MR. WEI, ASKED US TO CALL UP...
カチャ
"FRIEND" OF MINE, HUH? MAYBE AT ONE TIME HE *WAS,* FOR ALL I KNOW...
MUST BE HERE UNDER KAGAMI'S ORDERS NOW...SO IT'LL BE FOR ***REAL...***

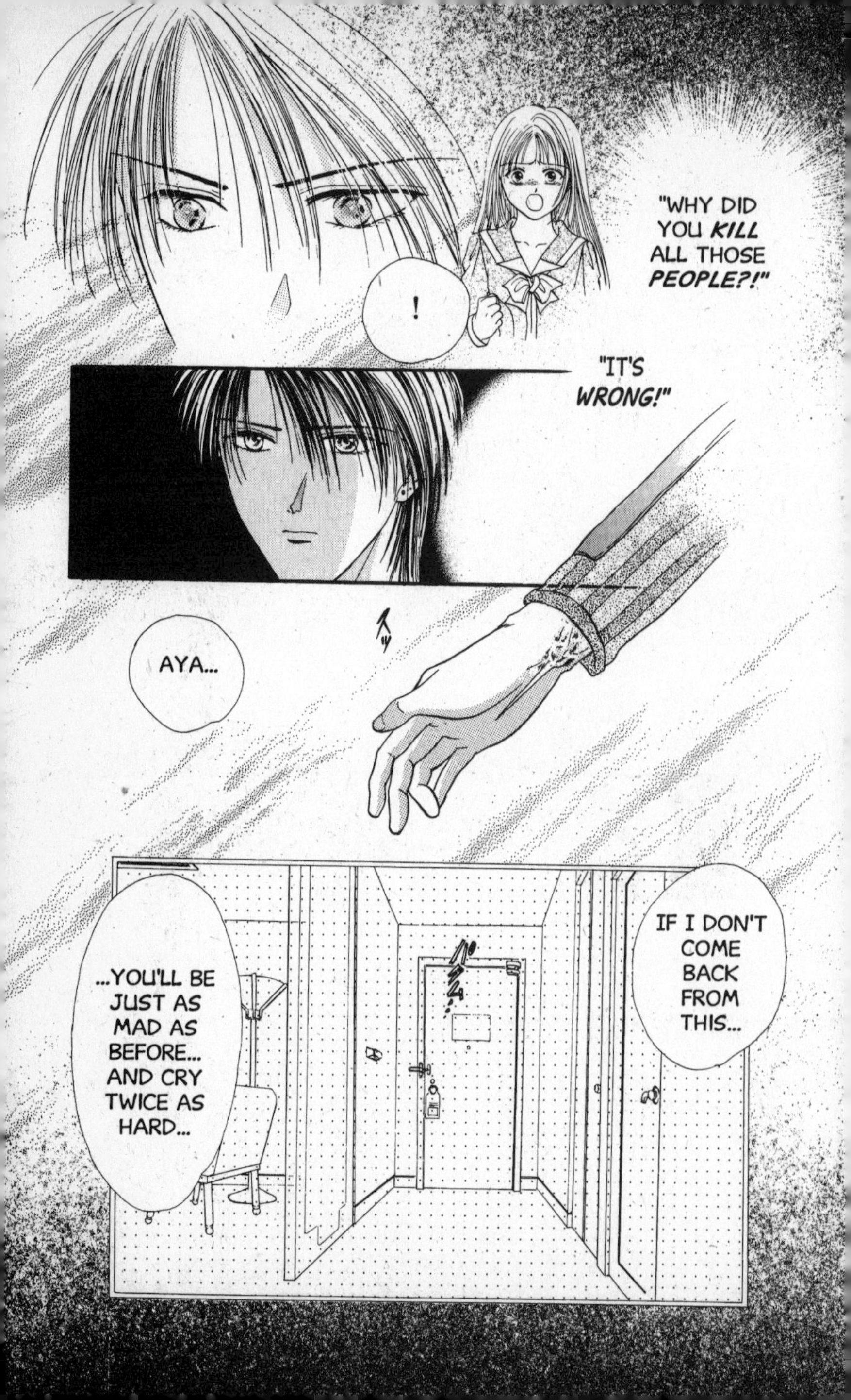
"WHY DID YOU *KILL* ALL THOSE *PEOPLE?!*"
!
"IT'S *WRONG!*"
AYA...
IF I DON'T COME BACK FROM THIS...
...YOU'LL BE JUST AS MAD AS BEFORE... AND CRY TWICE AS HARD...

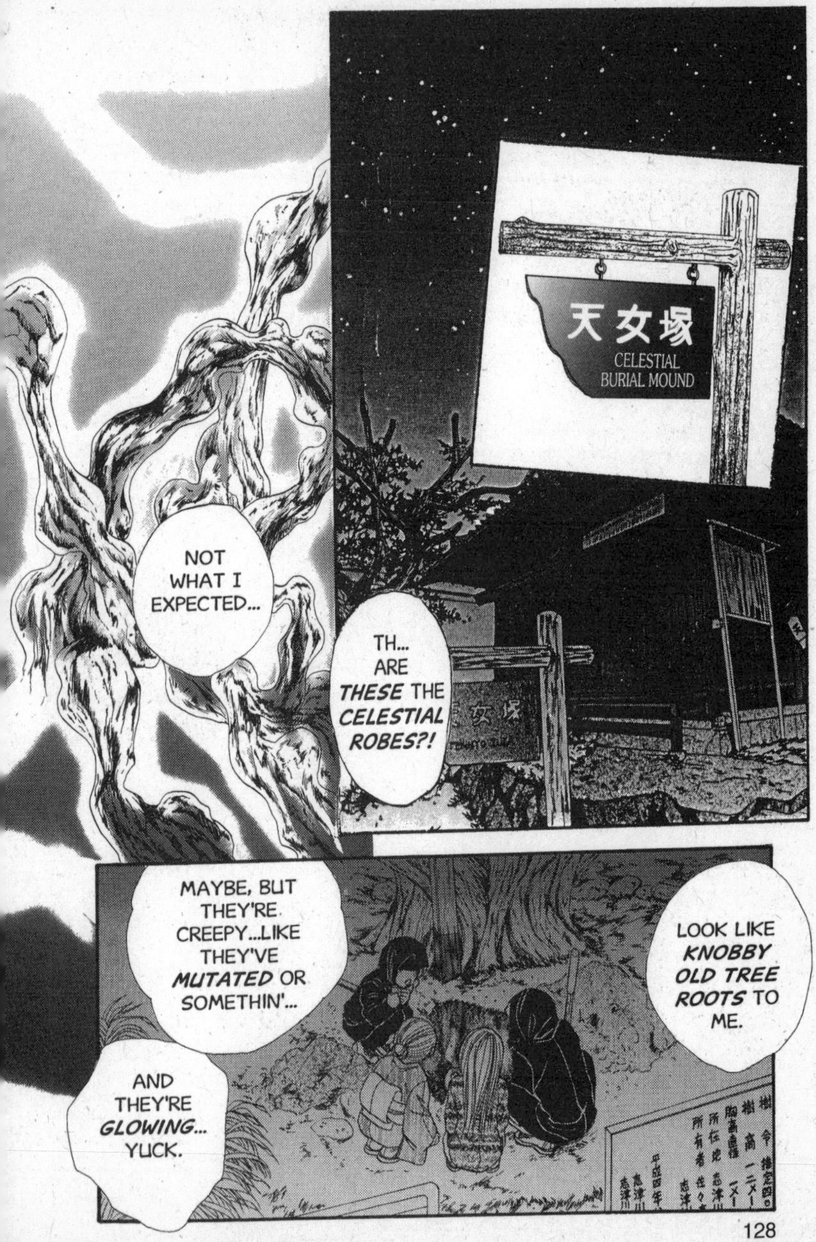
天女塚
CELESTIAL BURIAL MOUND
TH... ARE *THESE* THE *CELESTIAL ROBES?!*
NOT WHAT I EXPECTED...
LOOK LIKE *KNOBBY OLD TREE ROOTS* TO ME.
MAYBE, BUT THEY'RE CREEPY...LIKE THEY'VE *MUTATED* OR SOMETHIN'...
AND THEY'RE *GLOWING*... YUCK.

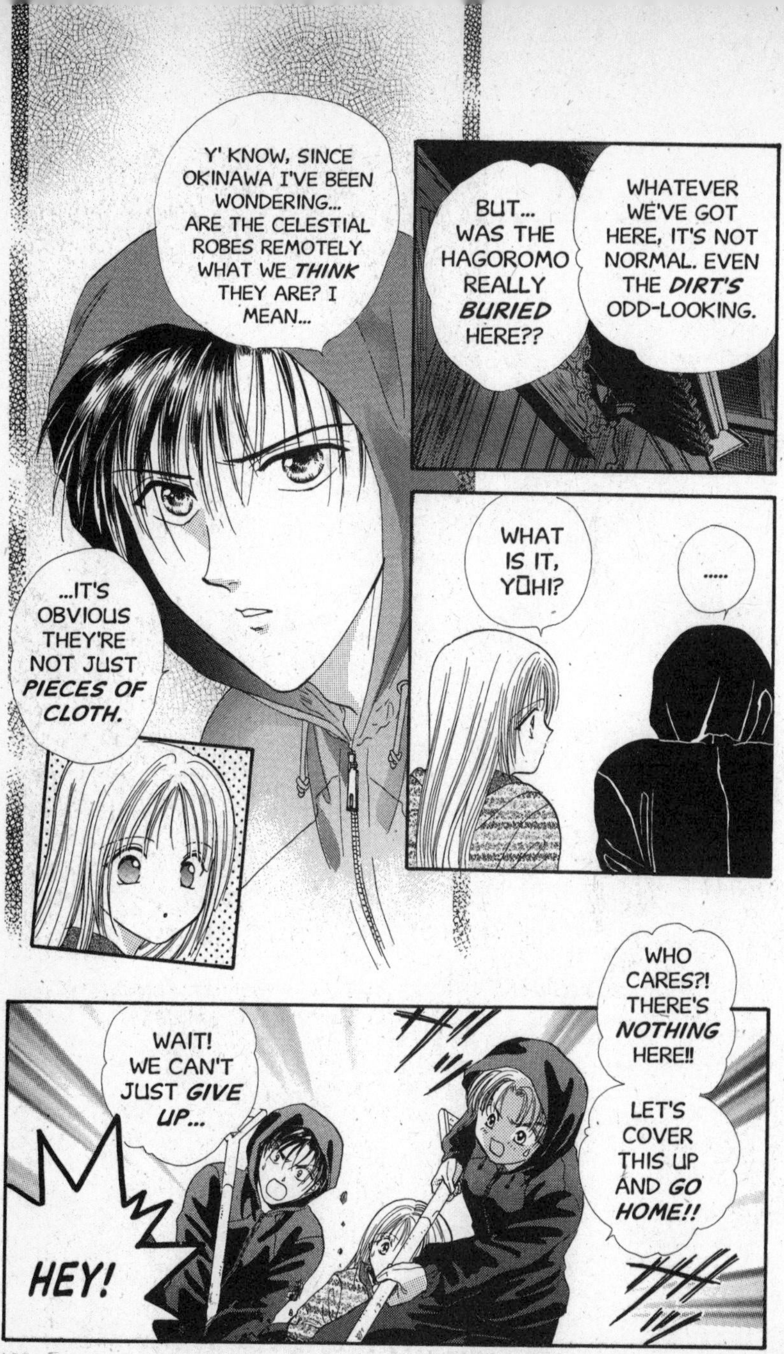

WHATEVER WE'VE GOT HERE, IT'S NOT NORMAL. EVEN THE *DIRT'S* ODD-LOOKING.
BUT... WAS THE HAGOROMO REALLY *BURIED* HERE??
.....
WHAT IS IT, YŪHI?
Y' KNOW, SINCE OKINAWA I'VE BEEN WONDERING... ARE THE CELESTIAL ROBES REMOTELY WHAT WE *THINK* THEY ARE? I MEAN...
...IT'S OBVIOUS THEY'RE NOT JUST *PIECES OF CLOTH.*
WHO CARES?! THERE'S *NOTHING* HERE!!
LET'S COVER THIS UP AND *GO HOME!!*
WAIT! WE CAN'T JUST *GIVE UP...*
HEY!

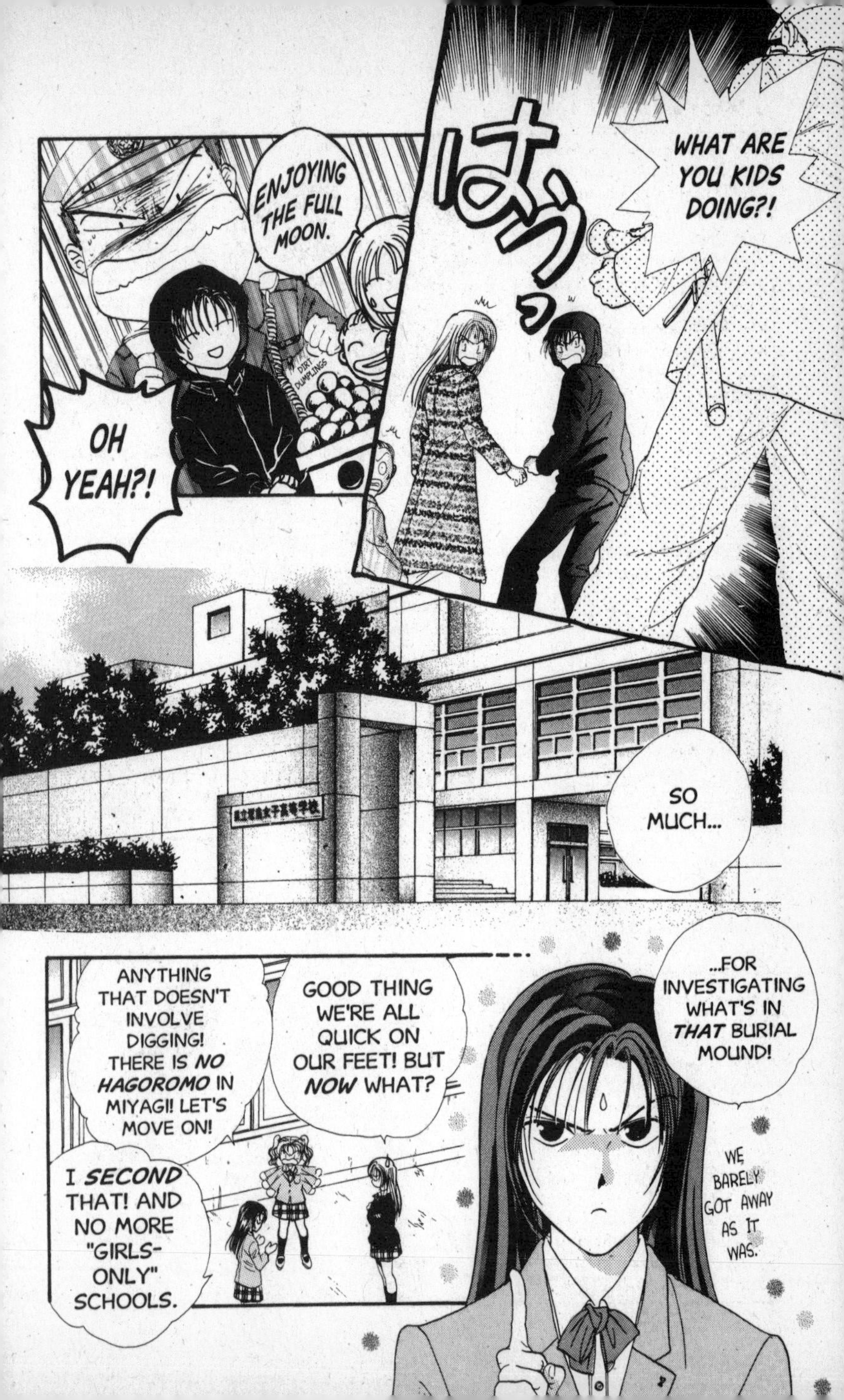
はうっ
WHAT ARE YOU KIDS DOING?!
ENJOYING THE FULL MOON.
DIRT DUMPLINGS
OH YEAH?!
SO MUCH...
...FOR INVESTIGATING WHAT'S IN *THAT* BURIAL MOUND!
WE BARELY GOT AWAY AS IT WAS.
GOOD THING WE'RE ALL QUICK ON OUR FEET! BUT *NOW* WHAT?
ANYTHING THAT DOESN'T INVOLVE DIGGING! THERE IS *NO HAGOROMO* IN MIYAGI! LET'S MOVE ON!
I *SECOND* THAT! AND NO MORE "GIRLS-ONLY" SCHOOLS.

✦ Maya ✦

Yūhi's a gentleman, really, for putting up with as much as he has. He **is**, after all, a healthy, **normal** teen. My assistants sympathize that he resists so much temptation—the boy's constantly frustrated. ◡̈ I guess it's just human nature to chase whatever's hard-to-get...which is why Aya can't help going after Tōya. She's attracted to his "mysterious" side! The strategy in love is to push hard forward...then pull back.

This close to the end of the volume, some of you may now be all like, **"Whoa!"** Aya has been always the pursuer, but I think that **slap** to Tōya may have opened his eyes a bit—at which point, he couldn't get his mind off her. That's how it **is** in relationships. If you want someone to like you, you should come on strong...then suddenly back off! Then the object of your affection will be consumed by thoughts of you. If there's **still** no reaction, well, then it's probably time to give up and move on. (Easy for me to say, tho', right?)

So, here we are—and it's taken Aya **seven volumes** to finally win Tōya's heart. No doubt Yūhi fans will complain, but that's how it goes! "Behind every smile are tears...." That's life. In every way. But there **will** be a twist...uh-oh. Wasn't I supposed to be talking about the **characters**?! Okay, then, let's do Ceres! She's actually pretty popular—lots of girl-readers admire her. (They do!) ...Well, I feel I've really "done it now" with this second half of Volume 7—it's gonna be interesting to see what happens. Signing off... (who **knows** what I'll do next!). See you in Volume 8.

BGM for this sidebar: [Yoko Kanno's] "Song to Fly" and Resident Evil 2 soundtrack.

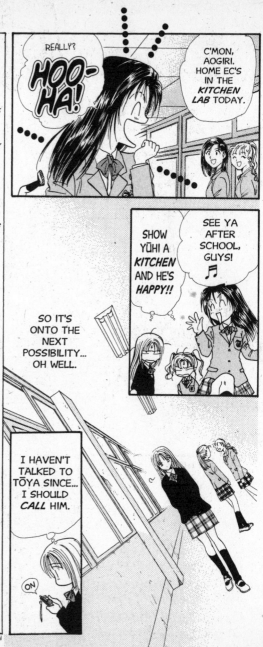

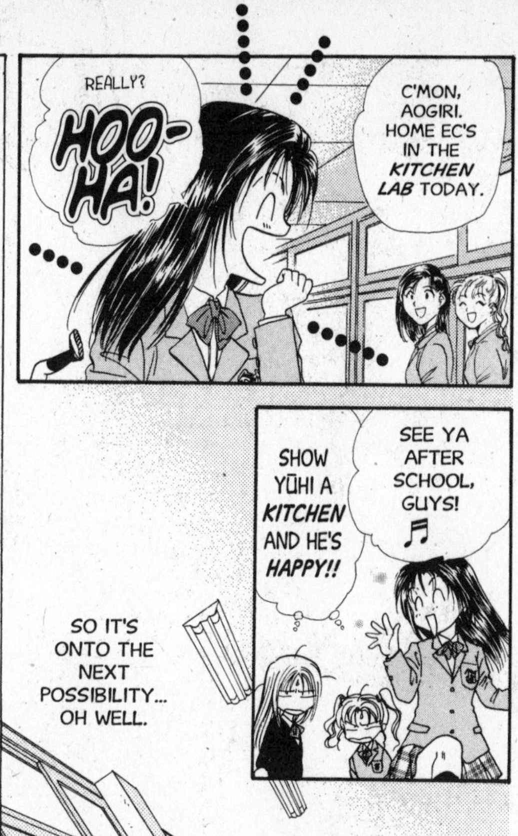
C'MON, AOGIRI. HOME EC'S IN THE *KITCHEN LAB* TODAY.
REALLY?
HOO-HA!
SEE YA AFTER SCHOOL, GUYS! ♫
SHOW YŪHI A *KITCHEN* AND HE'S *HAPPY!!*
SO IT'S ONTO THE NEXT POSSIBILITY... OH WELL.
I HAVEN'T TALKED TO TŌYA SINCE... I SHOULD *CALL* HIM.
ON

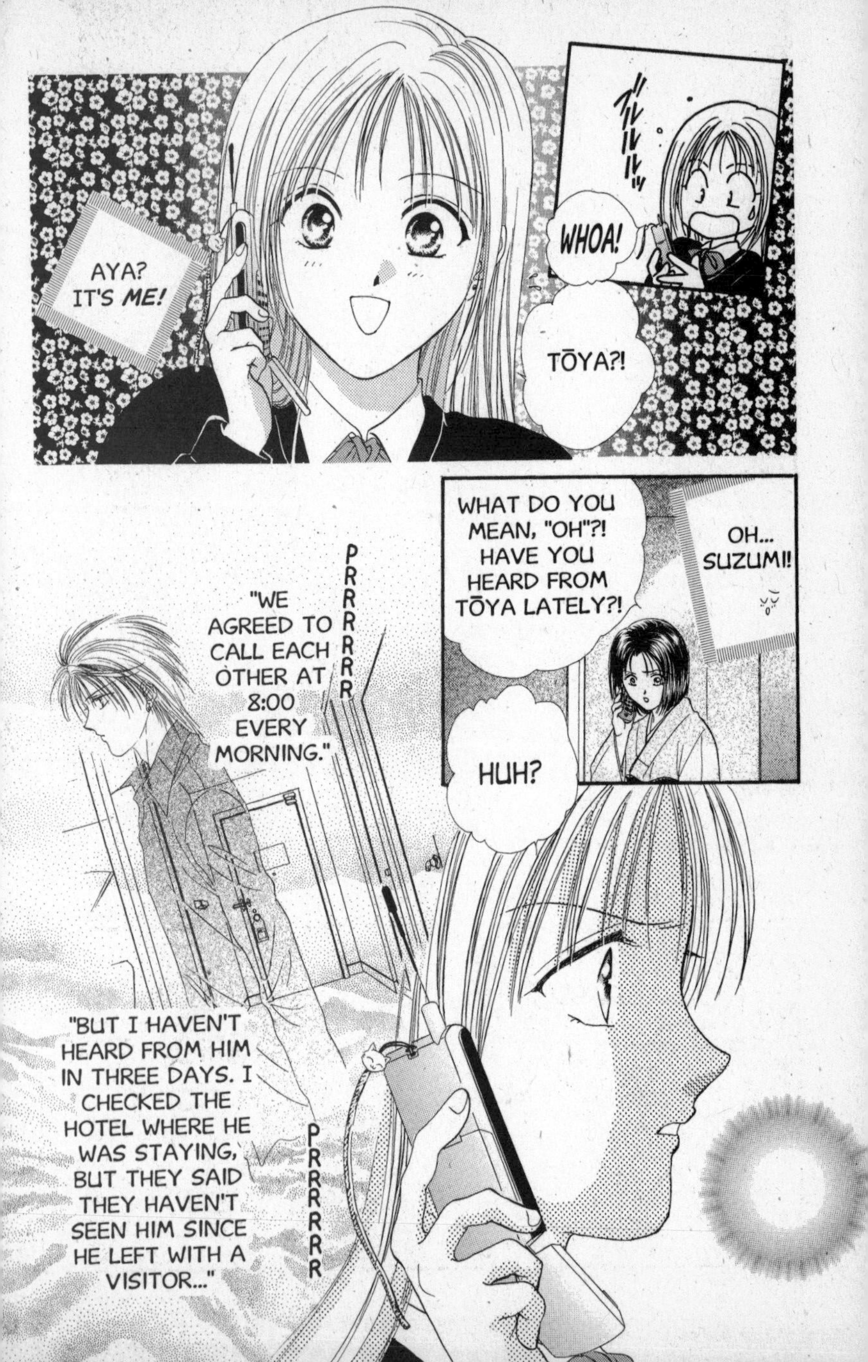
ブルルルッ
WHOA!
AYA? IT'S *ME!*
TŌYA?!
OH... SUZUMI!
WHAT DO YOU MEAN, "OH"?! HAVE YOU HEARD FROM TŌYA LATELY?!
HUH?
PRRRRRR
"WE AGREED TO CALL EACH OTHER AT 8:00 EVERY MORNING."
PRRRRRR
"BUT I HAVEN'T HEARD FROM HIM IN THREE DAYS. I CHECKED THE HOTEL WHERE HE WAS STAYING, BUT THEY SAID THEY HAVEN'T SEEN HIM SINCE HE LEFT WITH A VISITOR..."

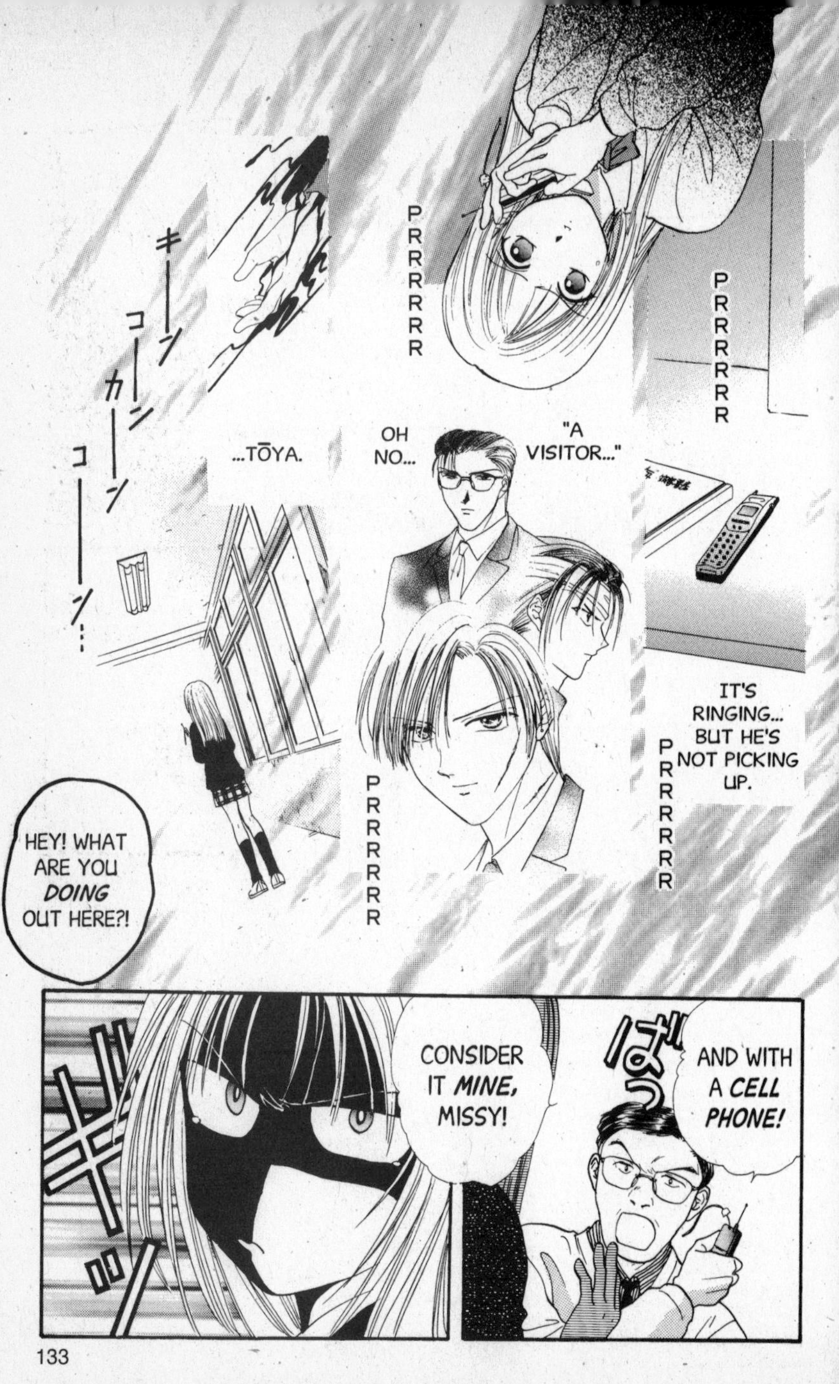
PRRRRRR
PRRRRRR
キーンコーンカーンコーン…
"A VISITOR..."
IT'S RINGING... BUT HE'S NOT PICKING UP.
PRRRRRR
OH NO...
PRRRRRR
...TŌYA.
HEY! WHAT ARE YOU *DOING* OUT HERE?!
ばっ
AND WITH A *CELL PHONE!*
CONSIDER IT *MINE,* MISSY!

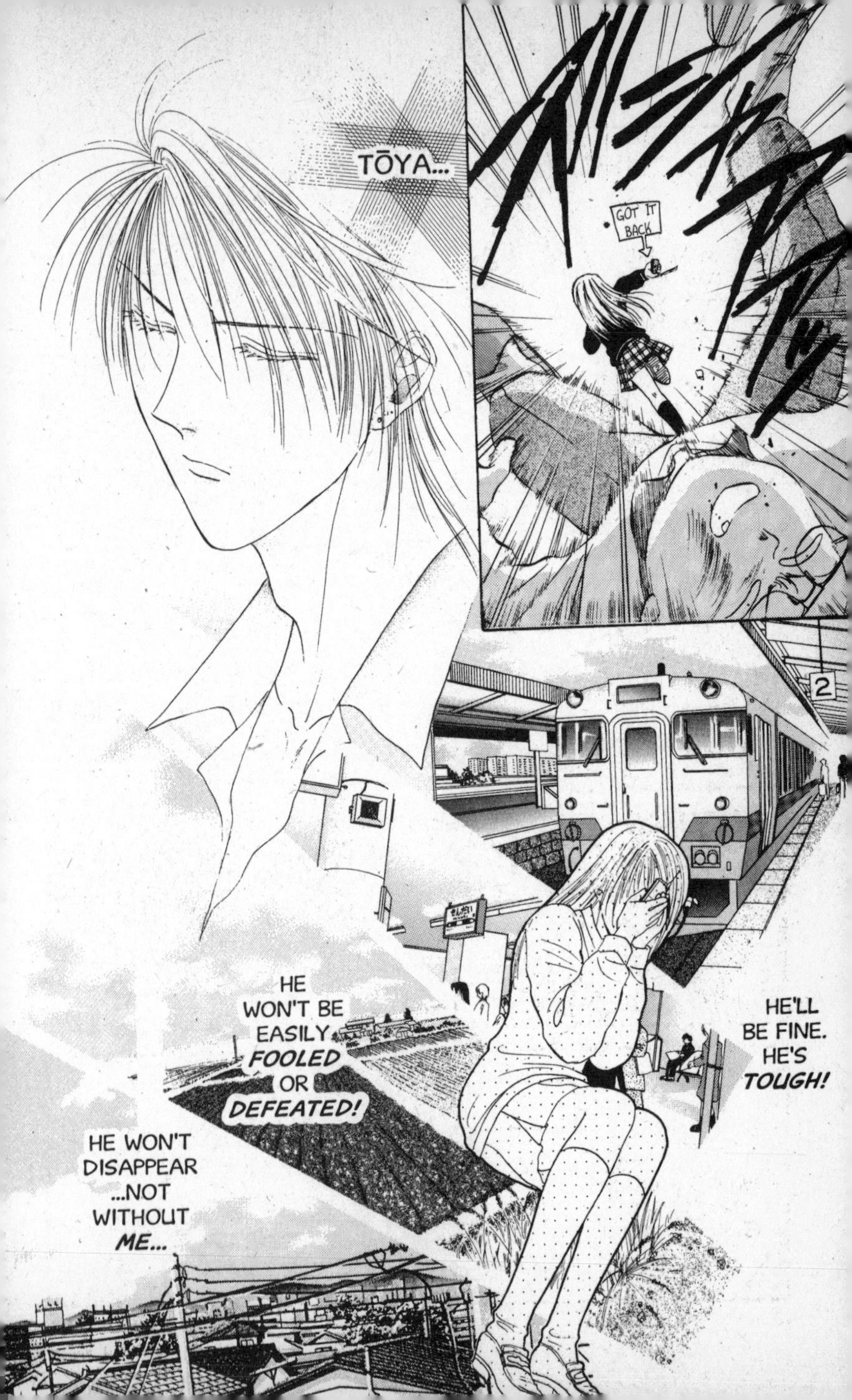
GOT IT BACK
TŌYA...
HE'LL BE FINE. HE'S *TOUGH!*
HE WON'T BE EASILY *FOOLED* OR *DEFEATED!*
HE WON'T DISAPPEAR ...NOT WITHOUT *ME*...

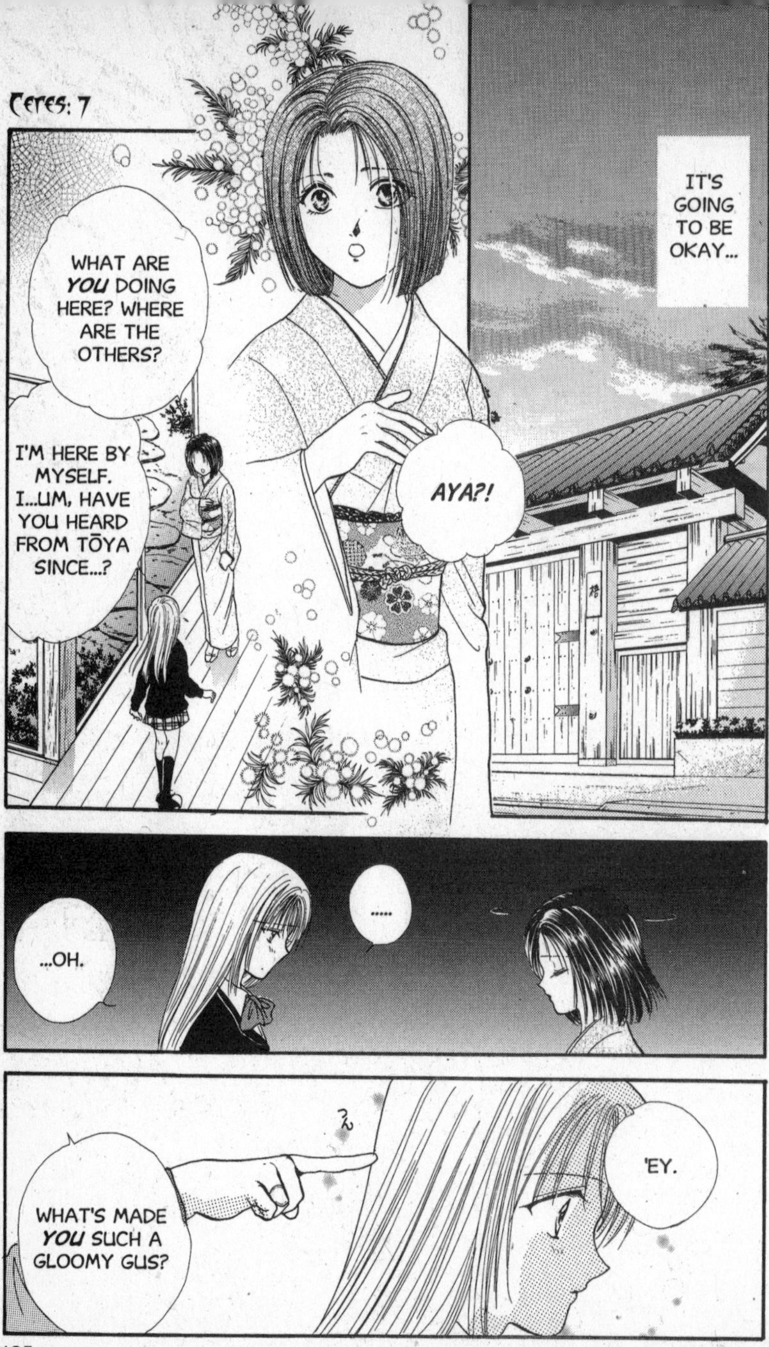
IT'S GOING TO BE OKAY...
AYA?!
WHAT ARE *YOU* DOING HERE? WHERE ARE THE OTHERS?
I'M HERE BY MYSELF. I...UM, HAVE YOU HEARD FROM TŌYA SINCE...?
......
...OH.
'EY.
つん
WHAT'S MADE *YOU* SUCH A GLOOMY GUS?

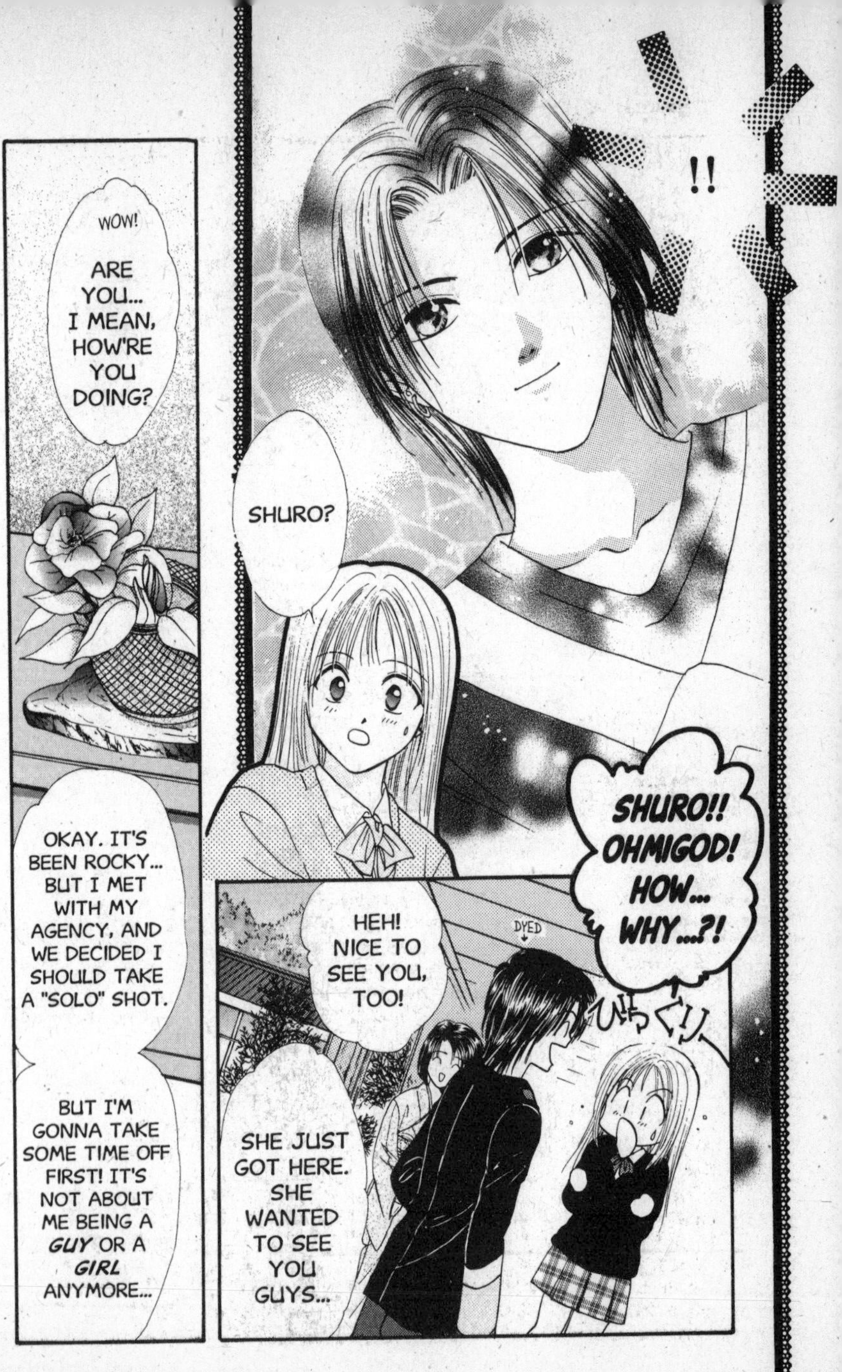
!!
SHURO?
SHURO!! OHMIGOD! HOW... WHY...?!
DYED
HEH! NICE TO SEE YOU, TOO!
SHE JUST GOT HERE. SHE WANTED TO SEE YOU GUYS...
WOW! ARE YOU... I MEAN, HOW'RE YOU DOING?
OKAY. IT'S BEEN ROCKY... BUT I MET WITH MY AGENCY, AND WE DECIDED I SHOULD TAKE A "SOLO" SHOT.
BUT I'M GONNA TAKE SOME TIME OFF FIRST! IT'S NOT ABOUT ME BEING A *GUY* OR A *GIRL* ANYMORE...

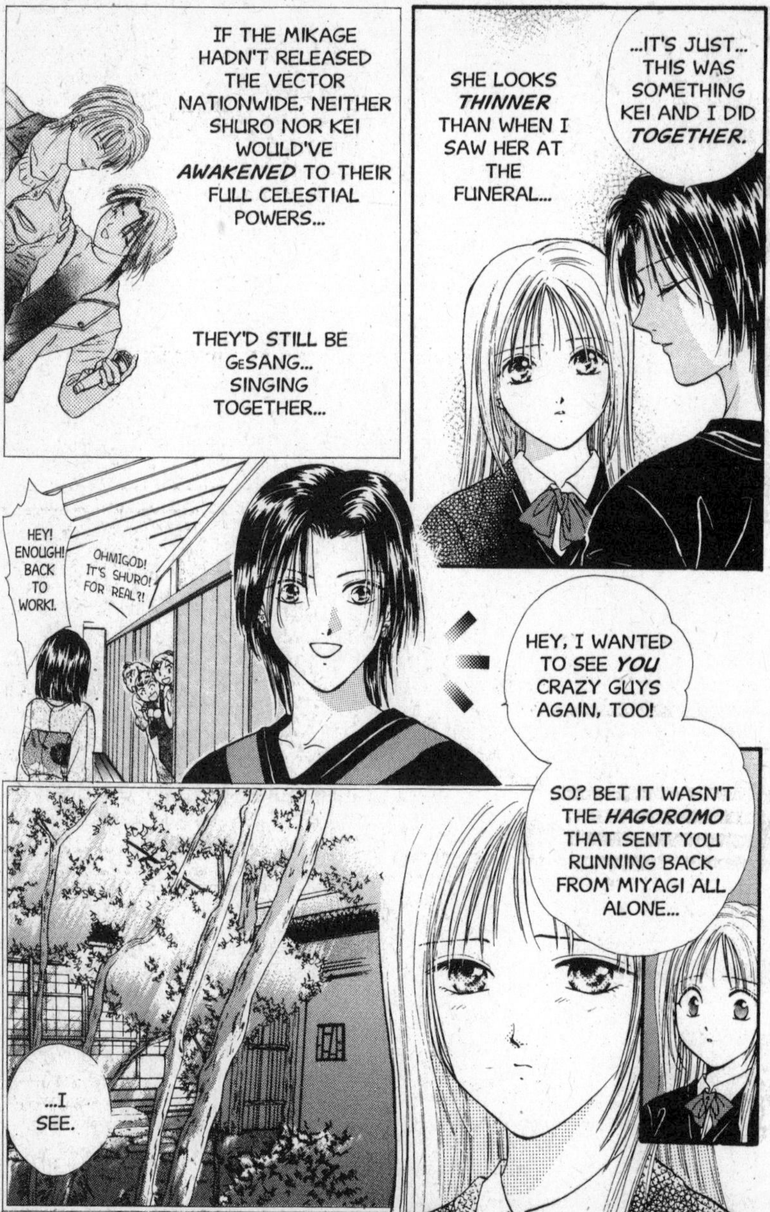
...IT'S JUST... THIS WAS SOMETHING KEI AND I DID *TOGETHER.*
SHE LOOKS *THINNER* THAN WHEN I SAW HER AT THE FUNERAL...
IF THE MIKAGE HADN'T RELEASED THE VECTOR NATIONWIDE, NEITHER SHURO NOR KEI WOULD'VE *AWAKENED* TO THEIR FULL CELESTIAL POWERS...
THEY'D STILL BE GESANG... SINGING TOGETHER...
HEY, I WANTED TO SEE *YOU* CRAZY GUYS AGAIN, TOO!
OHMIGOD! IT'S SHURO! FOR REAL?!
HEY! ENOUGH! BACK TO WORK!.
SO? BET IT WASN'T THE *HAGOROMO* THAT SENT YOU RUNNING BACK FROM MIYAGI ALL ALONE...
...I SEE.

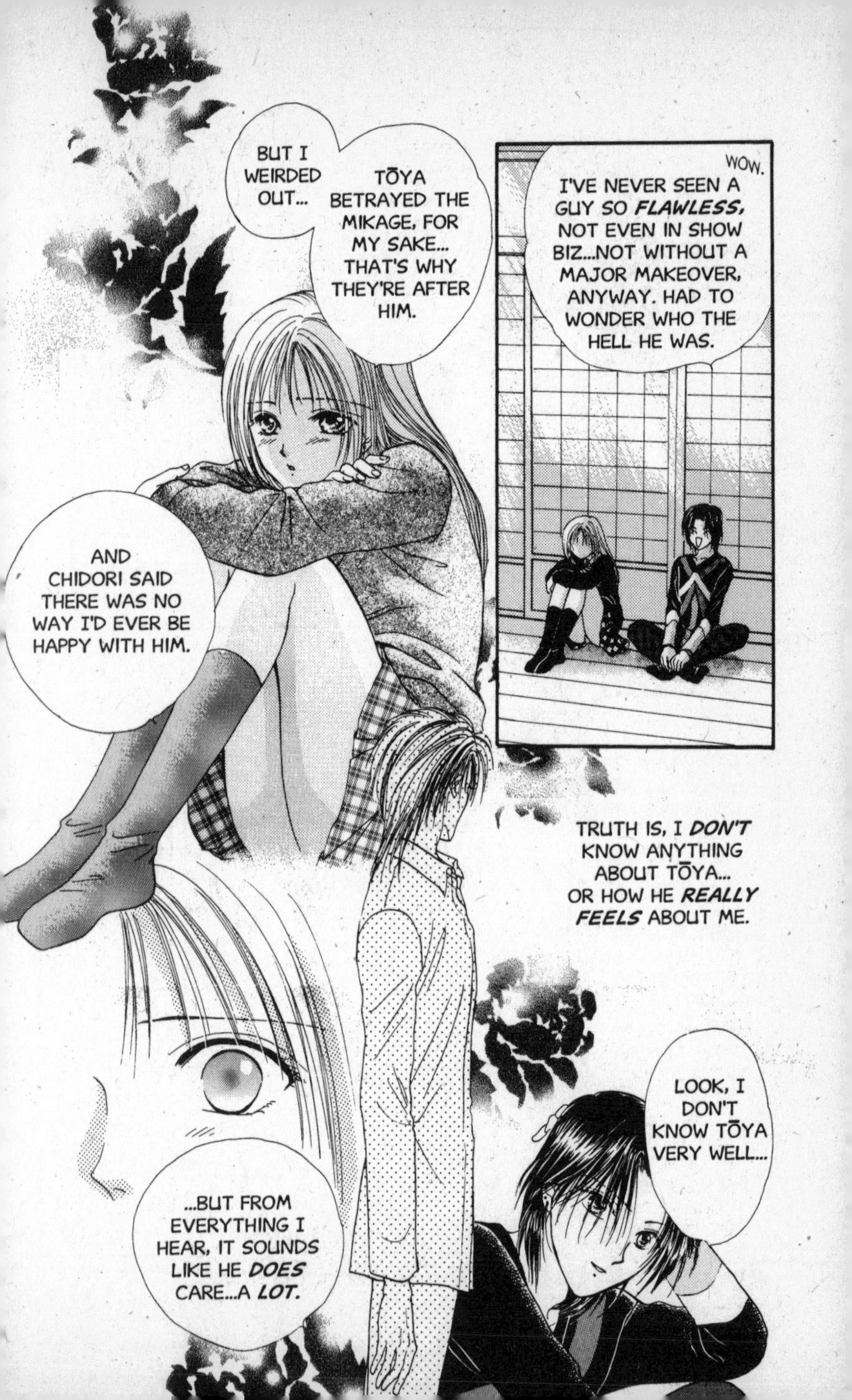
WOW.
I'VE NEVER SEEN A GUY SO ***FLAWLESS,*** NOT EVEN IN SHOW BIZ...NOT WITHOUT A MAJOR MAKEOVER, ANYWAY. HAD TO WONDER WHO THE HELL HE WAS.
TŌYA BETRAYED THE MIKAGE, FOR MY SAKE... THAT'S WHY THEY'RE AFTER HIM.
BUT I WEIRDED OUT...
AND CHIDORI SAID THERE WAS NO WAY I'D EVER BE HAPPY WITH HIM.
TRUTH IS, I ***DON'T*** KNOW ANYTHING ABOUT TŌYA... OR HOW HE ***REALLY FEELS*** ABOUT ME.
LOOK, I DON'T KNOW TŌYA VERY WELL...
...BUT FROM EVERYTHING I HEAR, IT SOUNDS LIKE HE ***DOES*** CARE...A ***LOT.***

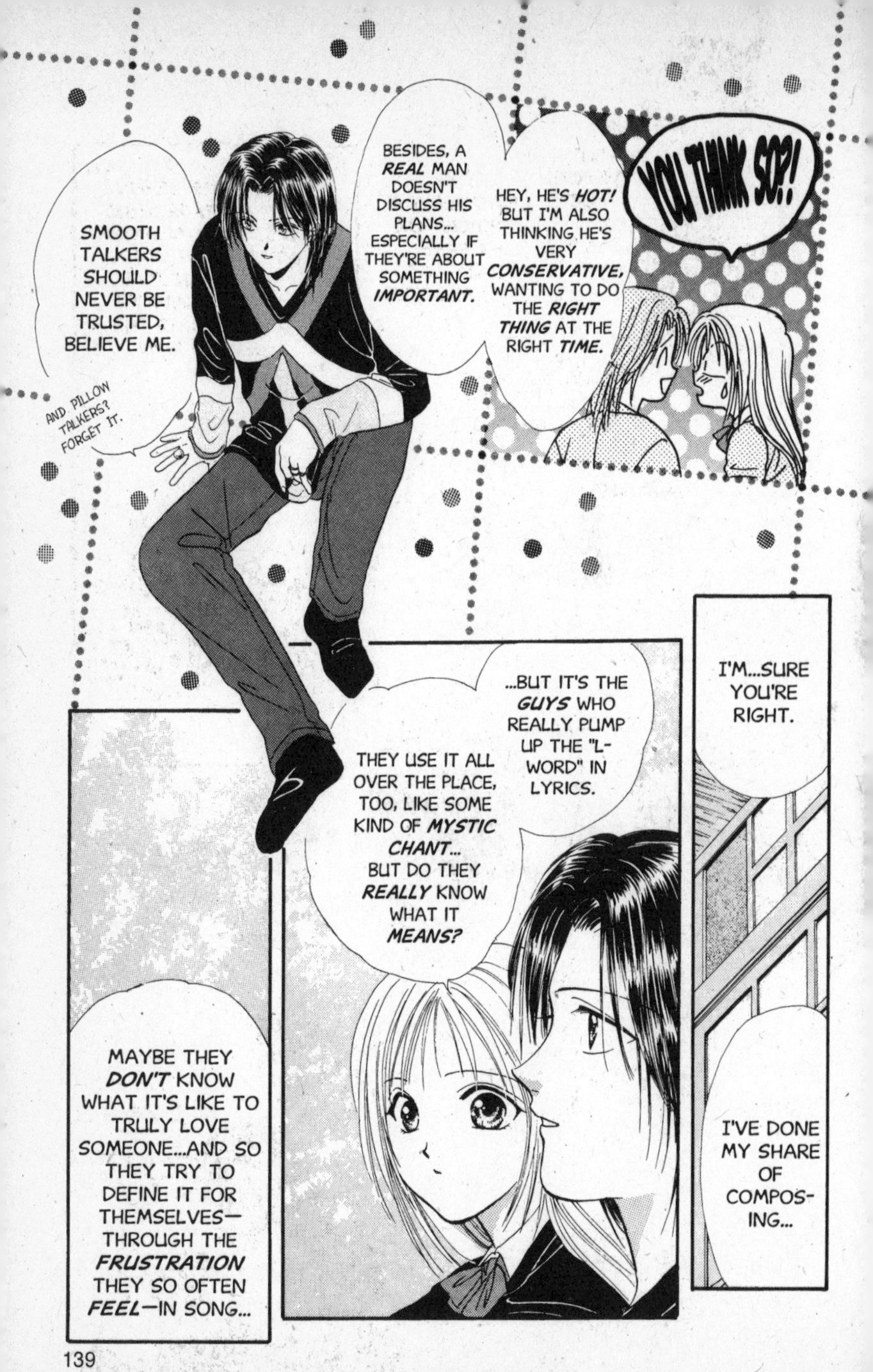
YOU THINK SO?!
HEY, HE'S HOT! BUT I'M ALSO THINKING HE'S VERY CONSERVATIVE, WANTING TO DO THE RIGHT THING AT THE RIGHT TIME.
BESIDES, A REAL MAN DOESN'T DISCUSS HIS PLANS... ESPECIALLY IF THEY'RE ABOUT SOMETHING IMPORTANT.
SMOOTH TALKERS SHOULD NEVER BE TRUSTED, BELIEVE ME.
AND PILLOW TALKERS? FORGET IT.
I'M...SURE YOU'RE RIGHT.
I'VE DONE MY SHARE OF COMPOS-ING...
...BUT IT'S THE GUYS WHO REALLY PUMP UP THE "L-WORD" IN LYRICS.
THEY USE IT ALL OVER THE PLACE, TOO, LIKE SOME KIND OF MYSTIC CHANT... BUT DO THEY REALLY KNOW WHAT IT MEANS?
MAYBE THEY DON'T KNOW WHAT IT'S LIKE TO TRULY LOVE SOMEONE...AND SO THEY TRY TO DEFINE IT FOR THEMSELVES—THROUGH THE FRUSTRATION THEY SO OFTEN FEEL—IN SONG...

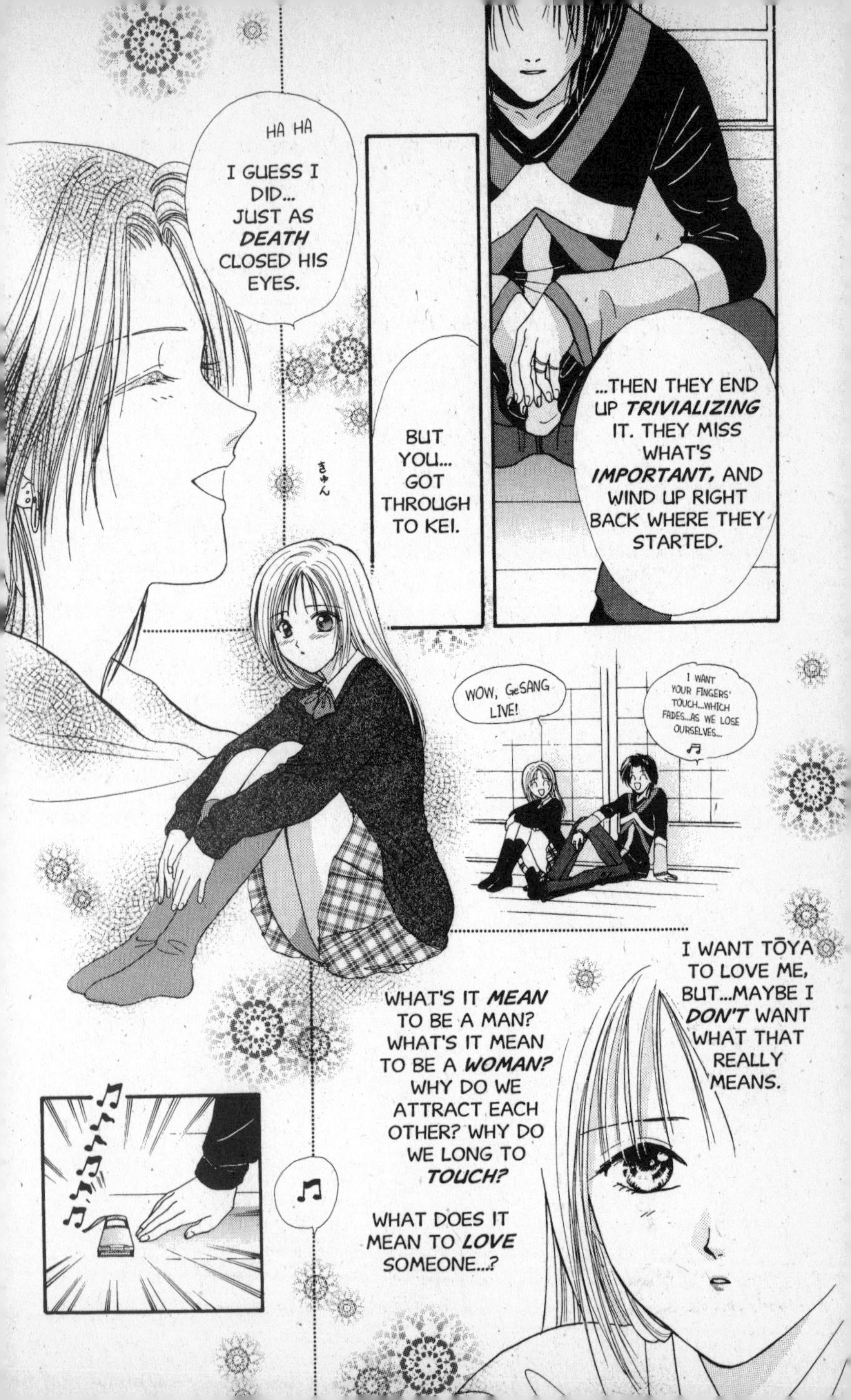
...THEN THEY END UP *TRIVIALIZING* IT. THEY MISS WHAT'S *IMPORTANT,* AND WIND UP RIGHT BACK WHERE THEY STARTED.
BUT YOU... GOT THROUGH TO KEI.
きゅん
HA HA
I GUESS I DID... JUST AS *DEATH* CLOSED HIS EYES.
I WANT YOUR FINGERS' TOUCH...WHICH FADES...AS WE LOSE OURSELVES... ♬
WOW, GeSANG LIVE!
I WANT TŌYA TO LOVE ME, BUT...MAYBE I *DON'T* WANT WHAT THAT REALLY MEANS.
WHAT'S IT *MEAN* TO BE A MAN? WHAT'S IT MEAN TO BE A *WOMAN?* WHY DO WE ATTRACT EACH OTHER? WHY DO WE LONG TO *TOUCH?*
WHAT DOES IT MEAN TO *LOVE* SOMEONE...?
♫

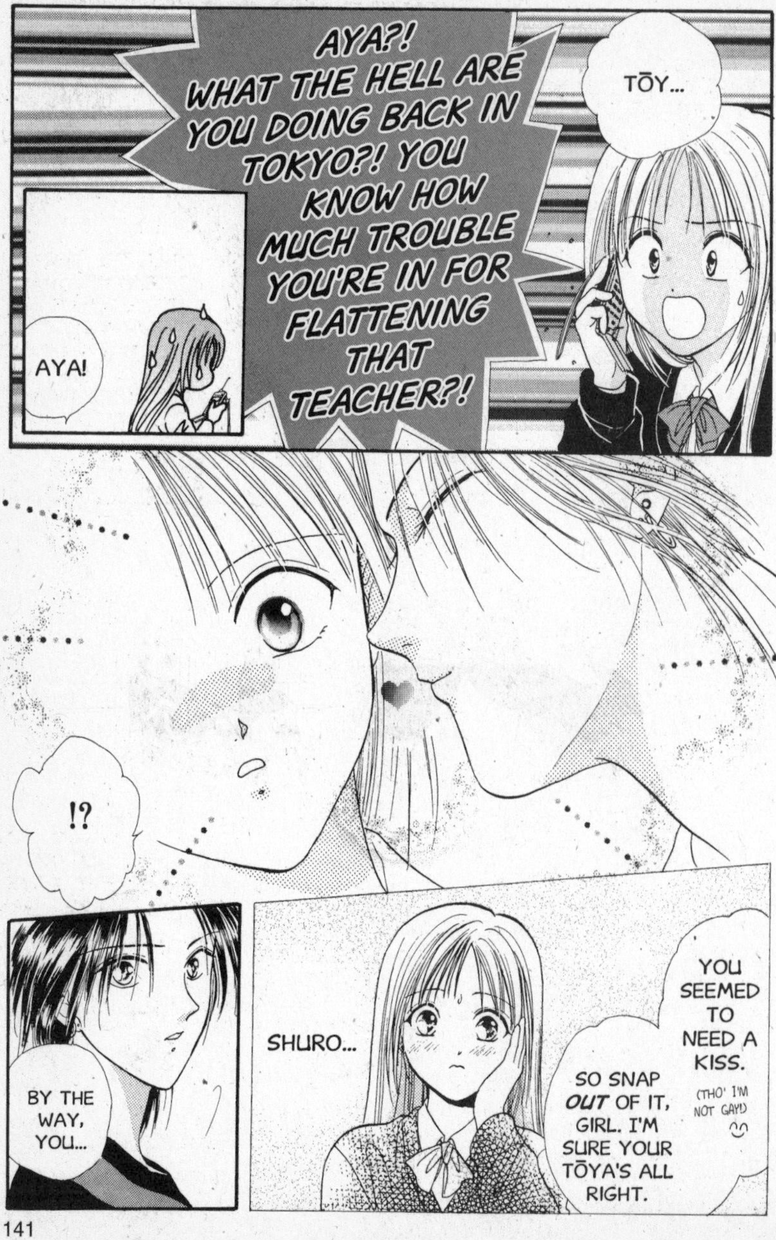
TŌY...
AYA?! WHAT THE HELL ARE YOU DOING BACK IN TOKYO?! YOU KNOW HOW MUCH TROUBLE YOU'RE IN FOR FLATTENING THAT TEACHER?!
AYA!
!?
YOU SEEMED TO NEED A KISS.
(THO' I'M NOT GAY!)
SO SNAP OUT OF IT, GIRL. I'M SURE YOUR TŌYA'S ALL RIGHT.
SHURO...
BY THE WAY, YOU...

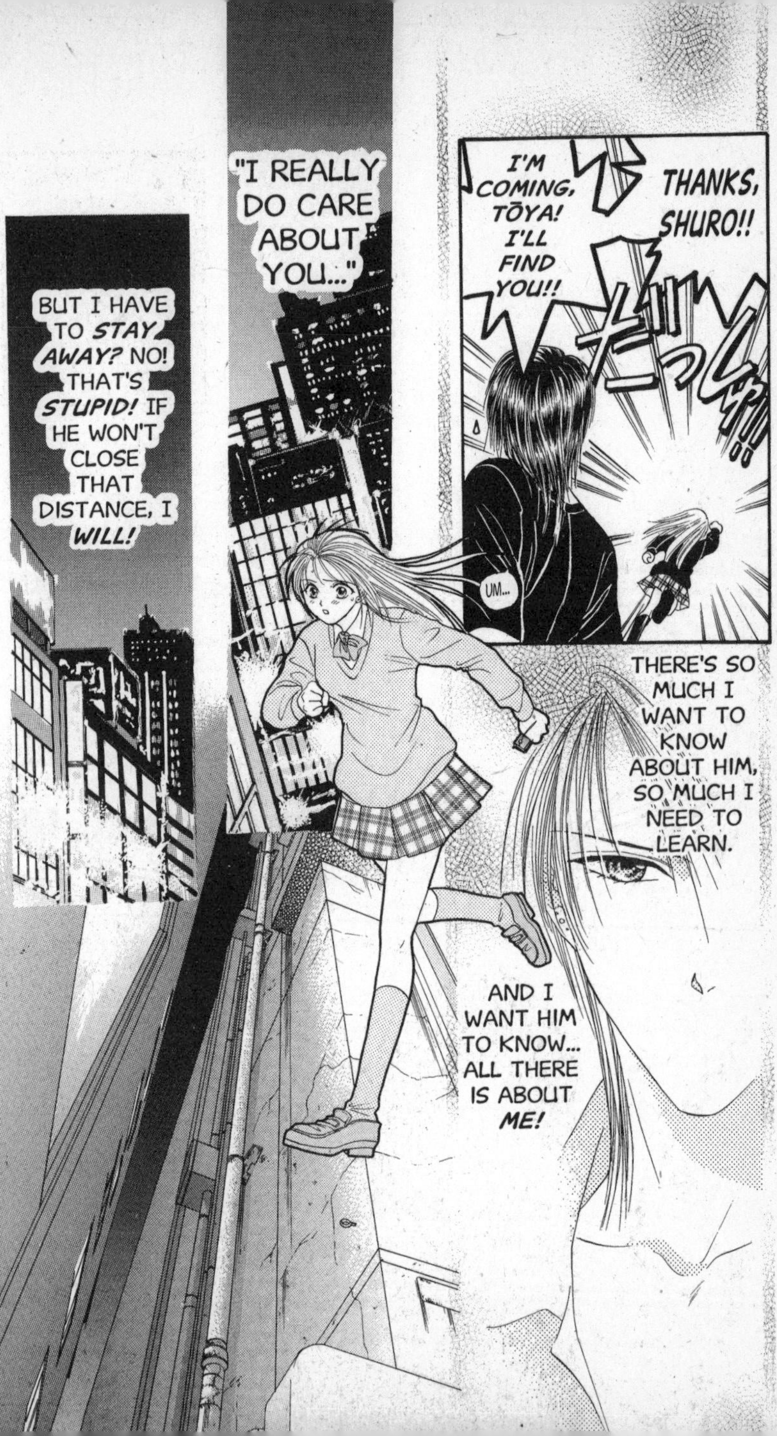
THANKS, SHURO!!
I'M COMING, TŌYA! I'LL FIND YOU!!
だーっしゅ!!!
UM...
THERE'S SO MUCH I WANT TO KNOW ABOUT HIM, SO MUCH I NEED TO LEARN.
AND I WANT HIM TO KNOW... ALL THERE IS ABOUT ME!
"I REALLY DO CARE ABOUT YOU..."
BUT I HAVE TO STAY AWAY? NO! THAT'S STUPID! IF HE WON'T CLOSE THAT DISTANCE, I WILL!

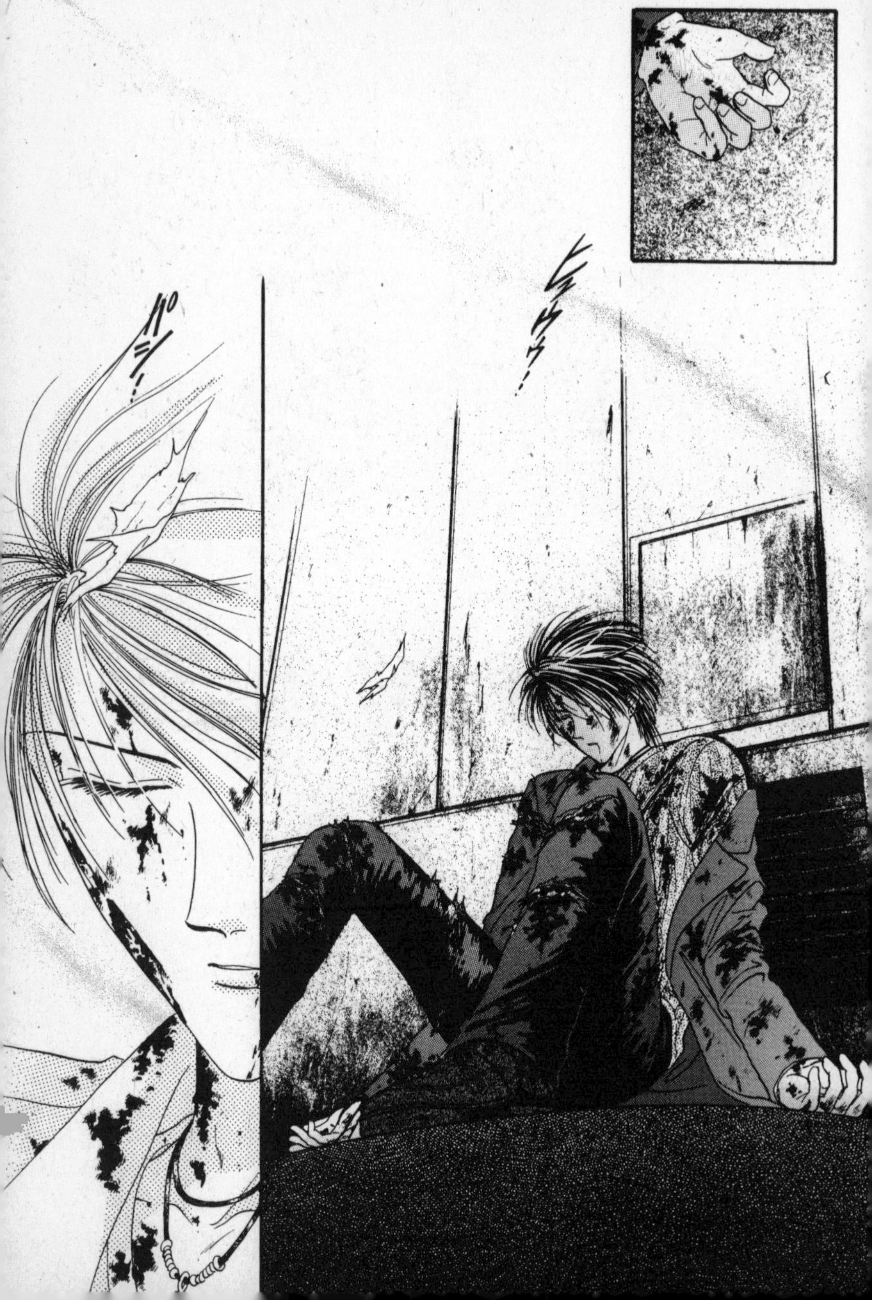
ヒュウウ…!
パシ…!

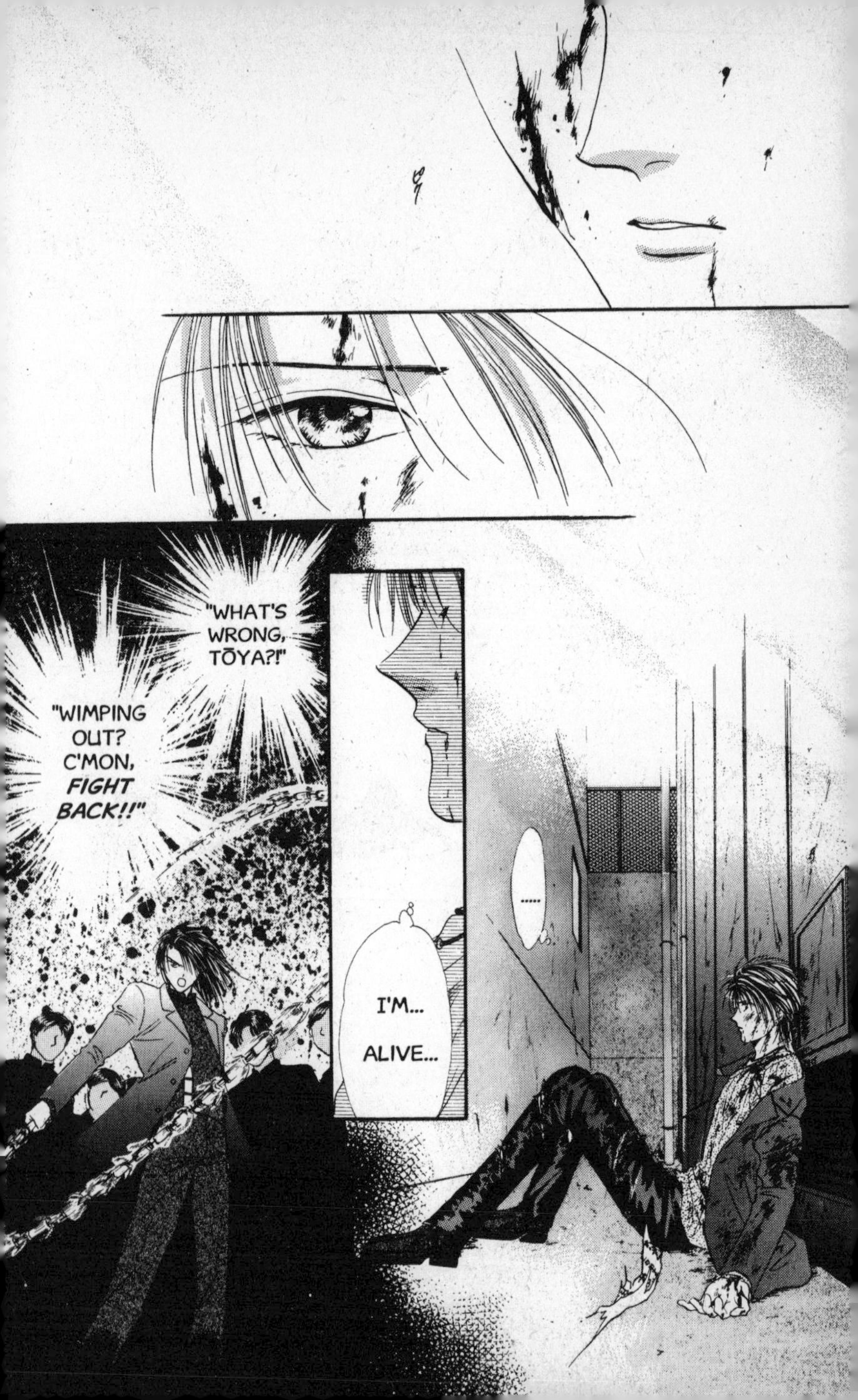
.....
I'M... ALIVE...
"WHAT'S WRONG, TŌYA?!"
"WIMPING OUT? C'MON, *FIGHT BACK!!*"

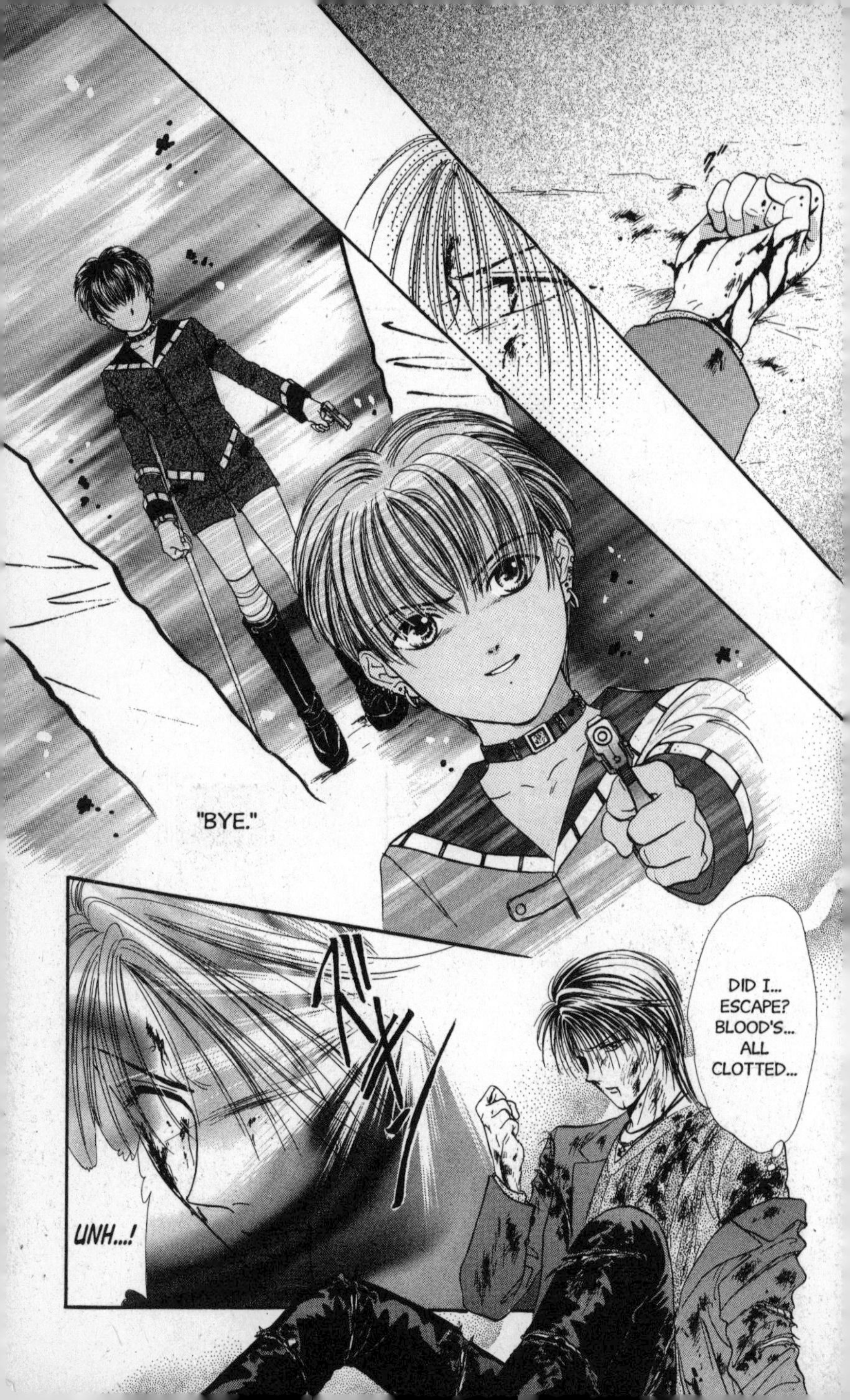
"BYE."
DID I... ESCAPE? BLOOD'S... ALL CLOTTED...
UNH...!

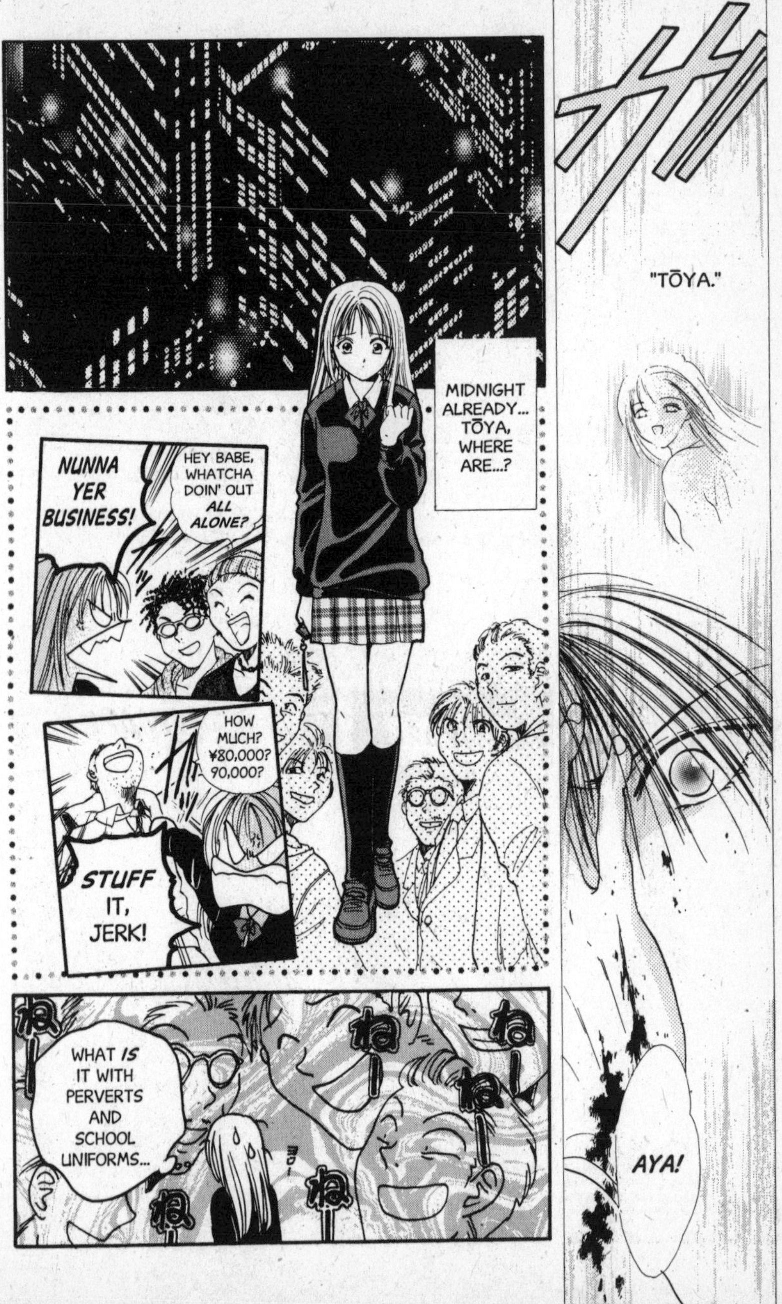
"TŌYA."
AYA!
MIDNIGHT ALREADY... TŌYA, WHERE ARE...?
HEY BABE, WHATCHA DOIN' OUT *ALL ALONE?*
NUNNA YER BUSINESS!
HOW MUCH? ¥80,000? 90,000?
STUFF IT, JERK!
WHAT *IS* IT WITH PERVERTS AND SCHOOL UNIFORMS...

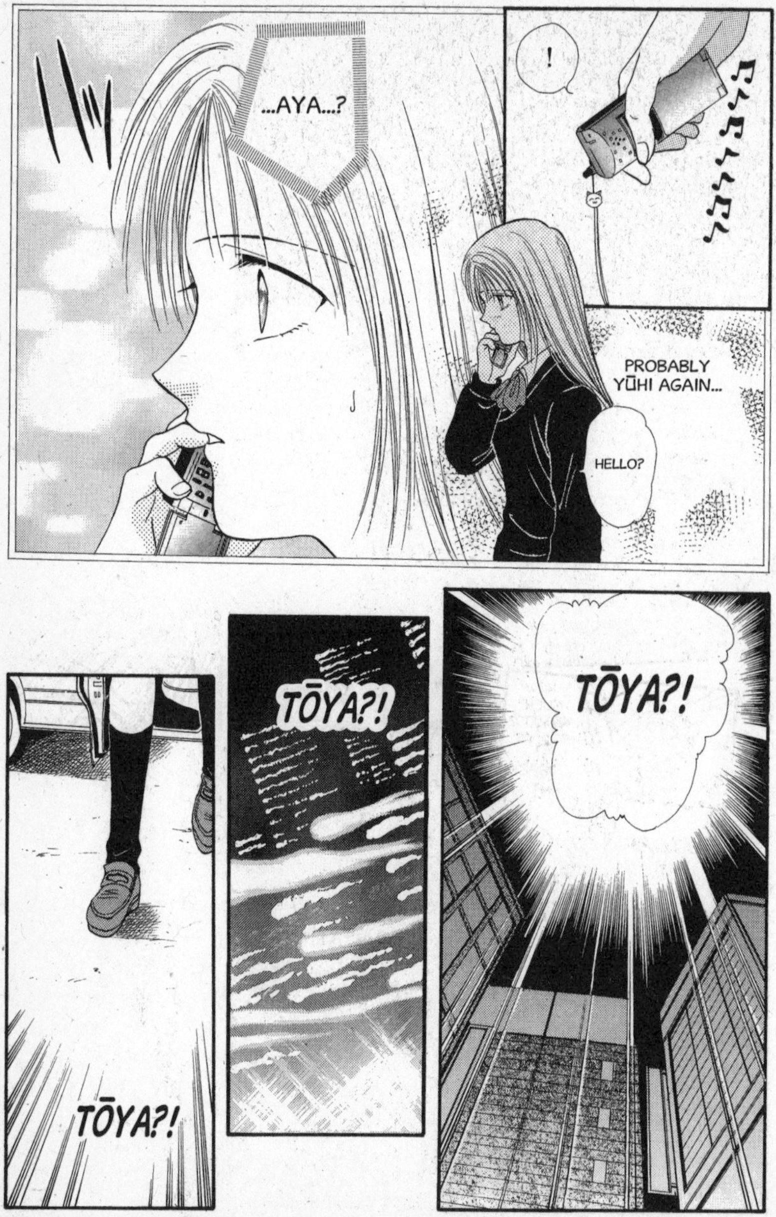
!
PROBABLY YŪHI AGAIN...
HELLO?
...AYA...?
TŌYA?!
TŌYA?!
TŌYA?!

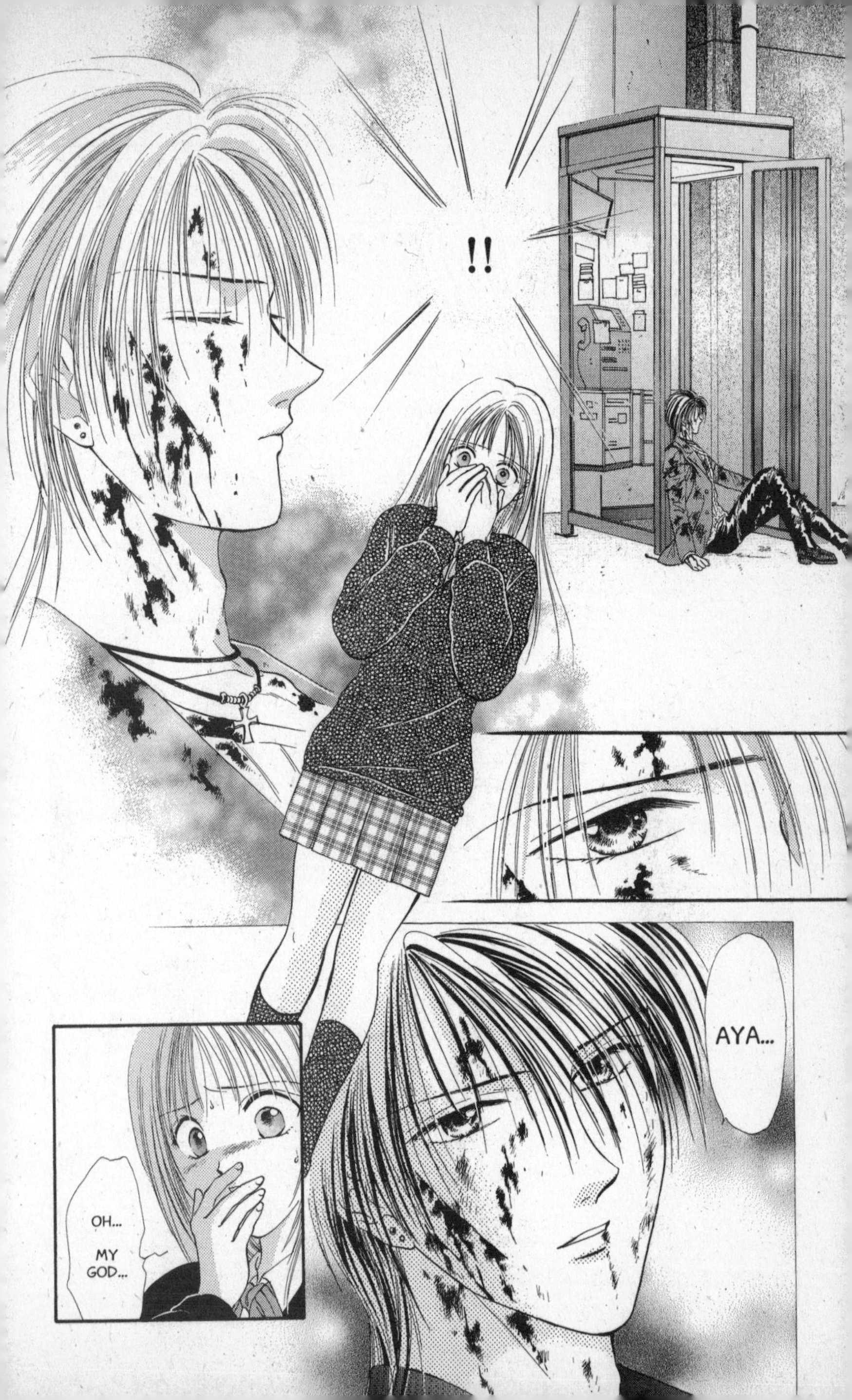
!!
AYA...
OH... MY GOD...

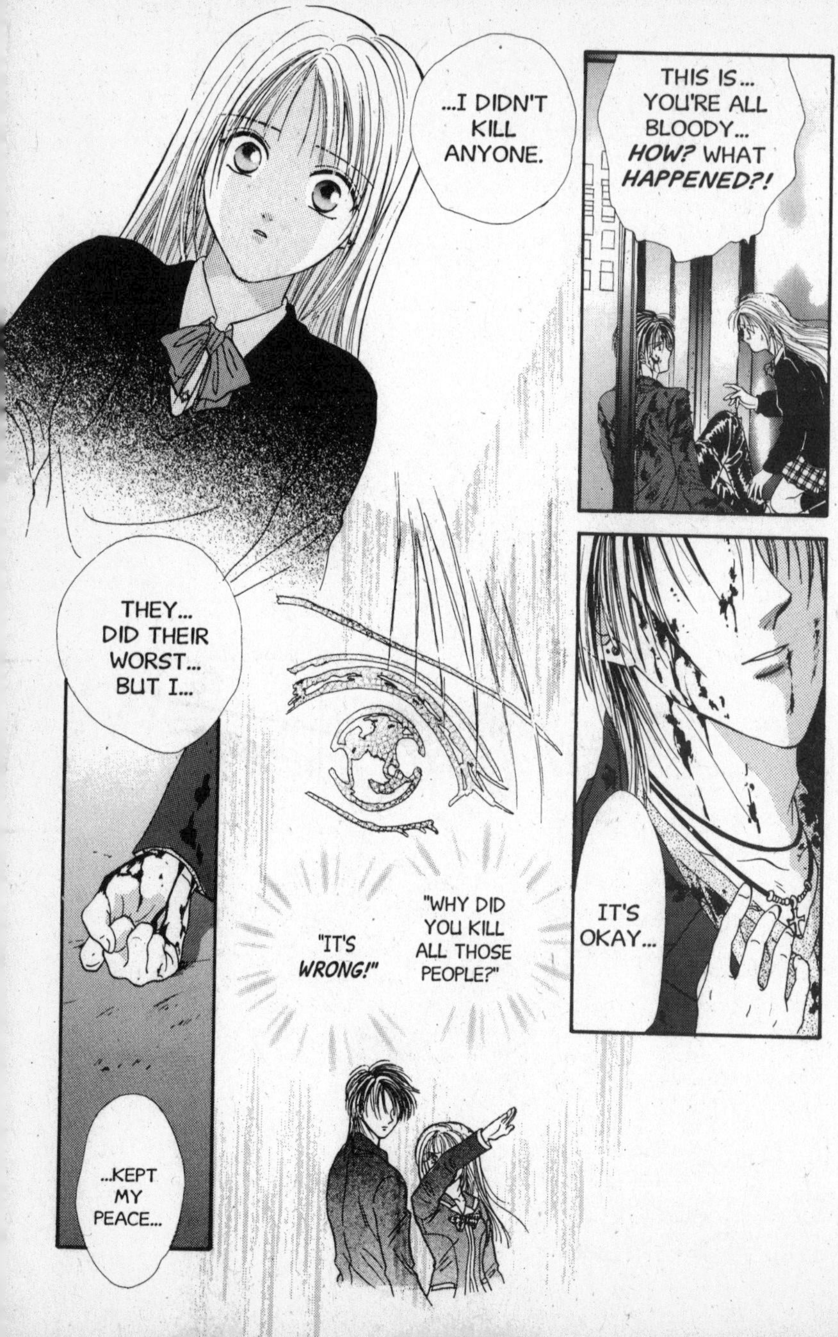
THIS IS... YOU'RE ALL BLOODY... *HOW?* WHAT *HAPPENED?!*
IT'S OKAY...
...I DIDN'T KILL ANYONE.
THEY... DID THEIR WORST... BUT I...
"WHY DID YOU KILL ALL THOSE PEOPLE?"
"IT'S *WRONG!*"
...KEPT MY PEACE...

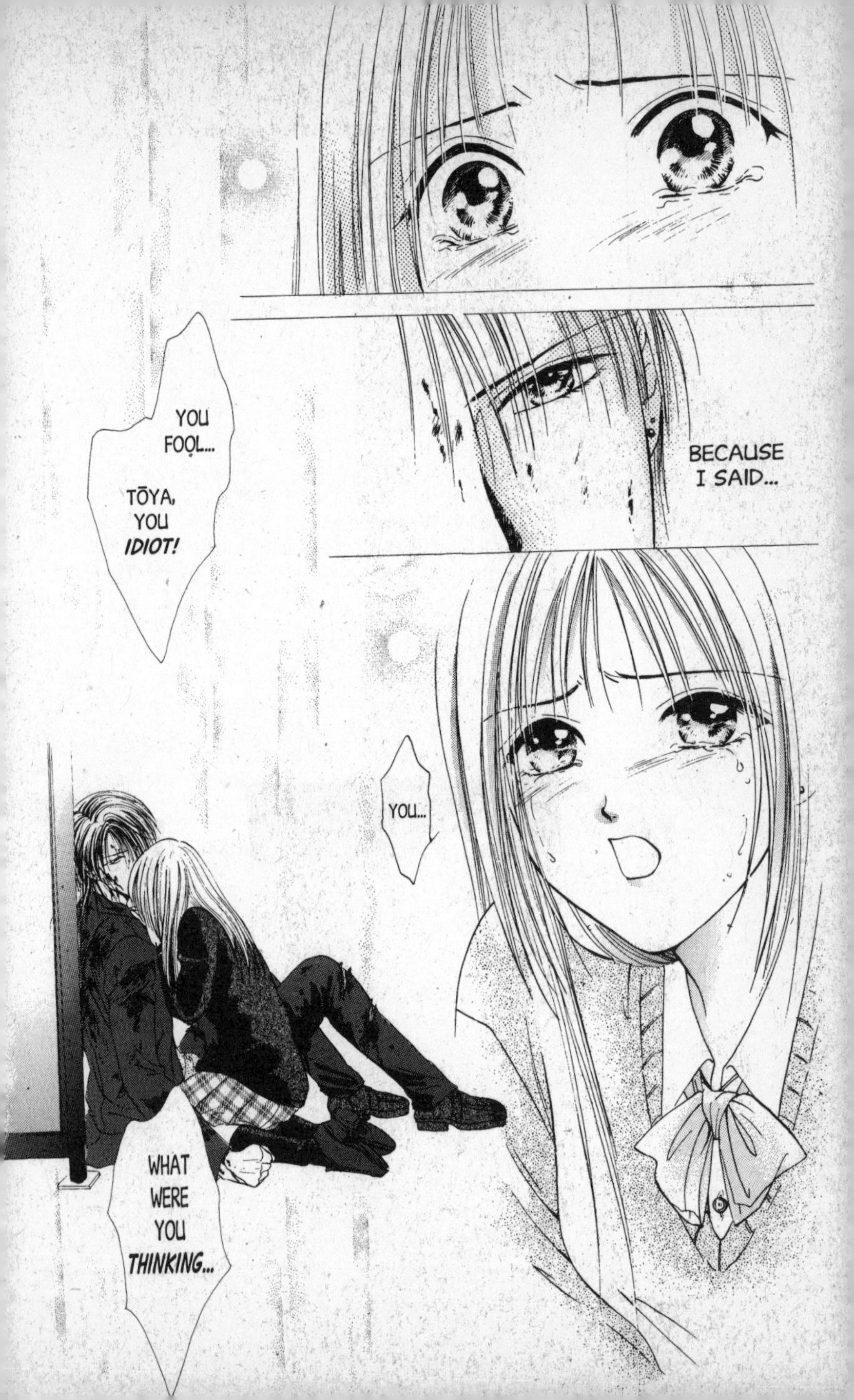
BECAUSE I SAID...
YOU FOOL... TŌYA, YOU IDIOT!
YOU...
WHAT WERE YOU THINKING...

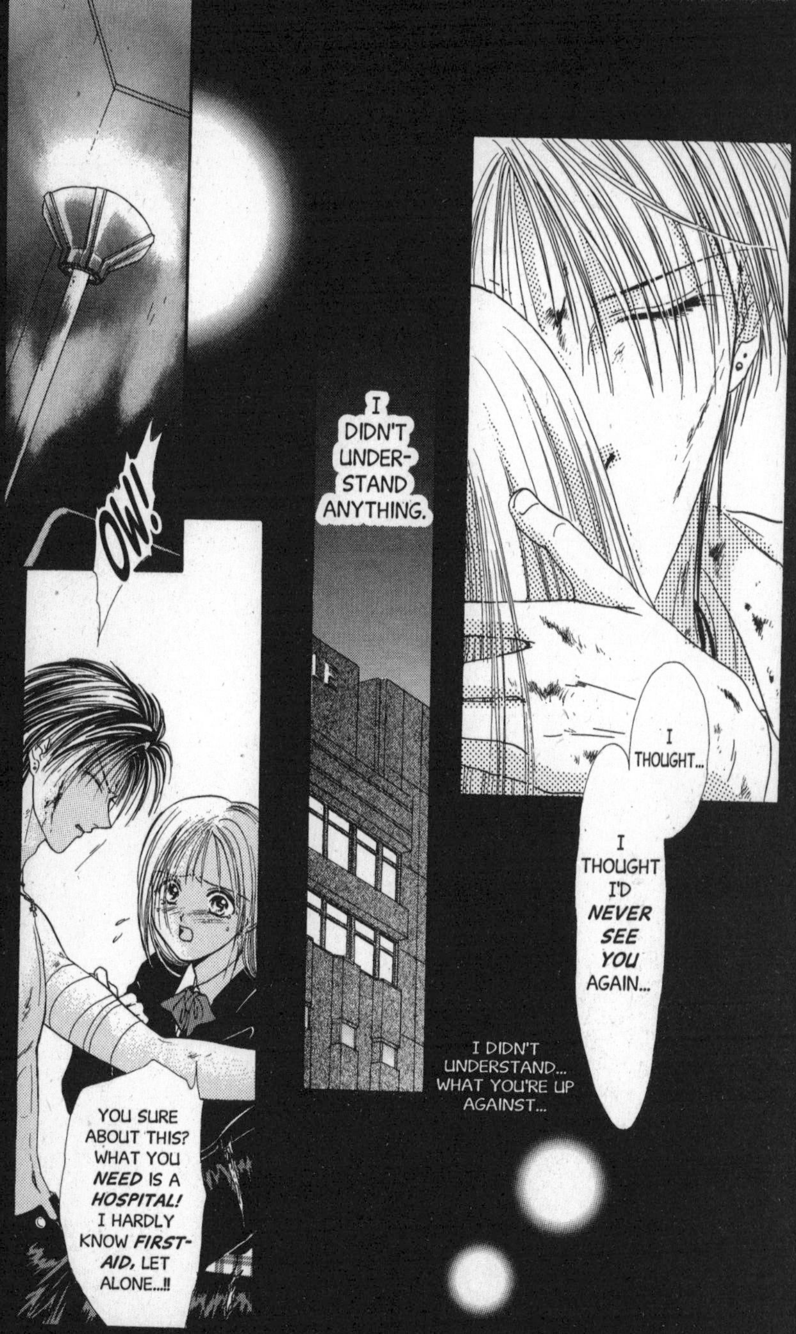
I THOUGHT...
I THOUGHT I'D NEVER SEE YOU AGAIN...
I DIDN'T UNDERSTAND... WHAT YOU'RE UP AGAINST...
I DIDN'T UNDER-STAND ANYTHING.
OW!
YOU SURE ABOUT THIS? WHAT YOU NEED IS A HOSPITAL! I HARDLY KNOW FIRST-AID, LET ALONE...!!

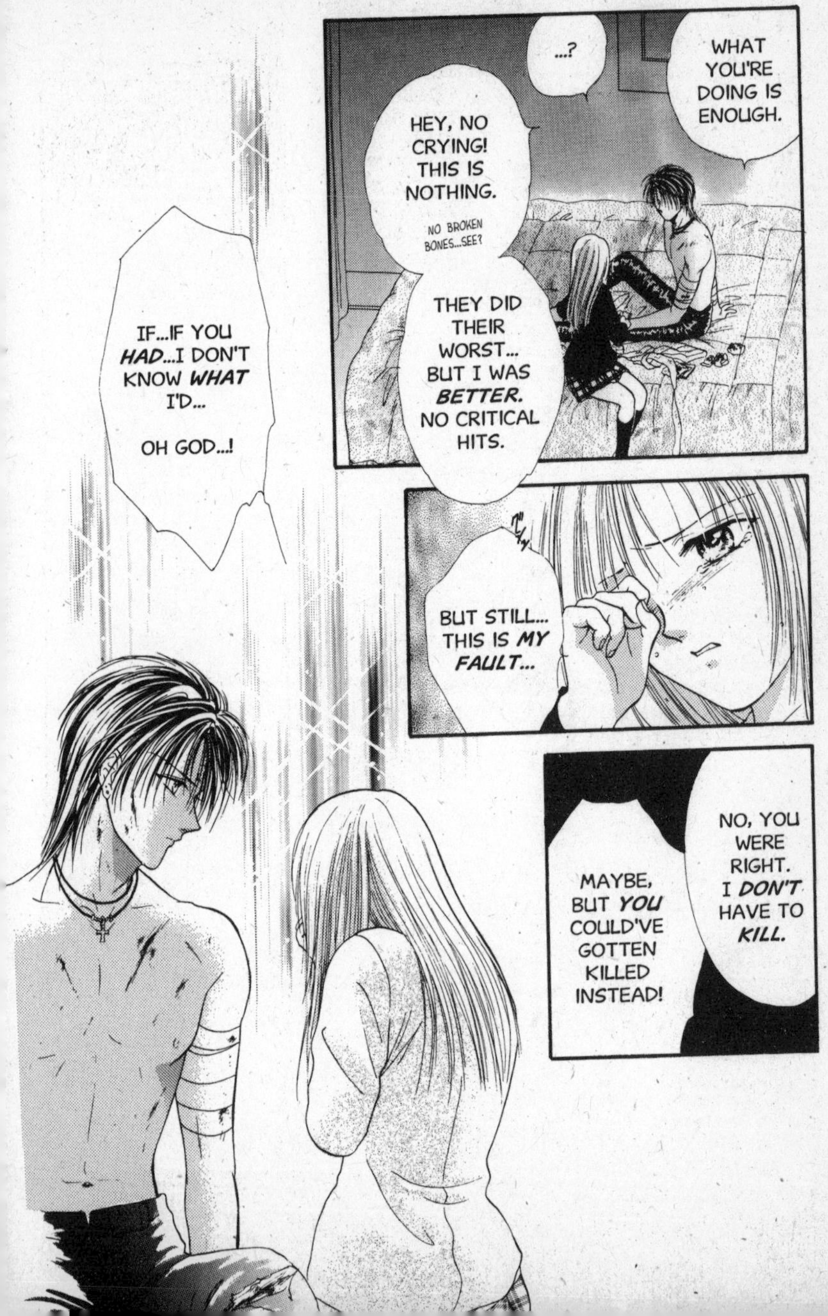
WHAT YOU'RE DOING IS ENOUGH.
...?
HEY, NO CRYING! THIS IS NOTHING.
NO BROKEN BONES...SEE?
THEY DID THEIR WORST... BUT I WAS *BETTER.* NO CRITICAL HITS.
BUT STILL... THIS IS *MY FAULT*...
NO, YOU WERE RIGHT. I *DON'T* HAVE TO *KILL.*
MAYBE, BUT *YOU* COULD'VE GOTTEN KILLED INSTEAD!
IF...IF YOU *HAD*...I DON'T KNOW *WHAT* I'D...
OH GOD...!

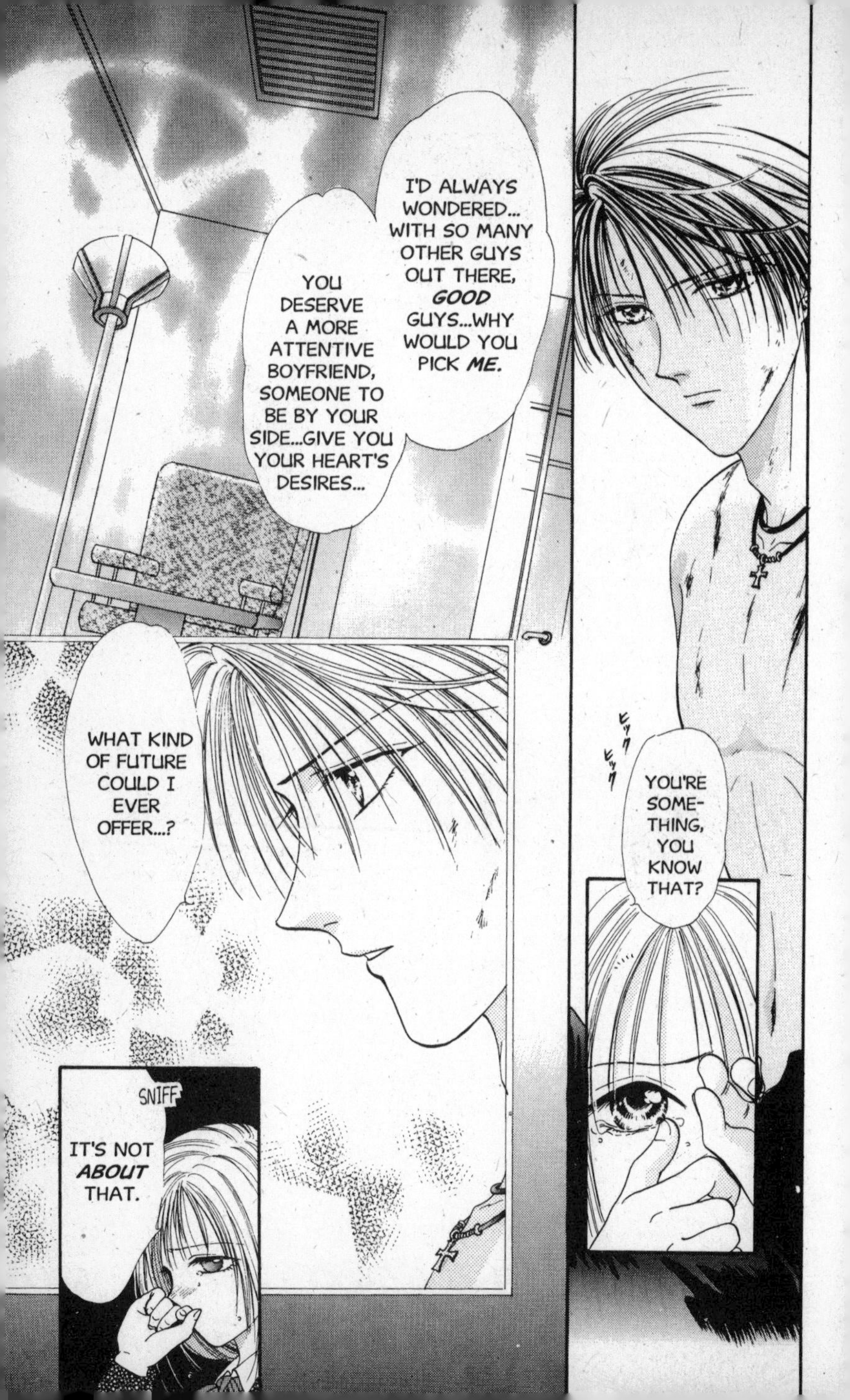
ヒック
ヒック
YOU'RE SOME-THING, YOU KNOW THAT?
I'D ALWAYS WONDERED... WITH SO MANY OTHER GUYS OUT THERE, *GOOD* GUYS...WHY WOULD YOU PICK *ME*.
YOU DESERVE A MORE ATTENTIVE BOYFRIEND, SOMEONE TO BE BY YOUR SIDE...GIVE YOU YOUR HEART'S DESIRES...
WHAT KIND OF FUTURE COULD I EVER OFFER...?
SNIFF
IT'S NOT *ABOUT* THAT.

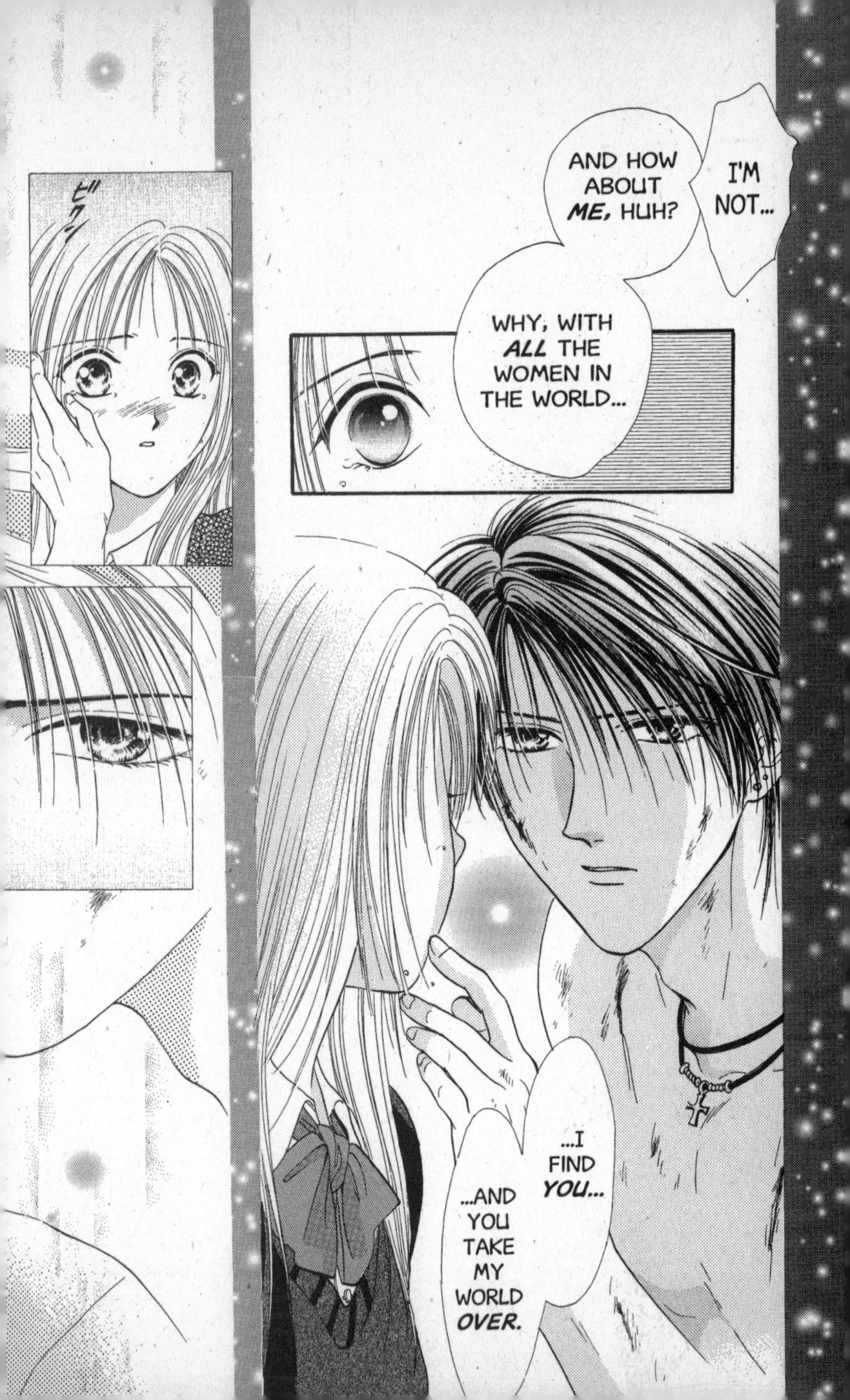
I'M NOT...
AND HOW ABOUT ME, HUH?
WHY, WITH ALL THE WOMEN IN THE WORLD...
...I FIND YOU...
...AND YOU TAKE MY WORLD OVER.
ビクッ

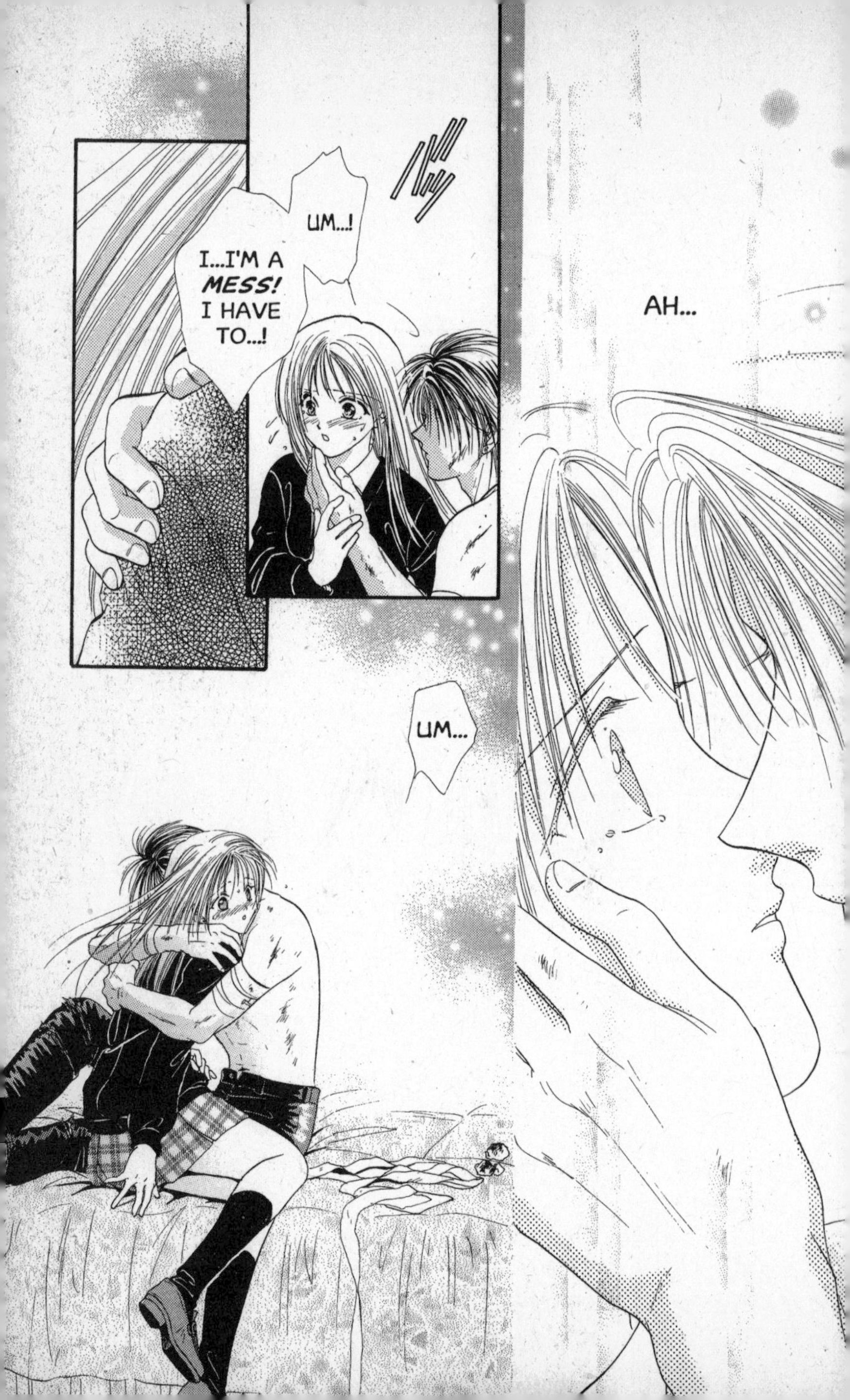

AH...
UM...!
I...I'M A MESS! I HAVE TO...!
UM...

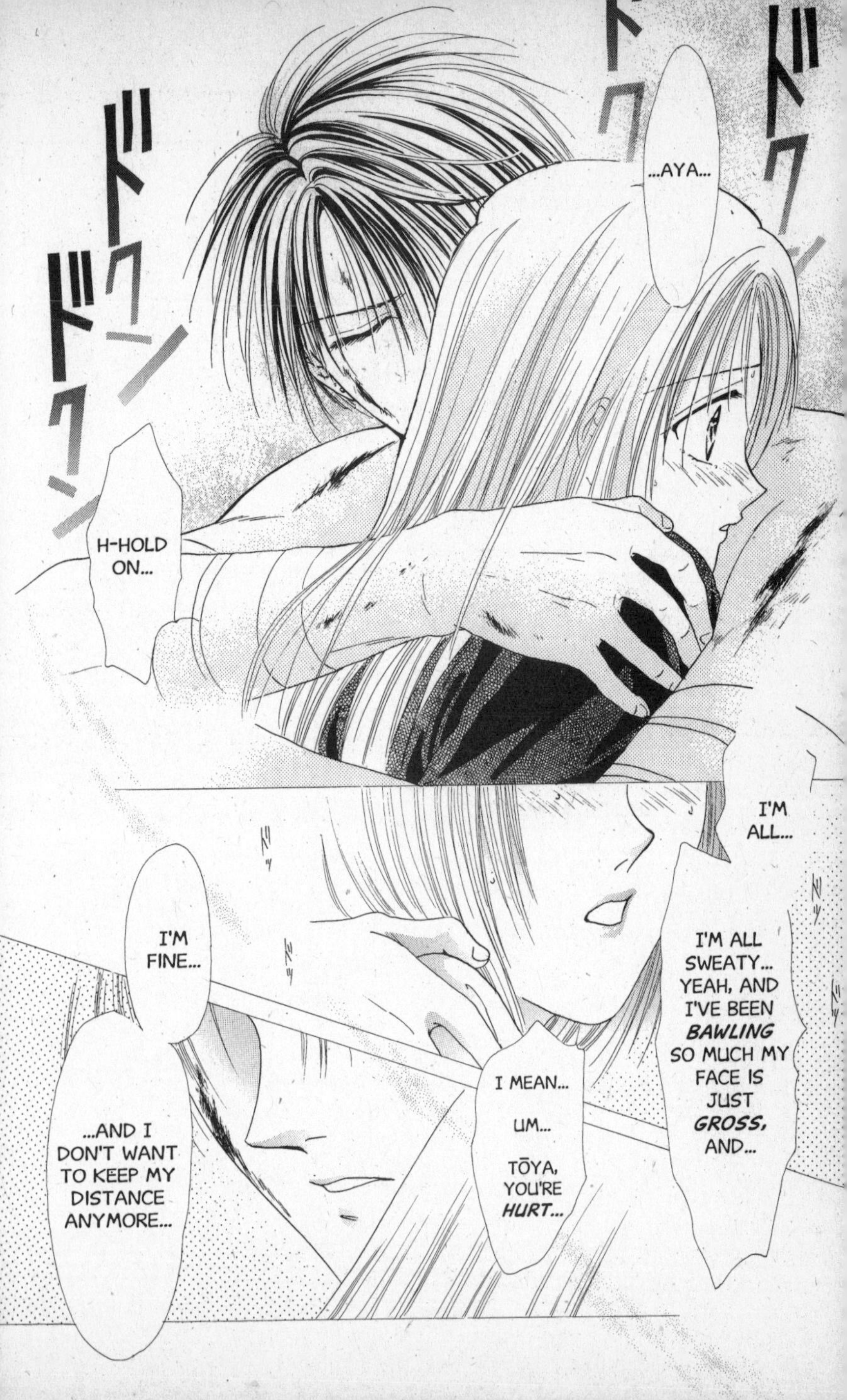
ドクン
ドクン
...AYA...
ドクン
ドクン
H-HOLD ON...
I'M ALL...
I'M ALL SWEATY... YEAH, AND I'VE BEEN *BAWLING* SO MUCH MY FACE IS JUST *GROSS,* AND...
I MEAN... UM... TŌYA, YOU'RE *HURT*...
I'M FINE...
...AND I DON'T WANT TO KEEP MY DISTANCE ANYMORE...

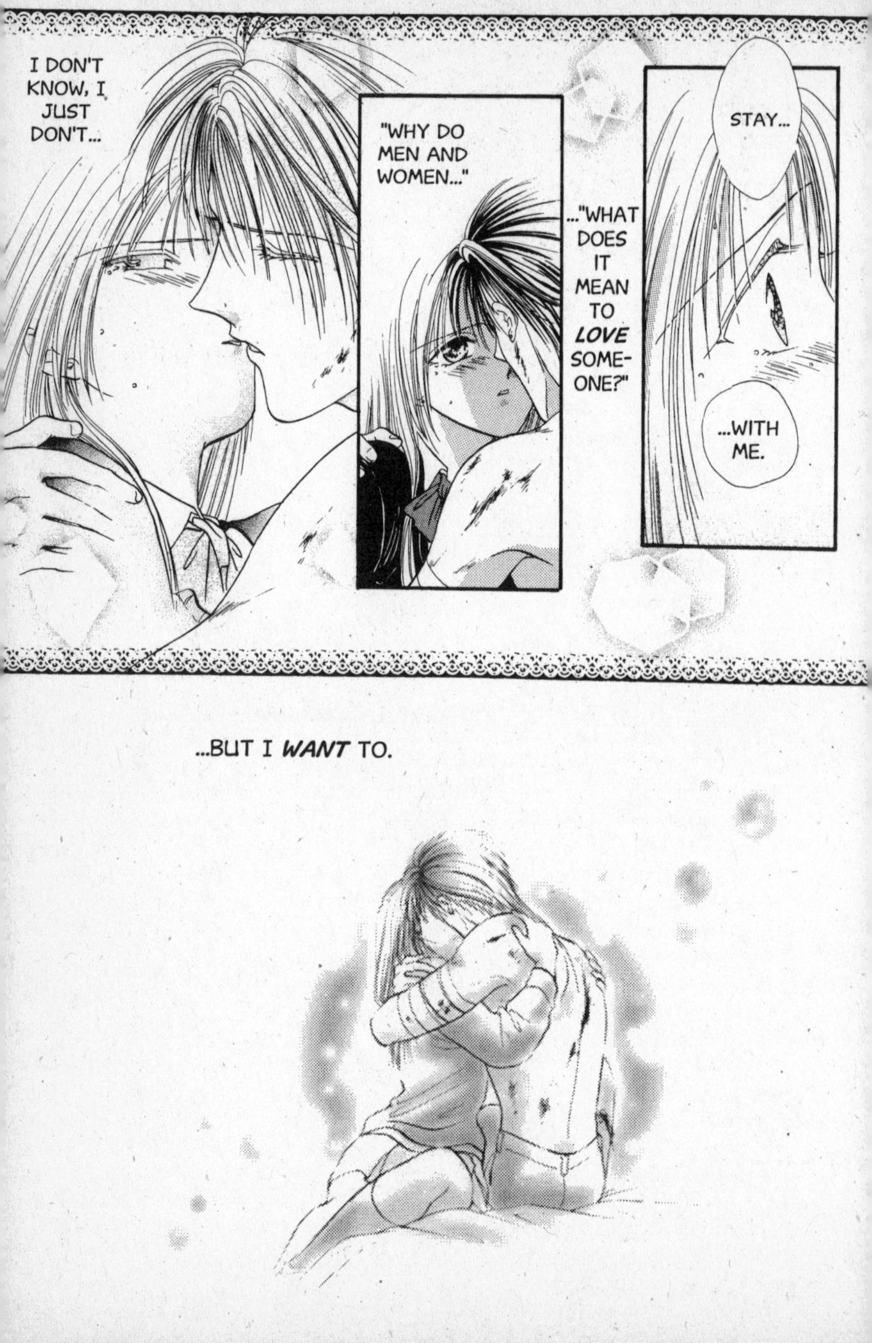
STAY...
...WITH ME.
"WHY DO MEN AND WOMEN..."
..."WHAT DOES IT MEAN TO *LOVE* SOMEONE?"
I DON'T KNOW, I JUST DON'T...
...BUT I *WANT* TO.

SHOW ME.

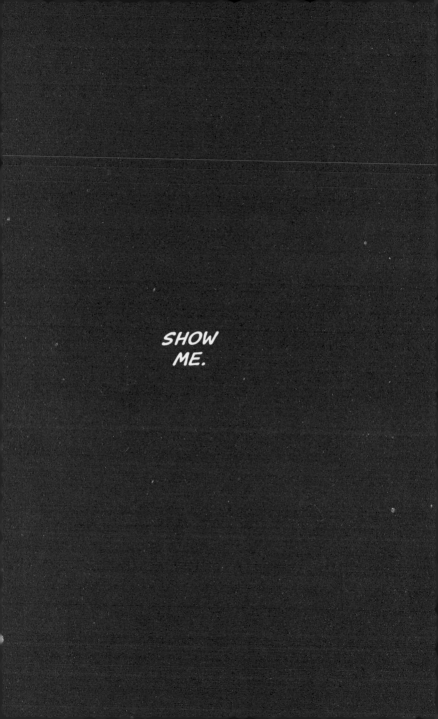

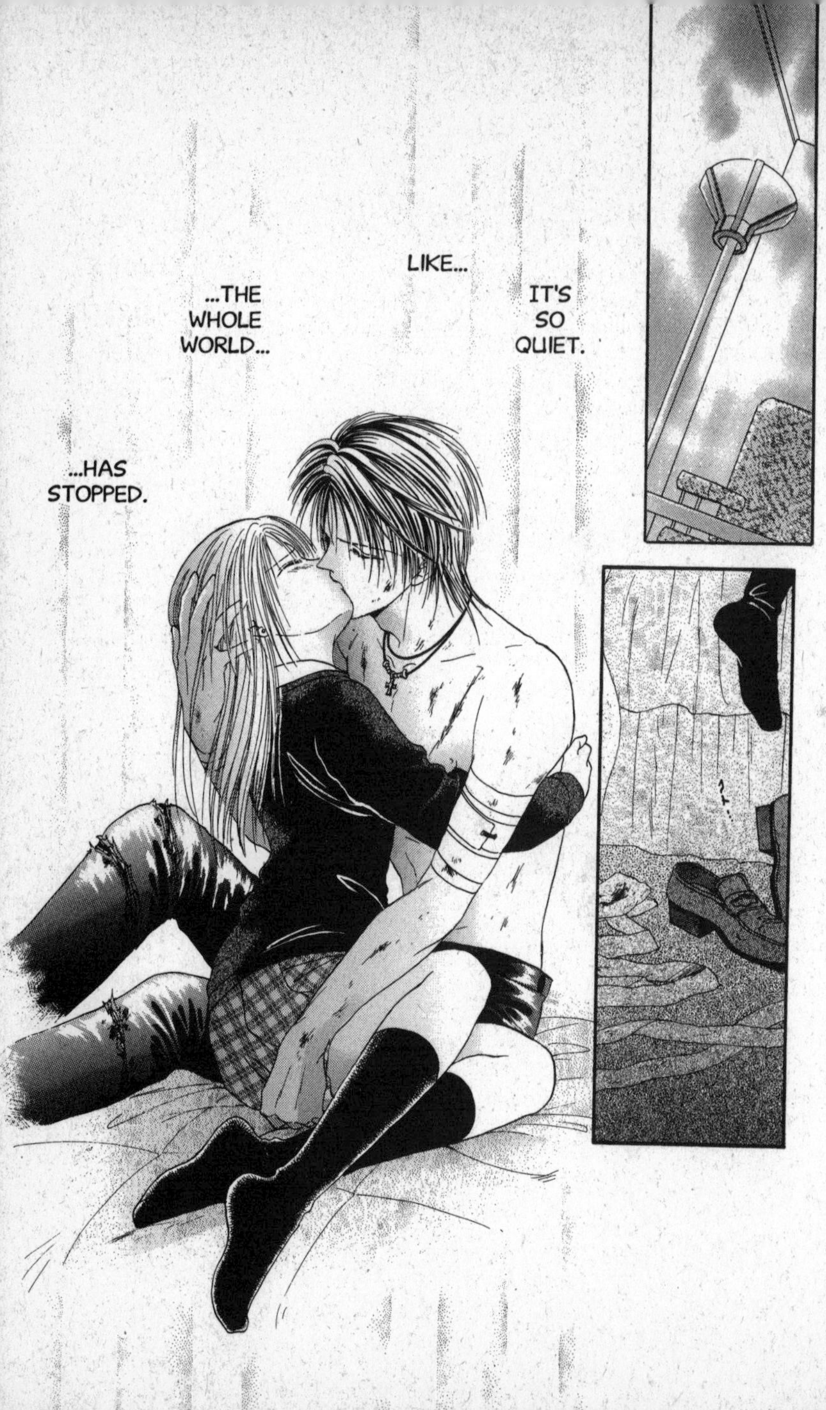
IT'S SO QUIET.
LIKE...
...THE WHOLE WORLD...
...HAS STOPPED.

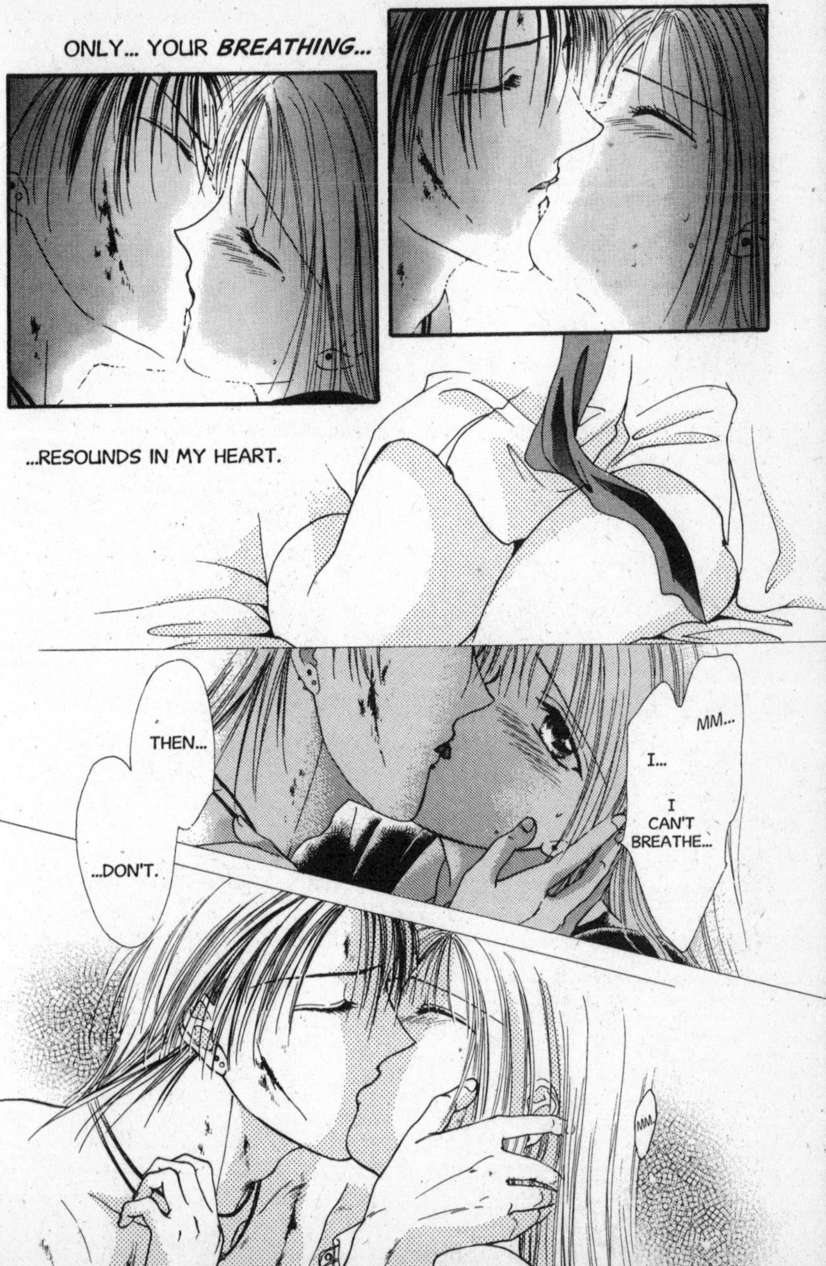
ONLY... YOUR BREATHING...
...RESOUNDS IN MY HEART.
MM...
I...
I CAN'T BREATHE...
THEN...
...DON'T.
MM.

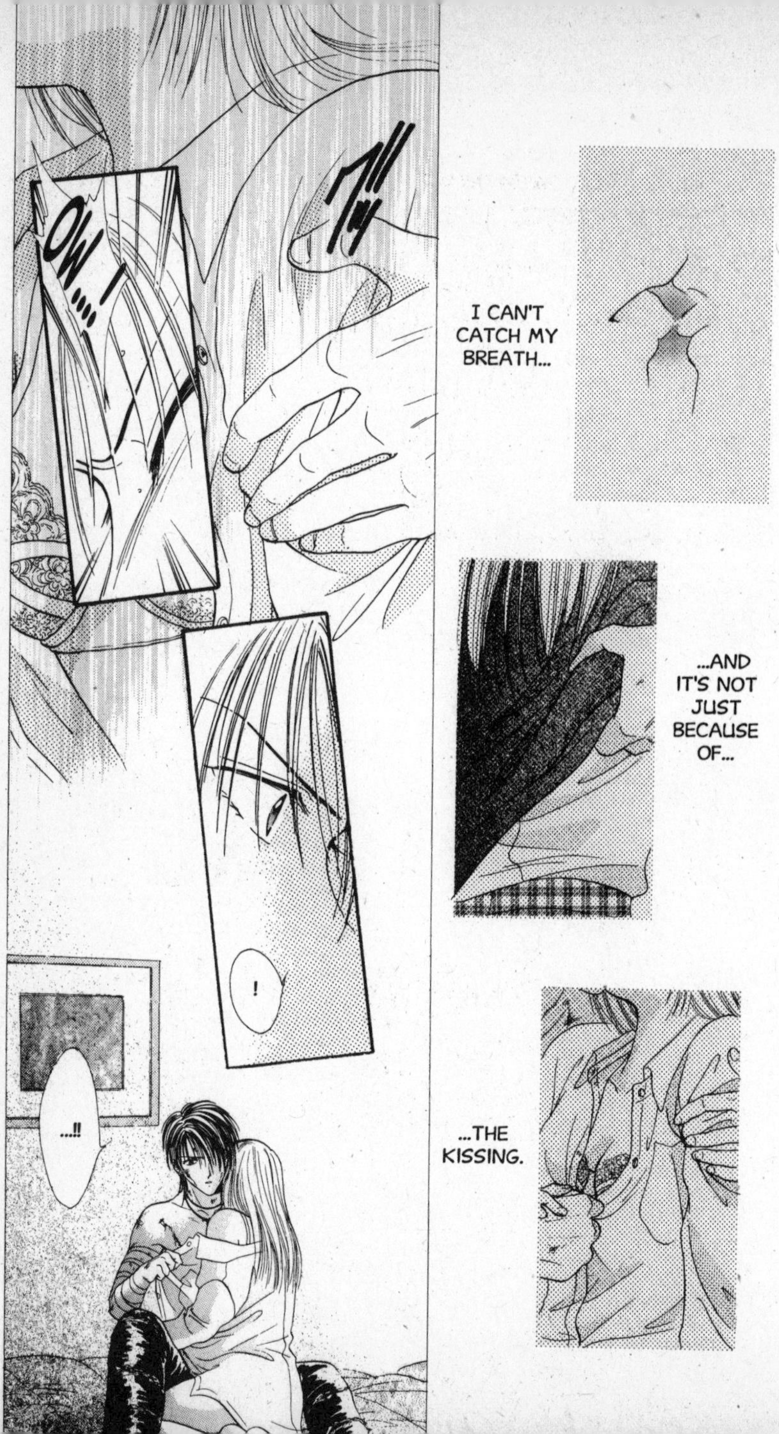
I CAN'T CATCH MY BREATH...
...AND IT'S NOT JUST BECAUSE OF...
...THE KISSING.
OW...!
!
...!!

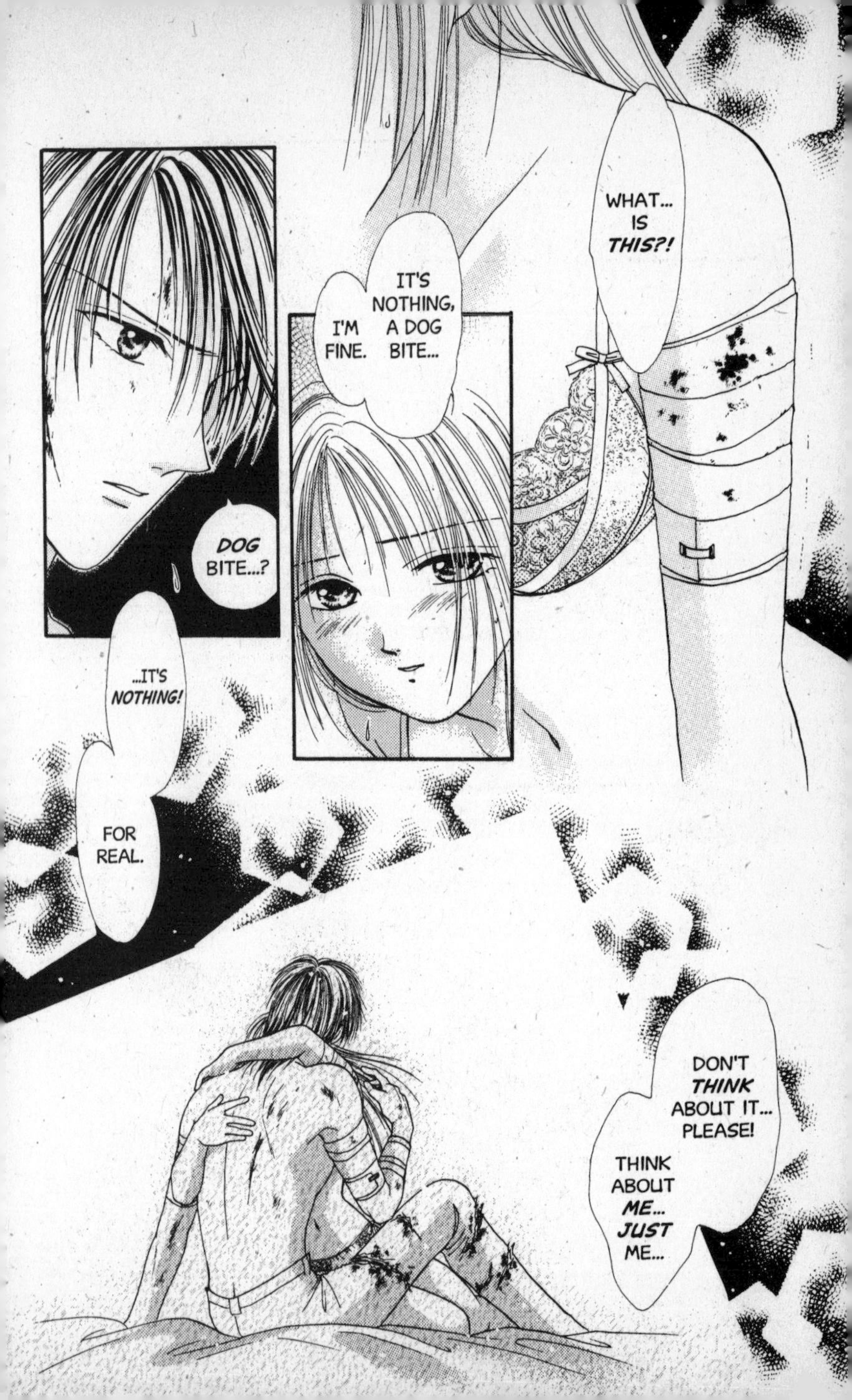
WHAT... IS *THIS?!*
IT'S NOTHING, A DOG BITE...
I'M FINE.
DOG BITE...?
...IT'S *NOTHING!*
FOR REAL.
DON'T *THINK* ABOUT IT... PLEASE!
THINK ABOUT *ME... JUST* ME...

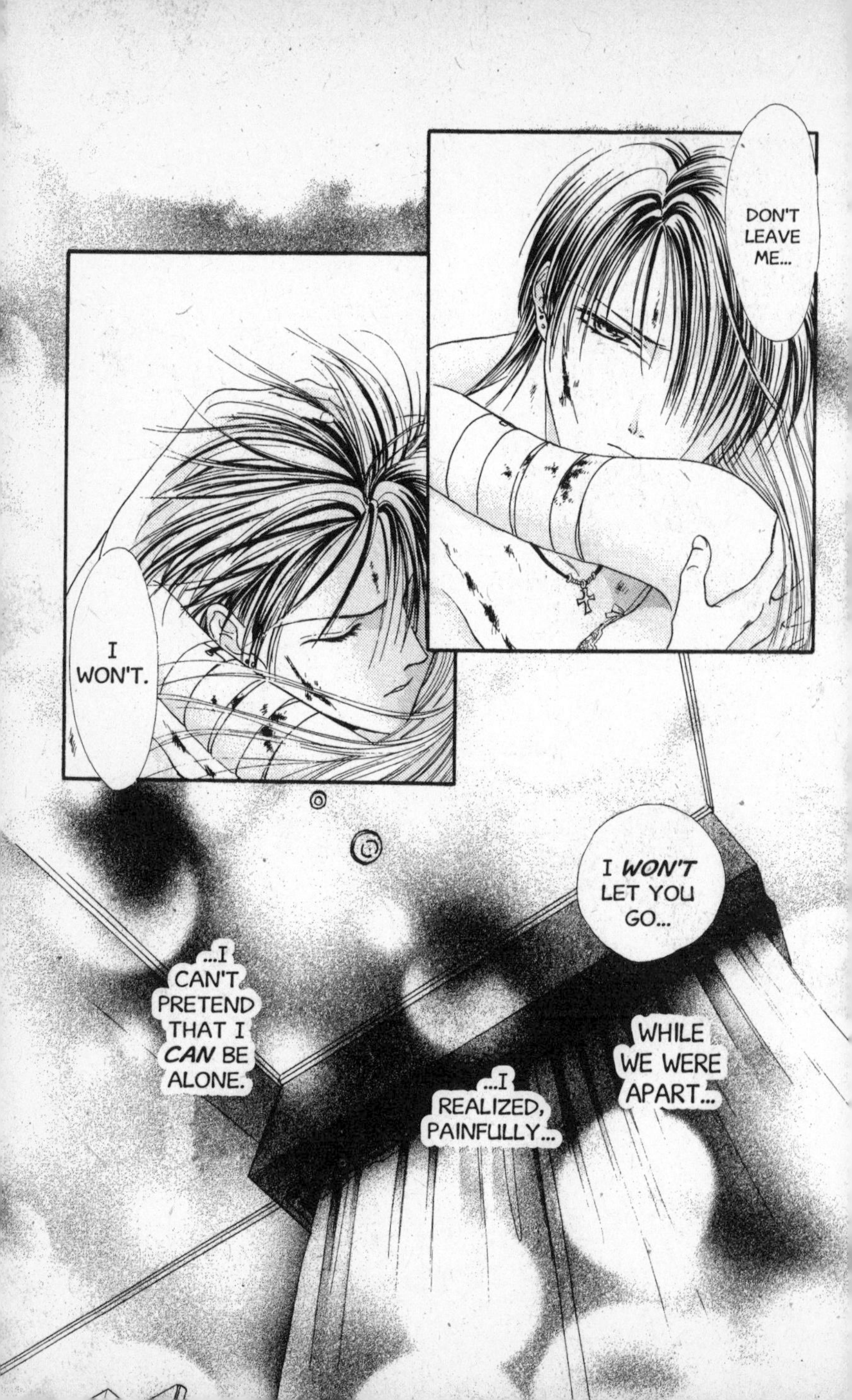
DON'T LEAVE ME...
I WON'T.
I *WON'T* LET YOU GO...
WHILE WE WERE APART...
...I REALIZED, PAINFULLY...
...I CAN'T PRETEND THAT I *CAN* BE ALONE.

kisses raining

breath mingling

limbs entwining

throat tightening

bodies melting

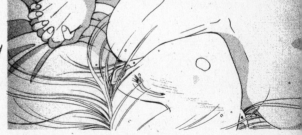

warmth piercing

sweet pain diffusing

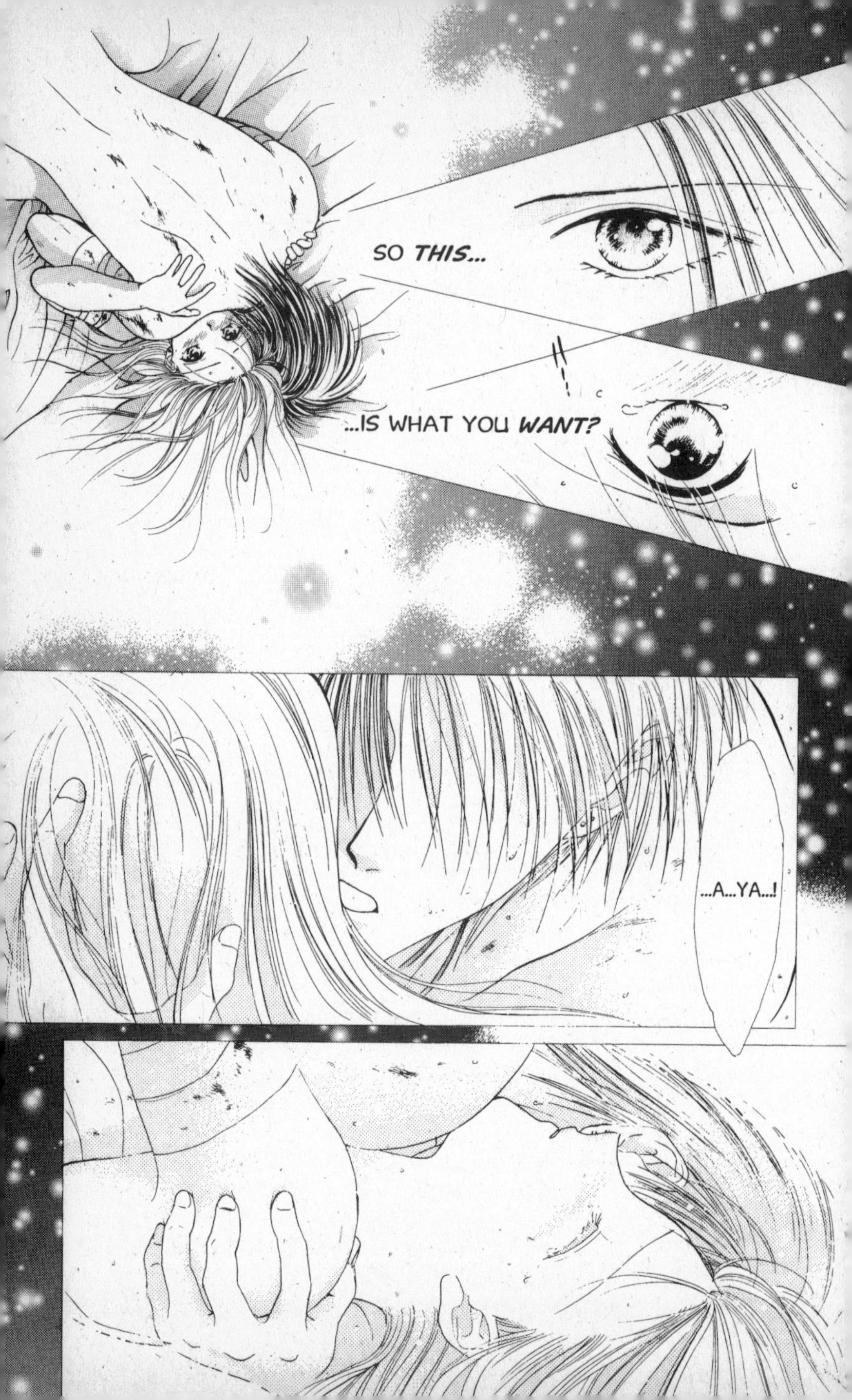
SO *THIS*...
...IS WHAT YOU *WANT*?
...A...YA...!

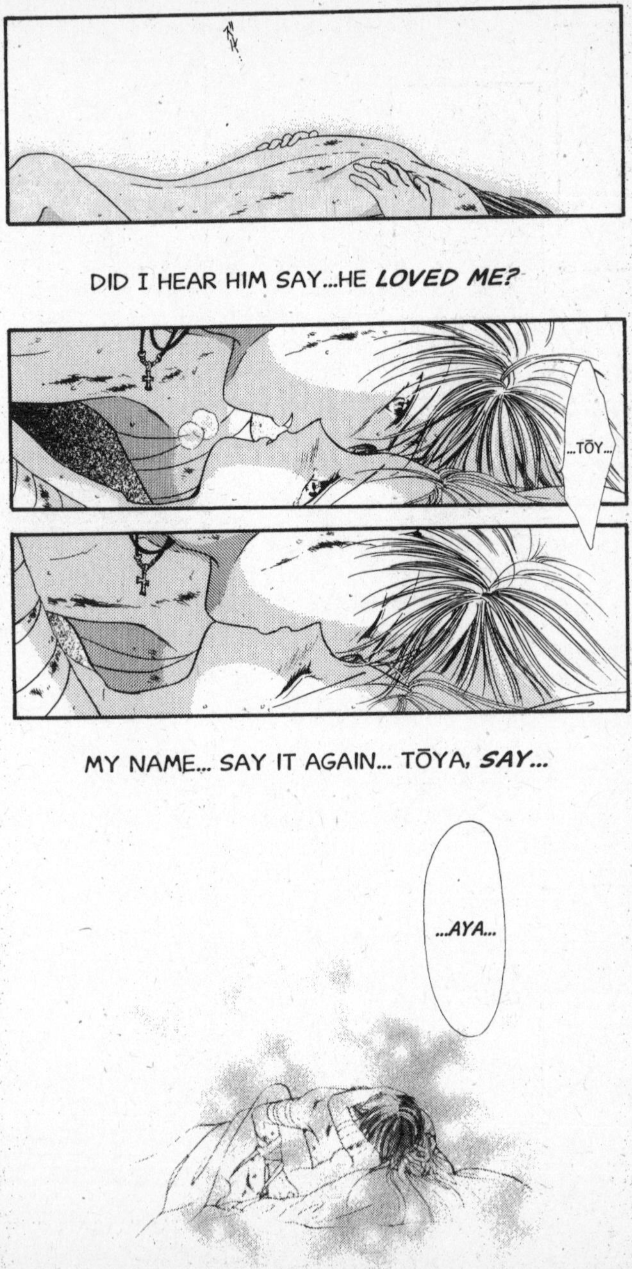
DID I HEAR HIM SAY...HE LOVED ME?
...TŌY...
MY NAME... SAY IT AGAIN... TŌYA, SAY...
...AYA...

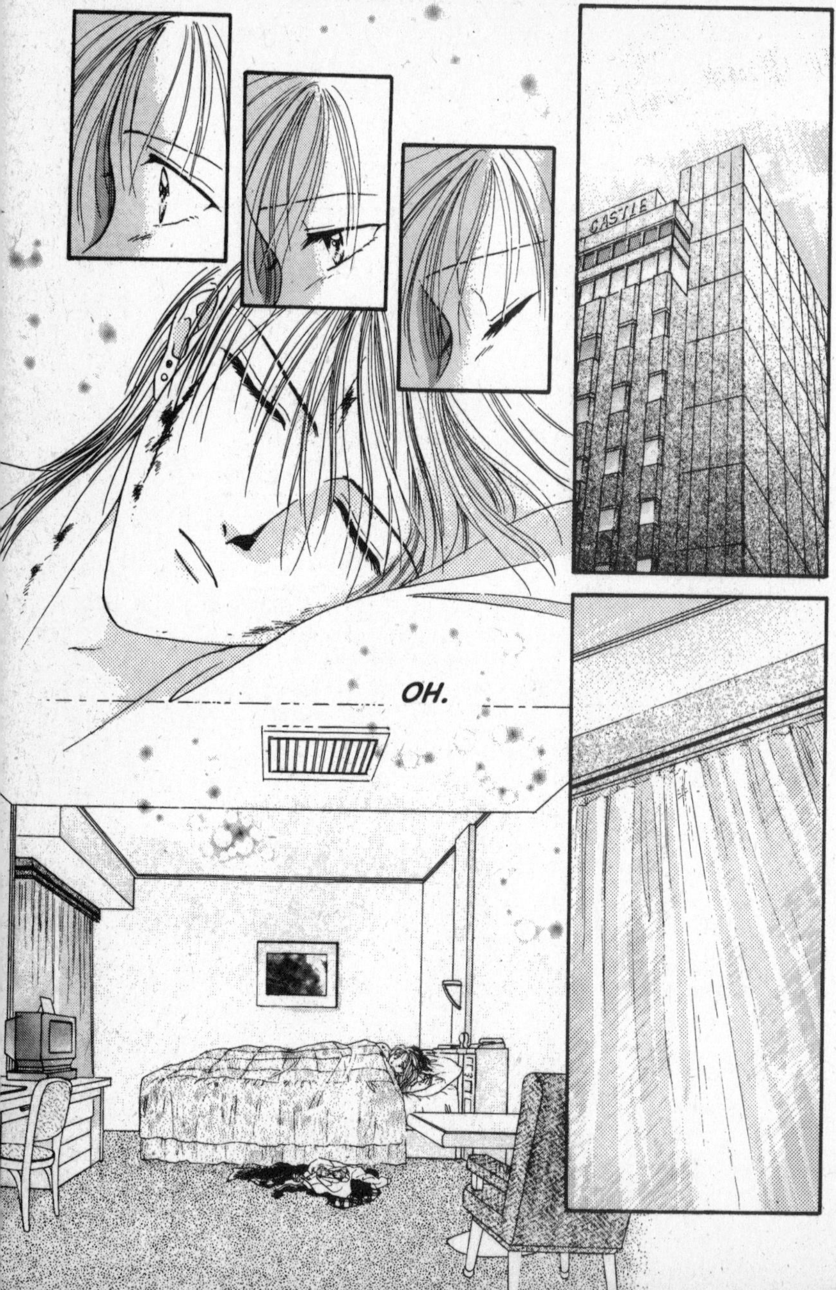
CASTLE
OH.

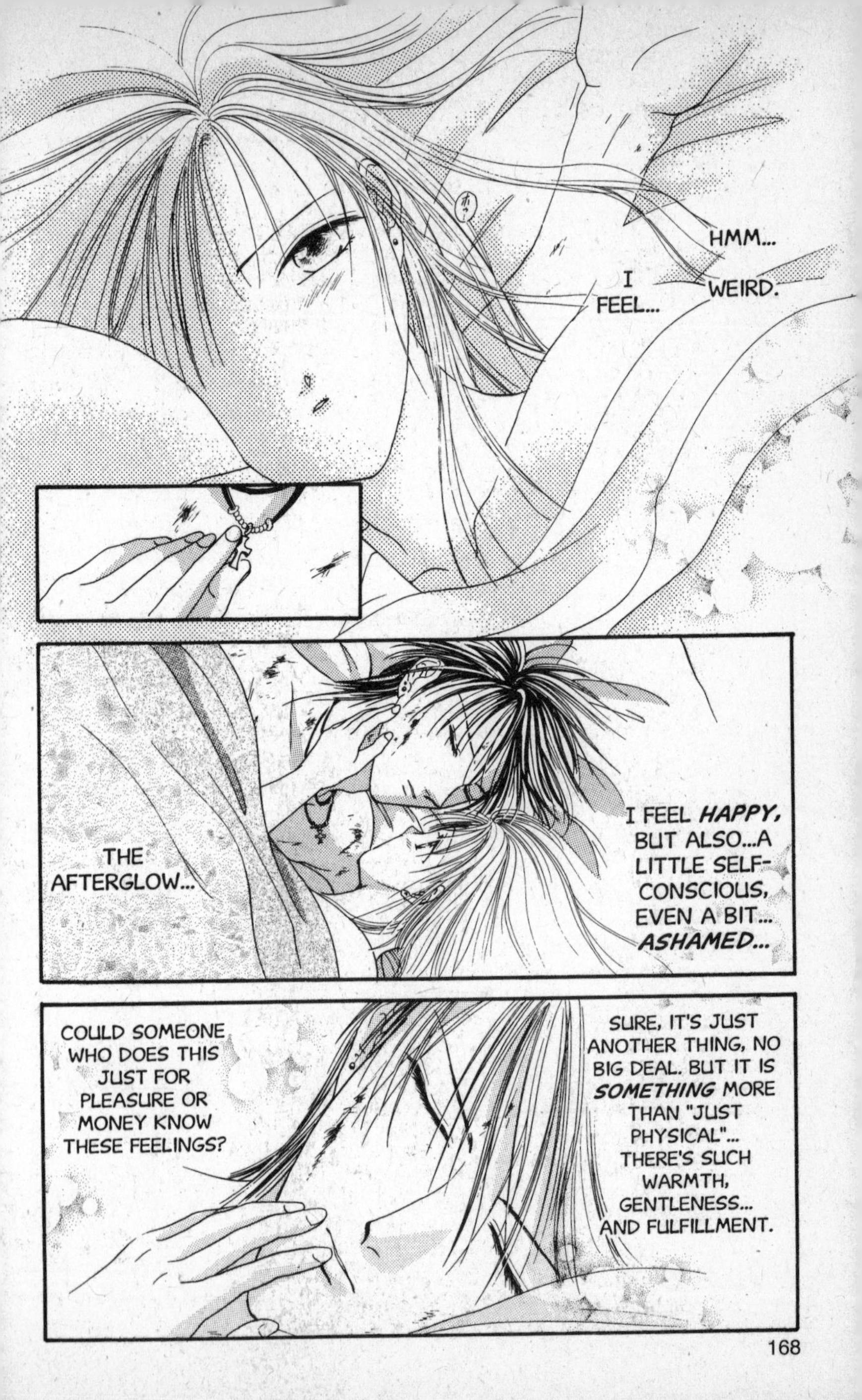
HMM...
I FEEL...
WEIRD.
I FEEL *HAPPY,* BUT ALSO...A LITTLE SELF-CONSCIOUS, EVEN A BIT... *ASHAMED...*
THE AFTERGLOW...
SURE, IT'S JUST ANOTHER THING, NO BIG DEAL. BUT IT IS *SOMETHING* MORE THAN "JUST PHYSICAL"... THERE'S SUCH WARMTH, GENTLENESS... AND FULFILLMENT.
COULD SOMEONE WHO DOES THIS JUST FOR PLEASURE OR MONEY KNOW THESE FEELINGS?

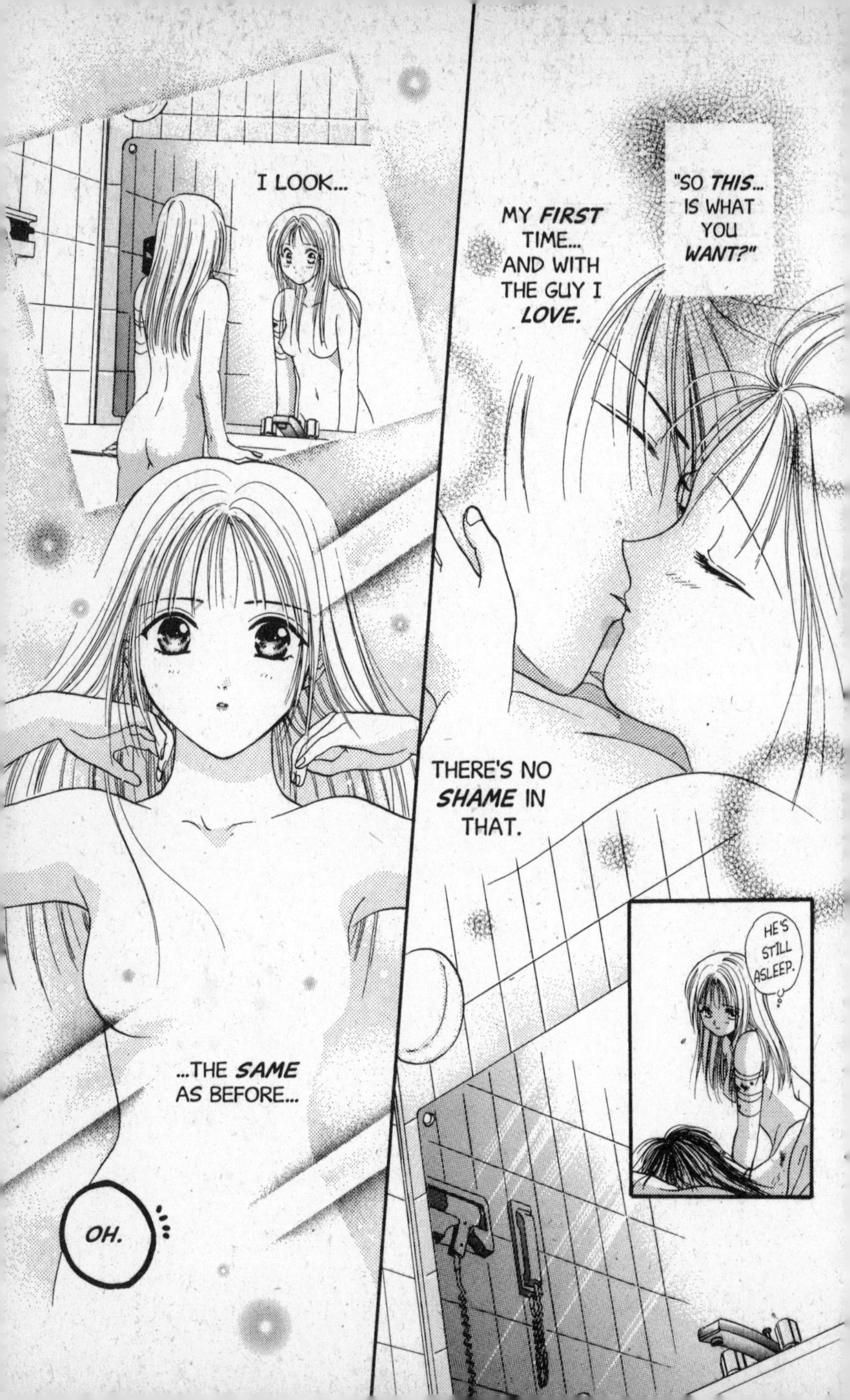
"SO THIS... IS WHAT YOU WANT?"
MY FIRST TIME... AND WITH THE GUY I LOVE.
THERE'S NO SHAME IN THAT.
HE'S STILL ASLEEP.
I LOOK...
...THE SAME AS BEFORE...
OH.

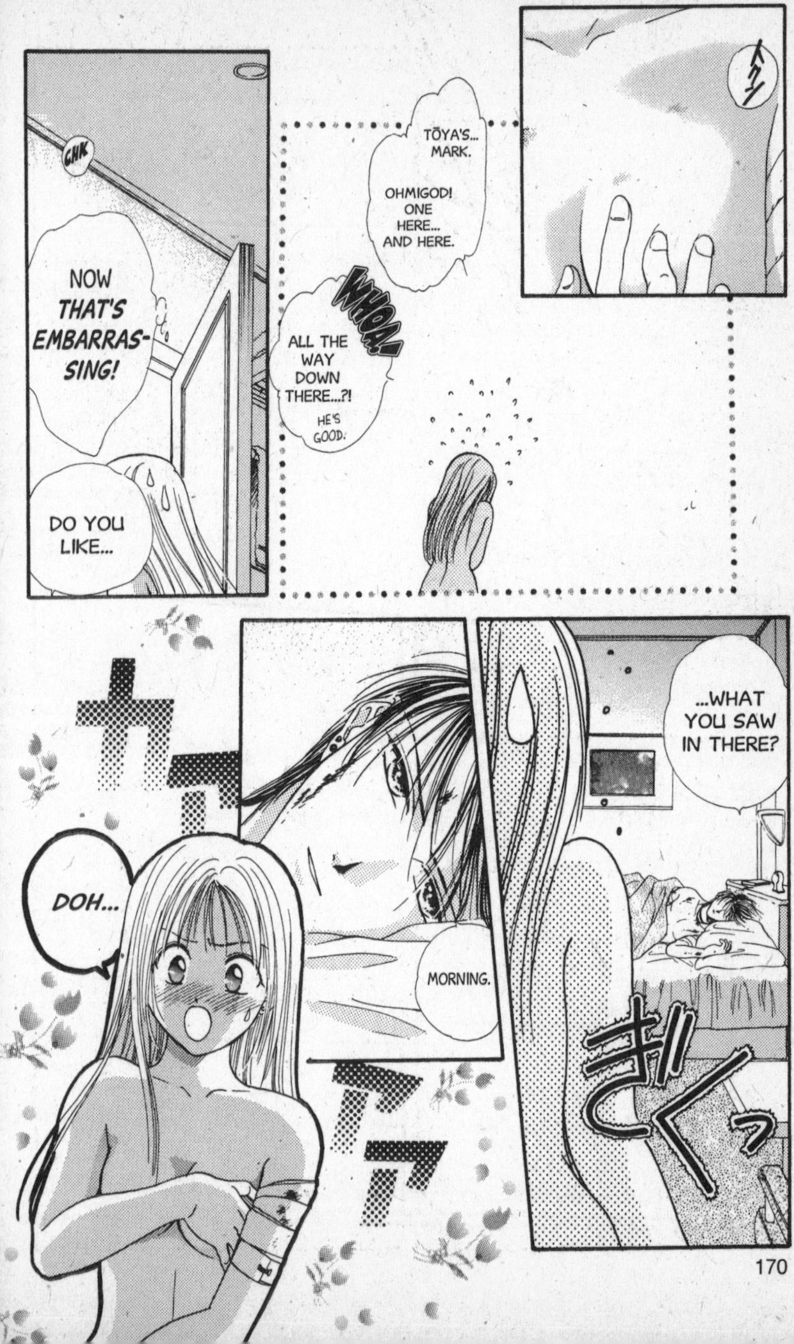
TŌYA'S... MARK.
OHMIGOD! ONE HERE... AND HERE.
WHOA!
ALL THE WAY DOWN THERE...?!
HE'S GOOD.
GHK
NOW THAT'S EMBARRAS-SING!
DO YOU LIKE...
...WHAT YOU SAW IN THERE?
ぎくっ
MORNING.
DOH...
カァァ

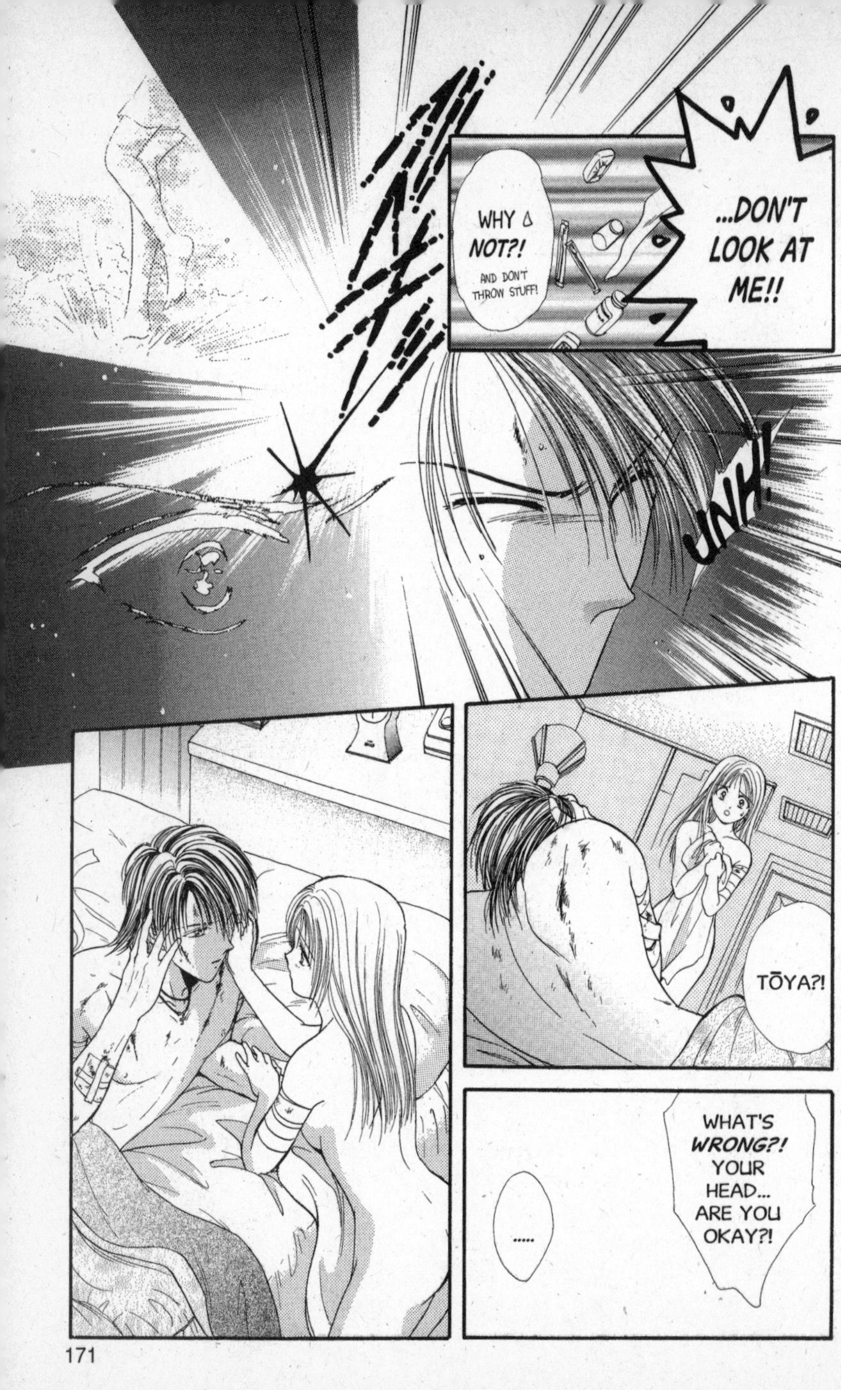
...DON'T LOOK AT ME!!
WHY NOT?! AND DON'T THROW STUFF!
UNH!
TŌYA?!
WHAT'S WRONG?! YOUR HEAD... ARE YOU OKAY?!
.....

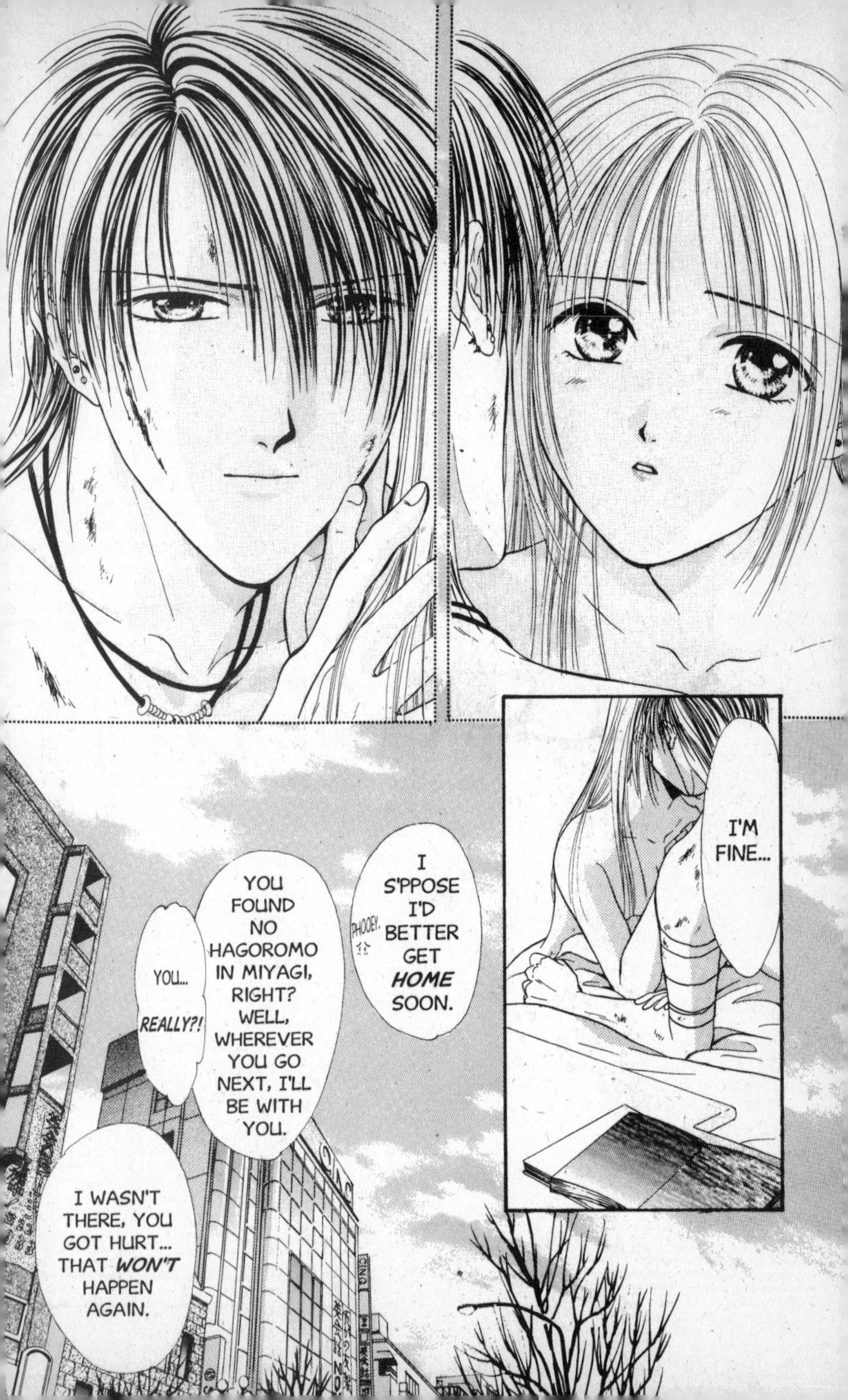
I'M FINE...
I S'PPOSE I'D BETTER GET HOME SOON.
PHOOEY.
YOU FOUND NO HAGOROMO IN MIYAGI, RIGHT? WELL, WHEREVER YOU GO NEXT, I'LL BE WITH YOU.
YOU... REALLY?!
I WASN'T THERE, YOU GOT HURT... THAT WON'T HAPPEN AGAIN.

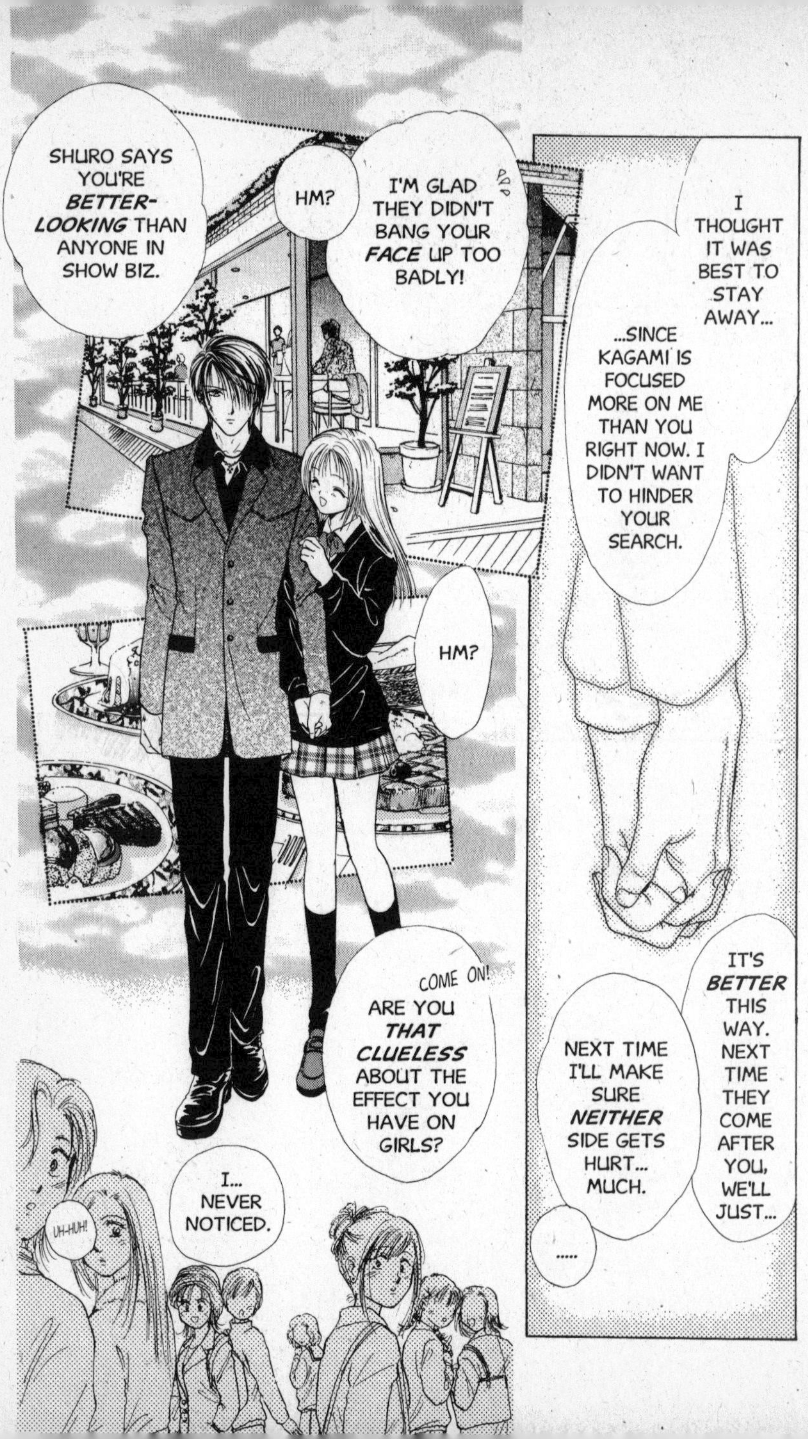
I THOUGHT IT WAS BEST TO STAY AWAY...
...SINCE KAGAMI IS FOCUSED MORE ON ME THAN YOU RIGHT NOW. I DIDN'T WANT TO HINDER YOUR SEARCH.
IT'S BETTER THIS WAY. NEXT TIME THEY COME AFTER YOU, WE'LL JUST...
NEXT TIME I'LL MAKE SURE NEITHER SIDE GETS HURT... MUCH.
.....
I'M GLAD THEY DIDN'T BANG YOUR FACE UP TOO BADLY!
HM?
SHURO SAYS YOU'RE BETTER-LOOKING THAN ANYONE IN SHOW BIZ.
HM?
COME ON!
ARE YOU THAT CLUELESS ABOUT THE EFFECT YOU HAVE ON GIRLS?
I... NEVER NOTICED.
UH-HUH!

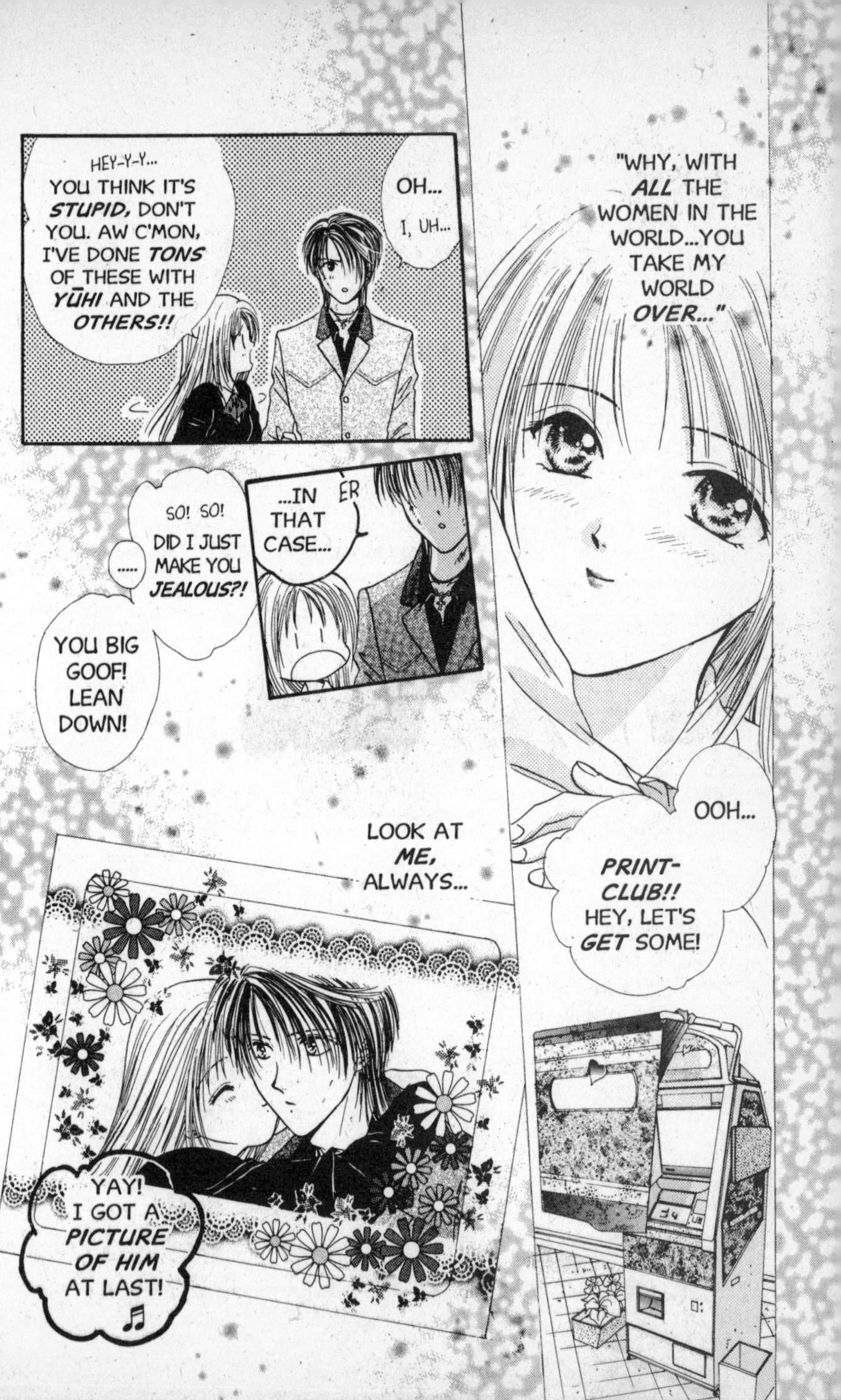

"WHY, WITH ALL THE WOMEN IN THE WORLD...YOU TAKE MY WORLD OVER..."
OOH... PRINT-CLUB!! HEY, LET'S GET SOME!
OH... I, UH...
HEY-Y-Y... YOU THINK IT'S STUPID, DON'T YOU. AW C'MON, I'VE DONE TONS OF THESE WITH YŪHI AND THE OTHERS!!
...IN THAT CASE...
ER
SO! SO! DID I JUST MAKE YOU JEALOUS?!
.....
YOU BIG GOOF! LEAN DOWN!
LOOK AT ME, ALWAYS...
YAY! I GOT A PICTURE OF HIM AT LAST! ♫

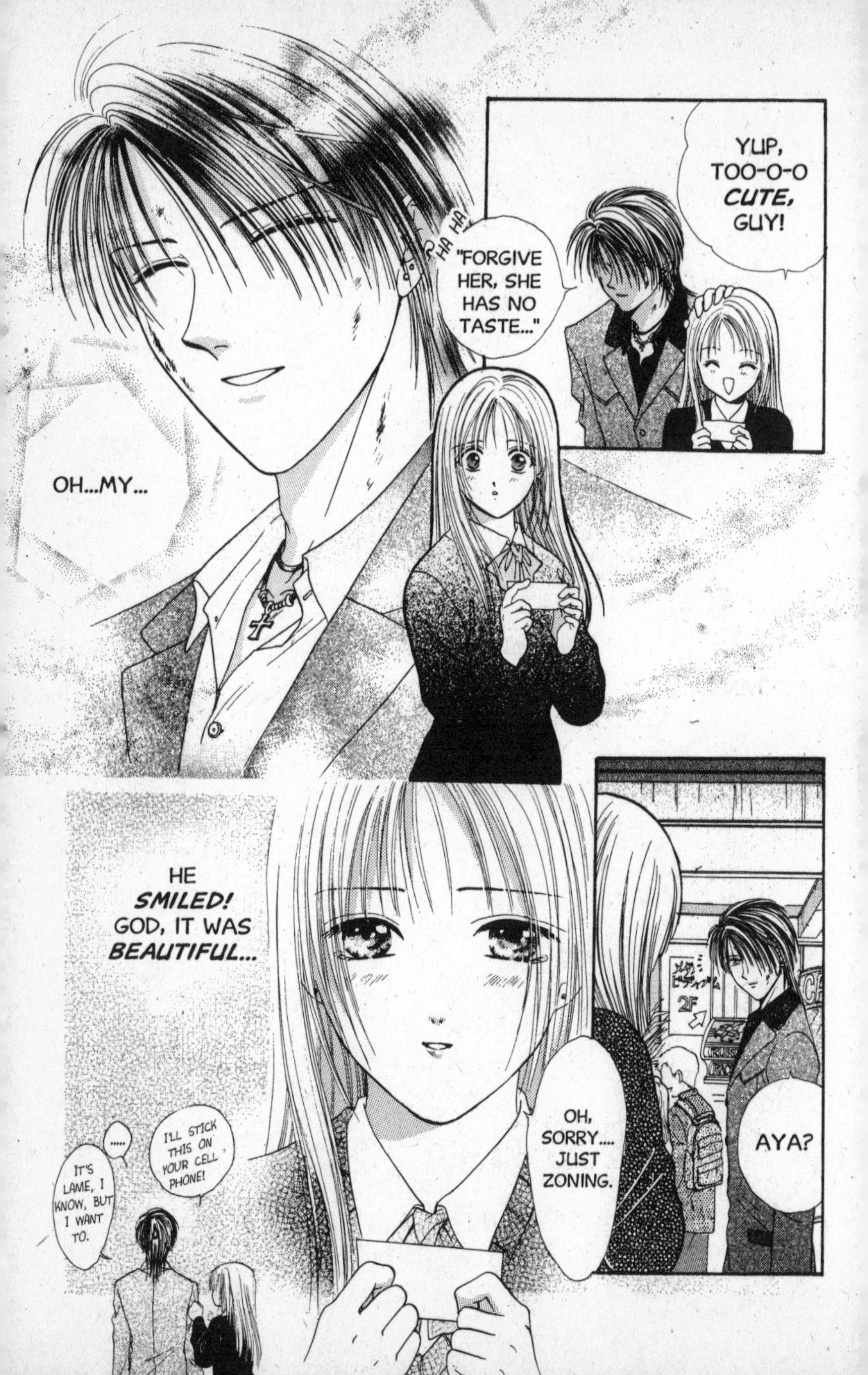
YUP, TOO-O-O *CUTE,* GUY!
HA HA
"FORGIVE HER, SHE HAS NO TASTE..."
OH...MY...
AYA?
2F
OH, SORRY.... JUST ZONING.
HE *SMILED!* GOD, IT WAS *BEAUTIFUL...*
I'LL STICK THIS ON YOUR CELL PHONE!
.....
IT'S LAME, I KNOW, BUT I WANT TO.

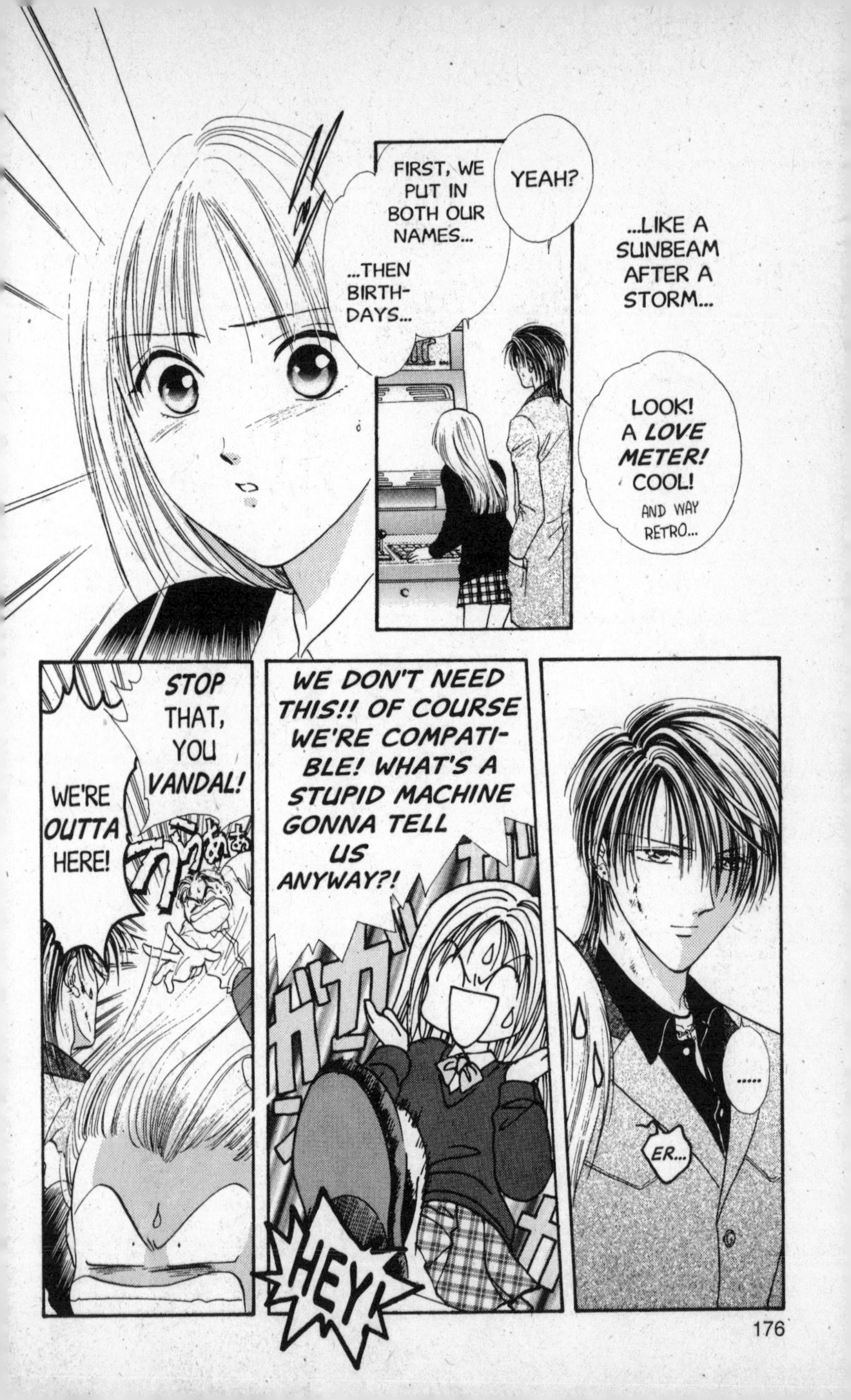

...LIKE A SUNBEAM AFTER A STORM...
LOOK! A *LOVE METER!* COOL!
AND WAY RETRO...
FIRST, WE PUT IN BOTH OUR NAMES...
YEAH?
...THEN BIRTH-DAYS...
.....
ER...
WE DON'T NEED THIS!! OF COURSE WE'RE COMPATI-BLE! WHAT'S A STUPID MACHINE GONNA TELL US ANYWAY?!
HEY!
STOP THAT, YOU *VANDAL!*
WE'RE *OUTTA* HERE!

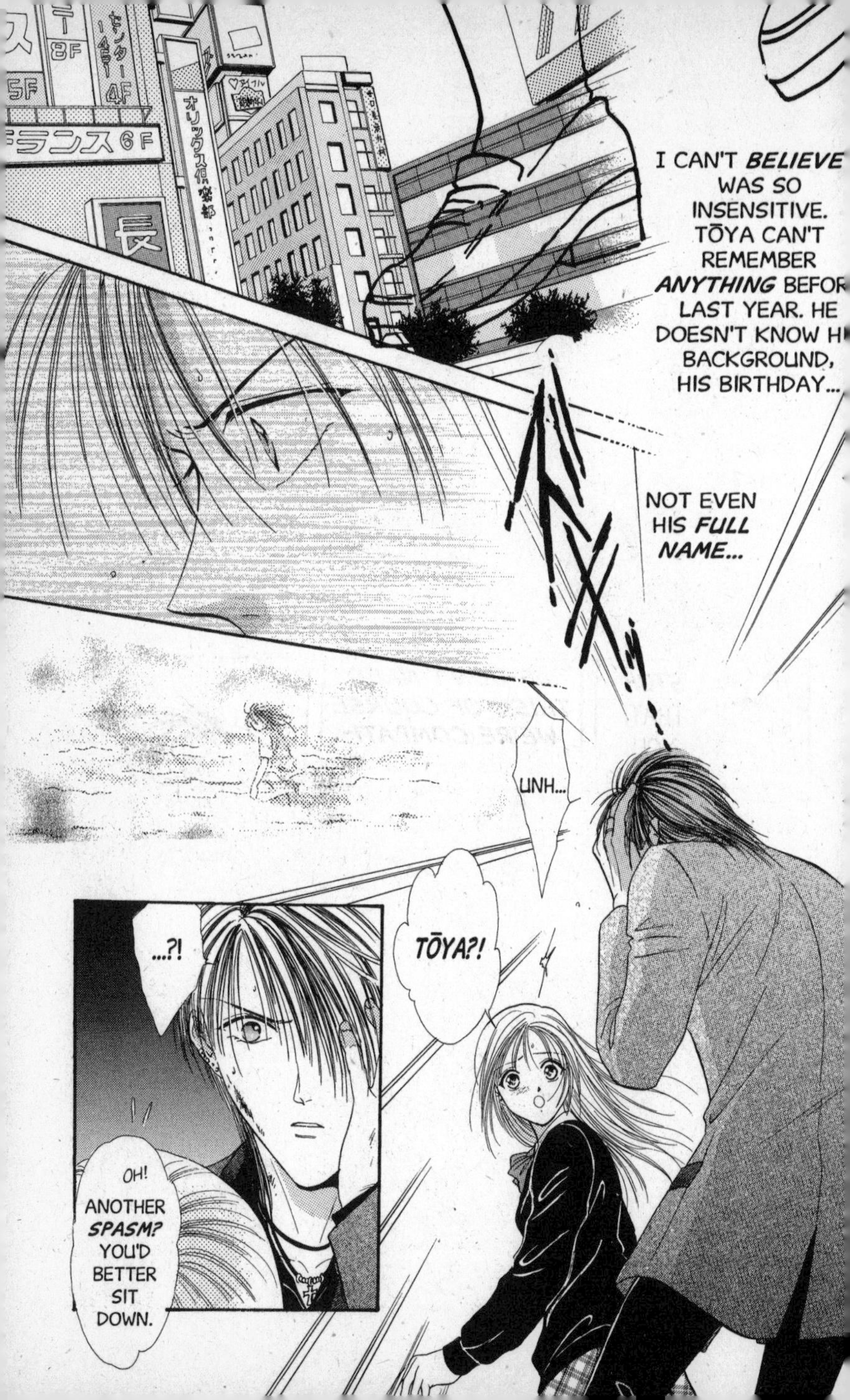
I CAN'T BELIEVE WAS SO INSENSITIVE. TŌYA CAN'T REMEMBER ANYTHING BEFOR LAST YEAR. HE DOESN'T KNOW H BACKGROUND, HIS BIRTHDAY...
NOT EVEN HIS FULL NAME...
UNH...
TŌYA?!
...?!
OH! ANOTHER SPASM? YOU'D BETTER SIT DOWN.

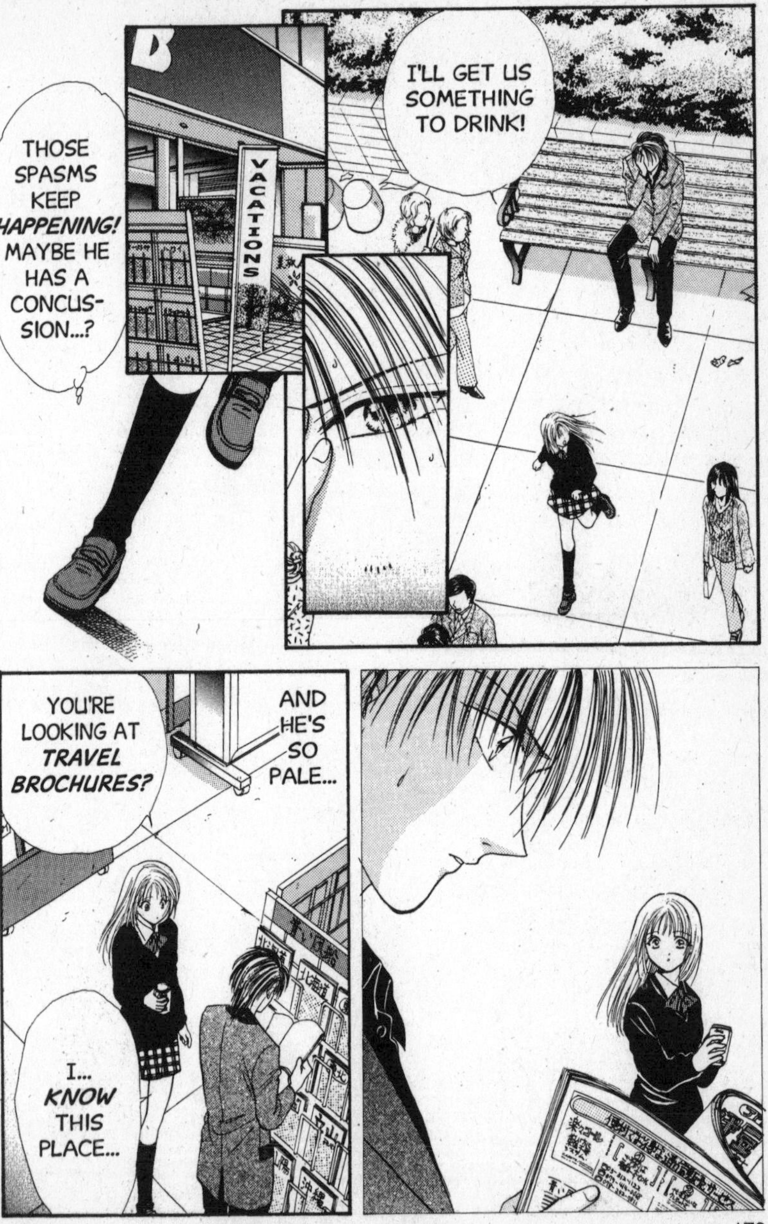
I'LL GET US SOMETHING TO DRINK!
THOSE SPASMS KEEP *HAPPENING!* MAYBE HE HAS A CONCUS-SION...?
VACATIONS
AND HE'S SO PALE...
YOU'RE LOOKING AT *TRAVEL BROCHURES?*
I... *KNOW* THIS PLACE...

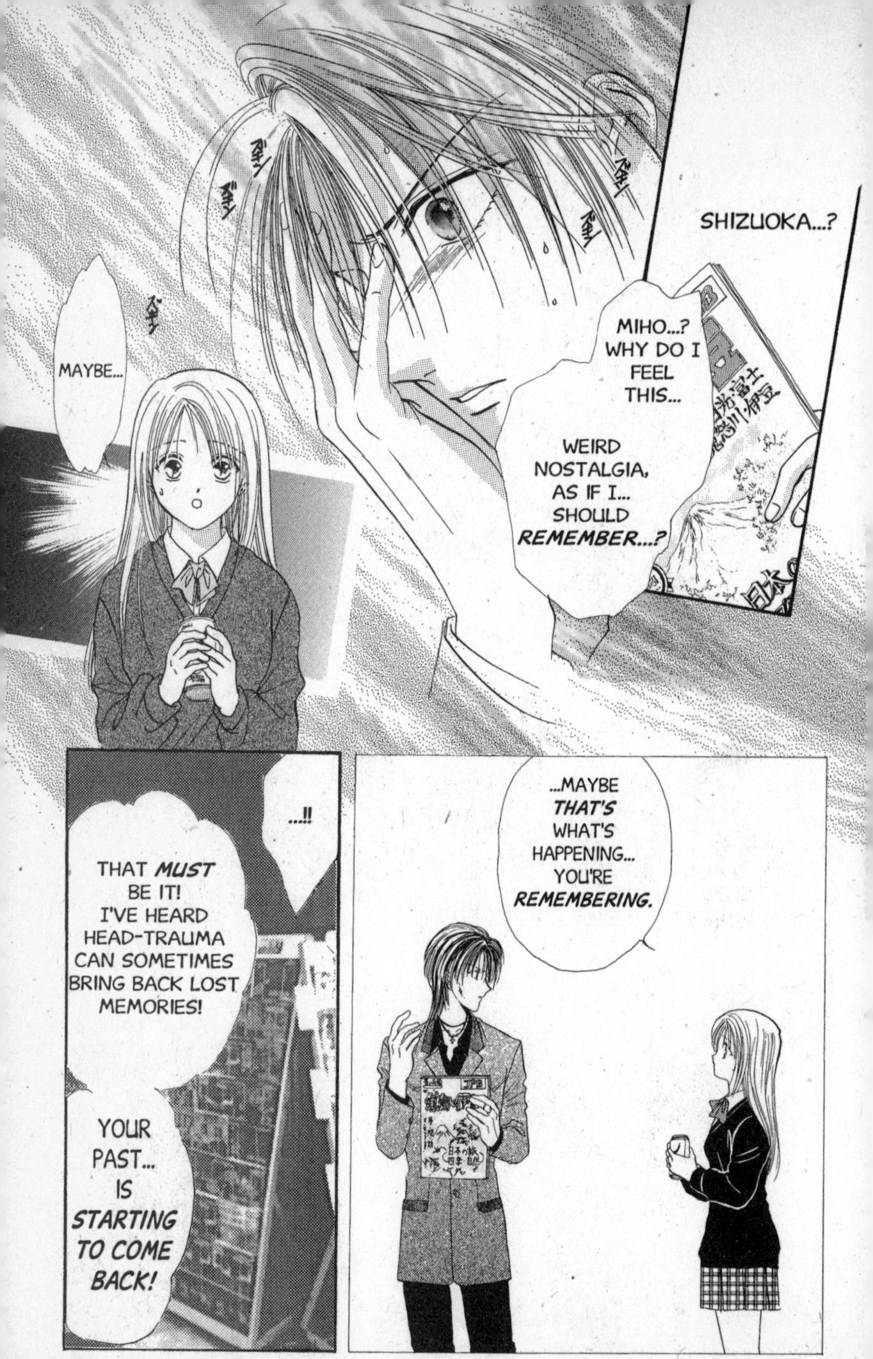
SHIZUOKA...?
MIHO...? WHY DO I FEEL THIS... WEIRD NOSTALGIA, AS IF I... SHOULD *REMEMBER...?*
MAYBE...
...MAYBE *THAT'S* WHAT'S HAPPENING... YOU'RE *REMEMBERING.*
...!!
THAT *MUST* BE IT! I'VE HEARD HEAD-TRAUMA CAN SOMETIMES BRING BACK LOST MEMORIES!
YOUR PAST... IS *STARTING TO COME BACK!*

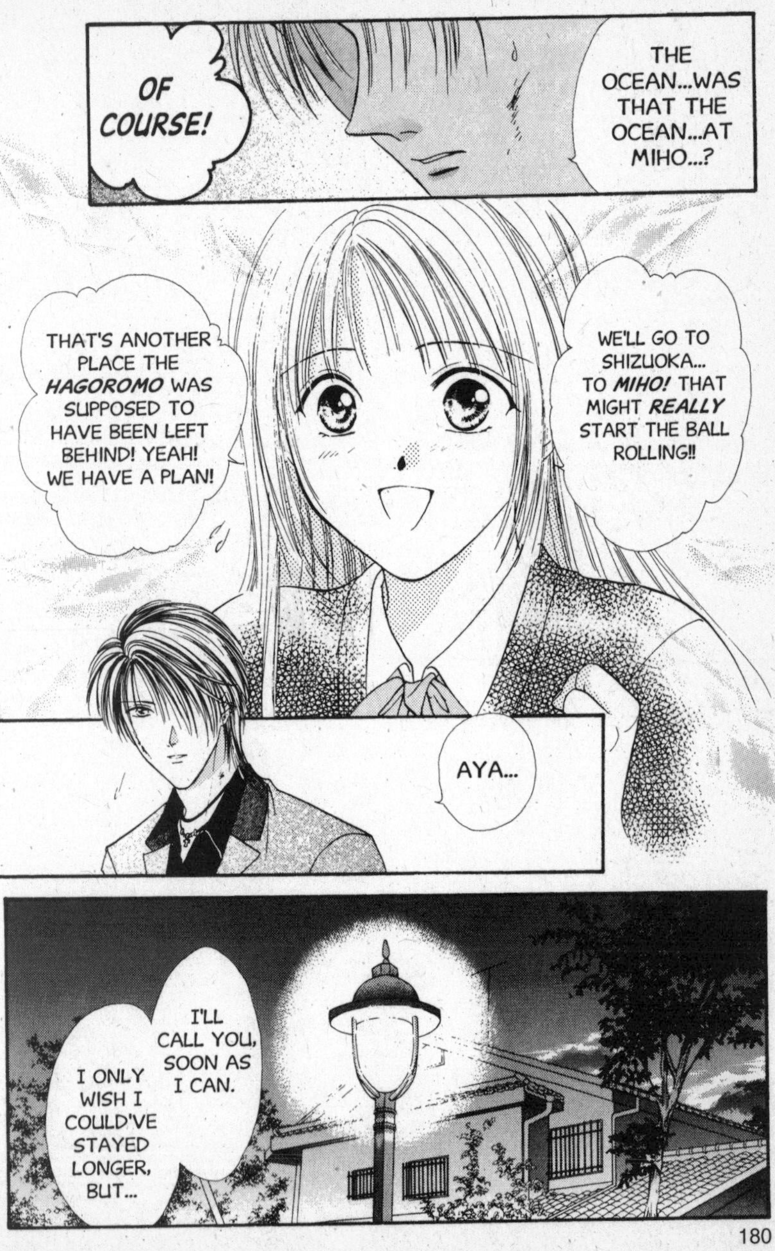
THE OCEAN...WAS THAT THE OCEAN...AT MIHO...?
OF COURSE!
WE'LL GO TO SHIZUOKA... TO MIHO! THAT MIGHT REALLY START THE BALL ROLLING!!
THAT'S ANOTHER PLACE THE HAGOROMO WAS SUPPOSED TO HAVE BEEN LEFT BEHIND! YEAH! WE HAVE A PLAN!
AYA...
I'LL CALL YOU, SOON AS I CAN.
I ONLY WISH I COULD'VE STAYED LONGER, BUT...

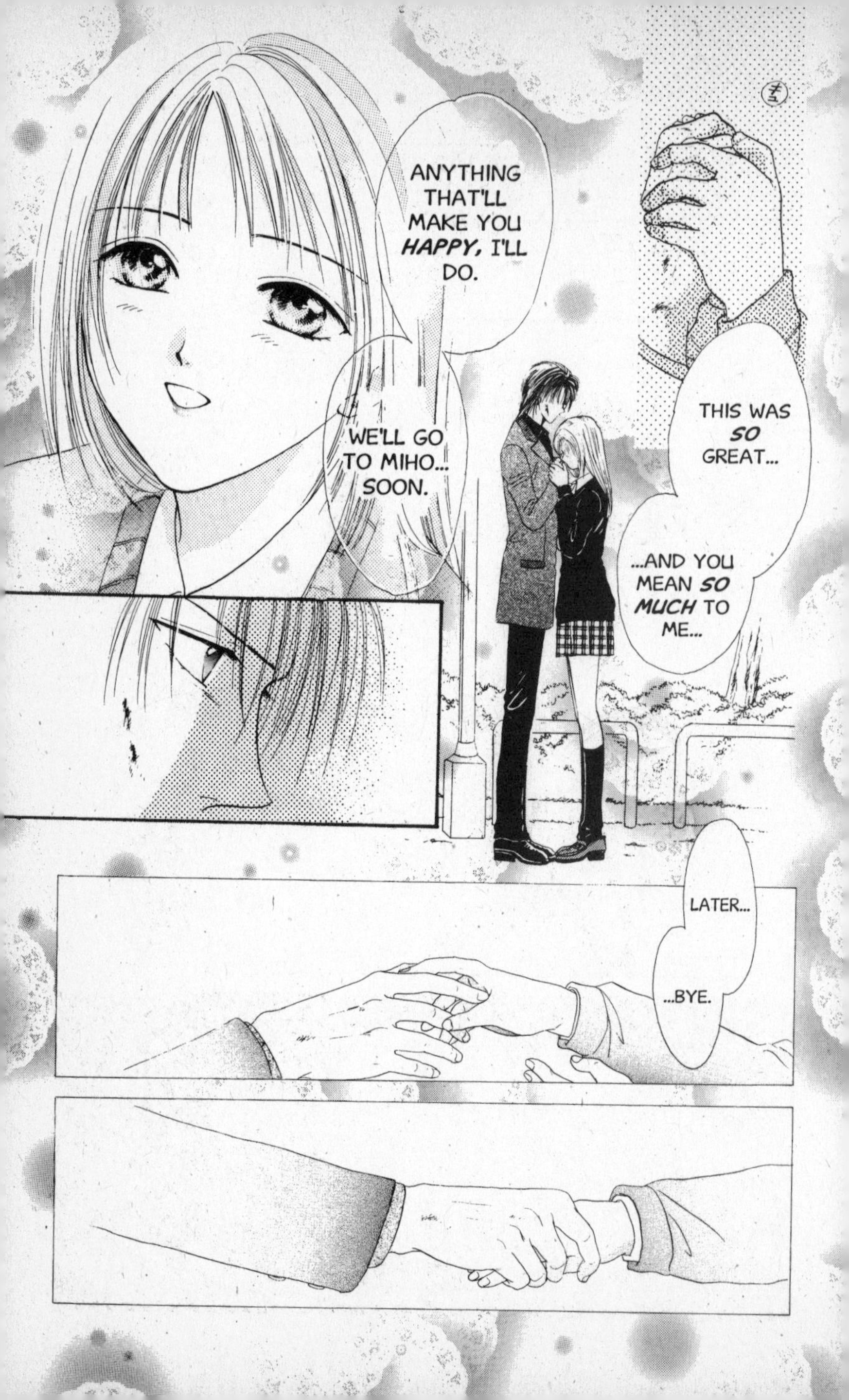
THIS WAS SO GREAT...
...AND YOU MEAN SO MUCH TO ME...
ANYTHING THAT'LL MAKE YOU HAPPY, I'LL DO.
WE'LL GO TO MIHO... SOON.
LATER...
...BYE.

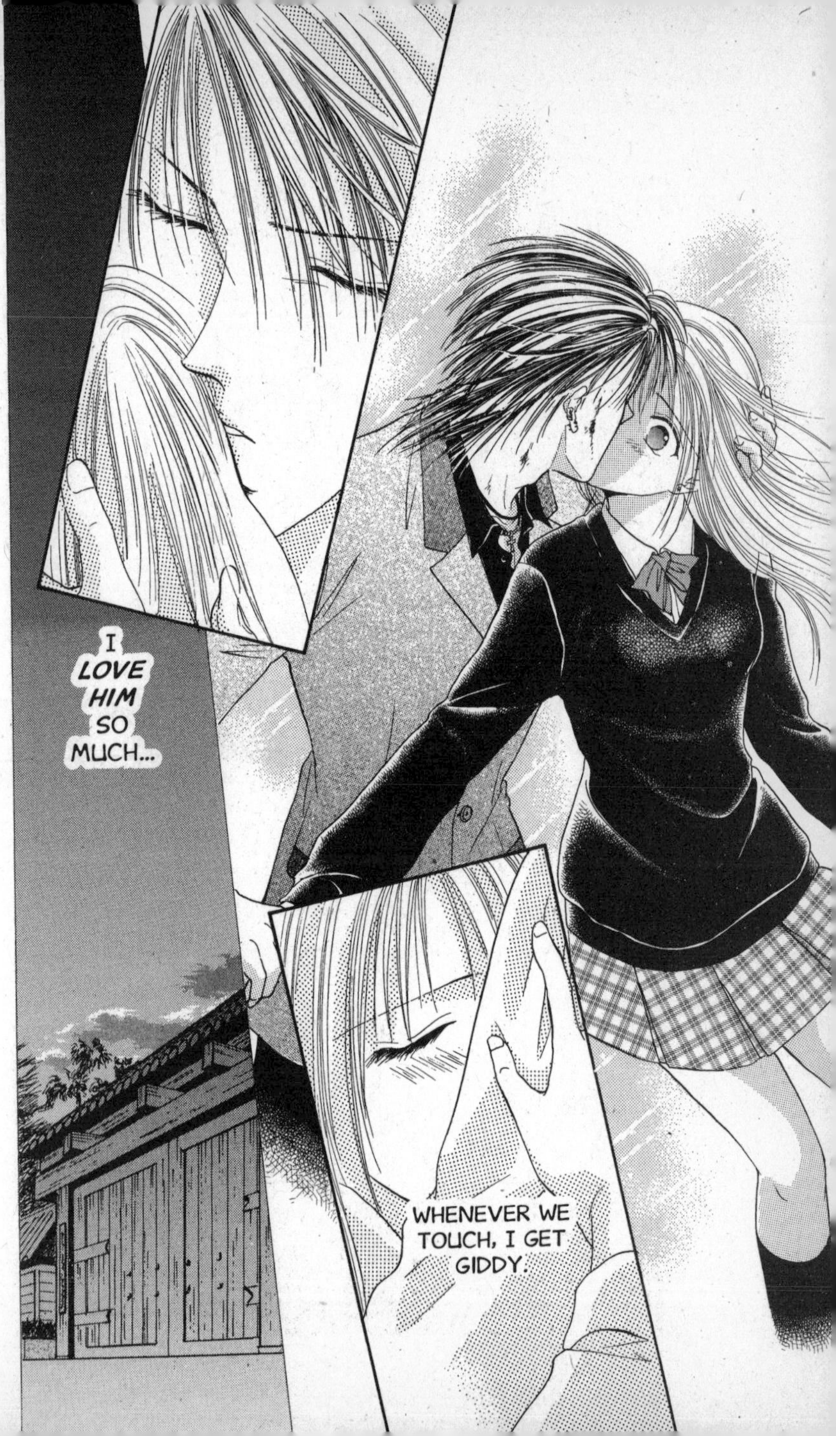
I *LOVE HIM* SO MUCH...
WHENEVER WE TOUCH, I GET GIDDY.

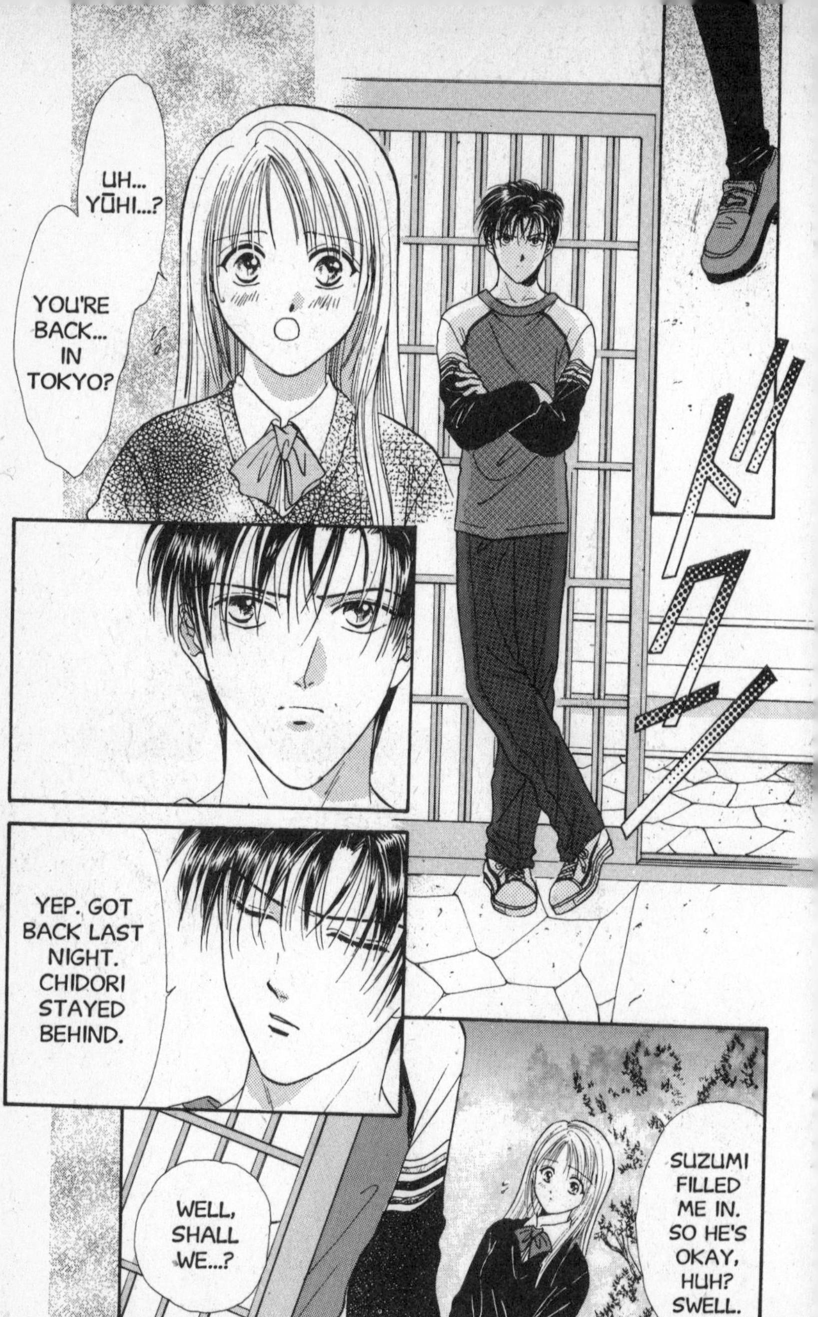
UH... YŪHI...?
YOU'RE BACK... IN TOKYO?
YEP. GOT BACK LAST NIGHT. CHIDORI STAYED BEHIND.
SUZUMI FILLED ME IN. SO HE'S OKAY, HUH? SWELL.
WELL, SHALL WE...?

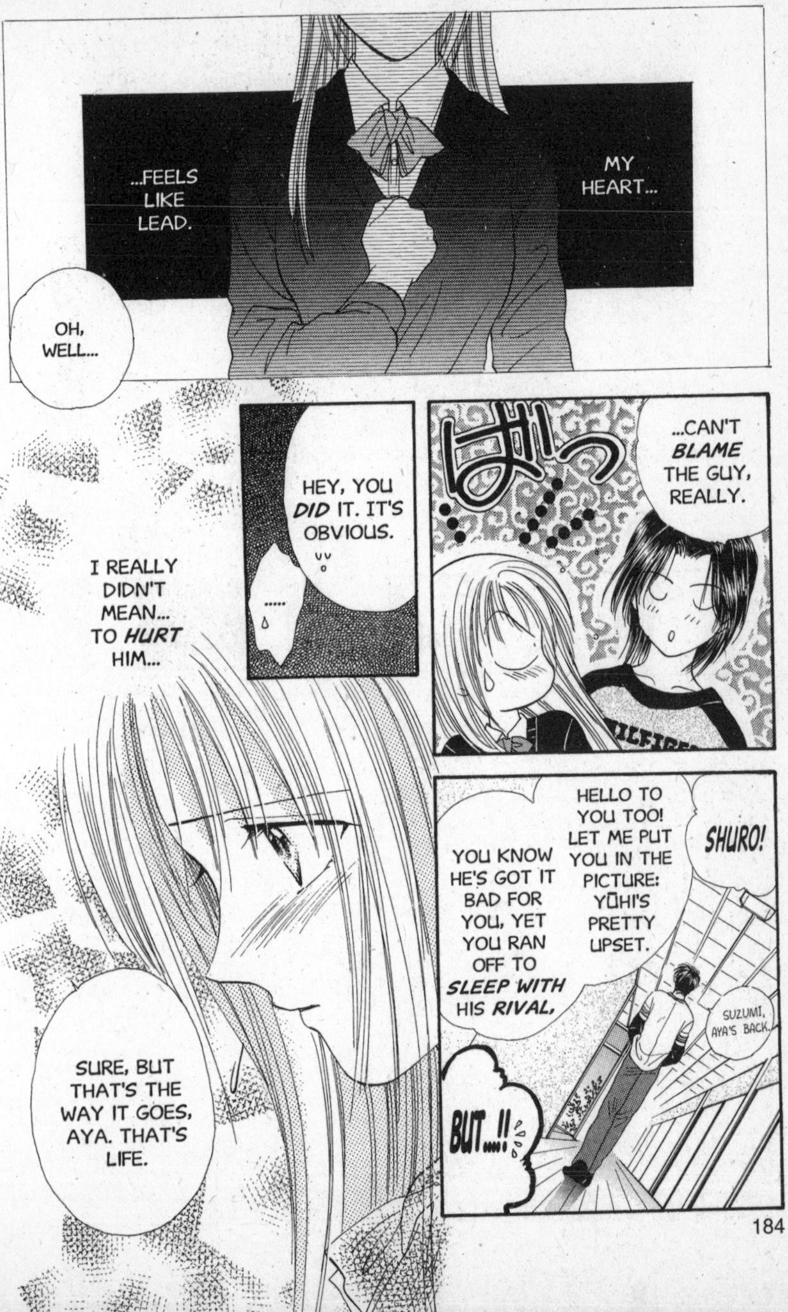
MY HEART...
...FEELS LIKE LEAD.
OH, WELL...
ぱっ
...CAN'T *BLAME* THE GUY, REALLY.
HEY, YOU *DID* IT. IT'S OBVIOUS.
.....
SHURO!
HELLO TO YOU TOO! LET ME PUT YOU IN THE PICTURE: YŪHI'S PRETTY UPSET.
YOU KNOW HE'S GOT IT BAD FOR YOU, YET YOU RAN OFF TO *SLEEP WITH* HIS *RIVAL,*
SUZUMI, AYA'S BACK.
BUT...!!
I REALLY DIDN'T MEAN... TO *HURT* HIM...
SURE, BUT THAT'S THE WAY IT GOES, AYA. THAT'S LIFE.

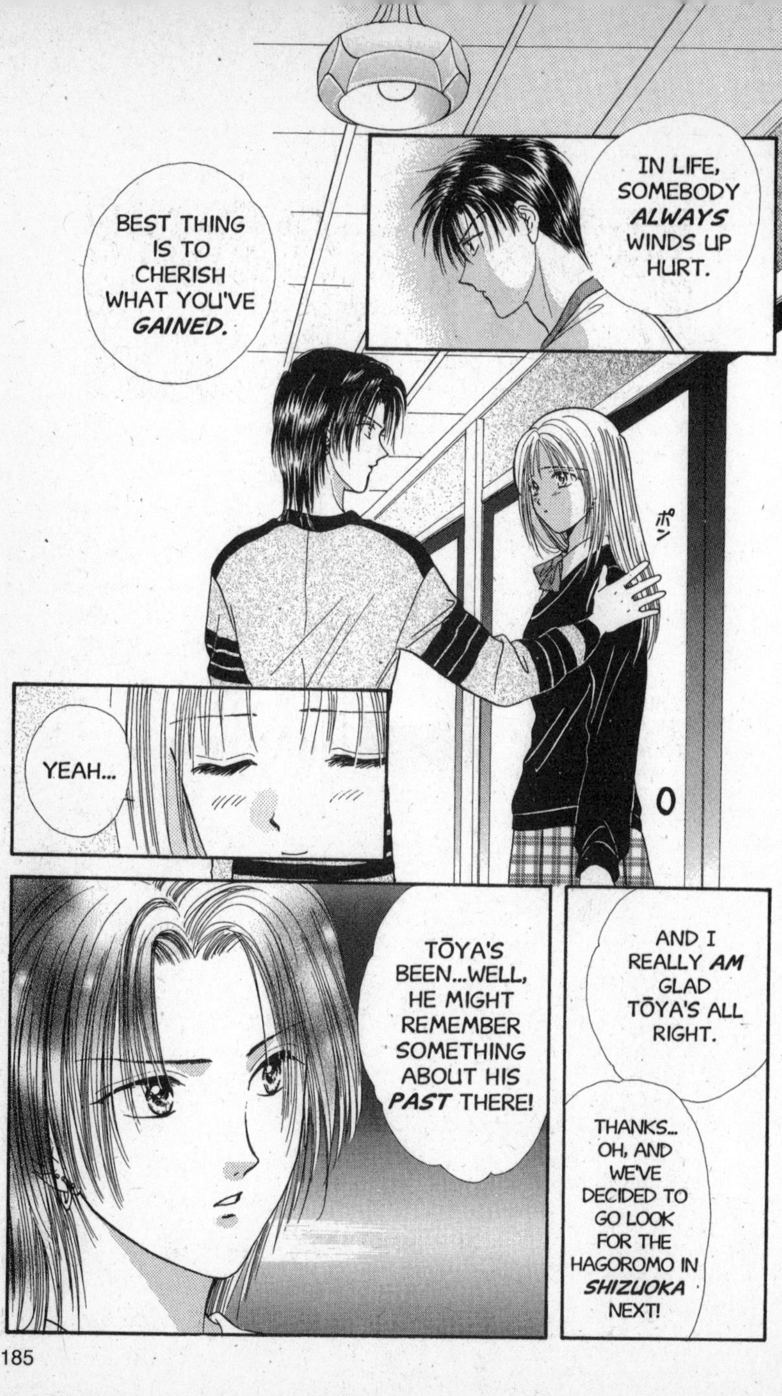

IN LIFE, SOMEBODY ***ALWAYS*** WINDS UP HURT.
BEST THING IS TO CHERISH WHAT YOU'VE ***GAINED.***
ポン
O
YEAH...
AND I REALLY ***AM*** GLAD TŌYA'S ALL RIGHT.
THANKS... OH, AND WE'VE DECIDED TO GO LOOK FOR THE HAGOROMO IN ***SHIZUOKA*** NEXT!
TŌYA'S BEEN...WELL, HE MIGHT REMEMBER SOMETHING ABOUT HIS ***PAST*** THERE!

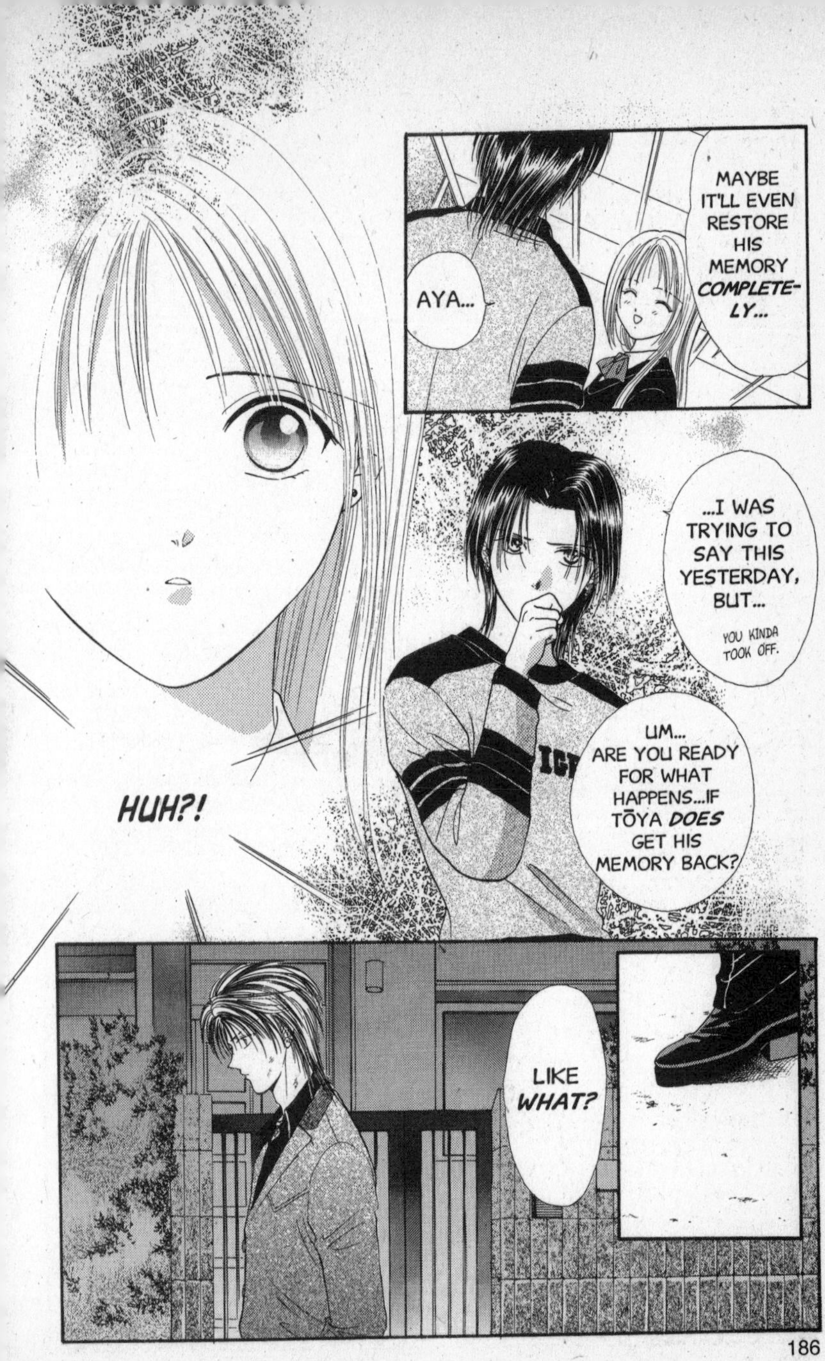

MAYBE IT'LL EVEN RESTORE HIS MEMORY *COMPLETE-LY...*
AYA...
...I WAS TRYING TO SAY THIS YESTERDAY, BUT...
YOU KINDA TOOK OFF.
UM... ARE YOU READY FOR WHAT HAPPENS...IF TŌYA *DOES* GET HIS MEMORY BACK?
HUH?!
LIKE *WHAT?*

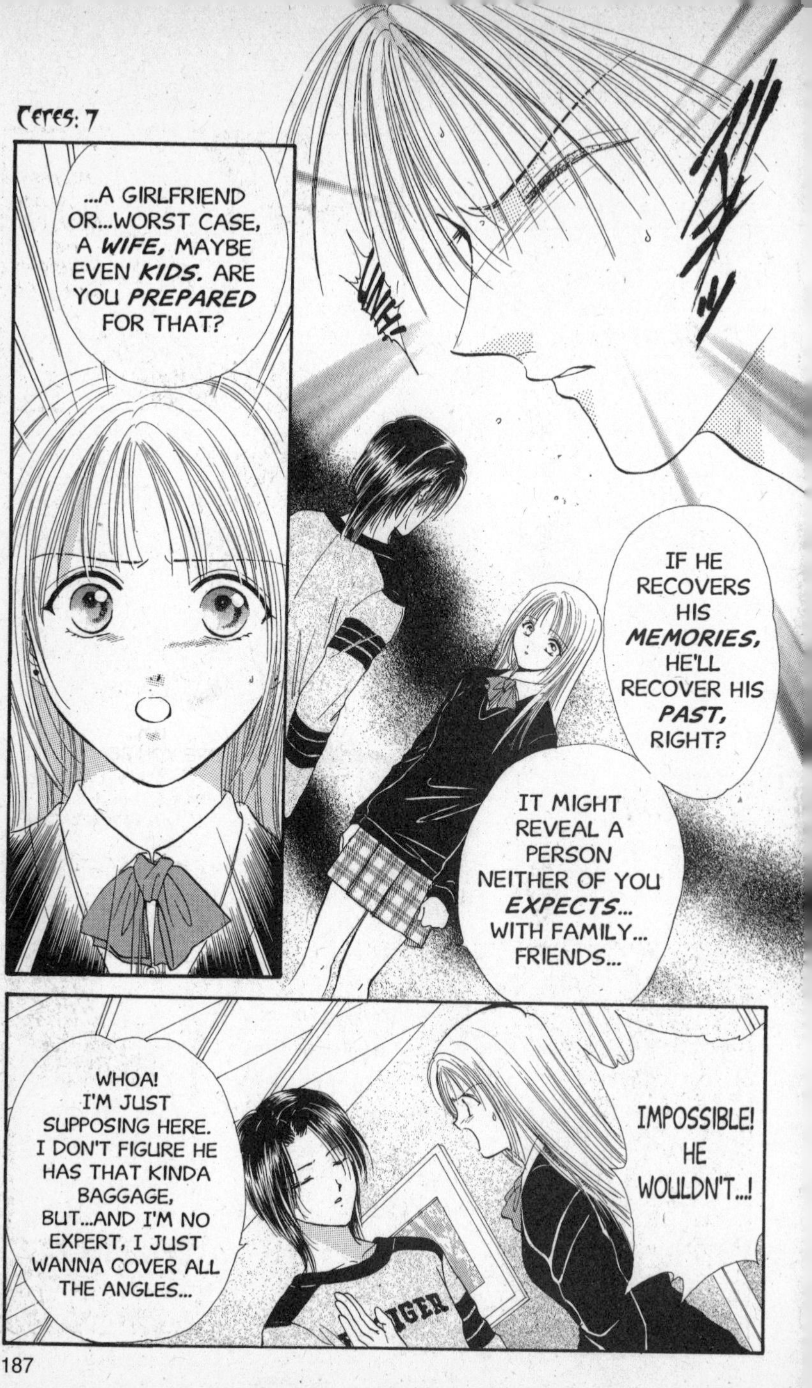
UNH!
IF HE RECOVERS HIS *MEMORIES,* HE'LL RECOVER HIS *PAST,* RIGHT?
IT MIGHT REVEAL A PERSON NEITHER OF YOU *EXPECTS...* WITH FAMILY... FRIENDS...
...A GIRLFRIEND OR...WORST CASE, A *WIFE,* MAYBE EVEN *KIDS.* ARE YOU *PREPARED* FOR THAT?
IMPOSSIBLE! HE WOULDN'T...!
WHOA! I'M JUST SUPPOSING HERE. I DON'T FIGURE HE HAS THAT KINDA BAGGAGE, BUT...AND I'M NO EXPERT, I JUST WANNA COVER ALL THE ANGLES...
IGER

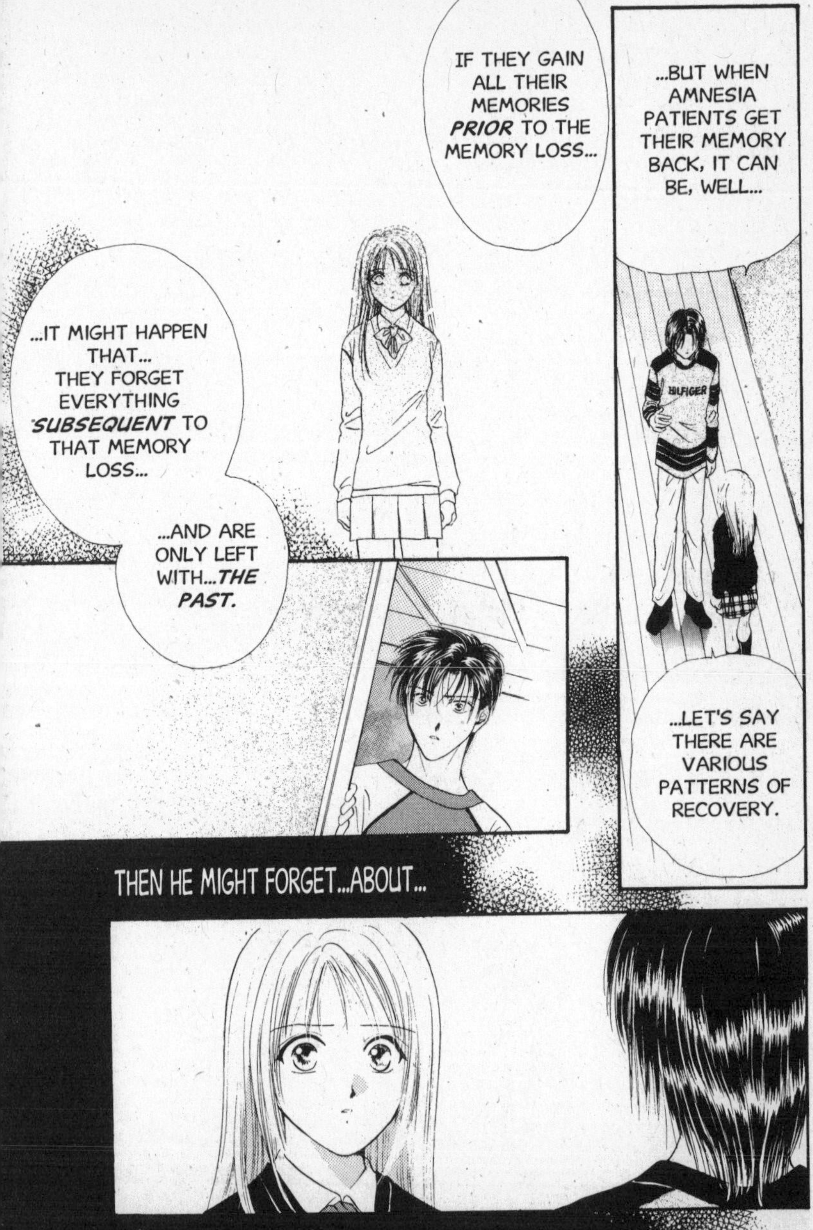
...BUT WHEN AMNESIA PATIENTS GET THEIR MEMORY BACK, IT CAN BE, WELL...
HILFIGER
...LET'S SAY THERE ARE VARIOUS PATTERNS OF RECOVERY.
IF THEY GAIN ALL THEIR MEMORIES *PRIOR* TO THE MEMORY LOSS...
...IT MIGHT HAPPEN THAT... THEY FORGET EVERYTHING *SUBSEQUENT* TO THAT MEMORY LOSS...
...AND ARE ONLY LEFT WITH...*THE PAST.*
THEN HE MIGHT FORGET...ABOUT...

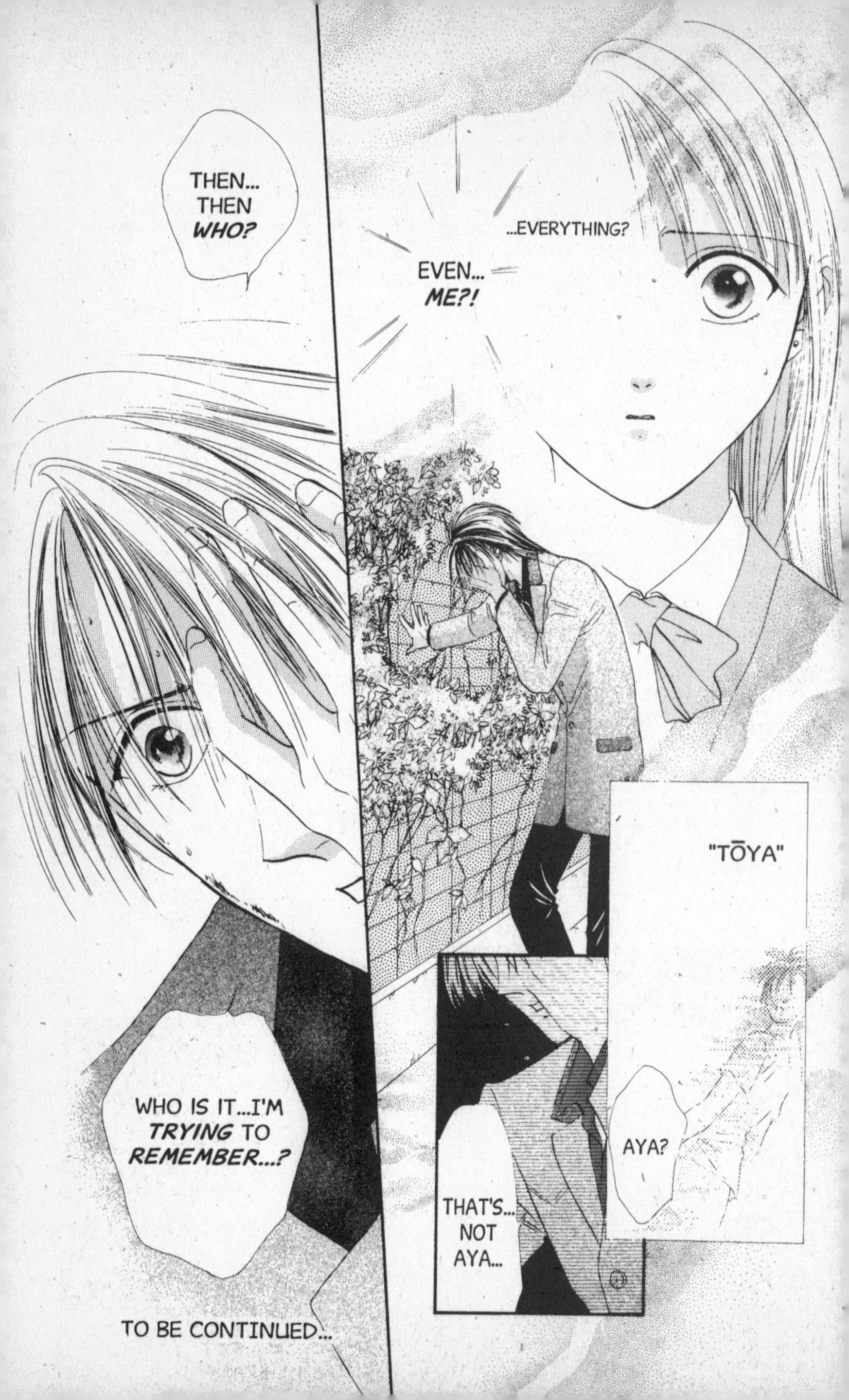
...EVERYTHING?
EVEN... ME?!
"TŌYA"
AYA?
THAT'S... NOT AYA...
THEN... THEN WHO?
WHO IS IT...I'M TRYING TO REMEMBER...?
TO BE CONTINUED...

The CERES Guide to Sound Effects

We've left most of the sound effects in CERES as Yuu Watase originally created them—in Japanese. VIZ has created this glossary to help you decipher, page-by-page and panel-by-panel, what all those foreign words and background noises mean. Use this guide to impress your friends with your new Japanese vocabulary. The glossary lists the page number then panel. For example, 3.1 indicates page 3, panel 1.

023.1 FX:Bishi ("thwap")
023.2 FX:Doza (heavy "thunk")
024.2 FX:Su (slight touch, movement)
024.5 FX:Doka ("boot")
024.6 FX:Pi ("beep")
025.2 FX:Do ("thud")
025.3 FX:Dosu ("thunk")
026.3 FX:Gigi (slice across flesh)
027.3 FX:Shu (displaced air)
027.5 FX:Za (quick movement)
028.2 FX:Zaza (displaced brush)
028.3 FX:Tata (running tread)
028.5 FX:Pashi (slap)
029.3 FX:Ga (tug)
031.2 FX:Rururuu (sniffling misery)
032.1 FX:Gyu (clench)
032.3 FX:Gu ("Urk!")
033.2 FX:Zaan (rolling waves)
033.3 FX:Goo (roar of plane)
034.3 FX:Boso (whisper)
034.5 FX:Dongara (clattering upset)
      FX:Gashan ("Crash!")
035.2 FX:Aroo (howl of dog)
036.4 FX:Basa ("fwap")
037.2 FX:Ruru ("Rrr...")
      FX:Gurururuuru ("Grrrr...")
037.3 FX:Garururuuru ("Growrrrr...")
      FX:Ba (quick movement)
037.4 FX:Gurururu ("Grrr...")
039.2 FX:Gurururu ("Grrr...")
039.3 FX:Gururururu ("Grrrr...")

007.2 FX:Jaki ("click" of chain)
008.1 FX:Kotsu Kotsu (footsteps)
008.3 FX:Kotsu Kotsu (footsteps)
008.4 FX:Kotsu (footstep)
009.1 FX:Pin Pon (doorbell)
009.5 FX:Gishi (creak)
      FX:Pin-Pon (doorbell)
010.1 FX:Cha (door)
010.3 FX:Chira (quick glance)
011.1 FX:Ku (stepping into shoe)
014.3 FX:Cha (door)
015.6 FX:Kyu (squeak of heel)
016.5 FX:Kin (metal)
017.1 FX:Za (taking positions)
017.2 FX:Gacha (door unlocking)
017.3 FX:Ba (quick emergence)
018.1 FX:Ba (shove)
018.2 FX:Batan ("thunk" sound)
018.3 FX:Da (dash)
      FX:Cha (door)
018.6 FX:Zaza (waves)
019.7 FX:Su (taking-up of gun)
020.1 FX:Don ("Blam!")
020.2 FX:Garan ("clatter")
020.4 FX:Biku (sharp exclamation)
020.5 FX:Byu (onrush of air)
021.2 FX:Ba (sudden movement)
021.4 FX:Zaza (slide)
021.5 FX:Dosu ("thunk")
022.2 FX:Tan (leap)
022.3 FX:To (easy landing)

058.2 FX:Niko (smile)
058.4 FX:Beshi ("whap")
058.5 FX:Ta ("trot")
060.3 FX:Ki'in (ringing in ear)
061.2 FX:Ho (long exhale)
061.5 FX:Doki ("ba-bump"; heartbeat)
062.3 FX:Pashi (grab, clasp, "snag")
062.4 FX:Gui (tug)
063.2 FX:Gyu (squeeze)
064.3 FX:Gyaaaaa (scream of fear, dismay)
064.4 FX:Buki (sudden, sharp throb)
065.4 FX:Rururu Garururu ("Rrr... Grrr...")
066.1 FX:Gururururu ("Grrrr...")
066.2 FX:Rurururu ("Rrrr...")
067.1 FX:Ba (sudden leap)
067.2 FX:Su (displaced air)
068.3 FX:Don (shove)
068.4 FX:Za ("splatter")
069.1 FX:Zuru ("slump")
069.4 FX:Ha (quick exhale [surprise])
070.1 FX:Garurururu ("Growrrrr...")
071.1 FX:Ba (sudden movement)
071.2 FX:Fu (fade-out)
071.3 FX:Pata ("slump")
072.3 FX:Gapo ("plonk")
072.4 FX:Piipoo Piipoo ("weeeoo, weeeoo [ambulance]")
073.4 FX:Gusu ("sniff")
075.2 FX:Koro ("roll")
075.4 FX:Koro Koro ("roll, roll")
078.1 FX:Gu (squeeze)
078.2 FX:Iteeeeee ("Yee-OUCH!")
078.3 FX:Ban Ban ("slam, slam")
078.4 FX:Ban ("slam")
078.6 FX:Patan ("sluh-SLAM!")
079.4 FX:Patan ("slam...")

040.1 FX:Guo ("Graugh!")
040.3 FX:Gyaaa (scream of horror, fear)
      FX:Bariin (crash)
040.4 FX:Bata Bata Bata Bata (hasty running)
      FX:Tan (door thrown-open)
044.2 FX:Kasha Kasha (snap snap)
045.3 FX:Za Za ("swish, swish")
045.4 FX:Koso ("Psst!")
046.1 FX:Doon (dramatic imminence)
046.2 FX:Gan Gan Gan (clanging shock!)
047.2 FX:Tata ("trot...")
047.5 FX:Ka—an Ko—on (class bell)
048.3 FX:Zui (leaning closer)
049.1 FX:Kya Kya (girlish giggling)
049.3 FX:Pita (sudden fall of silence)
050.1 FX:Katan ("clunk")
050.4 FX:Gurururu ("Grrr...")
050.5 FX:Garurururu ("Growrrrr...")
051.1 FX:Kyaaa (girlish scream of fear)
052.1 FX:Yoro (stagger, loss of balance)
052.2 FX:Ki—in Ko—on Ka—an (school bells)
053.1 FX:Hata (draws up short)
053.3 FX:Sa (sidestep)
053.4 FX:Sa (sidestep)
054.1 FX:Gashi ("glomp")
055.1 FX:Do-Do-Do ("vroom")
055.2 FX:Do-Do-Do ("vroom")
055.4 FX:Ba (sudden movement—suddenly stopped)
056.3 FX:Do-Da-Da-Da Dosaa ("Thump-thump-thump-WHAM!")
056.4 FX:Garan ("clatter")
056.5 FX:Zuru (slip, slide)
056.6 FX:Gapo ("plonk")
057.2 FX:Zawa Zawa (scandalized/concerned murmur)

079.6 FX:Pi Pi Pi Pi (dialing sounds)
081.1 FX:Pu (tentative dialing gesture)
081.3 FX:U— (keening wail)
082.5 FX:Kuun (dog's whimper)
083.3 FX:Poro ("plop")
084.1 FX:Hiso Hiso Hiso
(whispering ["psst"])
084.2 FX:Doki (heartbeat ["ba-bump"])
084.3 FX:Zawa (shocked murmur)
086.4 FX:Bikuu ("Urk!")
087.1 FX:Go ("bonk")
087.3 FX:Bashi Bashi Bashi
("Slap! Slap! Slap!")
087.5 FX:Hiri Hiri Hiri (throbbing sting)
090.3 FX:Kachi ("click")
FX:Gashan ("crash")
090.4 FX:Bashi ("Whack!")
091.1 FX:Gashan ("crash")
091.2 FX:Buru Buru (tremble, shake)
091.3 FX:Biku (flinching)
093.2 FX:Kacha ("click")
FX:Bibikuu ("Urk!"-type flinch)
094.1 FX:Pa (sudden "lean down")
095.3 FX:Dokun (heavy [exaggerated]
heartbeat)
097.1 FX:Kacha (door latch)
098.2 FX:Biku (flinch, exclamation)
099.2 FX:Ba (leap)
100.3 FX:Ga ("Chomp!")
101.2 FX:Ha (startled exhale)
101.3 FX:Biku (twitch, flinch)
101.4 FX:Don ("Zap!")
102.2 FX:Uooooo (pained howl)
103.2 FX:Wan Wan Wan (barking dog)
103.4 FX:Para ("flutter")
104.2 FX:Ooo Oooo Oo (hostile howl)
104.3 FX:Ku (pained exert)
105.3 FX:Gugu (straining effort)
106.3 FX:Gu Gu Gu (menacing strain)
107.1 FX:Pita (sudden stop)
107.2 FX:Ba (quick alertness)
FX:Gururuuru ("Grrr...")
107.3 FX:Fu (fading presence)
107.4 FX:Oro Oro (fretfulness)
109.2 FX:Ha (alert [startled] exhale)
109.4 FX:Giku (startled flinch)
110.1 FX:Gurururururu ("Grrrrr...")
110.3 FX:Ha (exhale)
110.4 FX:Zuzazazaza ("skud"-like slide)
112.1 FX:Ga ("Chomp!")
113.1 FX:Yoro ("stagger")
113.2 FX:Uuu ("snarl")
FX:Uuu ("snarl")
FX:Za (rasp of tongue on paw)
113.3 FX:Guo (snarling growl)
113.4 FX:Gau Gururururu Garuru
(dogs fighting)
114.2 FX:Fuwa ("float")
114.4 FX:Gyaun (yelping cry of pain)
115.1 FX:Biku (startled exclamation)
115.3 FX:Fu (fading presence)
116.1 FX:Ha Ha Ha Ha (panting exhales)
FX:Pero ("lick")
117.2 FX:Ba (release into air)
118.3 FX:Fuwa ("float")
120.1 FX:Kasha Kasha (clicking shutter)
120.2 FX:Zuki ("throb")
121.3 FX:Fun (snort of laughter)
123.4 FX:Kyoro Kyoko
(surreptitious glances)
124.1 FX:Za (shovel breaking earth)
124.2 FX:Zakku Zakku (digging shovel)
124.4 FX:Ha (shocked exhale)
125.3 FX:Para (flipped page)
126.3 FX:Kacha (phone in receiver)
126.5 FX:Su ("swip" of emerging blade)

127.3 FX:Su ("swip" of retracting blade)
127.4 FX:Patan (definitive closing door)
129.4 FX:Za Za (shovel in dirt)
130.1 FX:Hau (startled exclamation)
132.1 FX:Burururu (cell phone on "vibrate")
133.4 FX:Ki—in Ko—on Ka—an Ko—on (school chimes)
133.5 FX:Ba ("swipe")
133.6 FX:Gi (malevolent glare)
134.1 FX:Zushaaa ("Whuppah!")
135.4 FX:Tsun ("poke")
136.2 FX:Bikkuri ("Ohmigod!")
140.3 FX:Kyun ("twinge")
141.2 FX:Puchi (turning off phone)
142.1 FX:Dassha ("Dash!")
143.1 FX:Hyuuuu ("hwooo")
143.2 FX:Pashi ("fwap")
144.1 FX:Piku (alertness)
145.1 FX:Gu ("clench")
145.4 FX:Zukin ("throb")
146.1 FX:Za (a sudden bolt, as of electricity)
146.4 FX:Ka (surge, as of anger)
146.5 FX:Ga ("Pow!")
146.6 FX:Ne, Ne, Ne... ("C'mon-C'mon-C'mon...")
FX:Yoro (stagger, loss of equilibrium)
147.2 FX:Ha (startled exhale)
152.2 FX:Gushi (sniffly sob)
153.1 FX:Hikku Hikku (stifled sobs)
154.3 FX:Bikun (startlement)
155.2 FX:Ba (sudden turning-away)
156.1 FX:Dokun Dokun Dokun (heavy heartbeats)
156.2 FX:Do Do Do Do (rapid heartbeats)

159.2 FX:Koto (kicked-off [dropped] shoe)
161.2 FX:Gu ("squeeze")
165.2 FX:Ha (startled breath)
166.1 FX:Zuru ("slump")
168.1 FX:Ho (expelled breath, as in relief/contentment)
169.3 FX:Jii (fixed stare, gaze)
170.1 FX:Tokun (heartbeat)
170.3 FX:Cha (door latch)
170.5 FX:Giku (frozen startlement)
170.7 FX:Kaaaa (rising blush)
171.2 FX:Zuki (sudden stabbing pain)
174.3 FX:Boso (mumble, whisper)
176.3 FX:Ha (exclaimed breath)
176.5 FX:Gan Gan Gan ("Whack! Whack! Whack!")
176.6 FX:Uraaa ("Hey there!" "Yo!")
177.2 FX:Zukin (stabbing pain that lingers)
179.2 FX:Zukin Zukin Zukin Zukin (multiple, stabbing, lingering pains)
181.1 FX:Kyu ("squeeze")
183.1 FX:Dokun (heavy heartbeat ["lub-dub"])
184.2 FX:Ba (sudden "popping up" movement)
185.2 FX:Pon (friendly "pat")
187.1 FX:Zuki (stabbing pain)

Yuu Watase was born on March 5 in a town near Osaka, Japan, and she was raised there before moving to Tokyo to follow her dream of creating manga. In the decade since her debut short story, *PAJAMA DE OJAMA* ("An Intrusion in Pajamas"), she has produced more than 50 compiled volumes of short stories and continuing series. Her latest series, *ZETTAI KARESHI* ("He'll Be My Boyfriend"), is currently running in the anthology magazine *SHÔJO COMIC.* Watase's long-running horror/romance story *CERES: CELESTIAL LEGEND* and her most recent completed series, *ALICE 19TH,* are now available in North America, published by VIZ. She loves science fiction, fantasy and comedy.

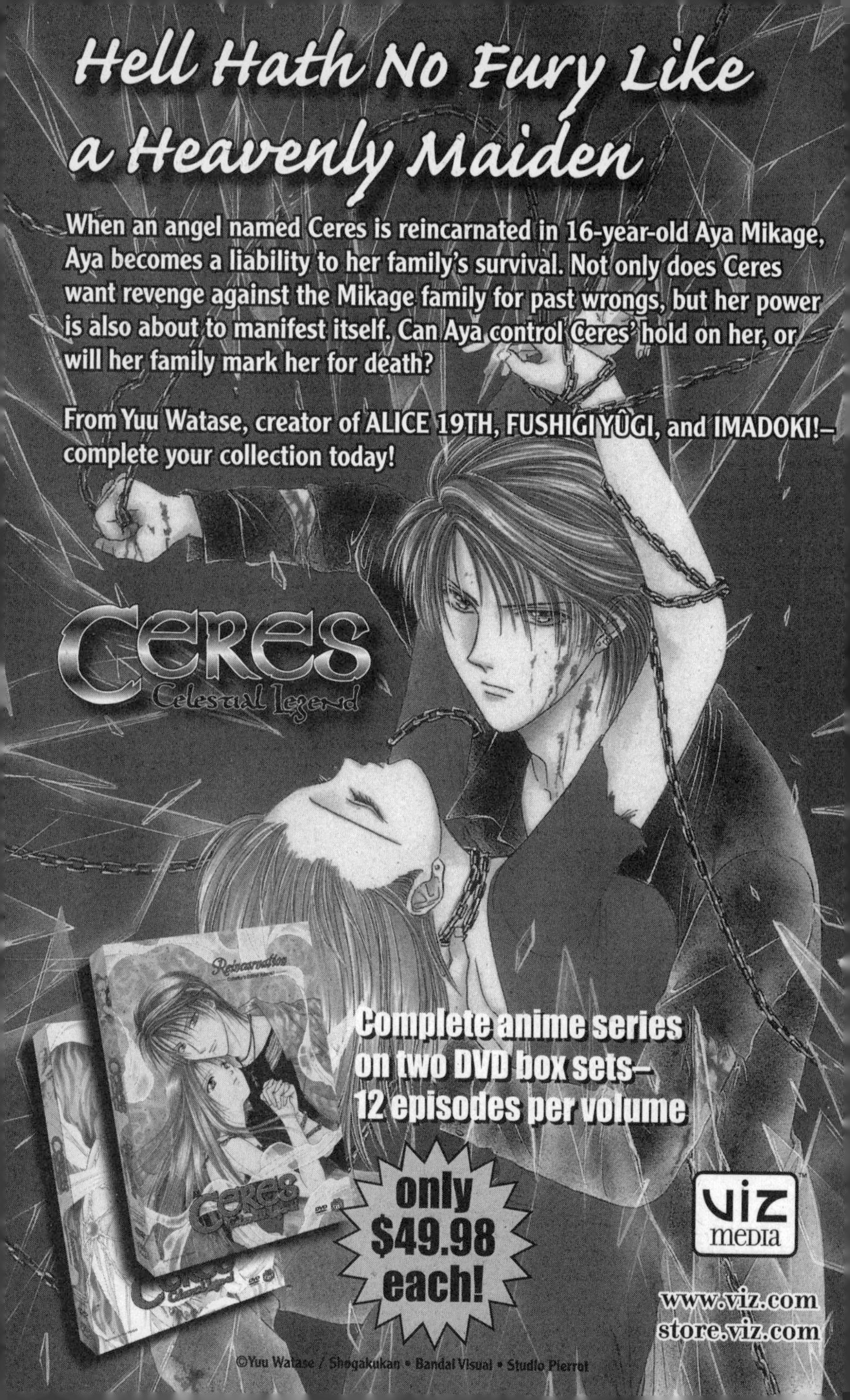
Hell Hath No Fury Like a Heavenly Maiden
When an angel named Ceres is reincarnated in 16-year-old Aya Mikage, Aya becomes a liability to her family's survival. Not only does Ceres want revenge against the Mikage family for past wrongs, but her power is also about to manifest itself. Can Aya control Ceres' hold on her, or will her family mark her for death?
From Yuu Watase, creator of ALICE 19TH, FUSHIGI YÛGI, and IMADOKI!–complete your collection today!
Ceres
Celestial Legend
Complete anime series on two DVD box sets–12 episodes per volume
only $49.98 each!
viz media
www.viz.com
store.viz.com
©Yuu Watase / Shogakukan • Bandai Visual • Studio Pierrot

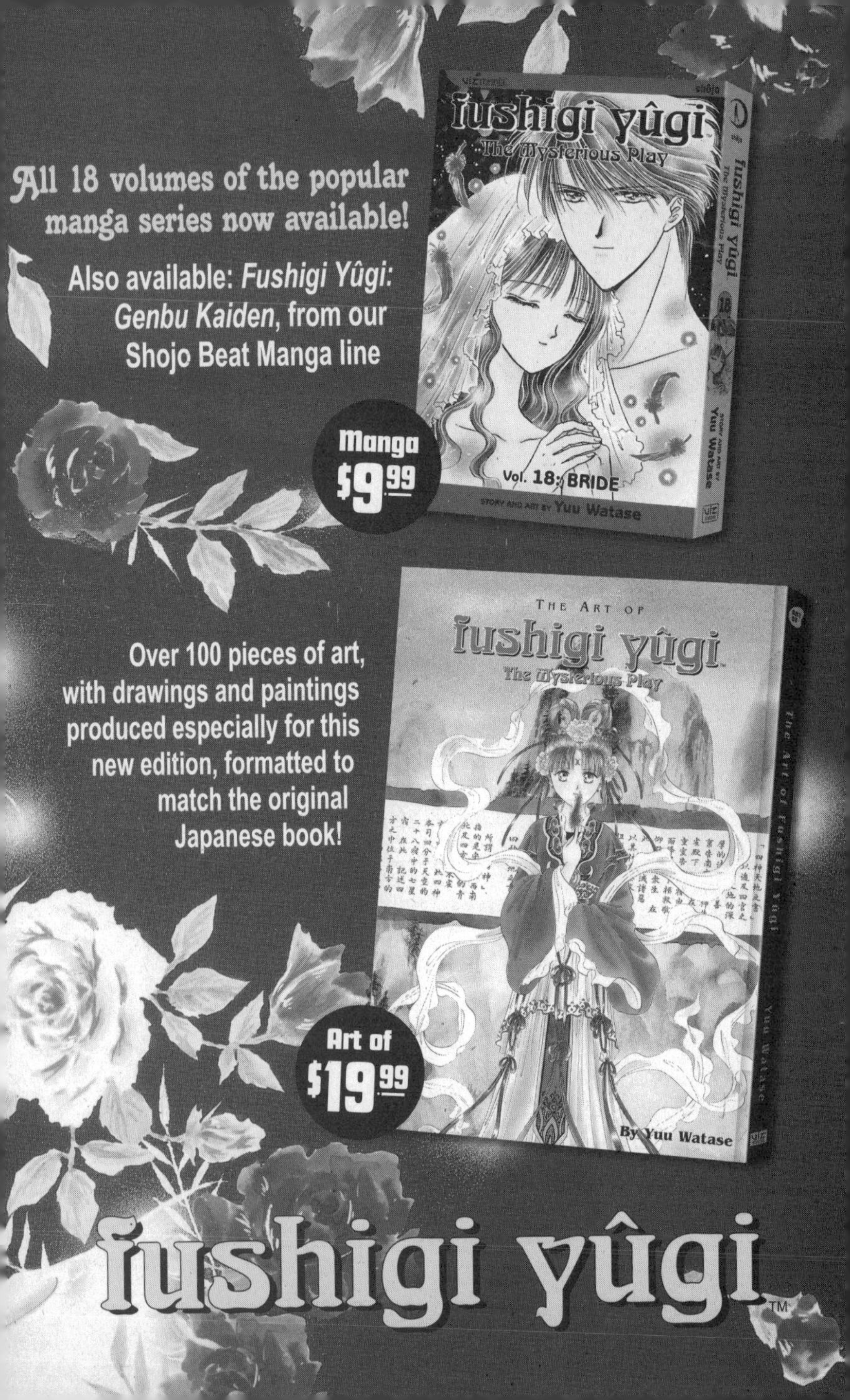
All 18 volumes of the popular manga series now available!
Also available: *Fushigi Yûgi: Genbu Kaiden*, from our Shojo Beat Manga line
fushigi yûgi
The Mysterious Play
Vol. 18: BRIDE
STORY AND ART BY Yuu Watase
Manga
$9.99
Over 100 pieces of art, with drawings and paintings produced especially for this new edition, formatted to match the original Japanese book!
THE ART OF
fushigi yûgi
The Mysterious Play
By Yuu Watase
Art of
$19.99
fushigi yûgi™

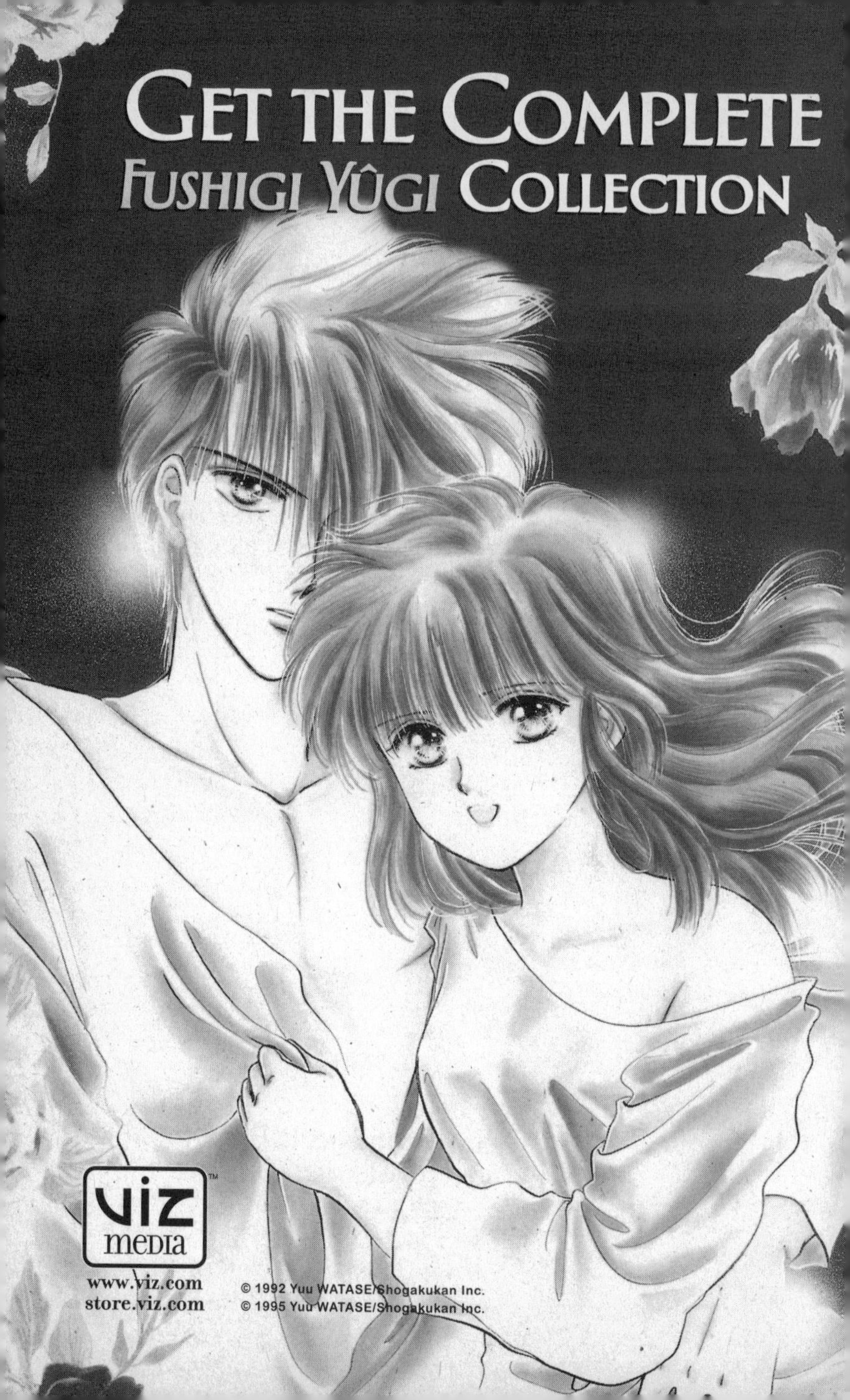
GET THE COMPLETE
FUSHIGI YÛGI COLLECTION
viz media
www.viz.com
store.viz.com
© 1992 Yuu WATASE/Shogakukan Inc.
© 1995 Yuu WATASE/Shogakukan Inc.

Collection

Complete your Angel Sanctuary collection—
buy the manga and art book today
at store.viz.com!

Read the epic saga
of forbidden love from the start—
the 20-volume manga series
now available.

A hardcover collection of illustrations
from manga volumes 1-8,
plus character info and an exclusive
interview with creator Kaori Yuki.

www.viz.com
store.viz.com